THE GRAND COLLABORATION

RELIGIOUS FREEDOM AND PUBLIC DIALOGUE
A Robert Nusbaum Center Series
Eric Michael Mazur and Kathleen M. Moore, Editors

The Grand Collaboration

Thomas Jefferson, James Madison, and
the Invention of American Religious Freedom

STEVEN K. GREEN

UNIVERSITY OF VIRGINIA PRESS

Charlottesville and London

Published in association with the Robert Nusbaum Center
at Virginia Wesleyan University

The University of Virginia Press is situated on the traditional lands of the Monacan Nation, and the Commonwealth of Virginia was and is home to many other Indigenous people. We pay our respect to all of them, past and present. We also honor the enslaved African and African American people who built the University of Virginia, and we recognize their descendants. We commit to fostering voices from these communities through our publications and to deepening our collective understanding of their histories and contributions.

University of Virginia Press
© 2024 by the Rector and Visitors of the University of Virginia
All rights reserved
Printed in the United States of America on acid-free paper

First published 2024

9 8 7 6 5 4 3 2 1

LIBRARY OF CONGRESS CATALOGING-IN-PUBLICATION DATA

Names: Green, Steven K. (Steven Keith), author.
Title: The grand collaboration : Thomas Jefferson, James Madison, and the invention of American religious freedom / Steven K. Green, University of Virginia Press.
Description: Charlottesville : University of Virginia Press, 2024. | Series: Religious freedom and public dialogue : a Robert Nusbaum center series | Includes bibliographical references and index.
Identifiers: LCCN 2024002734 (print) | LCCN 2024002735 (ebook) | ISBN 9780813951843 (hardcover) | ISBN 9780813951850 (paperback) | ISBN 9780813951867 (ebook)
Subjects: LCSH: Freedom of religion—United States. | Church and state—United States. | Constitutional law—United States. | Jefferson, Thomas, 1743–1826. | Madison, James, 1751–1836.
Classification: LCC KF4783 .G734 2024 (print) | LCC KF4783 (ebook) | DDC 342.7308/52—dc23/eng/20240129
LC record available at https://lccn.loc.gov/2024002734
LC ebook record available at https://lccn.loc.gov/2024002735

Cover art: Left pen, shutterstock.com/kylesmith; right pen, shutterstock.com/Philphot
Cover design: David Drummond

◖ CONTENTS ◗

◈ ACKNOWLEDGMENTS ◈

As this book is being published, the church-state jurisprudence of the United States Supreme Court—and as it goes, the church-state jurisprudence for the entire US judiciary—is in flux. Long-held assumptions and legal doctrines governing whether the government can fund religious-based education or refuse to fund the same, whether public school educators can engage in demonstratively religious conduct during a school activity, or whether religious institutions—and then private individuals and businesses raising religious claims—should be exempt from salutary public welfare laws have recently been jettisoned. The American principle of church-state separation, celebrated throughout much of the nation's history, endorsed by the Supreme Court in 1872, and then constitutionalized by the justices in 1947, has become a "dog's breakfast," according to a currently sitting justice. At the same time, jurists, scholars, and politicians have increasingly challenged the role of Thomas Jefferson and James Madison in framing the American regime of religious freedom.

This book, however, is not a rebuttal to what many perceive as a troubling trend in religion clause jurisprudence. Although as a law professor and legal advocate I hold a firm view on this issue, I came up with the idea for this book before the more recent Court terms that confirmed the resiliency of this trend. With this book, I have attempted to wear my professional historian's hat, to reexamine the legacy of Jefferson and Madison in their individual and collaborative capacities to "establish religious freedom" in the new nation, to employ the phrase from Jefferson's famous statute. I leave it to the book's readers to assess how well I have kept on that hat.

As for this book's preparation, I appreciate the support of the deans' office at Willamette University College of Law, through a faculty research grant and a sabbatical, and the assistance of the library staff at Willamette University. I also appreciate the conversations and suggestions from various colleagues over the past years, including Chris Beneke, John Ragosta, and David Sehat, as well as the recommendations from the anonymous reviewers of the manuscript. I also thank University of Virginia Press and the Robert Nusbaum Center for their willingness to invest in this project and for including it in their new series on Religious Freedom and Public Dialogue. And finally, I appreciate the ongoing love and support from my wife, Cindy, and our daughter, Elizabeth, in all my writing projects.

THE GRAND COLLABORATION

Introduction

O ne of the more iconic and recognizable memorials in Washington, DC, is the Jefferson Memorial, a neoclassical structure modeled after the Roman Pantheon that is situated on the Tidal Basin just south of the National Mall. In the center of the open-air interior stands an imposing, nineteen-foot statue of Thomas Jefferson. Surrounding the statue on the interior walls of the memorial are four panels with quotations of Jefferson. Although he had an extensive public career serving in various capacities—state legislator, delegate to the Continental Congress, governor, minister to France, secretary of state, vice president, and then president—and supporting myriad political causes, the panels are notable for the number of references to God and religion. The panel on the northwest interior wall contains an excerpt from Jefferson's 1786 Virginia Statute for Establishing Religious Freedom: "Almighty God hath created the mind free. . . . All attempts to influence it by temporal punishments or burthens . . . are a departure from the plan of the Holy Author of our religion." The quotations on the panel of the northeast interior wall are from multiple sources, including his *Notes on the State of Virginia:* "God who gave us life gave us liberty. Can the liberties of a nation be secure when we have removed a conviction that these liberties are the gift of God? Indeed I tremble for my country when I reflect that God is just, that his justice cannot sleep forever." On the panel of the southwest interior wall are excerpts from the Declaration of Independence, beginning with the second paragraph of that document: "We hold these truths to be self-evident, that all men are created equal, that they are endowed by their Creator with certain inalienable [*sic*] Rights, that among them are Life, Liberty, and the pursuit of Happiness." Only the panel on the southeast interior wall is devoid of any religious language. Finally, and more prominently, circling the interior of the dome on a frieze is another iconic statement by Jefferson concerning religion: "I have sworn upon the altar of God eternal hostility against every form of tyranny over the mind of man."[1] An uninformed visitor from a foreign country could be forgiven for mistaking the nation's third president for its most prominent religious thinker.

Any significance to the religious quotations contained inside the Jefferson Memorial can easily be discounted as reflecting the choices of the memorial commission appointed by President Franklin Roosevelt in 1934. The commission could have selected countless other statements by Jefferson, so, on their own, the quotations that do appear on the memorial cannot be taken as evidence of the importance of religious matters in Jefferson's life. Yet the words chiseled into its stone were far from insignificant sentiments to Jefferson—possibly one gauge is that of three accomplishments Jefferson directed to be engraved on his tombstone obelisk, one was his "Statute of Virginia Religious Freedom" (along with "Author of the Declaration of Independence" and "Father of the University of Virginia"). Those religious sentiments contained inside the memorial have gone far in creating a public image of the great man.[2]

Jefferson's image as a religious speculator is well deserved, as he thought about religious matters a lot—he "took religion seriously."[3] Indeed, his painstaking preparation of the "Jefferson Bible" and his extensive correspondence with John Adams and others about religious matters while in retirement suggest a person obsessed with discovering the essentials of religion and of Christianity in particular. Historian Edwin S. Gaustad asserted that "Thomas Jefferson was the most self-consciously theological of all America's presidents. . . . Jefferson could never dismiss the subject of religion. It mesmerized him, enraged him, tantalized him, alarmed him, and sometimes inspired him."[4]

There is no national memorial for James Madison, which is unfortunate considering his seminal role in the drafting of the US Constitution and the Bill of Rights, among other things. (The same could be said for John Adams, also denied a national memorial to commemorate his numerous accomplishments, something biographer David McCullough lamented.[5]) Perhaps it is as well, as Madison lacked Jefferson's flair for rhetorical flourishes, concentrating on his own talents for organization and detail. If a comparable memorial existed for Madison, however, at least two of its panels would necessarily include quotations from his *Memorial and Remonstrance,* written to build support for Jefferson's Bill for Establishing Religious Freedom, and the opening clause of the First Amendment: "Congress shall make no law respecting an establishment of religion, or prohibiting the free exercise thereof." According to Noah Feldman, "The subject that most animated James Madison was the freedom of religion and the question of its official establishment." Religion mattered for Madison too.[6]

One of the questions this book seeks to answer is "why?" Jefferson and Madison espoused ideas of Enlightenment rationalism and professed religious beliefs that placed them outside the boundaries of Christian orthodoxy. Why would two religiously heterodox and nominally observant men, immune from any threat of religious persecution due to their social standing and putative affiliation with the dominant Anglican Church, possess such a deep commitment to religious freedom and work so assiduously throughout their lives to advance that principle? (This book readily acknowledges the inherent danger with historians' evaluating the religiosity or piety of historical figures, considering that such definitions change over time as have the social conventions used to evaluate such matters. Still, neither man believed in many traditional Christian doctrines, either by contemporary standards or those of today.) To be sure, Jefferson's personal religious beliefs were attacked by political opponents during the 1796 and 1800 presidential elections, producing false charges that he was a "true infidel," a "professed deist," and an enemy of religion. But that was long after Jefferson had demonstrated his commitment to freedom of conscience and religious equality in writings such as his Bill for Establishing Religious Freedom (1777) and his *Notes on the State of Virginia* (1782).[7] Jefferson and Madison were members an elite class—including George Washington and Benjamin Franklin—whose outward demonstrations of latitudinarianism generally insulated them from challenges, which allowed them to dabble privately in rationalist and deistic thought without being questioned. Because neither Madison nor Jefferson faced the risks of a religious dissenter or had reason to empathize with the theology of evangelical enthusiasts, they seem unlikely candidates to emerge as the new nation's leading advocates of religious freedom. (Then again, perhaps those immunities and perspectives enabled them to become the nation's greatest proponents of religious freedom. If so, that still begs the question of why they cared.) As historian Jack N. Rakove observes, "To ask why the chief authors of the Declaration of Independence and the Constitution were so devoted to this cause provides a valuable point of departure for asking why religious freedom, in certain respects, became a right unlike no other—what made it so radically significant."[8]

To characterize Jefferson, and possibly Madison, as being nominally observant will likely draw criticism, as various biographers have insisted that Jefferson was personally pious and held "strong religious convictions," as one author writes. And Jefferson contributed generously to the support of churches, some of which advanced doctrines he disputed.[9] As is discussed here, this book does not deny that Jefferson exuded his own sense of piety or that both men held strong views about religion; both men also had a deep appreciation for the Bible and were versed in religious commentary. (In contrast to Jefferson's piety, historian Lance Banning called Madison's own religious faith a "puzzle," while Ralph Ketcham described Madison as "a rather passive believer."[10]) Yet, many authors have insisted that both men professed common deistic beliefs, if they were not deists themselves.[11] But even those who insist that Jefferson's and Madison's religious beliefs exclude them from the category of deists acknowledge that their heterodox views put them on the margins of traditional Christianity. Regardless of whether Jefferson and Madison held more conventional beliefs or were more personally devout than has been commonly thought, the question remains why they were so committed to advancing religious freedom in ways that did not benefit them directly, particularly since both men were occupied with so many other matters of nation-building. After all, this was a period when almost every issue about politics and governance was on the table and open for debate. With all the momentous issues concerning national survival that the founders had to address, it seems that matters of religion could be dealt with in due time.[12] But as Ketcham wrote about Madison, "There is no principle in all of Madison's wide range of private opinions and long public career to which he held with greater vigor and tenacity than this one of religious liberty."[13] The same can be said for Jefferson as well. This conundrum deserves exploring.

A second question this book seeks to address is how Jefferson's and Madison's evolving views about church and state complemented and reinforced each other. Their long political and personal alliance was truly a "great collaboration," as Adrienne Koch termed it several generations ago. Writing more recently, Jack Rakove called their relationship "the greatest friendship in American political history."[14] In no area was their collaboration greater than in their joint commitment to the cause of religious freedom. They worked together and separately to advance individual religious liberty, religious equality, and separation of church and state.[15] As such, this book departs from the views of those authors who have emphasized the differences in Jefferson's and Madison's approaches to matters of church and state at the expense of their similarities. Vincent Phillip Muñoz, for one, contends that Jefferson and Madison "disagreed about the separation of church and state and embraced different understandings of the right to religious liberty."[16] While some differences existed, they were minimal and complementary, rather than contradictory; "on fundamental constitutional matters their convictions converged."[17]

Scholars and commentators have debated the significance of that shared perspective ever since Supreme Court justices elevated Jefferson and Madison to the pantheon of expositors on the meaning of the Constitution's religion clauses. In 1947, in the first interpretation of the establishment clause by the modern Supreme Court, the justices unequivocally declared that the writings of Jefferson and Madison were authoritative for the purposes and meaning of that clause. Writing the majority opinion in *Everson v. Board of Education,* Justice Hugo Black emphasized the contributions of both men, famously highlighting Jefferson's statement that the establishment clause "was intended to erect 'a wall of separation between Church and State.'" The lead dissent, written by Justice Wiley Rutledge, focused chiefly on Madison's actions and writings—guided in no small part by the works of his friend and Madison biographer Irving Brant—going so far as to include Madison's *Memorial and Remonstrance* as an appendix to his opinion.[18] The following year, in the first case considering religious instruction in the public schools, the justices again declared that the Court's church-state jurisprudence would be guided by the examples of Jefferson and Madison.[19] Chief Justice Earl Warren later described the seminal impact of the two men on the Court's jurisprudence, writing that the justices considered "the [Virginia] act for establishing religious freedom, written by Thomas Jefferson and sponsored by James Madison, as best reflecting the long and intensive struggle for religious freedom in America, [and] as particularly relevant in the search for the First Amendment's meaning."[20]

At the time, however, detractors of the Court's decisions charged that the justices' reliance on Jefferson and Madison was misplaced, arguing that their church-state views were unrepresentative of most members of the founding generation. That debate has continued, with Justices Clarence

Thomas and David Souter engaging in a fierce exchange over that legacy in dueling opinions in 1995. As recently as 2022, Justice Neil Gorsuch referred derisively to "the so-called separation of church and state" that Jefferson and Madison were so central in promoting.[21]

Academic and popular authors have also debated whether Jefferson's and Madison's views about church-state matters were representative or are even relevant. After a lull following the initial Supreme Court decisions in the 1940s, the issue reemerged in scholarship in the 1980s and has not abated since. The intentions and beliefs (both ideological and religious) of Jefferson and Madison have been dissected and deconstructed. Some works have insisted that Jefferson and Madison were outliers when it came to views about church-state relations; others have insisted that their commitment to church-state separation was tactical (and political) rather than sincere; still others have disputed whether either man supported the model of separationism that has been attributed to them.[22] And then, as noted, some works have argued that Jefferson and Madison were more conventionally religious than has been assumed, implying that a higher degree of religiosity indicates less support for church-state separation. Longstanding assumptions about Jefferson's and Madison's commitment to advancing religious freedom and church-state separation have thus been called into question.[23]

Although there are a handful of dual biographies of Jefferson and Madison that discuss their long political collaboration, and individual biographies that examine the religious beliefs and intentions of Jefferson and Madison, no work exists that exclusively examines their collaboration in the cause of religious freedom.[24] This book expands on the existing coverage by addressing several questions: why were the two men so committed to advancing religious freedom and church-state separation, and how did their collaboration on this issue reinforce their separate commitments and collectively result in the invention of American religious freedom? And regardless of whether their views about religious freedom and church-state separation were representative of their times or were on the vanguard, this book asks whether various Supreme Court justices—including Hugo Black, Wiley Rutledge, William Brennan, David Souter, Stephen Breyer, and Sonia Sotomayor—were nonetheless perspicacious in embracing the Jeffersonian-Madisonian vision of church-state relations as best equipped for mediating conflict in an increasingly religiously pluralistic nation.[25] As Justice Souter asserted in 1995, Madison and Jefferson played "leading roles . . . in the drafting and adoption" of the principles underlying the religion clauses, such that their "authority on questions about the meaning of the Establishment Clause is well settled."[26] That claim, of course, has been challenged in more recent religion clause decisions. Still, the fact that critics of the Jeffersonian-Madisonian understanding of church-state separation spend considerable time contesting their true influence demonstrates the resiliency of their legacy. When it comes to considering the creation of American religious freedom, the essential role of Jefferson and Madison cannot be ignored.[27]

A note on terminology, and then a response to anticipated criticism. First, this book uses the phrase "religious freedom" to denote a broader concept than is indicated by the phrase "religious liberty." As used herein, "religious freedom" is meant to describe a social construct rather than an individual interest in the absence of a constraint on one's religiously motivated conduct. Religious freedom is a collectively shared condition that is represented in (and hopefully exemplified by) the nation's laws, customs, and institutions. It includes the idea of individual religious liberty but encompasses more. Thus, in examining Jefferson's and Madison's contributions to American religious freedom, the concept includes more than their actions that directly advanced the free exercise of religion, to use the constitutional phrase. While they were committed to making that a reality—as can be seen in Madison's successful amendment to the Virginia Declaration of Rights to substitute the words "free exercise" for George Mason's term "toleration"—their shared idea of religious freedom encompassed more: rights of conscience and free inquiry (religious and otherwise), the avoidance of religious conflict and divisiveness including the government's corruption of religion, a fear of religious majorities, a distrust of ecclesiastical power, the non-establishment of religion, and the secularity of government institutions and policies.

As for anticipated criticism, the first may be that the book's subtitle— "Thomas Jefferson, James Madison, and the *Invention* of American Religious Freedom"—gives short shrift to the much older and broader impulse that led to religious freedom in America. As numerous scholars have argued, religious freedom arose as a result of multiple factors and the efforts and commitments of many people. The long colonial and early national struggle to overcome religious persecution and the persistence of conscience-based dissent, bolstered by Protestant concepts of "soul liberty" and the "right of private judgment," were indispensable for developing the ideas of religious freedom that emerged in the revolutionary and postrevolutionary eras.[28]

This book does not dispute that narrative—had it not been for the ground-work laid by evangelicals, other dissenters, Enlightenment theorists, and Whig writers, Jefferson and Madison would have had little to work with. But this book maintains that the conception of religious freedom in America today owes itself to the distinct visions of Jefferson and Madison.[29] Even putting aside the hagiographic accounts by Supreme Court justices Wiley Rutledge and David Souter, American religious freedom today *is* the invention of Jefferson and Madison. This is not simply in its constitutional sense but in a popular cultural sense where we see divisions between those who assert the right to extend their "religious liberties" into the public realm and those who maintain that the privatization of religious expression is the only way to ensure a secular society free from religious divisiveness.

Criticism of the book's premise will also likely come from the opposite perspective, one that asserts that true American religious freedom was and continues to be unrealized—that American religious freedom is a myth, as David Sehat has written. As many scholars have demonstrated (including this author), for much of the nation's existence, religious freedom in the United States was enjoyed by white Protestants often to the exclusion of Native Americans, African slaves and free Blacks, Catholics, Jews, and other non-Christian groups. (And as slaveowners, Jefferson and Madison denied their enslaved workers any true sense of freedom of conscience.)[30] This too is indisputable. Yet, true religious freedom is a work in progress and an ideal to be achieved, particularly considering the ease with which a recent president successfully banned people from entering the United States based on their status as Muslims.[31] But it is the position of this book that the blueprint provided by Jefferson and Madison, one that Justice Felix Frankfurter once referred to as a "spacious conception," still offers a salutary mechanism for achieving an expansive vision of religious freedom.[32] In fact, it would violate the intentions of Jefferson and Madison to claim that their invention was completed or perfected during their lifetimes. Both men understood that there was a long arc toward achieving religious freedom and equality—that some inventions take time to be realized. Nonetheless, the United States' noble, and ongoing, experiment in achieving true religious freedom and equality and full freedom of conscience would have been still-born in the absence of the contributions of Jefferson and Madison.

The Setting

T homas Jefferson's and James Madison's lifelong dedication to the causes of religious freedom and liberty of conscience did not arise in a vacuum. It came about through their careful study of history—particularly of the European wars over religion that had concluded less than one hundred years earlier—of Enlightenment and Whig writings espousing freedom of conscience, of religiously themed commentaries and critiques of religious establishments, and through firsthand experience and observation. During their formative years—the 1750s and 1760s—the religious situation in colonial British America was experiencing new pressures and dynamic shifts. Controversies had broken out in nearly every colony between intrenched religious elites and religious dissenters, including disputes within many Protestant denominations between traditionalists and "New Light" enthusiasts. Anticlericalism—directed chiefly at the Church of England—was on the rise as were forms of rationalist deism. And as the political controversy between colonialists and British authorities unfolded during the 1760s, claims for civil and religious liberty became intertwined. This rich milieux provided the context for Jefferson's and Madison's intellectual development and their growing commitment to rights of conscience. One cannot understand their strong advocacy for religious freedom without first considering the religious situation in midcentury colonial America, generally, and in midcentury Virginia in particular.

Colonial America

According to popular folklore, the British American colonies were settled in large part by people fleeing religious persecution in Europe and searching for religious freedom. Once ensconced in North America, they established communities where faith could be freely practiced under a regime of religious toleration unmatched anywhere in the eighteenth-century world. This first claim is only partially true, and the experiences of the religious pilgrims are frequently exaggerated. For example, the majority of the settlers who traveled on the Mayflower—the "Strangers" as John Winthrop called them—were not Puritans. The second claim is largely a myth, though exceptions to the notoriously low standard for religious toleration did exist in parts of colonial America. Rather than British America being a haven for religious freedom, conformity to religious orthodoxy and uniformity of practice represented the general rule, perpetuating the dominant European tradition in the colonies.[1]

Nonetheless, by the middle of the eighteenth century, the religious diversity that existed in colonial America was unmatched by any place in Christendom. Puritans—Calvinist dissenters to the Church of England—had settled in New England, and Catholics—along with Anglicans—had colonized Maryland. Anglicans predominated in the southern colonies, though chiefly in the Tidewater areas. Quakers dominated parts of central North Carolina; Huguenots—French Calvinists—had settled around Charleston, South Carolina; while Lutherans, Moravians, Presbyterians, and Jews settled in Savannah, Georgia. As is commonly known, Quakers colonized Pennsylvania with their leader, William Penn, recruiting immigrants from the German states, bringing in Lutheran, German Reformed, Brethren, Moravian, and Mennonite migrants. Presbyterians also settled in the middle colonies making them the most religiously pluralistic region. And then New York was a polyglot of Dutch Reformed, Presbyterian, Lutheran, Anglican, and Jewish residents.[2] Unquestionably, many of these people migrated to the colonies in search of greater religious freedom or to escape religious persecution, some forms being more overt than others. Yet other people, including some from the above groups, immigrated to the colonies drawn by available land and greater economic opportunities, though in Europe such opportunities were often hampered by one's status as a religious dissenter. While religion permeated colonial culture in a manner that would seem quite oppressive today, for many colonialists religious consid-erations were of secondary concern to economic matters.[3]

Despite this unparalleled religious diversity, religious freedom was not the rule, nor was religious toleration common in many areas. Nine of the thirteen colonies maintained religious establishments, meaning forced tax-ation to support the dominant orthodox church (chiefly Congregational in New England and Anglican in the South), with many civil privileges turning on one's religious affiliation. Failure to pay the tax or assessment meant that dissenters were subject to fines, distrait of property, or even imprisoned. All colonies imposed behavioral codes consistent with the practices of the dominant Protestant body's theology, although enforcement varied widely, particularly in the backcountry. The New England colonies and Virginia and South Carolina enforced Sabbath attendance and fined recalcitrants for failure to attend the established churches.[4]

Even though the 1689 Act of Toleration technically legalized religious dissent, it did not prohibit colonial authorities from imposing conditions for establishing meetinghouses and licensing requirements for dissenting clergy. In the 1720s and 1730s, pressure from the British government forced resistant colonial assemblies to lift some of the harsher penalties for reli-gious dissenters and grant them property rights and, arguably, exemptions from paying taxes to support the established church. But in New England and the South, authorities frequently required petitioners to prove their membership in a recognized church with a full-time minister before the tax could be assigned to the dissenting church. As historian Chris Beneke has observed, even with greater toleration of dissenting churches, "dissenters were still expected to keep a lid on their religious opinions, only worshiping 'privately,' 'soberly,' and 'indoors,'" and not to undermine the authority of the established church.[5] So, as Jack Rakove has written, "the conventional assumptions about the value of preserving religious orthodoxy and unifor-mity thus persisted into the early decades of the eighteenth century. Religion dissent was a form of disease or infection that authorities should quarantine or suppress."[6]

Several factors arising in the eighteenth century nurtured an impulse of recognizing greater religious freedom in America. Some were intellec-tual; others were practical. The first factor that fostered the idea of greater toleration, if not religious freedom, was the rich intellectual tradition that came out of the Enlightenment and then continued in the mid-eighteenth century through Whig political theories. The Enlightenment arose on the heels of the Scientific Revolution of the seventeenth century; scientific philosophers such as Francis Bacon, Baruch Spinoza, and Isaac Newton had endeavored to identify universal natural laws of science that operated free from the mysteries and constraints of religious dogma. Freedom of thought and inquiry were necessary prerequisites for scientific discovery, which implied that civil authorities should have limited authority to enforce religious orthodoxy and conformity thereto. Building on the foundation laid by such philosophers, Enlightenment theorists emphasized the necessity of freedom of conscience and religious toleration so that human reason and observation could operate fully.[7]

A leading Enlightenment writer for many members of the founding generation—particularly for Thomas Jefferson and James Madison—was John Locke.[8] In addition to his highly influential writings about government, Locke wrote extensively about religious toleration and freedom of conscience, chiefly in his *Letter on Toleration,* though related discussions appeared in his *Essay Concerning Human Understanding.* Locke published his *Letter* in 1689, coinciding with the passage of the Act of Toleration. Although ostensibly published in support of the act, Locke wrote his treatise earlier while exiled in Holland, where he had associated with religious dissenters. As a result of this experience, Locke's argument for toleration went beyond merely indulging deviations from religious orthodoxy, which was the assumption underlying the act.[9]

The salient themes in Locke's *Letter* were that there was a firm distinction between religious and civil authority, that civil authorities lacked all power over religious matters, and that religious judgments could not be compelled. Locke understood religious belief to be a matter that existed solely between a person and God. The "conscience of each individual and the salvation of his soul" was something "for which he is accountable to God only." Knowledge, religious and otherwise, was acquired by reason and persuasion—"true and saving religion consists in the inward persuasion of the mind"—but coercion was ineffective to change people's minds: "Human understanding . . . cannot be compelled by any outward force." As such, "every man is entitled to admonish, exhort, convince another of effort, and lead him by reason to accept his own opinion." Following naturally on those principles, the state had no interest in legislating religious matters. A political commonwealth was "constituted only for preserving and advancing [people's] civil goods." As a result, "the care of souls is not committed to the civil magistrate. . . . It is not committed to him by God . . . nor can any such power be vested in the magistrate by men." Accordingly, Locke wrote, "The civil power ought not to prescribe articles of faith, or doctrines, or forms of worshipping God, by civil law." Locke never called for disestablishing the Church of England, reaffirming the importance of a Christian state, but that was the logical extension of his argument. His insistence on separate realms of authority for the state and the church presaged the idea of church-state separation; as he wrote, the "church itself is absolutely separate and distinct from the commonwealth and civil affairs. The boundaries on both sides are fixed and immovable."[10]

Other Enlightenment writers who influenced members of the founding generation and wrote about freedom of conscience and toleration included Baron Montesquieu, Voltaire, and Lord Bolingbroke. Montesquieu was likely the only Enlightenment writer to match Locke's stature among the founders, in no small part for his advocacy for separation of powers.[11] Like Locke, Montesquieu advocated different spheres of temporal and spiritual authority. Those "things that prejudice the tranquility or security of the state . . . are subject to human jurisdiction," he wrote. "But in those which offend the Deity, where there is no public act, there can be no criminal matter, the whole passes between man and God, who knows the measure and time of His vengeance." Rather than seeking religious conformity, "when the legislator has believed it a duty to permit the exercise of many religions, it is necessary that he should enforce also a toleration among these religions themselves."[12] Voltaire also advocated for "the unalterable rights of conscience" and "freedom of reason." The sovereign, Voltaire wrote, "has no right to employ force to lead men to be religious, which essentially presumes choice and liberty. My opinions are no more dependent on authority than my sickness or my health."[13]

Lord Bolingbroke was not as familiar to American readers as Locke or Montesquieu, but his writings greatly influenced the formation of religious ideas of a young Jefferson. Although chiefly a critic of religious orthodoxy and the authenticity of scripture, Bolingbroke promoted the ability of people to freely acquire religious knowledge through empirical study rather than by following religious dogma.[14] These writers, among others, connected empiricism and reason with rights of conscience in ways that challenged the necessity of religious uniformity. "The ideas and writings of the leading secular thinkers of the European Enlightenment," wrote Bernard Bailyn, "were quoted everywhere in the colonies, by everyone who claimed a broad awareness."[15]

Reinforcing Enlightenment arguments in favor of religious tolerance and freedom of conscience were the writings of Whig polemicists of the mid-eighteenth century. Whigs criticized royal authority and corrupt ministerial power, including the privileges of the Anglican Church. Among other issues, Whig writers advocated for freedom of conscience, greater religious toleration, and a lessening of dogmatism within traditional Christianity. The Whig conception of tolerance extended beyond dissenting Protestants to include Arians, Unitarians, Atheists, Jews, Muslims, and even Catholics.[16] Two influential Whig writers were Thomas Gordon and John Trenchard, authors respectively of the *Independent Whig* and *Cato's Letters*, the latter pamphlet subtitled "Essays on Liberty, Civil and Religious, and Other Important Subjects." Firm believers in religious tolerance and freedom of conscience, Trenchard and Gordon opposed all authority over individual religious exercise, whether that came from church officials or civil authorities. In *Cato's Letters*, no. 60, Trenchard set out the Whig argument for religious liberty: "Every Man's Religion is his own; nor can the Religion of any Man, of what Nature or Figure soever, be the Religion of another Man, unless he also chooses it; which Action utterly excludes all Force, Power or Government. . . . [Religion] is independent upon all human Directions, and superior to them; and consequently uncontroulable by external Force, which cannot reach the free Faculties of the Mind, or inform the Understanding, much less convince it."[17] Expressing a similar sentiment in the *Independent Whig*, Gordon asserted that "religion is a voluntary Thing; it can no more be forced than Reason, or Memory, or any Faculty of the Soul. To be devout against our Will is an Absurdity. . . . We have no Power over the Appetites of others, no more than over their Consciences." Trenchard's and Gordon's criticisms of clerical authority and religious establishments, and their advocacy of freedom of conscience, found a receptive audience among colonists with the outbreak of political conflict with Great Britain in the 1760s.[18]

Later Whig writers who advocated for religious reform and greater toleration included Richard Price and Joseph Priestley, both well known among the founders. Price was a British clergyman and founder of early Unitarianism who supported American independence. A prolific writer of political pamphlets, his American subscribers included Benjamin Franklin, John Adams, Thomas Jefferson, and Thomas Paine. Price wrote in one of his popular pamphlets that "RELIGIOUS LIBERTY signifies the power of exercising, without molestation that mode of religion we think best, or making decisions of our own consciences, respecting religious truth."[19] Priestley, also a clergyman with Unitarian leanings, corresponded with many members of the founding generation before fleeing to America in 1794. He called for the repeal of the Test and Corporation Acts (which limited officeholding to communicants of the Anglican Church) and disestablishing the Church of England. In an early book, *Essay on the First Principles of Government* (1768), Priestley called the "union of civil and ecclesiastical power" an "unnatural mixture." "All human establishments," he insisted, "obstruct freedom of inquiry in matters of religion, by laying an undue bias upon the mind. . . . They are, therefore, incompatible with the genius of christianity."[20] Together, the arguments of Enlightenment and Whig writers presented a strong rebuttal to the presumption favoring religious conformity. By synthesizing Enlightenment ideas into their critiques of royal authority and religion, Whig writers, "more than any other single group, . . . shaped the mind of the American Revolutionary generation."[21]

Still, on its own, this intellectual tradition was insufficient to overcome the forces that perpetuated conformity and denied true religious freedom. It took matters of a more practical nature to move colonial society beyond "mere toleration" of religion to an acceptance of the merits of religious freedom and equality.[22]

Other factors that worked to undermine religious conformity were the growing religious diversity and the availability of land. Whether sanctioned by colonial authorities or not, religious dissenters were often able to establish farms and communities in backcountry areas. Distance and isolation hampered efforts at enforcing conformity of practice and uniformity of faith; suppression of dissent in such instances was simply not effective. (And colonial authorities were often happy for dissenting communities to serve as buffers between Native Americans on the frontier and the more populated settlements in the East.) By experiencing a sense of freedom, dissenters became emboldened to resist conforming pressures when they did arise, causing them to demand not just mere toleration but actual religious freedom and equality. As discussed below in more detail, Scots-Irish Presbyterians settled Virginia's Shenandoah Valley and parts of the Piedmont where Jefferson and Madison were raised, ensuring their exposure to religious dissenters.[23]

Related to the geographical dispersion of religious dissent was a fourth factor that presented a significant challenge to the forces of religious conformity. Beginning in the late 1730s and extending into the next decade, colonial America experienced a series of popular religious revivals, commonly called the Great Awakening. The revivals were in reaction to the lethargic worship and stale doctrines of orthodox Calvinist and Anglican Churches; presenting an alternative, the revivals emphasized an enthusiastic and personal religious experience of being "born again"—they were the birthplace of American evangelicalism. At the same time, the revivals nurtured ideas of religious freedom by emphasizing a "right to private judgment" on religious matters, free from the direction and control of church authorities. This liberating aspect of the revivals invited challenges to religious authority and helped to break down religious uniformity. Before long, congregations and denominations divided between those who supported the "new methods" and those that did not, commonly called "New Lights" and "Old Lights." New denominations emerged—New Side Presbyterians, Separate Baptists, and eventually Methodists—with itinerate ministers committed to spreading God's word among the unchurched and those disaffected members of orthodox churches.[24]

As the activities of evangelical itinerates expanded and they established churches, conflicts with authorities arose over the licensing of meetinghouses and clergy. Not only did the orthodox churches face competition for members; the dissenters also attacked the privileges, authority, and abuses of the established clergy and the church-state systems that sustained them. This only reinforced the inclination of authorities to increase efforts to impose religious conformity. Renewed persecution of dissenters then facilitated their claims for liberty of conscience and religious toleration, if not outright religious freedom. Even so, most dissenters did not embrace greater toleration based on magnanimity but rather out of self-interest; over time, however, the desire to be free from constraints of the dominant church led to a willingness to afford the same privileges to others. As Sidney Mead wrote, "On the question of religious freedom for all, there were many shades of opinion in [dissenting] churches, but all were practically unanimous on one point: each wanted freedom for itself. And by this time it had become clear that the only way to get it for themselves was to grant it to all others."[25]

One persuasive argument that freedom of conscience—or the right to private judgment—was preferable to uniformity appeared near the end of the revivals after the Connecticut Assembly enacted a law restricting the activities of itinerate preachers in the colony. In 1744, Elisha Williams, a Congregational minister and judge, wrote a pamphlet titled *The Essential Rights and Liberties of Protestants: A Reasonable Plea for the Liberty of Conscience and the Right of Private Judgment in Matters of Religion* in opposition to the law. While not an enthusiast himself, Williams offered a compelling argument on behalf of religious freedom that combined both theological and Enlightenment rationales for freedom of conscience. Man was a "moral & accountable being," he wrote, and in order to be "accountable for himself, he must reason, judge and determine [belief] for himself." It followed from that premise that "every man has an equal right to follow the dictates of his own conscience in the affairs of religion. Every one is under an indispensable obligation to search scripture for himself. . . . And as every Christian is so bound, so he has an unalienable right to judge wherever it leads him; even an equal right with any rulers be they civil or ecclesiastical." This led Williams to insist that religious establishments were inconsistent with true liberty of conscience, a novel idea for the time. Civil officials lacked authority to determine "modes and circumstances of worship by legal injunctions; because this would interfere with the right of private judgment that belongs to Christians." For Williams, "*Every claim of power* inconsistent with this right (as the making such a human establishment of religion of which we are speaking) is an encroachment on the Christian's liberty." As a result, "unity, or uniformity in religion is not necessary to the peace of a civil state"; in fact, such "legal establishments have a direct contrary tendency to the peace of a Christian state." Williams's pamphlet so upset fellow members of the Connecticut Standing Order than it cost him reelection to the supreme court the following year. But his strong argument, melding theological and Enlightenment concepts, indicated how the idea of religious freedom was evolving.[26]

A final event that impacted colonialists' thinking about the tension between religious uniformity and liberty involved a decades-long controversy over an effort to appoint an Anglican bishop in the American colonies. The Church of England in colonial America operated under the authority of the bishop of London; no Anglican bishop resided in America, which meant that oversight of parishes fell to civil authorities and vestries, and domestically trained clergy had to travel to England for ordination. These inconveniences led church officials in England and the colonies to call for the appointment of an American bishop. Protestant dissenters—chiefly Congregationalists and Presbyterians—feared that an American bishopric would include all of the ecclesiastical authority associated with an established church, which would be to the detriment of their "voluntary" systems. The initiative, arising in midcentury, coincided with what many dissenters perceived as new, more aggressive measures by the Anglican Church in the colonies, facilitated by the evangelizing activities of the Society for the Propagation of the Gospel in Foreign Parts. Anglican officials had established the society in the early 1700s to proselytize Indigenous Natives, slaves, and non-adherents, but by midcentury it sought to extend Anglican authority throughout the colonies by proselytizing members of dissenting Protestant churches. These actions distressed Old Lights and New Lights alike who felt their right to religious coexistence was under threat.[27]

In response, dissenting clergy mounted a counterattack on Anglican officials, charging that they were seeking to inhibit religious freedoms. In 1750, Boston Congregational minister Jonathan Mayhew delivered a sermon, *A Discourse Concerning Unlimited Submission and Non-Resistance to the Higher Powers,* which asserted that resistance to civil and religious authorities was "lawful and glorious" when their dictates violated "the commands of God." "A spirit of domination is always to be guarded against, both in church and state," Mayhew wrote, such that people could "refuse to comply with any *legal establishment of religion,* because it is a gross perversion and corruption." Although he did not condemn religious establishments outright, he emphasized that "ecclesiastical tyranny" is "the most cruel, intolerable, and impious of any" form of tyranny.[28] Mayhew's sermon was quickly printed in pamphlet form, and it caused a sensation in New England and throughout the colonies, even making "a noise in Great Britain." Mayhew's *Discourse* "was read by everybody; celebrated by friends, and abused by enemies," John Adams later recounted. For many people, the *Discourse* first articulated the idea of resistance to tyrannical civil and religious authority.[29]

Contributing to growing anticlerical and antiestablishment sentiments among colonialists were efforts by Anglican authorities to assert the church's preeminence in New York at the expense of other religious groups. In 1751, Anglican leaders set their sights on seizing control of a newly authorized

college for New York City, King's College.[30] The machinations elicited
outcries from New York's dissenting religious community, led by William
Livingston, publisher of the *Independent Reflector*. Modeled after the *Independent Whig*, the *Reflector* criticized clerical authority and religious establishments while it promoted freedom of conscience and religious exercise.
Religious establishments were perpetuated "by the unutterable Miseries
of PRIEST-CRAFT," which throughout history had "reduc[ed] Nations and
Empires to Beggary and Bondage" and people to "Vassalage," Livingston
wrote.[31] In another essay, he expounded on church-state relations:

> Matters of Religion relate to another World, and have nothing to do
> with the Interest of the State. The first resides in the Minds and Consciences of Men; the latter in the outward Peace and Prosperity of the
> Public. It is the Business of the civil Power, to see that the Common-
> Wealth suffer no Injury. . . . But provide he hurt no Man, every Subject
> has a Right to be protected in the Exercise of the Liberty of thinking
> about Religion, as he judges proper, as well as acting in Conformity
> thereto.[32]

Even though King's College was eventually chartered as an Anglican institution, the controversy exacerbated relations between Anglican authorities and New York's dissenting communities, contributing to anticlerical
attitudes. In retirement, James Madison reflected how during his student
years at Princeton between 1769 and 1772, William Livingston served as
a trustee and that students read copies of the *Independent Reflector*, which
Madison "admired for the energy and eloquence of their composition."[33]

Efforts to establish an Anglican bishopric continued into the next decade, spilling into the mounting political conflicts between the colonists and
Parliament. In the late 1760s, Congregationalist minister Charles Chauncy
picked up where Mayhew had left off, charging in a series of pamphlets that
an Anglican bishopric would be to the detriment of religious dissenters and
their rights of conscience:

> We are in principle against all civil establishment in religion. It does
> not appear to us that God has entrusted the State with a right to
> make religious establishments. . . . We claim no right to desire the
> interposition of the State to establish that mode of worship, [church]
> government, or discipline we apprehend is most agreeable to the mind

of Christ. . . . Episcopalians . . . want to be distinguished by having bishops upon the footing of a state establishment. The plain truth is, by the Gospel-charter, all professed Christians are vested with precisely the same rights; nor has one denomination any more right to the interposition of the civil magistrate in their favor than another.[34]

Chauncy, like other Congregationalists, distinguished the New England system of assessments for supporting "public worship," ostensibly justified as maintaining public morals rather than as promoting any particular religious doctrine, from a formal establishment associated with the Church of England. New England Baptists like Isaac Backus, who were forced to undergo the byzantine process of obtaining licenses and exemption certificates from parish clerks, saw little difference between the Anglican establishment that Chauncy criticized and the Congregationalist one that sustained him.[35] Contradictions aside, the Bishop Controversy caused people to question the merits of religious uniformity and to align themselves with the right of private judgment on religious matters. It also highlighted the dangers of clerical authority, fostering a growing anticlericalism among dissenters and the nominally churched. Writing later in life, John Adams asserted that "the apprehension of Episcopacy contributed . . . as much as any other cause to arouse the attention, not only of the inquiring mind, but of the common people" to the revolutionary cause. "The objection was not merely to the office of a bishop, though even that was dreaded, but to the authority of parliament, on which it must be founded." Historian Patricia U. Bonomi maintains that the Bishop Controversy of the 1750s to 1770s "easily consumed as much paper as the Stamp Act dispute" of 1765.[36]

Considered together, these various factors and events caused a growing cross-section of people, not merely religious dissenters, to question the utility of religious uniformity and conformity of belief. Yet, despite these pressures on the colonial establishments for greater religious freedom, writes historian Jon Butler, "as late as the very eve of the Revolution, not a single American colony sanctioned religious freedom, meaning—as even contemporaries understood the term—freedom to worship any supernatural being." Nonetheless, these impulses set the stage for more people of the revolutionary era to advocate not merely for toleration of varieties of religious belief but for true religious freedom and equality.[37]

Colonial Virginia

The religious situation in prerevolutionary Virginia deserves separate consideration because, in the words of historian John A. Ragosta, "our sense of religious freedom was largely developed in Virginia." This is due in no small part to the familiar, ten-year struggle to disestablish the Church of England in Virginia between 1776 and 1786, an episode documented in two decisions by the United States Supreme Court in the late 1940s. Additionally, the commonwealth served as the primary referent for Jefferson's and Madison's ideas about religious freedom, not only during their formative years but also as the place where they worked to make those ideas become a reality.[38]

Unlike the New England colonies and Pennsylvania, Virginia was not settled by people seeking greater religious freedom, nor was the colony established in order to create a "godly" society. "Virginia's colonization was not a flight from England by people pushed to the political and religious margins of their homeland," writes one scholar; in essence, "the founding of Virginia was hardly permeated by the aura of religion."[39] To be sure, the early charters and legal documents contain multiple religious affirmations, as do many surviving letters and written accounts. The Virginia Charter declared an express religious purpose of bringing "the Christian religion to such people, as yet live in darkness and miserable ignorance of the true knowledge and worship of God."[40] In addition, the early government imposed a strict behavioral code ("Dale's laws") consistent with Christian principles that was as severe as any found in Puritan New England. In a culture imbued with religious customs and traditions, however, religious language was common in official documents, particularly if one wanted to secure the patronage of powerful authorities, both civil and clerical. And the purpose of Virginia's code was not necessarily to increase piety; rather, it was designed to stabilize the colony at a critical time through a rigorous policing of behavior while distinguishing "civilized" English settlers from the "uncivilized" American Natives. Most crucial, the code helped to promote a degree of religious uniformity that authorities simply assumed was necessary for orderly society.[41]

From the beginning, the Church of England was presumed to be established in Virginia, a fact the House of Burgesses made official in 1632. With the colony's emphasis on stability and conformity, Virginia was not a receptive place for religious dissenters. Catholic clergy were banned, and in 1640 the assembly required all officials to take an oath of allegiance and supremacy to the king and the Anglican Church, which effectively excluded Catholics from officeholding. Colonial leaders also harassed clergy and lay people with Puritan leanings, even during the Commonwealth, with Governor William Berkeley expelling the more ardent Calvinists from the colony in the late 1640s. With the arrival of Quakers in the late 1650s, the assembly passed an "Act for the Suppression of Quakers" (1659)—"an unreasonable and turbulent sort of people"—which imposed a one-hundred-pound fine for anyone who brought Friends into the colony or permitted their religious services to be held on their property. Quakers were regularly fined or imprisoned until the assembly repealed the law in 1688 in anticipation of the Act of Toleration.[42]

Despite these repressive actions—or possibly because of them—Virginia was relatively free of open religious conflict until the 1740s. That does not mean Virginia's religious establishment was particularly healthy during its early years. The colony suffered from a chronic shortage of clergy and parishes in the backcountry.[43] Ineffective administration of the church was due in part to the lack of a bishop in the American colonies. What this meant, particularly in Virginia, is that decision-making over church parishes was made by local vestrymen, composed of the local elite, or by the House of Burgesses, which was dominated by vestrymen. Even more than in England, Virginia operated an Erastian form of religious establishment where the state controlled the church. According to Rhys Isaac, "The very essence of the establishment was the vestry. This was a powerful and jealously guarded institution which served as an immediate embodiment of social order, both secular and religious." The vestry hired the parish minister, controlled his salary, and even set the theological tone for each local church. In contrast, the clergy were relatively powerless and depended on the landed elite for financial support and respect. The clergy existed at the level of a "client status" to the gentry. Clergy were not rewarded for their degree of piety or their ability to inspire devotion among parishioners but rather for reinforcing the social status quo.[44] Lay control of the parishes, and of Virginia's religious establishment, meant that the latter chiefly served secular goals: order, stability, and uniformity. So, despite the pervasiveness of religious customs and traditions in the culture, the tone of Virginia society in the early eighteenth century was "highly secular" for the time.

"Institutionalized religion found its principal expression in services as appointed by the Book of Common Prayer," wrote Isaac. "But churchgoing in Virginia had more to do with expressing the dominance of the gentry than with inculcating piety or forming devout personalities."[45]

By the mid-eighteenth century, the condition of the Anglican Church had improved with the number of parishes growing to approximately one hundred, most staffed with clergy. At the same time, the church was firmly established and growing in power and control, in line with the colony's well-entrenched political hierarchy. Parish clerks collected taxes from all landowners, including from religious dissenters, for the support of Anglican clergy and church buildings (the small number of German Lutherans in the northern Shenandoah Valley region were allowed to apply the tax toward their own churches).[46] Dissenting clergy and their meetinghouses had to obtain licenses from the General Court in Williamsburg in order to operate, and few were granted. Vestries were responsible for reporting violators of behavioral laws and for controlling poor relief and the care of orphans, the latter requiring additional taxation. Only Anglican clergy could baptize children and perform marriages, which had significant legal consequences for inheritance. And finally, laws required attendance at Anglican parish worship on threat of a fine. In his study of late colonial court records, John Ragosta documented that the most common offense in a majority of counties was for "missing church." Accordingly, in the years leading up to the American Revolution, "no British colony was more protective of its established church, nor more abusive of religious dissenters."[47]

Despite the relative health and power of Virginia's Anglican establishment, tensions persisted between the gentry and Anglican clergy. Clergy resented the control that the vestry exercised over the operation of parishes and their renumeration, while many gentry looked down on the ministers sent from England, most of whom were of lower social standing or of questionable repute. Matters came to a head in the late 1750s when clergy complained about two acts by the House of Burgesses that reset their rate of pay, with the clergy eventually prevailing through an appeal to the Lords of Trade in London. The controversy, termed the "Parson's Cause," ended up damaging the reputation of the clergy while it fueled a rise in anticlericalism in Virginia that never fully subsided.[48]

According to a 1748 law, clerical salaries were set at sixteen thousand pounds of tobacco to be paid through the local parish assessments. That meant that the true value of ministers' compensation fluctuated depending on the supply and price of tobacco. In the late 1750s, tobacco prices rose dramatically due to a shortage, which appeared to create a financial windfall for the clergy. In response, the House of Burgesses—dominated by vestrymen—passed the "Two-Penny Act," which valued a pound of tobacco at two pence (significantly under market value) and permitted payment of the assessment in currency or forms other than tobacco. After the house and Governor's Council rejected the clergy's petitions to rescind the act, the clergy dispatched an agent to London to plead their cause before the bishop of London and the Board of Trade. That action, according to Rhys Isaac, "cast the clergy in the role of treacherous enemies of the colony" through their willingness to sacrifice Virginia's self-governance for their own financial benefit.[49] The "artifice [of the clergy] to bring their evil Machinations to Perfection," wrote planter Richard Bland in defense of the assembly, made them "a Disgrace to the Ministry" and deserving of "the Contempt of the People." After succeeding on their appeal in England to have the Two-Penny Act disallowed, several clergy further damaged their reputations by suing to recover the full value of the tobacco owed to them. The suits were generally unsuccessful as resentful jurors refused to award damages. In one famous case involving Reverend James Maury—who had been a tutor for Thomas Jefferson—a young Patrick Henry defended the vestry by attacking the greed of the clergy, with him then charging that the king, "by disallowing Acts of this salutatory nature, [far] from being the father of his people [has] degenerated into a Tyrant, and forfeits all rights to his subjects' obedience." Henry's incendiary speech convinced the jury to award Maury one pence in damages, and it established Henry as a leading force in Virginia politics. Overall, the Parson's Cause controversy tarnished the image of Anglican clergy and fed an anticlericalism that would extend into Virginia's disestablishment some twenty-five years later.[50]

Around that time, the number of religious dissenters in Virginia was growing, spurred by the after-effects of the Great Awakening. Small numbers of Regular Baptists and German Lutherans had resided in Virginia since the early 1700s, in the southeast and upper Shenandoah Valley, respectively. With the awakening, however, religious enthusiasts began to appear in the valley and Piedmont areas. In the early 1740s, New Side Presbyterian itinerates followed an earlier migration of Scots-Irish settlers, finding among them a receptive audience that resented the Virginia gentry and their Anglican establishment.[51] In addition to calling for spiritual renewal, the evangelists frequently stirred up trouble by preaching about the incompetence and decadence of the established clergy. As one Anglican critic of the evangelists acknowledged, "There were many [Anglican clergy] who preached a dry orthodoxy and frigid morality; but that was not enough. Dissenters came and gave hungry souls something else, though often mixed with what was not the Gospel." Edmund Randolph, in a historical essay written in 1809, provided a more sympathetic assessment: "The Presbyterian clergy were indefatigable. Not depending on the dead letter of written sermons, they understood the mechanism of haranguing." Civil and religious authorities took greater notice when Presbyterian itinerates began infiltrating the central and Tidewater areas and attracting large crowds, as happened in Hanover County in 1743. Authorities pushed back on the activities, insisting that before itinerates could preach they had to obtain licenses; otherwise, they were "liable to be bound to their good Behavior and treated as Vagabonds by the Justice of the Peace."[52]

For several years, New Side itinerates faced resistance from civil and religious authorities, with the former refusing to grant licenses to preach and then sanctioning those offenders. In 1745, in James City Parish (outside the capital of Williamsburg), disaffected Anglicans invited an itinerate Presbyterian minister, John Roan, to preach in their house for several days. According to an account, Roan "inveighed against the clergy of the Established Church with great freedom, charging them not only with neglect of their official duties, but with gross moral delinquencies." The civil and religious authorities heard about the activity, and the latter secured an indictment against Roan for blasphemy and "vilifying the Established Religion in diverse sermons . . . before a numerous audience unlawfully assembled." Roan fled to Pennsylvania before he could be arrested, but the court nonetheless issued an order forbidding any meetings of "Moravians, Muggletonians, and New Lights." Several people who had attended the informal meetings were fined for unlawful assembly.[53] Prompted by such persecution, in 1747 Presbyterian leader Samuel Davies petitioned the General Court to grant licenses for four Presbyterian meetinghouses, which were finally granted through the intervention of the governor. However, the status of Presbyterian churches and ministers remined tenuous, which forced Davies to travel to England in 1753 to obtain an opinion from the British attorney general that the Act of Toleration applied in Virginia and did not impose any limitations on the number of dissenting meetinghouses that could be licensed. Not until the 1760s, with Presbyterians firmly entrenched in Virginia and rising in social standing, did authorities give up on efforts to restrict their churches.[54]

Separate Baptists, who began appearing in central Virginia in the late 1750s, encountered even greater resistance and persecution from authorities than did the Presbyterians. Like the New Side Presbyterians, the Separate Baptists came out of the revivals of the Great Awakening, many initially being "Separatist" New Light Congregationalists before finding a home in the Baptist tradition. The upstart Separate Baptists were more evangelical and firmer in their Calvinist beliefs than the Regular and General Baptists. In addition, Separate Baptist itinerates were usually less educated than Presbyterian ministers, and their evangelical message commonly appealed to people of lower social standing, particularly when the itinerates showed little deference to the civil and religious authorities. According to one account, the Baptists' "strong convictions of the necessity of conversions to God, . . . [of] Repentance [and] justification by faith . . . appealed to the hearts of men. . . . Multitudes became believers under their fervent exhortations." The resulting growth of Baptist congregations was unparalleled. The first Separate Baptist church was formed in central Virginia in 1767; by 1770, there were six Baptist churches, and four years later there were reputedly over fifty congregations.[55]

For theological reasons, most Separate ministers refused to petition authorities for certificates to preach or for licenses for their meetinghouses. Not merely defiant of authority, Baptists did not hesitate to cause public annoyance with their evangelizing. As one complainant commented, the Baptists were "great disturbers of the peace, [and] they cannot meet a man upon the road but they must ram a text of Scripture down his throat."[56] In addition to defying civil authority, Baptist leaders condemned the Anglican clergy for their "loose and immoral deportment" and the gentry for their lax lifestyle and social practices, drawing the ire of both groups. Equally concerning for the gentry, Baptist itinerates evangelized among Black slaves, which threatened to undermine the control that masters exercised over the enslaved. (Presbyterian and then Methodist itinerates also evangelized Blacks but not to the extent of Baptists.) As a result, almost as soon as Baptists made their presence known in Virginia, civil and religious authorities began to persecute Baptists with a vengeance. According to one contemporary history,

"Magistrates and mobs, priests and sheriffs, courts and prisons all vainly combined to divert [the Baptist itinerates] from their object."[57]

Persecution broke out almost immediately. Anglican clergy, supported by local sheriffs and possies, broke up unauthorized Baptist meetings, assaulted ministers and congregants, and then fined the former for preaching without a license and the latter for being absent from Anglican worship. As another early account related matters, "Baptists never knew when they assembled whether they would be permitted to proceed in a peaceable manner, or to have their service barbarously broken up, without any protection from the civil authorities."[58] One infamous incident occurred in 1771 when an Anglican parson, accompanied by his clerk and the local sheriff, broke up a Baptist Sunday meeting. As the preacher, John Waller, led the congregation in a hymn, the Anglican parson ran "the but end of his whip into Waller's mouth and silenced him." When Waller then attempted to pray, the clerk dragged him from the stage, beat his head on the ground, with the sheriff horsewhipping Waller some twenty times, scarring him for life. That same year four additional Baptist itinerates were attacked and beaten at other meetings in Virginia.[59]

The first imprisonment of Baptist ministers for preaching without a license apparently occurred in January 1768, involving four men, including the same John Waller. Charged with disturbing the peace, the magistrates offered them release if they promised not to preach in the county for one year. The Baptists refused, and they were imprisoned in the Fredericksburg jail where they reputedly preached and sang hymns through the bars, often to hostile crowds. One preacher was released after four weeks, while Waller and the other two served an additional three weeks in jail. In 1771, Waller and other Baptist preachers were again imprisoned for several weeks for "not having an Episcopal Ordination to Teach or Preach the Gospel," and for engaging in actions "destructive to the Peace of Society to the subversion of all Religious establishment." According to John Ragosta, between 1768 and 1778, more than fifty Baptist ministers were imprisoned for preaching without a license with at least that many dissenters arrested, indicted, fined, or otherwise persecuted for engaging in Baptist worship.[60]

One of these incidents of Baptist imprisonment had a significant impact on a young James Madison. In early 1774, having recently returned to Virginia from college in Princeton, New Jersey, Madison discovered that a handful of Baptist ministers had been arrested and were being held in a nearby jail. In a letter to his college friend William Bradford, Madison railed against the ongoing religious persecution that was taking place in Virginia. "There are at this time in the adjacent county not less than five or six well-meaning men in close Gaol for publishing their religious sentiments which in the main are very orthodox," Madison wrote. Remarking on the different treatment of religious dissenters in tolerant Philadelphia (where Bradford lived), Madison added that "I want again to breathe your free air . . . but [I] have nothing to brag of as to the state and liberty of my [colony]." So, Madison concluded, "I leave you to pity me and pray for Liberty of Conscience to revive among us."[61] The imprisonment of the Baptists no doubt influenced Madison's developing views about religious freedom and left a lasting impression on him. Later in life he recounted the event, writing that he "spared no exertion to save them from imprisonment, and to promote their release from it." The Baptists' stance for religious liberty, Madison wrote, "obtained for [me] a lasting place in the favor of that particular sect." Persecution of the Baptists would not subside until the Revolutionary War with the enactment of the Virginia Declaration of Rights, the suspension of the religious assessment, and the need to secure support among religious dissenters for the patriot cause. But as Rhys Isaac wrote, "The rapid rise and uncompromising style of the New Light Separate Baptists brought on Virginia's first full-scale debate on religious liberty."[62]

By the advent of the American Revolution, therefore, religious controversy had been embroiling Virginia for three decades. The colony's religious diversity was expanding while the Anglican establishment was becoming more entrenched and hostile to challenges to its privileged position. The more Anglican officials and their allies lashed out, the more emboldened the dissenters became. These actions only added to the growing anticlericalism fueled by the church's internal difficulties represented through the Parson's Cause and the Bishop Controversy. This was the religious situation that Jefferson and Madison observed during their formative years, laying the foundation for their political engagement on these issues in the 1770s.

ㅣ〇 TWO 〇ㅣ

Thomas Jefferson's Background

S ince the mid-nineteenth century, jurists and historians alike have proclaimed Jefferson's and Madison's preeminent role in the development of the American ideas of religious freedom and separation of church and state. In 1879, Chief Justice Morrison Waite praised the contributions of Jefferson and Madison in securing disestablishment in both Virginia and at the federal level, declaring that their actions represented the "authoritative declaration of the scope and effect of the [First] amendment." Some seventy years later, Justice Hugo Black asserted that the two men "played such leading roles" in "the drafting and adoption" of the First Amendment, a sentiment later echoed by Justice William Brennan, who called them "the architects of the First Amendment." Scholars have generally agreed.[1]

Critics of that narrative exist, however, and they have commonly raised three counterarguments to this narrative. The first more or less accepts the conventional understanding of Jefferson's and Madison's vision of church-state separation, and of their religious heterodoxy, but argues that the two men's views were not representative of most members of the founding generation. In support of this position, critics point to the ubiquity of religious rhetoric and the prevalence of official acknowledgments of religion during the founding period. They note that even supporters of disestablishment, such as the Baptists, generally did not call for a *separation* of church and state.[2] The second response disputes that they were religiously heterodox and conveys them as holding more conventional religious views or at least being more sympathetic to religion's role in civil society. This response focuses on their upbringings and the religiously infused education the two men received at college. It asserts not only that religion significantly informed their political and world views but that Jefferson and Madison remained religiously pious throughout their lives, particularly in their later years.[3] The third critique relies on a handful of seeming contradictions in Jefferson's and Madison's approaches to church-state matters to refute claims that they agreed on the principles of separation and religious freedom. Critics note that Jefferson and Madison supported legislation approving days of public thanksgiving and punishing Sabbath violations, with Jefferson even supporting federal monies for a Catholic priest for an Indian tribe. Like the second critique, this response asserts that Jefferson and Madison were not as committed to a secular ideal or to church-state separation as has traditionally been portrayed.[4]

Aspects of these critiques are not without merit. When it came to ideas of church-state relations, Jefferson and Madison were clearly on the vanguard; according to Jack Rakove, on matters of religion and social order, "Jefferson and Madison marked the advanced edge of American thinking."[5] Unquestionably, many leaders of the founding generation were more conventionally religious and more accommodating of church-state intermixing. That should not be surprising considering the general acceptance of religion as being necessary for maintaining order and promoting morality and public virtue. Yet, Jefferson and Madison were not alone in their progressive views either, with contemporaries from various communities—evangelical dissenters, latitudinarians, rationalists—agreeing on essential points, particularly that religious establishments inhibited rights of conscience. Also, the fact that Jefferson and Madison were not always consistent in their approach to church-state separation and religious equality does not necessarily undermine their commitments to those principles; we must remember that they did not have the advantage of hindsight but were figuring out applications of these principles as they encountered them. We should always hesitate before judging the actions of historical figures by modern standards.[6]

And finally, efforts to marginalize Jefferson and Madison as religious outliers or, alternatively, to "rehabilitate" them as conventional Christians are chiefly distractions. Despite their religious heterodoxy, neither Jefferson nor Madison can accurately be characterized as a deist, at least in the sense as that belief has come to be understood today.[7] Conversely, the fact that both men adhered to certain essential principles of Christianity throughout their lives should not obscure the fact that they departed in significant ways from the Protestant orthodoxy of the day; neither does their religious essentialism contradict their strong convictions in favor of freedom of conscience and the separation of church and state, any more than it turns them into conventional Christians. Indeed, it would have been unusual if their upbringing and exposure to the religious forces and events of the time had not informed their perspectives about church-state matters. Their education and experiences complemented other secular referents that culminated in a comprehensive, and relatively consistent, approach to church-state matters throughout their lives.

A Political, Personal, and Principled Friendship

Historians have long noted the close, lifelong friendship and political collaboration between Jefferson and Madison. Adrienne Koch's dual biography of the men carries the subtitle "The Great Collaboration," with her writing that Jefferson and Madison had a "warm personal friendship" that was "fortified by [a] close political collaboration." A more recent dual biography calls their relationship a "fifty-year-long personal bond that guided the course of American history."[8] This is not just the opinion of modern-day historians; contemporaries recognized their close collaboration as well. According to John Quincy Adams, "Mr. Madison was the intimate, confidential, and devoted friend of Mr. Jefferson, and the mutual influence of these two mighty minds upon the other is a phenomenon."[9] Indeed, their friendship and political alliance extended throughout their adult lives, with them exchanging over 2,300 pieces of correspondence over the half-century, their last occurring two months before Jefferson's death on July 4, 1826, and concerning the operations of the University of Virginia.[10] While their close relationship and intellectual symbiosis can easily be overstated, the weight of evidence supports this narrative. In one of his final letters to Madison, an ailing Jefferson thanked him "for the friendship which has subsisted between us, now half a century, and the harmony of our political principles and pursuits, have been sources of constant happiness to me thro' that long period." "There was an irresistible, even magnetic, attraction," wrote James Morton Smith, "that pulled the two together into a harmonious relationship, one that easily withstood the stresses and strains that occasionally surfaced between them."[11]

That symbiosis began even before the two men met. As young children, Jefferson and Madison were raised under similar circumstances, on slave-labor plantations on the Piedmont frontier of colonial Virginia. Both were scions of the new planter elite, and both received a similar early education from tutors who were Anglican clergy. Even though they were born and raised approximately thirty miles apart, Jefferson and Madison apparently did not meet until October 1776, when the former was thirty-three years old and the latter twenty-five. (Coincidentally, a classmate of Jefferson's at his second tutelage with Reverend James Maury was Madison's cousin, also named James Madison, who would go on to become the Episcopal bishop of Virginia after the Revolution, so Jefferson was familiar with the Madison clan.)[12] The friendship did not coalesce until 1779 when Jefferson was governor of Virginia and Madison served on his executive Council of State. As Madison wrote later, "With the exception of an intercourse in a session of the Virginia Legislature in 1776, rendered slight by the disparity between us, I did not become acquainted with Mr. Jefferson till 1779, when being a member of the Executive council, and he the Governor, an intimacy took place." That began the forty-seven-year-long "personal bond" that continued until Jefferson's death. As Madison remarked afterward, that friendship "was for life" and "was never interrupted in the slightest degree for a single moment."[13]

Before considering that collaboration, however, this chapter examines Jefferson's background and the formation of his religious opinions in his earlier years. The next chapter considers Madison's background in the formation of his religious opinions. Subsequent chapters address whether and how those opinions may have evolved in later years.

Jefferson's Upbringing and Early Religious Views

A commentator on Jefferson's religious beliefs once observed that "the task of examining the religious ideas of Thomas Jefferson is not an easy one." For one, Jefferson was reticent to discuss his religious views or for them to be made public. "Say nothing of my religion," he wrote John Adams in 1817. "It is known to God and myself alone." As Jefferson informed another friend, "I have ever thought religion a concern purely between our god and our consciences, for which we were accountable to him. . . . I never told my own religion, nor scrutinised that of another."[14] His insistence on privacy was based on a deeply held commitment to individual freedom of conscience but also resulted from having experienced unfounded attacks on his beliefs throughout much of his adult life. Yet, as examined in a later chapter, in retirement Jefferson frequently referred to, if not defended, his religious inclinations in correspondence to friends and acquaintances. Because of this desire to protect but then justify his beliefs, "Jefferson's religion has long fascinated and vexed students of his career." The result, according to biographer Merrill D. Peterson, is that "in the twentieth century, Jefferson's religion has been the subject of more articles, many of them scholarly, than any other topic except his politics; and the great majority have attempted to demonstrate that he was *some* kind of Christian."[15]

Thomas Jefferson was born on April 13, 1743, at Shadwell plantation in Albemarle County, Virginia, to Peter and Jane Randolph Jefferson. Peter Jefferson, a "middle rank" man of "means and enterprise," had patented one thousand acres of wilderness land at the edge of the Blue Ridge Mountains in 1735, clearing a portion for planting and building a modest home. He eventually acquired another six thousand acres and over one hundred slaves for cultivating tobacco. (At his father's death, Jefferson would inherit approximately five thousand acres and fifty-two slaves.) Even though the Jeffersons could trace their lineage in Virginia back several generations, Jefferson's mother, Jane, hailed from a more prominent family—the Randolphs—whose relatives assumed leading roles in Virginia society and politics. Peter Jefferson was ambitious, however, rising in status to that of a local squire and magistrate while serving as vestryman for the local Anglican parish.[16]

As the last fact suggests, young Thomas was baptized an Anglican, a religious affiliation he never renounced. Despite his father's position as a vestryman, however, there is little to indicate that Jefferson's family was anything more than nominally religious. Local gentry assumed the role of vestrymen as a prerogative, which chiefly indicated the holder's social standing, and with Charlottesville having no church building, Anglican worship was irregularly held during Jefferson's childhood. Still, it can be assumed that in his early years Jefferson was instructed in the orthodox doctrines and rites of the Church of England.[17] For five years, beginning at the age of nine, Jefferson was tutored in the home of Anglican minister William Douglas, who in addition to instructing in religion taught "the rudiments of the Latin and Greek languages," as well as French. Douglas was apparently an uninspiring tutor, and after Peter Jefferson's untimely death in 1757, the fourteen-year-old Jefferson began a two-year tutelage under

Anglican minister James Maury, who Jefferson called "a correct classical scholar."[18] Biographer Dumas Malone described Maury as a rigid church-man who was "bitterly intolerant" of religious dissenters. "It is obvious that [Jefferson] did not get from Maury his ideas about the relations between church and state," Malone wrote. "Nor did the future advocate of religious freedom get from this teacher any germinal ideas about the just treatment of dissenters."[19] In his *Autobiography*, written in 1821, Jefferson does not men-tion the intensity of the religious instruction he received under the two tu-tors, though there is little doubt that he studied the Bible as he was able to cite scripture with ease throughout his life.[20]

Still, instruction in the Bible and church doctrines, which was central to all education at the time, does not necessarily indicate any degree of reli-gious devotion. Two of his earlier letters offer contrasting perspectives. In a 1763 letter to a friend, John Page, Jefferson provided a conventionally reli-gious, if not dour, view of human condition, writing that "perfect happiness was never intended by the deity to be the lot of any one of his creatures in this world." The only method "to fortify our minds against . . . calamities and misfortunes" of life was "to assume a perfect resignation to the divine will, to consider that whatever does happen, must happen . . . and to proceed with a pious and unshaken resignation till we arrive at our journey's end, where we may deliver up our trust into the hands of him who gave it, and receive such reward as to him shall seem proportioned to our merit."[21] Whether such a conventional religious view reflected an early flirtation with orthodoxy or a restatement of the prevailing social conventions is impossible to assess. Years later, however, in a letter to a French friend, Jefferson admitted that he "had never sense enough to comprehend" the "ritual of the church in which I was educated," and that he had had "difficulty of reconciling the ideas of Unity and Trinity . . . from a very early part of my life."[22]

Whether the young Jefferson experienced a "religious crisis" that caused him to "reject . . . his ancestral Anglican creed" and embrace "instead a vaguely defined natural religion," as some biographers have suggested, or that he simply underwent a normal questioning of rote doctrine, the next phase of his life ushered in an exploration into religious heterodoxy that he would maintain for the remainder of his life.[23] In 1760, seventeen-year-old Jefferson matriculated in the College of William and Mary in Williams-burg, the colonial capital. At the time, William and Mary had approxi-mately a hundred students at various levels and seven faculty, all but one an Anglican minister. Jefferson had the "great good fortune" to study under (and be mentored by) Scotsman William Small, professor of mathematics, science, and natural philosophy and the sole nonclerical member of the faculty. Small was a devotee of the Scottish Enlightenment and of rational free inquiry, a man whom Jefferson praised as having "an enlarged and liberal mind." Later in life, Jefferson referred to Small as his surrogate father and declared that "to his enlightened & affectionate guidance of my studies while at College I am indebted for every thing."[24] Jefferson shortly became a junior participant in soirees held by the town's intellectual triumvirate—Small, lawyer George Wythe, and Lieutenant Governor Francis Fauquier—with Jefferson's presence making it a "partie quarreé." Wythe was a disciple of John Locke and along with Fauquier held deistic religious views. Jefferson later called them "inseparable friends, and with their frequent dinners with the governor . . . [I] heard more good sense, more rational and philosophical conversations than in all my life besides." Under their influence, Jefferson likely came to question many core Christian doctrines.[25]

Following graduation, Jefferson apprenticed under Wythe studying law. At the same time, he continued with his study of the classics, philosophy, and foreign languages. Wythe would have a lifelong influence on Jefferson, later writing that Wythe was "devoted to liberty and the natural and equal rights of man" and was "neither troubled [by], nor perhaps trusted anyone with his religious creed." Wythe, Jefferson noted with admiration, "left to the world the conclusion that that religion must be good which could produce a life of such exemplary virtue."[26] Years later, Anglican apologist Bishop William Meade wrote derisively that "Mr. Jefferson, and Wythe, . . . did not conceal their disbelief in Christianity," even though they took part "in the[ir] duties as vestrymen."[27]

During this apprenticeship, Jefferson began expanding his commonplace book—a compilation of excerpts from poetic, philosophical, and historical works—likely started while a student under Reverend Maury. Historians consider Jefferson's commonplace book to be a significant piece of historical evidence as it offers insight not only into what he read but also as to what material he considered to be intellectually significant if not profound. Of all the excerpts, the largest number of entries are from Viscount Henry St. John Bolingbroke's *Philosophical Works,* a total of fifty-four, amounting to over ten thousand words and constituting approximately 40 percent of the book.[28] Bolingbroke was an advocate of human reason and a critic of religious orthodoxy, and associated with the likes of Voltaire and Montesquieu in the early eighteenth century. Bolingbroke's writings challenged many traditional Christian doctrines, including the Incarnation and Virgin Birth of Jesus, his divinity, the miracles, and of acquiring understanding of God through revelation rather than reason. Bolingbroke was a thorough-going materialist, a critic of clerical authority, and a skeptic of the authenticity of many biblical accounts. On the whole, according to historian Eugene R. Sheridan, *Philosophical Works* was "a veritable summa of rationalistic criticisms of revealed religion." The excerpts Jefferson included in his commonplace book concern many of Bolingbroke's harsher critiques: Jesus's divinity and redemptive mission, the authenticity of miracles and scripture, the later corruption of Christian principles, and the need for human reason to mediate religious questions. Significantly, Jefferson's entries from Bolingbroke represent the only works that concern Christianity.[29]

It is impossible to gauge the full significance and impact of Jefferson's reading and regurgitation of Bolingbroke's heterodoxy. Jefferson was likely introduced to *Philosophical Works* by Governor Fauquier, who admired Bolingbroke, so the latter's writings may have merely reinforced Jefferson's developing views about religion. Still, most historians believe that "Bolingbroke's contribution to Jefferson's religious ideas was profound." As another historian has written, "No single influence was stronger on Jefferson's formation and none was more continuous."[30] That influence can be seen in a number of letters Jefferson later wrote to various acquaintances where he recommended reading Bolingbroke's *Philosophical Works*. And more telling, "for at least the next two decades, Jefferson's religious views departed in no significant respect from those of Bolingbroke." Even later in life, Jefferson's admiration for Bolingbroke remained strong, calling him an "enem[y] of the priests & Pharisees of [his] day. . . . His political tracts are safe reading for the most timid religinist, his philosophical, for those who are not afraid to trust their reason with discussions of right and wrong." At least until the late 1790s when Jefferson encountered the writings of Joseph Priestley, "Bolingbroke's works accurately reflect[ed] [Jefferson's] own considered opinion of Christianity."[31]

By the late 1760s, Jefferson had concluded his apprenticeship with Wythe, been admitted to the Bar of the General Court, and elected to the House of Burgesses. By that time, Jefferson had adopted a form of religious rationalism, one that judged religious doctrines, biblical principles, and the scripture itself by what survived the test of reason. At that point, Jefferson had rejected the Virgin Birth, the divinity of Jesus, his miracles, and his redemptive mission; the denial of the Trinity and the authenticity of the epistles of the Bible were positions that aligned him with deist thought. According to his second cousin Edmund Randolph—who served with Jefferson in George Washington's cabinet as attorney general and succeeded him as secretary of state—Jefferson was adept "in the ensnaring subtleties of deism and gave it, among the rising generation, a philosophical patronage; which repudiates as falsehoods those [biblical] things unsusceptible of strict demonstration." Based on conventional understandings of the day, Jefferson was not a Christian, nor does it appear that he thought of himself as one at that time, at least in the sense of what he observed about Christian practice in the larger society.[32]

It would be wrong, however, to declare as some authors have that "by 1771, Christianity held little or nothing that attracted him" or that Jefferson was a deist in the model of Thomas Paine. Even at this early age, Jefferson was a committed moralist who believed in accordance with Scottish philosopher Lord Kames that God had endowed in each person the ability to distinguish right from wrong and, if allowed to use that faculty, to choose the former over the latter. Moral sense needed cultivating, however, by giving people access to uncorrupted ethical and religious principles. Writing to Robert Skipwith in August 1771, Jefferson observed that "exercise produces habit; and in the instance of which we speak, the exercise being of the moral feelings, produces a habit of thinking and acting virtuously." When considering what to study and read, Jefferson recommended that "every thing is useful which contributes to fix us in the principles and practice of virtue."[33] Years later, Jefferson still adhered to this belief in a moral sense. Writing to his nephew Peter Carr in 1787, Jefferson declared that "man was destined for society. His morality, therefore, was to be formed to this object. He was endowed with a sense of right and wrong merely relative to this. This sense is as much as part of his nature as the sense of hearing, seeing, feeling; it is the true foundation of morality. . . . The moral sense, or conscience, is as much a part of man as his leg or arm."[34] Jefferson believed that the true value of any religion depended on the moral standards it promoted rather than the doctrines it taught.[35]

Jefferson thus became a theistic "religious essentialist": he accepted only those religious beliefs that promoted a moral life and improved the conditions of society. A benevolent and providential God, the ethical teachings of Jesus, and some form of rewards and punishments after death were essential elements for a religion that would promote morality.[36] He listed several of these in some fragmentary notes compiled in 1776. "The [essentials] fundamentals of Xty. as found in the gospels are 1. Faith. 2. Repentance," Jefferson noted. The lessons "from our Savior's mission" were "1. the knolege of one god only. 2. a clear knolege of their duty, or system of morality, delivered on such authority as to give it sanction. 3. [that] the outward forms of religious worship [were] to be purged of that farcical pomp & nonsense with which they were loaded. [and] 4. an inducement to a pious life, by revealing clearly a future existence in bliss, & that it was to be the reward of the virtuous." For Jefferson, these fundamentals were found "in the preaching of our savior, which is related in the gospels"; in contrast, the epistles contained biases of their writers "promiscuously mixed with other truths."[37] Even then, he did not consider the gospels to be inspired—they contained too many unverified claims such as the miracles. Rather, the Bible was a human history that contained numerous errors. The "new testament . . . is the history of a personage called Jesus," he told his nephew Carr. Accordingly, he should "read the bible, then as you would read Livy or Tacitus," or other classical histories, with a healthy skepticism. And "those facts in the bible which contradict the laws of nature, must be examined with more care." That advice was not just limited to reading the Bible but also for considering all religious claims. "You must lay aside all prejudice on both sides" of any religious issue, Jefferson advised Carr, "and neither believe nor reject any thing because any other person, or description of persons have rejected or believed it." This last statement was of course a swipe at the authority of clergy and church doctrine. When it came to religion, "It is too important, and the consequences of error may be too serious" not to question authority: "shake off all the fears and servile prejudices under which weak minds are servilely crouched."[38]

Those religious essentials that were convincing also had to withstand the scrutiny of reason. "Reason and free inquiry are the only effectual agents" for discovering truth, Jefferson wrote in his *Notes on the State of Virginia*, as they would "support true religion by bringing every false one to their tribunal, to the test of their investigation." Everywhere that "reason and experiment have been indulged . . . error has fled before them."[39] He gave the same advice to his nephew: "Fix reason firmly in her seat, and call to her tribunal every fact, every opinion. Question with boldness even the existence of a god; because, if there be one, he must more approve the homage of reason, than that of blindfolded fear." Even if that inquiry brought about a negative answer, he told Carr, "do not be frightened . . . by any fear of it's consequences. If it ends in a belief that there is no god, you will find incitements to virtue in the comfort and pleasantness you feel in it's exercise." In the end, "Your own reason is the only oracle given you by heaven, and you are answerable not for the rightness but uprightness of the decision."[40]

So, by early adulthood, Jefferson had rejected many of the central doctrines of Christianity: the Virgin Birth, the divinity of Jesus and his substitutional atonement for humankind, the Trinity, the inspiration of the Bible, and then those mysterious and supernatural components of Christianity contained in the Bible and in church doctrine. As Annette Gordon-Reed and Peter S. Onuf note, Jefferson "rejected all the miracles in the Bible, seeing them as distractions from the real message that the philosopher, who he deliberately called 'Jesus of Nazareth' brought to the world." All religious doctrines and beliefs had to be judged in the tribunal of free inquiry and reason.[41] Even with these views, Jefferson continued to attend Anglican worship, reputedly brining his worn prayer book. In 1772, he married Martha Wayles Skelton in a ceremony performed by an Anglican minister, and his children were all baptized in the Church of England. He was appointed a vestryman, though there is no indication he partook in those duties. Jefferson also developed a friendship with Reverend Charles Clay, the evangelical-leaning rector of Charlottesville's St. Anne's Church, the construction of which Jefferson contributed to financially.[42] Some authors have argued that because Jefferson engaged in these conventional practices, he held more traditional Christian views, notwithstanding his writings. At most, however, they indicate that Jefferson was not hostile to religion generally or to all organized religion or all clergy, or that he perceived any serious inconsistency between his idiosyncratic beliefs and participating in the religious ceremonies and traditions of the day.[43]

Jefferson's Early Musings on Religious Freedom

Jefferson's insistence that reason was essential for discovering religious truths implied an individual freedom to exercise that reason. His belief that early church leaders and then clergy had perpetuated many orthodox (i.e., false) doctrines for their own benefit and power also led him to embrace free inquiry and to reject the authority of ecclesiastical organizations, including those supported by the state. Early on, Jefferson did not express the degree of anticlericalism that he would exhibit later in life or tie it as directly to the need for religious freedom and disestablishment. But Jefferson had observed the rise in anticlericalism associated with the Parson's Cause and had read Bolingbroke and the writings of Whig critics about the wealth, indolence, and corruption of clergy. By the mid-1770s, he was integrating that inclination into his call for greater religious freedom.

Jefferson's commitment to religious freedom grew out of and was central to his general commitment to free inquiry and freedom of conscience. Even though the latter was commonly manifested in the right to choose which religious tenets to believe—the right of private judgment on matters concerning religion—for Jefferson, the conscience right was broader and included the ability to use one's mind to arrive at whatever conclusions reason led to. This included the right not to hold religious beliefs, as he had informed his nephew Peter Carr. As William Lee Miller asserted, "For Jefferson, religious liberty was part of that larger liberty (larger to him—larger and also smaller to many believers), freedom of the *mind*." Jefferson's commitment to religious freedom must thus be considered together with his advocacy for a secular university, for public education, for freedom of the press, and with his interest in discovering the natural laws of science.[44]

Jefferson's early embrace of religious freedom likely resulted from his exposure in college to Enlightenment writers such as Locke and Lord Shaftesbury and to the influence of the triumvirate of Small, Wythe, and Fauquier, who embraced reason and free inquiry while demonstrating degrees of religious heterodoxy. In Jefferson's 1771 letter to Robert Skipwith suggesting books for a private library, he recommended Locke for his "conduct of the mind in search of truth." That admiration continued throughout Jefferson's life; some forty years later, he referred to "Bacon, Newton, & Locke" as "my trinity of the three greatest men the world had ever produced," in part for their advocacy of freedom of inquiry. Unlike Madison, there is no indication that Jefferson embraced the value of religious freedom after observing the persecution of religious dissenters, though he must have heard of their occasional plight simply by growing up in the Piedmont with its considerable number of Presbyterian and Baptist dissidents. Jefferson's statement in his *Autobiography* that the "unrighteous compulsion, to maintain teachers of what [the dissenters] deemed religious errors, was grievously felt during

the regal government, and without a hope of relief," suggests some awareness of that persecution.⁴⁵

Like many contemporaries, Jefferson celebrated the tradition of civil and
religious liberty that reputedly existed in colonial America, with him writing
in his 1775 "Declaration of the Causes and Necessity of Taking Up Arms"
that "our forefathers, inhabitants of the island of Great-Britain . . . left their
native land, to seek on these shores a residence for civil and religious freedom." As discussed in the previous chapter, as the political crisis with Great
Britain unfolded in the 1770s, many colonialists justified the revolution on
the need to protect not only their civil rights but their religious rights as
well. Summing up the sentiment shared by many Americans, Thomas Paine
in *Common Sense* identified the goals of the rebellion as "securing freedom
and property to all men, and above all things, the free exercise of religion,
according to the dictates of conscience."⁴⁶

A detailed, early musing of Jefferson's about the value of religious freedom is found in his fragmentary notes prepared in the autumn of 1776 when
he was a member of the House of Delegates' Committee on Religion, which
was tasked with revising Virginia's religious laws. The notes show considerable reliance on Locke, particularly his *Letter on Toleration*. "Why persecute for difference in religion," Jefferson asked rhetorically, and "how far
does the duty of toleration extend?" The answers to the initial inquiry were
first, to correct people from their heretical positions and from committing
"gross vices," and second, to prevent the spread of opinions contrary to
orthodox Christianity that might interfere with the "salvation of souls." As
Jefferson continued with sarcasm, "The fantastical points for which we generally persecute are often very questionable." Paraphrasing Locke, Jefferson
wrote that society was constituted for "preserving [man's] civil interests"
such as life, health, liberty, and property. The "magistrate's jurisdn. extends
only to civil rights and from these considerations." The people had "not
given him the care of souls . . . because no man has [the] *right* to abandon
the care of his salvation to another." Not only did civil officials lack jurisdiction over religious matters, Jefferson continued, "no man has *power* to let
another prescribe his faith. faith is not faith witht. believing." Because the
"life & essence of religion consists in the internal persuasion or belief of the
mind . . . no man can conform his faith to the dictates of another." Accordingly, "External forms [of wor]ship, when [imposed] against our belief, are
hypocrisy [and im]piety."⁴⁷

As for the second inquiry, the question of why to tolerate religious differences, Jefferson again echoed Locke, asserting that a church was "a *voluntary* society of men, joining [themselves] together of their own accord, in order to the [publick] worshipping of god in such a manner as they judge [accept]able to him & effectual to the salvation of their souls." This situation inevitably promoted a variety of opinions about religious matters, and "from the dissensions among sects themselves arises necessarily a right of chusing & necessity of deliberating to which we will conform." And if we desire the ability to "chuse for ourselves, we must allow others to chuse also, & so reciprocally[,] this establishes religious liberty." In addition, Jefferson asserted, any error in belief affected only the person holding those beliefs: "If any man err from the right way, it is his own misfortune, no injury to thee." Therefore, he concluded, "we have no right to prejudice another in his civil enjoiments because he is of another church." Because religious compulsion implicated the core of a right of conscience and free inquiry, "[co]mpulsion in religion is distinguished peculiarly from compulsion in every other thing."[48]

Despite drawing on Locke to inform his ideas about religious freedom, Jefferson was not willing to be constrained by what he saw as limitations in Locke's proposals. Jefferson noted that Locke had not extended the benefits of toleration "to those who entertain opinions contrary to those moral rules necessary for the preservation of society." Included in that category were those, among others, whose "obedience is due to some foreign prince, or who will not own & teach the duty of tolerating all men in matters of religion, or who deny the existence of a god"—in essence, Catholics, atheists, and religious fanatics (though Locke believed Jews and Muslims should be tolerated). This troubled Jefferson, who believed that Christians historically had "distinguished [themselves] above all people who have ever lived for persecutions." The granting of "mere toleration" to religious dissenters had actually produced "the reverse," Jefferson wrote. "It is the refusing *toleration* to those of a different opn which has produced all the bustles & wars on account of religion. It was the misfortune of mankind that during the darker centuries the Xn priests[,] following their ambition & avarice & combining with the magistrates to divide the spoils of the people, could establish the notion that schismatics might be ousted of their possessions & destroyed. This notion we have not yet cleared ourselves from." Here, we see early expression of his lifelong anticlericalism—that entrenched clergy were largely responsible for oppressing freedom of conscience and private judgment on matters of belief while aligning with civil authorities to persecute nonconformists. Jefferson thus noted that all people owed a debt to Locke's ideas, which were "a great thing to go so far" as they did, "but where he stopped short, we may go on."[49]

Jefferson elaborated on the views from his notes five years later in his query on "Religion" in his *Notes on the State of Virginia*.[50] Jefferson had reassessed his rosy view of the colonial tradition of religious liberty, now writing how immigrants to the colonies had "cast their eyes on these new [colonies] as asylums of civil and religious freedom, but they found them free only for the reigning sect." Focusing on Virginia, he alleged that the Anglican church had "show[n] an equal intolerance" in the colony as the church had practiced in England. Listing several laws that shored up the Virginia establishment, Jefferson charged the arrangement had created a form of "religious slavery" for those dissenters who had "lavished their lives and fortunes for the establishment of their civil freedom." In his *Notes*, Jefferson reiterated the two grounds for supporting religious freedom that he had identified earlier. First, again relying on Locke, he repeated the jurisdictional argument—that civil rulers "can have authority over such natural rights only as we have submitted to them. The rights of conscience we never submitted." And because the state's only interest was to protect against *civil* injuries, nonconforming religious opinions caused no injury to the state. As he continued with a statement that his political opponents would later use against him, Jefferson declared, "It does me no injury for my neighbor to say there are twenty Gods, or no God. It neither picks my pocket nor breaks my leg." The second ground was that religious compulsion was injurious to reason and freedom of conscience, which were the only tools for discovering true religion. "Reason and free inquiry are the only effectual agents against error," whereas "truth cans stand by itself." Picking up on his earlier musings, Jefferson insisted that uniformity of religious belief and practice was simply unattainable based on human nature and the lessons of history: "Millions of innocent men, women and children, since the introduction of Christianity, have been burnt, tortured, fined, imprisoned; yet we have not advanced one inch toward uniformity. What has been the effect of coercion? To make one-half the world fools, and the other half hypocrites."[51]

"But is uniformity of opinion desirable?" he asked rhetorically. On the contrary, Jefferson wrote, answering his own question, "difference of opinion is advantageous in religion." He pointed to the examples of Pennsylvania and New York, which "have long subsisted without any establishment at all." Religion "of various kinds" "flourish[es] infinitely" while "their harmony is unparalleled. . . . They have made the happy discovery, that the way to silence religious disputes is to take no notice of them." Although the *Notes* were designed to provide the reader with an overview of the geography, climate, and customs of Virginia, Jefferson could not resist deviating from facts into opinions when writing his particular query.[52]

There is one other significant piece of Jefferson's earlier works that people have claimed reflects his political theology—that writing, of course, is the Declaration of Independence. Unlike his *Notes on the State of Virginia* (or the Bill for Establishing Religious Freedom), the Declaration does not contain an argument on behalf of religious freedom. It may, however, reflect Jefferson's assumptions about the philosophical basis for political rights and the legitimacy of government (with the caveat that the Declaration was a joint project, with Jefferson penning the draft, committee members Benjamin Franklin and John Adams suggesting changes, and then Congress as a whole making thirty-nine changes. Adams would later remark that "Congress cut off about a quarter part of it, as I expected they would, but they obliterated some of the best of it and left all that was exceptionable").[53]

The Declaration of Independence has been scrutinized and dissected more than any other document of American history. That is in no small part due to the Declaration's association with the birth of the United States and the widely accepted notion that it sets out the nation's essential republican values.[54] The purpose of discussing it here is not to examine the various ideological sources for its political assumptions but to consider whether it offers insight into Jefferson's ideas about the relationship between religion and government. Initially, it must be remembered that the Declaration was chiefly a listing of grievances against the British government and a justification for breaking political ties with the home country, through armed resistance if necessary. The document had "one thing, and one thing only" to accomplish, wrote William F. Dana, "and that was, a justification of the separation of the Colonies from Great Britain."[55] Second, the language of the Declaration had to inspire and unite the colonialists—to convince those wavering minds that independence was the only solution to the year-long armed conflict and to rally all others to the patriot cause. One of the means of accomplishing the latter was to state the case in stark and compelling terms—that the cause met with God's providential will and had God's blessing. And finally, religious language and imagery, and appeals to God, were ubiquitous in the political documents and writings of the time—even the works of Thomas Paine are full of religious allusions: "Our independence with God's blessing we will maintain against all the world," Paine declared in *The American Crisis II*. Consequently, it would have been remarkable if such a seminal document, one designed to explain and justify severance with Britain, had omitted claims of God's approval.[56]

With these cautions in mind, the language and arguments of the Declaration are "an example of the moderate form of the Enlightenment." Its terms, "self-evident" truths and "unalienable rights," evoke the rationalist natural-rights theory that "all human beings can perceive, understand, and act upon consensual, universal truths."[57] The document contains four deific references. Most familiar to people is language in the Declaration's second paragraph, which states, "We hold these truths to be self-evident; that all men are created equal; that they are endowed by their Creator with certain unalienable rights." Possibly less familiar, the initial paragraph speaks of the colonists' possessing "the separate and equal station to which the Laws of Nature and of Nature's God entitle them." After listing the various grievances against Britain, the Declaration concludes with an appeal to "the Supreme Judge of the world" and a claim to having "a firm reliance on the protection of divine Providence."[58] All of these references have a distinct natural-rights ring to them—they are not necessarily appeals to or acknowledgments of a Christian god. It is important to note, however, that Jefferson's initial draft included only the initial phrase "Laws of Nature and of Nature's God." After sharing the draft with Franklin and Adams, the phrase "endowed by their Creator" was substituted in place of Jefferson's original language of "that from the equal creation they derive rights inherent and inalienable." Some scholars have maintained that Franklin suggested adding the reference to a "Creator" while others believe the evidence is more equivocal. Jefferson's initial wording of truths being "sacred and undeniable" was also dropped in favor of the familiar phrase "We hold these truths to be self-evident." The final two references—"Supreme Judge of the World" and "divine

Providence"—were added to the document by members of Congress before the Declaration's final approval.[59]

Jefferson was therefore responsible for the first deific reference of "Nature's God," and then possibly for the declaration that "unalienable rights" are "endowed by [their] Creator." Even if the latter reference was suggested by Franklin, Jefferson likely agreed with the sentiment that natural rights were at an initial point implanted in humans by the god of nature—as Jefferson wrote in his 1774 *Summary View of the Rights of British America*, "The god who gave us life, gave us liberty at the same time." According to historian Allen Jayne, for Jefferson rights "were part of man's inner nature or being, even though God created that nature or being." As Jefferson wrote years later in an apparent reference to the Declaration, "evidence of . . . natural right[s], like that of our right to life, liberty, the use of our faculties, the pursuit of happiness, is not left to the feeble and sophistical investigations of reason but is impressed on the sense of every man." Thus, rights "did not need to be rationally derived from considering the nature of man and God and God's will; they emerged as feelings from man's inner nature or being once God put them there."[60]

As for the phrase Jefferson clearly did author, historian John Fea writes that "'Nature's God' was a term used often by eighteenth-century deists who upheld the belief that God created the world; instilled it with natural laws of science, morality, and politics; and allowed it to function based on those laws without any further divine intervention."[61] As discussed, Jefferson was never a true deist, though he was influenced by deistic writings and his theology was aligned with many deistic beliefs. Jayne elaborates on the meaning of "Nature's God": "'Nature's God' of the Declaration, like the laws of nature, was not made known to humanity by God's exclusive revelation or the custodians of such revelation, whether church or priestcraft. 'Nature's God' could be detected with the reason of each individual human being. Jefferson, by referring to 'Nature's God,' thereby departed from the Old and New Testament in giving reason precedence over revelation as a means of gaining knowledge of God."[62] Although Jefferson's conscious choice of these terms reflected his theological perspective, as well as his political views about the source of natural rights informing republican government, the terms "Nature's God" and "Creator" were sufficiently vague and common in popular discourse; as a result, both rationalists and the religiously orthodox could affirm the concept that there were natural laws and rights that had at some point originated from God.[63]

An argument could be made that the other two deific references in the Declaration added by members of Congress indicated more conventional religious ideas. "Supreme Judge of the World" could be interpreted as an affirmation of traditional Christian doctrine that people will be held morally accountable by God upon death; however, heterodox believers including Jefferson, Adams, and Franklin accepted various aspects of a future state of rewards and punishments. And while the reference to divine providence was also more conventional, it could appeal to orthodox and heterodox believers alike. Allusions to the interposing of providence were ubiquitous during the revolutionary era and found their way into the rhetoric of deists like Franklin and Paine, as well as that of Jefferson and Madison. Still, these more conventional references to God "were conspicuously missing in Jefferson's draft," asserted Pauline Maier, and Jefferson likely would have preferred their omission. As he later told Madison, while Congress was making changes, he "was writhing a little under the acrimonious criticisms on some of its parts."[64]

Jefferson's idea of religious freedom enunciated in the Declaration was therefore subtle but profound. The god of nature had endowed each individual with natural rights, the ability to reason, and an inner sense to discern those rights. Having created the laws of nature, Nature's God would not contradict God's own laws or interfere with the ability of people to use their rational faculties to discover religious truth. If God "has made it a law in the nature of man to pursue his own happiness," Jefferson wrote in a statement that applied to religion as well, "he has left him free in the choice of place as well as mode."[65] This implied that there were no legitimate intermediaries between God and the individual in this search for religious truth, whether those were civil authorities or clergy. And because all people were "created equal" by Nature's God and entitled to "equal station" in the exercise of their rights, including religious rights, no religion was entitled to a preferred status in society. Finally, Jefferson's deific references in the Declaration are consistent with the rationally theistic worldview he held in his mid-thirties. By that time, Jefferson's ideas about Christianity, the attainment of religious knowledge, the basis for religious freedom residing in free inquiry, and the evils of religious establishments all reflected his considerable thought about the matter.[66]

By 1780, Jefferson's ideas about religious faith and religious freedom were well formed. Central to both was his firm belief in free inquiry and freedom of conscience. Both of those values encompassed more than a freedom of religion, but religious freedom was an essential manifestation of those values. Jefferson's ideas about these matters would remain relatively consistent for the remainder of his life, though he later came to realize that his heterodox religious beliefs could fit within a framework of a rational, primitive Christianity.

James Madison's Background

The development of James Madison's religious beliefs and ideas about freedom of conscience and religious freedom deviated from that of Thomas Jefferson more than it paralleled it. Even though, as noted, Madison and Jefferson grew up in the same region of Virginia under similar circumstances as scions of landed gentry, the formative components that influenced their religious attitudes differed greatly, arising chiefly through their different college experiences. While Jefferson benefited from—and was greatly influenced by—his mentoring by the deistic triumvirate of William Small, George Wythe, and Francis Fauquier in Williamsburg, Madison's collegiate experience was considerably more traditional. Madison's earlier speculations about religion also were more conventional than those of Jefferson. That they ended up sharing similar perspectives about religion and its role in civil society is part of the remarkable story of their collaboration.

Madison's Upbringing and Early Religious Views

Like Thomas Jefferson, James Madison was born into one of the first European families to settle the Virginia Piedmont. Unlike Jefferson, Madison's prominent lineage drew chiefly from his father's side; one great grandfather (James Taylor) had patented over thirteen thousand acres in what would become Orange County in 1722, whereas his paternal grandfather from a different line (Ambrose Madison) had obtained five thousand areas nearby in 1728, eventually establishing a plantation that would become Montpelier.

(The paternal side of Madison's family would produce two US presidents: Madison and his distant cousin Zachary Taylor.) Madison was born on March 16, 1751, the first child to James Madison Sr. and Nelly Conway Madison. As a member of the landed gentry, James Madison Sr. served as a vestryman for the Anglican parish, which in addition to managing church affairs included responsibility for collecting religious tax assessments and enforcing moral behavioral codes, including Sabbath conduct and observance. As vestryman, James Sr. would also have been tasked with enforcing the laws requiring the licensing of dissenting ministers and their meeting-houses. While there is no record of James Sr.'s activities in this regard, persecution of Baptists did occur in neighboring Culpepper and Spotsylvania Counties in the 1760s, so it is likely that a young Madison was aware of the plight of religious dissenters.[1]

Madison's earliest schooling was in a local plantation school where he received rudimentary instruction in reading, writing, and arithmetic. In 1761, at the age of ten, Madison was sent to be tutored by Reverend Donald Robertson, a Scots-born Anglican minister educated at the University of Edinburgh, whom Madison would recall as "a man of extensive learning, and a distinguished Teacher." There, in addition to instruction in the basics, Robertson introduced Madison to the Greek and Roman classics and foreign languages, including Latin. After five years, and apparently needing or desiring additional study to prepare for college, Madison returned home for two more years of tutoring by Reverend Thomas Martin, who was rector of the nearby Anglican church. Martin was a recent graduate of the College of New Jersey at Princeton, which was operated by New Side Presbyterians. Martin likely influenced Madison's decision to choose Princeton over the College of William and Mary, though Madison's father may also have been motivated by the declining reputation of William and Mary after the departure of Jefferson's mentor William Small. (Historian Mark Noll asserts that James Madison Sr. sent his son to Princeton based on Reverend John Witherspoon's reputation as a friend of religious freedom. Conversely, Bishop William Meade claimed that the Madisons may have chosen Princeton because of the prevalence of skepticism at William and Mary at the time.) The already sickly Madison also wrote that he attempted to avoid the Tidewater areas because of their unhealthy climate. Whatever the reasons for choosing Princeton over Willian and Mary, the decision had a significant impact on Madison's intellectual and philosophical development.[2]

Madison arrived in Princeton, New Jersey, in 1769. The college had been established some quarter century earlier by New Side Presbyterian leaders for the purpose of training their clergy. At the time of Madison's matriculation, Princeton was the most rigorous and dynamic college in the colonies.[3] This was due in part to its new president, John Witherspoon, who had come to Princeton only a year earlier from Scotland. Educated at the University of Edinburgh, Witherspoon adhered to the "common-sense" school of the Scottish Enlightenment, though in Scotland he had resisted both the moderating trend in the established Scottish church and the secularizing strain of the Scottish Enlightenment represented by David Hume and Adam Smith. Despite professing orthodox Calvinist beliefs, Witherspoon possessed two notable characteristics: he opposed ecclesiastical authority and was committed to having students exercise their own judgment in arriving at religious and philosophical conclusions. During Witherspoon's presidency, the college's stated goal was that "care is to be taken to cherish the spirit of liberty, and free enquiry, and not only to permit, but even to encourage their right to private judgment, without presuming to dictate with an air of infallibility, or demanding an implicit assent to the decisions of the preceptor." As a result, even though religious ideas permeated much of the curriculum, "the college with pride guaranteed 'free and equal Liberty and Advantage of Education [to] any Person of any religious Denomination whatsoever.'"[4]

When Madison arrived at Princeton he found himself "at the center of the English dissenting tradition in North America," wrote biographer Ralph Ketcham. The intellectual environment at the college "took for granted the pattern of thought . . . [that] had opposed religious establishment, ecclesiastical hierarchy, courtly influence, and every other manifestation of privileged and therefore easily and inevitably corruptible power." Witherspoon and the Princeton faculty aligned themselves with the growing political resistance movement to Great Britain, interacting with opposition leaders such as John Dickinson and William Livingston, the latter's *Independent Reflector* being read by Madison and other Princeton students.[5] Unquestionably, during his three years at Princeton Madison also received regular instruction in Calvinist doctrine. Witherspoon did not hide his beliefs about the sinful nature of humans and the redemptive power of God; nonetheless, while emphasizing the inclination toward human depravity he maintained that people had the potential for goodness. Based on his adherence to common-sense philosophy, Witherspoon asserted that "the whole Scripture is agreeable to sound philosophy," thereby refuting rationalists like David Hume and Lord Shaftesbury who rejected portions of the Bible as unsound.[6]

The fact that Madison and other students received instruction in religious doctrine that permeated much of Princeton's curriculum was not unusual, however, as all education at the time—primary and collegiate—had a strong religious thrust. The more important focus should be on breadth of the nonreligious curriculum. Despite criticizing writers such as Shaftesbury and Hume—that "infidel writer"—Witherspoon had his students read Enlightenment and Whig authors including Hugo Grotius, Samuel von Puffendorf, Jean-Jacques Burlamaqui, Thomas Hobbes, James Harrington, Locke, Algernon Sidney, Montesquieu, Smith, and Voltaire, ensuring that they had a wide exposure to various ideas.[7] One work on religion that apparently impressed Madison was Dr. Samuel Clarke's *A Discourse Concerning the Being and Attributes of God* (1704), where Clarke, a proponent of a forerunner to Unitarianism, sought to prove the existence of God through reason. Some fifty years later, Madison would praise Clarke's approach to rational religion. Citing Clarke's work, Madison wrote that while the "arguments which enforce [the existence of God] can not be drawn from too many sources, . . . it will probably always be found that the course of reasoning from the effect to the cause, 'from nature to nature's God,' will be of the more universal & more persuasive application." Ketcham maintains that despite the religious atmosphere at Princeton, "much of the Christian aspect of Madison's schooling was relatively perfunctory and he seems never to have been an ardent believer himself." Other historians, however, argue that Princeton's Calvinist orientation strongly influenced Madison's attitudes toward religion generally and human nature in particular.[8]

Madison graduated from Princeton in 1771 but remained there for part of another year of additional study under Witherspoon in Hebrew, theology, and law.[9] Madison returned to Montpelier in 1772 where for two years he tutored his younger siblings and attended to his delicate health, what some historians have identified to be a form of epilepsy.[10] At this point, Madison was unsure of a vocation, though he apparently considered and rejected both the ministry and law. It was during the next two years that Madison ruminated about religion in ways that suggest the influence of three years of schooling at a Calvinist institution. One document from the period is a collection of notes on biblical commentary, which contains entries regarding the gospels and traditional church doctrines, copied from William Burkitt's 1724 book, *Expository Notes, with Practical Observations, on the New Testament of Our Lord and Saviour Jesus Christ.* Commenting on these notes, nineteenth-century biographer William C. Rives claimed that they "evince[d] a close and discriminating study of the sacred scriptures," and that Madison "seems to have searched the Scriptures daily and diligently." Madison's entries include references to the Resurrection and Virgin Birth of Jesus, among other traditional doctrines, though most concern moral subjects. Whether the notations on orthodox doctrine reflect Madison's own beliefs at the time, they do indicate an interest in religious study. Biographer Irving Brant believed Madison's intense interest in the Bible and theology during this period arose out of a fear of illness and early death. Whatever the motivation, Madison would never sound more religiously conventional than he did at this time.[11]

In 1772, shortly after returning to Virginia, Madison began exchanging letters with his close friend and Princeton classmate William "Billey" Bradford, who lived in Philadelphia. Much of the correspondence dealt with longings for their college days and shared uncertainties about their future careers. In an October letter to Madison, Bradford wrote that he "propose[d] making History & Morality my studies the ensuing winter," but that in his "present disposition" he was "so far from expecting Happiness hereafter that I look for little but trouble & anxiety." In a dour response—likely reflecting his ongoing study of religious texts and his preoccupation with his health—Madison told Bradford that they should not expect to experience "ordinary Happiness and prosperity till we feel the convincing argument of actual disappointment." Possibly revealing a sense of religious inevitability, Madison wrote that he could "not determine whether we shall be much the worse for [disappointment] if we do not allow it to intercept our views towards a future State." Remarking that he felt "dull and infirm," such that he did "not expect a long or healthy life," Madison was already thinking about life after death. He advised Bradford that "a watchful eye must be kept on ourselves lest while we are building ideal monuments of Renown and Bliss here[,] we neglect to have our names enrolled in the Annals of Heaven." He advised his friend that during his study of history and morals to remember "to season them with a little divinity now and then."[12]

In an exchange of letters the following year, Madison and Bradford debated the merits of choosing the ministry as a career, a profession several of their classmates had chosen. "Could I think myself properly qualified for the ministry," Bradford asked rhetorically, though he was now leaning "betwixt Law[,] Physic [medicine] and Merchandize." (Bradford would choose law, eventually becoming attorney general of the United States.) After commenting on "the fortitude & Zeal with which" their friends had "enter[ed] on the ministerial Duties," Madison expressed regret at Bradford's decision not to pursue the ministry, writing that he could "only condole with the Church on the loss of a fine Genius and persuasive Orator. I cannot however suppress thus much of my advice on that head that you would always keep the Ministry obliquely in View whatever your profession be." Madison continued that he "thought there could not be a stronger testimony in favor of Religion" than for those men who chose secular careers "and are rising in reputation and wealth, publicly to declare their unsatisfatoriness by becoming fervent Advocates in the cause of Christ."[13]

In other letters to Bradford that demonstrated the seriousness with which Madison took matters of religion and morality, he expressed disdain with people's frivolous captivation with "those amusing Studies[:] Poetry wit and Criticism Romances Plays." Madison wrote that "I find them loose in their principals," and he criticized those "encourage[r]s of free enquiry even such as destroys the most essential Truths." They were, he concluded, "enemies to serious religion."[14] This criticism of free inquiry is remarkable coming from the same person who would become a fierce advocate for freedom of conscience and religious liberty; possibly it reflects the lingering influence of Witherspoon, who warned students against reading ephemeral works dangerous to sound religion and morality. Finally, some fifty years later in one of Madison's few letters that expressed any religious inclinations, he wrote, "A belief in a God All powerful wise & good, is so essential to the moral order of the world & to the happiness of man, that arguments which enforce it can not be drawn from too many sources, nor adapted with too much solicitude to the different characters & capacities to be impressed with it."[15]

What conclusions are to be drawn from these brief but apparently conventional expressions of religious faith? Because Madison wrote so rarely about inspirational religion or his own beliefs later in life, these short statements could indicate his lifelong private views about religion, or they could merely represent transitory sentiments. The terms "future State" and "Annals of Heaven" reveal a belief in an afterlife, and his praise for those "fervent Advocates in the cause of Christ" suggests a positive view of the mission of

Christianity. Those sentiments, taken together with his Calvinist-oriented education at Princeton and his postgraduate study in religion under Wither-spoon, could indicate that Madison was more conventionally religious than has commonly been depicted.[16] In a hagiographic biography written in 1859, William C. Rives declared that Madison's education and writings revealed an "elevated strain of religious sentiment" containing "a due attention to the oracles of Divine truth." Writing at the same time, William Meade claimed that while Madison was a student at Princeton, a "great revival took place" in which he had participated. Meade related that after Madison's death, acquaintances insisted that Madison believed "the Christian system to be divine."[17]

A handful of modern scholars have drawn similar conclusions. "Madison's writings reflect the strict, ordered rationality characteristic of eighteenth-century Calvinist training," writes Garrett Ward Sheldon. He was "a person of deep Christian faith, who integrated his religious beliefs and perspectives with his political thought and views of society and government." Mary-Elaine Swanson insists that Madison's early writings about religion indicate that "the Presbyterian view of man and government played a prominent role in his intellectual development. . . . The religious ideals Madison ab-sorbed at Princeton played an important role in all of his contributions to America's political history."[18] Finally, Martha Nussbaum calls Madison "a devout and curious believer," though she does not indicate the basis for that conclusion or whether it was a lifelong position.[19]

There is simply a lack of compelling evidence indicating that Madison held conventional religious beliefs, or that they significantly informed his political philosophy, beyond that brief period following Princeton. After his exchanges with Bradford, "Madison's discussion, never extensive, of his own religion would later fall away into total silence," wrote William Lee Miller. By 1774, religious themes in their letters gave way, replaced by po-litical concerns related to the growing tensions with Great Britain.[20] Even though Madison viewed his personal beliefs as a private concern, he had myriad opportunities to mention them in correspondence with his close friends and intimates, particularly in his extensive discussions with Jeffer-son about religious matters, but he declined to declare any statement of faith. Madison scholar Jack Rakove speculates, "One might suppose that the absence of any overt religious expression is itself a tacit form of re-pudiation because religiously devout individuals are rarely quiet about their convictions."[21] Although Madison never disaffiliated from the Anglican Church, he reportedly never partook in communion or entered into full membership.[22] And despite writing about an "all powerful, wise, and good" god being "essential to the moral order of the world" in the above-quoted 1825 letter, Madison did not clarify whether the statement represented his own beliefs or those of Samuel Clarke, who was, as noted, an early advocate of *rational* Christianity. In that same letter, Madison questioned the human ability to arrive at ultimate religious truths and asserted the futility of seeking to find "the self-existence of an invisible cause possessing infinite power, wisdom & goodness."[23] Even Meade acknowledged that Madison's "religious feelings . . . seems to have been short lived" after college, based on his "political associations with those of infidel principles, of whom there were many in his day" (a likely reference to Jefferson). In his one meeting with Madison before his death, Meade noted that their discussion "left the impression on my mind that his creed was not strictly regulated by the Bible." As much as Meade, like Rives, wanted to portray Madison as a man of Christian devotion, he could not.[24]

Despite his apparent ambivalence to a personal faith, Madison maintained friendships and cordial relationships with religious figures throughout his life—particularly with his cousin Episcopal bishop James Madison, who also held generous views about religious freedom—though later in life the politician expressed some disdain for clergy and "enthusiasts." As discussed in the following chapter, those cordial and working relationships with religious figures appear to have been motivated by his commitment to the principle of religious freedom rather than arising from any shared beliefs. David L. Holmes describes Madison's beliefs for most of his life as a "Deistic form of Anglicanism," whereas Rodney A. Grunes calls them "consistent with 'Liberal Christianity' (Unitarianism) and Deism." Ralph Ketcham concludes that Madison was at best "a passive believer," though "it seems probable that Madison [maintained] a deep personal attachment to some general aspects of Christian belief and morality."[25]

Even though Madison apparently rejected his early orthodox leanings in favor of a life of casual heterodoxy, some authors have maintained that his Calvinist education had a lingering impact on his political philosophy, represented chiefly through his pessimistic view of human nature and of the need for political checks on human conduct to control factionalism.[26] At Princeton, Madison received a heavy dose of Calvinist doctrine about human fallibility and depravity. In his lectures, Reverend Witherspoon argued that the Bible gives a "clear and consistent account of human depravity," which began with the fall of Adam and continued to the present. Human sinfulness represented "an opposition and transgression to the law of God." Therefore, an overriding purpose of government was to control humans' innate selfishness, which led to factionalism, which would undermine government itself. "It sems plainly the point of view in every human law," Witherspoon wrote, "to bridle the fury of human inclination, and hinder one from making a prey of another."[27] Some authors have argued that Madison promoted this distinctly Calvinist view of human depravity in several of his writings, including in the Federalist essays. Garrett Ward Sheldon, for instance, writes that as a result of Witherspoon's tutelage, Madison "adopted the Calvinist view of human nature: the predominance of sin, selfishness, and rebellion against God leading to man's domination of others." The conclusion that these scholars seek to draw is that Madison's view of faction, and his proposed constitutional solutions of separation of powers and checks and balances, reflected a religious worldview rather than one based on more secular, rationalist ideas.[28]

Madison's thoughts about human nature and factionalism appear most prominently in his Federalist essays, though the matter comes up in other political writings.[29] As Madison declared darkly in Federalist no. 55, "There is a degree of depravity in mankind which requires a certain degree of circumspection and distrust." This propensity was "sown in the nature of man."[30] In other Federalist essays, Madison referred to the dangers presented to representative governments by human "ambition" and "self-love," while he argued for the need "to control the caprice and wickedness of man."[31] His most comprehensive account of human nature and the challenges it presents to self-governance is found in Federalist no. 10. There, Madison related the concern shared by many contemporaries: "Complaints are everywhere heard from our most considerate and virtuous citizens . . . that our governments are too unstable, that the public good is disregarded in the conflicts of rival parties, and that measures are too often decided, not according to the rules of justice and the rights of the minor party, but by the superior force of an interested and overbearing majority." A "candid review of our situation," Madison noted, "will not permit us to deny that they are in some degree true." The reasons why people act out of selfishness rather than on behalf of the common good were several: innate self-preservation, ambition, and the fallibility of reason but also because of a diversity in human faculties and the unequal distribution of property. All of this "ensure[d] a division of the society into different interests and parties," which led to political factionalism. "Human passions, have, divided mankind into parties, inflamed them with mutual animosity, and rendered them much more disposed to vex and oppress each other than to co-operate for their common good."[32]

Madison saw two potential solutions for this dilemma: to remove the causes of factionalism or to control its effects. The first was not realistic, as it would run counter to innate human nature and impinge on personal liberty. "As long as the reason of man continues fallible, and he is at liberty to exercise it, different opinions will be formed." The second was the only plausible solution, but "neither moral nor religious motives can be relied on as an adequate control" on the undesirable effects of factionalism, he wrote.[33] As he elaborated in Federalist no. 51, the answer for mitigating factionalism while protecting liberty was to ensure a multiplicity of interests and sects that would check each other: "The degree of security [for free government] will depend on the number of interests and sects; and this may be presumed to depend on the extent of country and number of people comprehended under the same government." The political solution for ameliorating the passions of human nature, therefore, was to protect a diversity of interests while dividing or separating the possession of power and to maintain a system of checks and balances. As Madison concluded in a famous passage, it was likely

> a reflection on human nature, that such devices should be necessary to control the abuses of government. But what is government itself, but the greatest of all reflections on human nature? If men were angels, no government would be necessary. If angels were to govern men, neither external nor internal controls on government would be necessary. In framing a government which is to be administered by men over men, the great difficulty lies in this: you must first enable the government to control the governed; and in the next place oblige it to control itself.[34]

The foregoing aside, Madison's view of human nature was not completely negative. Humans had an innate ability to rise above their baser instincts. While acknowledging in Federalist no. 55 "a degree of depravity in mankind," Madison also insisted that "there are other qualities in human nature which justify a certain portion of esteem and confidence." He rejected the argument "that there is not sufficient virtue among men for self-government"; republican government "presupposes the existence of these qualities in a higher degree than any other form."[35] Madison expressed similar sentiments in his arguments at the Virginia ratifying convention. He refused to accept either proposition—that elected representatives would either exhibit "exalted integrity and sublime virtue" or "do every mischief they possibly can." Human nature was complex, with people acting out of "duty, gratitude, interest, [and] ambition" at various times. "But I go on this great republican principle, that the people will have virtue and intelligence to select men of virtue and wisdom. Is there no virtue among us? If there be not, we are in a wretched situation." No structural forms of checks and balances "can render us secure." So, to "suppose that any form of government will secure liberty or happiness without any virtue in the people, is a chimerical idea."[36]

Madison's writings in the Federalist thus reflect a realistic view of human nature within a political context. It has an undeniable Calvinist ring to it. Yet, it would be surprising (and unusual) if Madison had not derived some of his ideas about the fallibility of human nature and people's inclination toward selfishness from his schooling and exposure to religious doctrine. Religion, and religious ideas concerning moral subjects, exercised a significant influence on the culture and on people's worldviews. However, claims of an overwhelming religious influence on Madison's understanding of human nature and his justifications for divided government can be easily overstated; contrary to what some have claimed, his Federalist essays do not "mimic Protestant theology" and are not paeans to Calvinism.[37] Negative views of human nature—of self-interestedness, ambition, and avarice—were held not only by Calvinists but by other Christian groups and then by people who subscribed to Enlightenment and Whig ideas. Indeed, in his *Two Treatises of Government,* John Locke spoke of the "Vanity and Ambition of Man" and the "baseness of Human Nature," which was easily "corrupted with Flattery." Expressing a similarly negative view, John Trenchard wrote about the "Corruption and Malignity of Human Nature," which was subject to the "worst Appetites, his Luxury, his Pride, his Avarice, and Lust for Power." Trenchard spoke of the need "to put Checks upon those who would otherwise put Chains upon [others]."[38] David Hume also wrote extensively about human nature and the need to control political factions. Historians have long noted the connections between Hume's writings and Madison's Federalist no. 10.[39]

Another aspect that undercuts the argument for a significant religious influence on Madison's conception of faction and human nature in the Federalist essays is that he, like Hume, perceived that religious sects constituted the most pernicious type of faction to be controlled. As Douglass Adair wrote, "Hume was primarily concerned with 'priestly parties' and bigots who fought over abstract political principles."[40] And Madison offered a considerably nonreligious solution for controlling faction: political mechanisms rather than promoting public piety or encouraging Christian redemption. As he wrote in Federalist no. 10, "Neither moral nor religious motives can be relied on as an adequate control."[41] Finally, the founders' conception of separation of powers is widely attributed to Montesquieu, among other Enlightenment writers, rather than to religious sources.[42]

Consequently, during the founding period there was a high degree of consensus about the fallibility of human nature, the dangers of self-interested factions, and the need for political solutions in order for government to succeed. Calvinists and rationalists shared aspects of this critique, though the latter took a more positive view of the ability of people to affect solutions without the assistance of God. Madison fit within this latter camp. People therefore naturally had "reliable innate abilities to apprehend the truth, both in the physical world and in the sphere of morality." In the words of historian George M. Marsden, "At the very root of the eighteenth-century political theory on which the United States government was founded is a distinctively anti-Calvinist view of human nature. Virtually all the prevailing political thought of the day in America was based on the assumption that the light of natural reason was strong enough to reveal the eternal principles of God's law to any unprejudiced right-thinking person. Depravity, it seemed, may have touched the wills of humans, but it was no longer considered to have blinded their intellect."[43] Madison was, in a sense, an optimistic realist, acknowledging the baser inclinations of human nature, which necessitated political checks, but also believing that people had the innate ability to strive for virtue. Although Madison's ideas about human nature and factionalism were likely influenced by his early religious education, they also reflected a variety of intellectual traditions.

Madison's Early Expressions about Religious Freedom

Madison's earliest ideas about religious freedom came from two sources: his time and studies at Princeton and his observation of the persecution of religious dissenters. The New Side Presbyterians who founded Princeton identified closely with the Protestant dissenting tradition—in a sense, the very operation of the college was an ongoing statement of that tradition. Reverend Witherspoon had resisted religious hierarchies in Scotland, bringing that passion with him to America, and its faculty had aligned with the opposition in the Anglican Bishop Controversy. In addition to hearing Witherspoon rail against religious hierarchies and persecution, Madison was taught about the importance of a right of private judgment in religious matters and of freedom of conscience. Finally, through his study of Enlightenment and Whig critics of religious orthodoxy and uniformity, such as Spinoza, Voltaire, Locke, Hume, and Smith, Madison would have gained an appreciation for the secular intellectual arguments favoring religious freedom, beginning with the value of free inquiry.[44] So, as William Lee Miller noted, by experiencing the antiestablishment and dissenting strain of Protestantism at Princeton, Madison had "a knowledge of and sympathy with the tradition of dissent that Jefferson did not have and few other major figures in the nation's founding would have."[45]

Back in Virginia, both before and after college, Madison was likely aware of the persecution of religious dissenters. As stated, although there is no record that Madison's father participated in enforcing religious licensing requirements or church attendance, the younger Madison must have known of the duties of vestrymen to promote religious uniformity and to protect the dominant position of the Anglican Church. Madison's earliest statements regarding religious freedom appeared in his correspondence with his college friend Billey Bradford. Approximately a year into their letters concerning their ongoing studies and career plans, Madison asked Bradford to prepare him a "scetch" about the "Origins & fundamental principals" of the Pennsylvania Constitution regarding "your religious Toleration." Madison asked his friend to address the following inquiries: "Is an Ecclesiastical Establishment absolutely necessary to support civil society in a supream Government? & how far it is hurtful to a dependant State?" The phrasing of the first inquiry likely indicated that Madison had been rereading Hume's *History of England*.[46] Before Bradford could reply with his assignment—which he never did—Madison wrote him another letter containing two revealing observations. The first answered his own rhetorical question, apparently spurred on by reports of the Boston Tea Party and Philadelphia's own refusal to permit the unloading of a similar shipment of British tea. Madison revealingly tied the growing British infringements on political liberties with concerns for religious liberty: "If the Church of England had been the established and general Religion in all the Northern Colonies as it has been among us here and uninterrupted tranquility had prevailed throughout the Continent, It is clear to me that slavery and Subjection might and would have been gradually insinuated among us." Madison's point appeared to be that rather than religious establishments being a salutary influence on civil society, they accomplished the opposite: a "Union of Religious Sentiments begets a surprizing confidence and Ecclesiastical Establishments tend to great ignorance and Corruption all of which facilitate the execution of mischievous Projects."[47]

After digressing to discuss Princeton friends and careers (again), Madison returned to the subject of religious establishments. Commenting on the entrenched Anglican establishment in Virginia, Madison wrote that he "want[ed] again to breathe your free Air" of Pennsylvania. "I expect it will mend my Constitution & confirm my principles. I have indeed as good an Atmosphere at home as the Climate will allow: but have nothing to brag of as to the State and Liberty of my Country [Virginia]. Poverty and Luxury prevail among all sorts: Pride ignorance and Knavery among the Priesthood and Vice and Wickedness among the Laity." The basis for that anticlerical remark is unknown—possibly it reflects the young Madison's encounter with a local member of the Anglican clergy. The indolence of Virginia's Anglican clergy was "bad enough," Madison continued. "But It is not the worst I have to tell you." "That diabolical Hell conceived principle of persecution rages among some and to their eternal Infamy the Clergy can furnish their Quota of Imps for such business. This vexes me the most of any thing whatever. There are at this [time?] in the adjacent County not less than 5 or 6 well meaning men in close Gaol for publishing their religious Sentiments which in the main are very orthodox."[48] As discussed earlier, Madison was relating the imprisonment of several Baptist ministers in Culpepper County for failing to obtain licenses to preach, something he had possibly witnessed or knew of from secondhand reports. He obviously was disgusted with the situation and was struggling for a longer-term solution to remedy the injustice. The cause was clear, however: it was from the inherent oppression of religious establishments. Here was a practical example of what Reverend Witherspoon had warned about during Madison's studies at Princeton. As he concluded his letter to Bradford, "I leave you to pity me and pray for Liberty of Conscience to revive among us."[49]

Bradford replied two months later, commiserating with his friend that he was "sorry to hear that Persecution has got so much footing among you." "Persecution is a weed that grows not in our happy soil [Pennsylvania]," Bradford remarked, "and I do not remember that any Person was ever imprisoned here for his religious sentiments however heretical or unepiscopal they might be."[50] Madison responded immediately, revealing that the matter still bothered him. He related that the Virginia Assembly was about to consider a petition from the "Persecuted Baptists," with possible support from the Presbyterians, "for greater liberty in matters of Religion." Madison doubted the petition would succeed because the majority of legislators were "too much devoted to the ecclesiastical establishment to hear of the Toleration of Dissentients." Railing once more against the Anglican establishment, he remarked that "the Clergy are a numerous and powerful body [and] have great influence at home by reason of their connection with & dependence on the Bishops and Crown and will naturally employ all their art & Interest to depress their rising Adversaries." The true villains in this situation were not necessarily the Anglican clergy but members of the House of Burgesses, most of whom were vestrymen bent on retaining their power and privileges. Because both were empowered by the Anglican establishment, however, Madison conflated the two.[51]

Historians have pointed to this episode as foundational for Madison's ideas about religious freedom. There can be little doubt that the Baptists' imprisonment impacted Madison's perspective; later in life, he recounted the event in his *Autobiography,* claiming to have been "under very early and strong impressions in favor of Liberty both Civil & Religious. [My] devotion to the latter is found in a particular occasion for its exercise in the persecution instituted in [my] County as elsewhere belonging to the sect of Baptists." The Baptists' stance for religious liberty, Madison wrote, "obtained for [me] a lasting place in the favor of that particular sect."[52]

There is one other revealing passage in his last letter to Bradford. As he had discussed in his previous letter, Madison again commended the religious freedoms that existed in Pennsylvania, telling his friend how Bradford was privileged to live in a state "where those inestimable privileges are fully enjoyed and public has long felt the good effects of their religious as well as Civil Liberty." Madison then raised another argument on behalf of greater religious freedom. He suggested that freedom invited immigration, resulting in the flourishing of industry, virtue, commerce, and the arts. Madison attributed these salutary attributes to the "inspiration of [religious] Liberty" which existed in that state. In contrast, he wrote, "Religious bondage shackles and debilitates the mind and unfits it for every noble enterprise every expanded prospect." Here was a practical argument for religious freedom, one that transcended the abolition of tyranny and the promotion of religious conscience. Religious freedom and equality created a political and economic climate that enhanced the wellbeing of all members of that society. Rather than representing a threat to social order as advocates of uniformity claimed, religious diversity with an accompanying equality would create a stable, industrious society.[53] At this young age, Madison was already formulating comprehensive arguments about church-state matters that would benefit him in the struggles ahead.

So, on the cusp of entering his life of public service in the mid-1770s, Madison had already developed his initial beliefs and justifications for religious freedom. Freedom of inquiry to discover knowledge and then the freedom of conscience to maintain those beliefs were essential natural rights, values that could only be maintained under a system of religious freedom. Religious establishments and the clergy and laity who sustained them were impediments to the realization of these values. At this stage, the younger Madison's ideas about church-state orderings were still not as developed as those of Jefferson, who was eight years Madison's senior. Even so, their views about free inquiry, freedom of conscience, and of the injustices of religious establishments were remarkably similar, even though they had yet to meet. That meeting, and the beginning of their long collaboration, would occur in 1776 through their joint service in the new Virginia House of Delegates.

◈ FOUR ◈

The First Collaboration

Virginia Disestablishment, Part 1

T he decade-long struggle in Virginia to expand liberty of conscience, guarantee religious equality, and disestablish the Anglican Church (and effectively all religions) has been extensively covered in scholarly and popular literature. It has also received considerable attention from members of the Supreme Court.[1] As noted in the introduction, commentators have disagreed over how to interpret the relevant documents and the ultimate resolution of the struggle—the enactment of Jefferson's Bill for Establishing Religious Freedom. Commentators have also disputed the broader significance of the Virginia disestablishment experience, of its relevance to the church-state settlements in other states, and its influence on the enactment of the First Amendment to the Constitution. Detractors of church-state separation and critics of the traditional Jeffersonian-Madisonian narrative have charged that the Virginia struggle has received unwarranted attention, due largely to the purportedly slanted historicism of Supreme Court justices and their separationist allies.[2]

To be sure, Virginia was not the only state to modify its church-state arrangement during the fifteen years between the Battle of Bunker Hill and the drafting of the First Amendment; other states, particularly those in New England, adopted other conceptions of church-state interactions.[3] Despite the attention that people have given to the Virginia episode, it overstates matters to claim it "served as a model for other American states, both old and new."[4] Thomas J. Curry is closer to the mark in writing that "most other states did not soon accept the same definitive solution [as Virginia], especially of abandoning [religious] tests, so Virginia cannot be said to have

served as a model for them." Even separationist-leaning scholars acknowledge that Virginia's comprehensive solution to church and state was in the
vanguard.[5]

With that proviso in mind, the Virginia episode was nonetheless highly
consequential, not only for that state's development but for its impact on
evolving perspectives about church-state matters, both contemporaneous
and subsequent to the episode. Virginia was the largest and most populous state, home to many prominent national figures, and a state whose example mattered. John Adams grudgingly acknowledged that status, writing
that Virginians "think they have a right to take the lead, and the Southern
States and middle States too, are too much disposed to yield it to them."[6]
As discussed, Virginia had the most entrenched and intolerant religious
establishment at the beginning of the Revolution. Within a decade, it had
transformed its political situation into one that promoted the highest degree
of religious freedom in human history. "Virginia's decision to embrace religious freedom provided an important example for the rest of the nation,"
writes John Ragosta, if not to the world, even if its example was not copied
immediately. And as Curry added, "In the nature and variety of the internal
debates that led up to its ultimate decision [to disestablish], Virginia was
a microcosm of the ferment taking place throughout the new nation." The
later nationalization of the Virginia Statute for Establishing Religious Freedom "reflected a major change in the social and religious composition of
the American people." The principles it announced, even if not replicated
exactly in other states, established the bar for measuring conceptions of
religious freedom, at that time and later.[7]

In studying the Virginia struggle there is a tendency to break it into
segments—to portray the passage of the Virginia Declaration of Rights in
1776 and the enactment of Jefferson's bill a decade later as separate, free-
standing events.[8] This, of course, was not how Jefferson, Madison, and their
contemporaries viewed the matter, including those who favored the public
support of religion. Rather, the Virginia struggle was one continuous event,
stretching from before the Revolution until disestablishment in 1786. While
activity surrounding it ebbed and flowed in response to the war and other
pressing matters of governance, religious dissenters kept pressure on the
issue throughout the decade.[9] There is also a tendency to view disestablishment in Virginia as a foregone conclusion, which it was not. Many people
considered Patrick Henry's compromise proposal—for a *general* assessment

to benefit *all* denominations—as a salutary move away from the traditional, single-church establishment that had existed in Virginia for a century and a half. Presbyterians changed their minds on the merits of Henry's proposal more than once, and it almost passed—initially, it *did* pass on a preliminary vote. While it is speculative, had the Virginia Assembly enacted Henry's general assessment bill in lieu of Jefferson's bill, chances are the related provisions of the Kentucky and Tennessee constitutions would also have varied, and New England might not have disestablished when and as it did.[10] Considering the way in which later generations lauded the statute, the development of church-state relations might have been quite different had it not passed (and Justices Hugo Black and Wiley Rutledge would have been denied their primary pieces of ammunition when adopting separationism as the constitutional model 160 years later). Whether participants in the struggle were aware of its significance at the time, much hung in the balance on the outcome in Virginia.[11]

The Virginia Declaration of Rights

In May 1776, twenty-five-year-old James Madison arrived in Williamsburg, newly elected to represent Orange County in Virginia's provincial convention. One purpose of the session was to draft a form of government for the independent commonwealth of Virginia. The colonial rebellion, now a revolution, had been waging for over a year, and any realistic hope of reconciliation with Great Britain was over. That same month, the Continental Congress, sitting in Philadelphia, had passed a resolution urging the colonies to formerly reorganize as states; Virginia, though, had needed no encouragement, as it had been operating under a provisional government, now headed by Edmund Pendleton, since the departure of royal governor Lord Dunmore the year before.[12]

Arriving in the capital, Madison fell into the role of a junior delegate, deferring to his seniors and not participating in the convention debates; as he wrote later, "Being young & inexperienced, I had of course but little agency in those proceedings." After the convention voted to instruct its delegates to the Continental Congress—Thomas Jefferson and Richard Henry Lee—to formally propose independence from Britain, it organized a committee to draft a constitution and declaration of rights for the new state. Members of the committee included Pendleton, Patrick Henry, Robert Carter Nichols,

Edmund Randolph, and George Mason, with Madison added later. The highly respected Mason became the primary drafter of the declaration, with its opening statement announcing in Lockean terms that "all men are by nature equally free and independent."[13] Protecting conscience and religious practice were rights on people's minds, with "A Dissenter to the Church of England" writing in the *Virginia Gazette*, urging people to "to petition their rulers for the removal of that yoke, that in these scarce times is becoming more grievous, in paying the established clergy, and being still obliged to have the solemnization of matrimony performed by them."[14] The sixteenth article of the declaration addressed religion, with Mason's draft asserting, "That religion, or the duty which we owe to our CREATOR, and the manner of discharging it, can be directed only by reason and conviction, not by force or violence; and therefore, that all men should enjoy the fullest toleration in the exercise of religion, according to the dictates of conscience, unpunished and unrestrained by the magistrate unless, under colour of religion, any man disturb the peace, the happiness, or safety of society." The article concluded by declaring that it was "the mutual duty of all to practice Christian forbearance, love and charity, towards each other."[15]

Madison, with his exposure to Princeton's dissenting tradition and his recent encounter with the imprisoned Baptist ministers in Culpepper County, was troubled by Mason's use of the word "toleration," which he saw as falling short of guaranteeing full religious freedom and equality. As Madison explained later in life, he proposed an amendment "with a view, more particularly to substitute for the idea expressed by the term 'toleration,' an absolute and equal right of all to the exercise of religion according to the dictates of conscience." Mason, an enlightened student of history, likely chose the word out of familiarity with Locke's *Letter on Toleration* and envisioned it in the most generous terms. Writing to Mason's grandson some fifty years later, Madison graciously remarked that Mason had "inadvertently" chosen the "term being of familiar use, [from] the English Code," without necessarily meaning to impose any limitations. Still, Madison felt the term could be easily misconstrued.[16]

Madison drafted an amendment to Mason's language, substituting "all men are equally entitled to the full and free exercise of it according to the dictates of Conscience" for Mason's term "toleration." Madison's amendment omitted Mason's closing clause of a "mutual duty of all to practice Christian forbearance, love and charity, towards each other," which could indicate his belief that government should not encourage any religious duties, even salutary ones. More significant, however, Madison added the following: "and therefore that no man or class of men ought, on account of religion to be invested with peculiar emoluments or privileges; nor subjected to any penalties or disabilities." Although the language was subtle, the clause would have effectively disestablished the Church of England by prohibiting any privileges it possessed and forbidding enforcing an assessment on dissenters. Madison had Patrick Henry introduce his amendment for him; Henry had possibly not read the amendment closely, as when challenged by pro-establishment delegates about whether he intended to disestablish the Anglican Church, he demurred and the amendment failed.[17] Madison then wrote a substitute amendment which provided that "all men are equally entitled to enjoy the free exercise of religion, according to the dictates of conscience" while omitting the offending clause. This time Madison had Edmund Pendleton, a pro-establishment Anglican, sponsor the amendment for him, and the measure passed and was included in article 16 of the Declaration of Rights.[18]

Madison proposed one other potentially significant change from Mason's draft, which as originally written provided protection "unless, under colour of religion, any man disturb the peace, the happiness, or safety of society." Madison's second amendment would have narrowed that exemption to situations where "the preservation of equal liberty and the existence of the State are manifestly endangered." This would have required a much stronger justification before the state could restrict religious exercise; mere disturbance of the peace, which Baptists were famous for, might still receive protection. In the end, neither clause was included in the final version of article 16.[19]

This episode reveals two important aspects about Madison at this early stage of his career. First, it indicates he was already thinking comprehensively about church-state matters. Madison was not satisfied with a society in which people enjoyed the "the fullest toleration" of religion but wanted a condition of full religious freedom and equality where no person was privileged by virtue of their religious status. That condition could only occur through a complete disestablishment that ended all emoluments, privileges, disabilities, and penalties. Second, the episode reveals "Madison the strategist," a talent he would use throughout his public career. Madison was willing to propose a broader goal but then accept a compromise that still moved matters forward. Although John Ragosta is correct that the outcome indicated the members of the convention were not yet willing to disestablish the Anglican Church, that idea had been introduced for later consideration. And Madison was able to secure support for free exercise over mere toleration—in his words, the acknowledgment of "freedom of conscience to be a *natural and absolute* right"—a concession that some pro-establishment delegates had likely not been prepared to accept. Possibly unbeknownst to pro-establishment forces, the affirmation of an equal enjoyment of free exercise of religion led dissenters to argue that that guarantee was irreconcilable with maintaining a religious establishment. Rather than resolving the difficult "religion issue," the declaration merely set the stage for further deliberations.[20]

With Madison's proposed amendments, the collaboration with Jefferson had begun, even though the two men had yet to meet. In the early summer of 1776 Jefferson was in Philadelphia. Despite the pressing matters there, Jefferson was eager to return to Virginia to participate in establishing a new government for "his country." Jefferson wrote to the provisional government requesting to be recalled for "a short time" because the activity of the Virginia convention was "a work of the most interesting nature and such as every individual would wish to have his voice in."[21] Unsuccessful in that request, Jefferson proceeded to write three drafts of a proposed constitution for Virginia. In those drafts, which were too late to be considered by the convention, Jefferson proposed a provision that "all persons shall have full and free liberty of religious opinion; nor shall any be compelled to frequent or maintain any religious institution." So, writing approximately at the same time as Madison, Jefferson also advocated disestablishment for the new state of Virginia. Jefferson's language of "full and free liberty of religious opinion" was arguably not as comprehensive as Madison's guaranteeing the equal enjoyment of free *exercise* of religion according to "the dictates of conscience," though Jefferson would likely have insisted that the "full liberty of religious opinion" necessarily included the ability to freely apply one's opinions. While Thomas Buckley was correct that neither Madison's nor Jefferson's proposal would have fully severed the relationship between the Virginia government and the Anglican Church—in particular, the ability of the legislature to regulate church matters or the status of ecclesiastical law—both men were already thinking along similar lines, recommending initial steps to dismantle the establishment and guarantee full religious freedom.

The Declaration of Rights was a significant advance in the cause for religious freedom, fundamentally altering the status of religious dissenters in Virginia, but as Madison, Jefferson, and those dissenters understood, it was only the first step toward achieving full religious equality and freedom of conscience.[22]

The First Collaboration: The Committee on Religion

After spending the summer back in Orange County, Madison returned to Williamsburg in October 1776 to assume his position in the new House of Delegates. One of the primary tasks of the session, besides securing Virginia's contribution to the war effort, was to revise the British laws and those enacted by the old House of Burgesses that still governed many legal relationships, such as property ownership and inheritance rights. Madison was eventually appointed to one of the leading committees dealing with legal revision, the Committee on Religion. There, for the first time, he met Jefferson, who had returned from Philadelphia. Jefferson was a delegate from Albemarle County and already a member of the Committee on Religion. Here was the beginning of an acquaintance that would grow into a lifelong friendship and partnership.[23]

Even before the session commenced, the legislature was inundated with petitions from Presbyterians and Baptists seeking to expand the protections contained in the Declaration of Rights; despite being "the magna carta of our Commonwealth," the declaration had failed to resolve Virginia's religious establishment or address the legal privileges the Anglican Church still enjoyed. Baptists had submitted a petition near the end of the spring convention, but it was too late to impact article 16. In it, the Baptists laid out the grievances they had been raising for more than a decade: it pleaded that "they be allowed to worship God in their own way, without interruption; that they be permitted to maintain their own ministers, and none others; [and] that they be married, buried, and the like, without paying the clergy of other denominations." The petition represented the Baptists' more immediate concerns, which might explain why they stopped short of requesting disestablishment outright.[24]

Any such hesitation to seek full disestablishment was gone in the various petitions filed that fall. As one petition asserted, the signers had been deprived of their "birthright" of "equal liberty . . . in that by taxation[,] their property hath been wrested from them and given to those from whom they receive no equivalent." They had "long groaned under the burden of an ecclesiastical establishment," and they prayed "that this, as well as every other yoke, may be broken." Another petition, this one from Prince Edward County southwest of Richmond, praised article 16 as "the rising sun of religious liberty" but then asked the legislature "to complete what is so nobly begun" in order to fully "relieve them from a long night of ecclesiastical bondage." To accomplish this, the petition pleaded that "without delay, all church establishments might be pulled down, and every tax upon conscience and private judgment abolished." This result would "raise religious as well as civil liberty to the zenith of glory, and make Virginia an asylum for free inquiry, knowledge, and the virtuous[ness] of every denomination." This last petition was reputedly written by Reverend Samuel Stanhope Smith, president of the Presbyterian Hampden-Sydney Academy and former Princeton classmate of James Madison. Biographer Ralph Ketcham speculated that Madison may have assisted with the petition based on its rationalist language and the fact that Madison served as a trustee of Hampden-Sydney where his younger brother William attended.[25]

The house journal contains entries of approximately a dozen petitions and memorials from religious dissenters: Presbyterians, Baptists, and even Lutherans, who, though permitted to have their taxes applied to their own ministers, were still required to support the local Anglican vestry. One Baptist petition famously became known as the "Ten-Thousand Name" petition for the number of signatories.[26] Another notable memorial came from the Hanover Presbytery, which asserted that Presbyterians had been subjected to "invidious and disadvantageous restrictions" by being forced "annually [to] pay large taxes to support an establishment from which their consciences and principles oblige them to dissent." Because "our blessed Savior declares his kingdom is not of this world," it continued, it does not "appear that the gospel needs any such aid." In contrast to the Baptist petitions, the Hanover memorial raised not only religious arguments but ones based on rationalistic grounds. While the taxation and restrictions of the establishment infringed on their rights of "private judgment," such rules and duties also violated Presbyterians' "natural rights" to "freedom of inquiry." In Lockean fashion, the memorial asserted that the authority of civil government extended only to protecting life, liberty, and property, whereas religious obligations could only be directed by individual "reason and conviction." Echoing other dissenting petitions, the Presbyterians tied the political struggle with Britain to one to abolish religious tyranny: "Certain it is that every argument for civil liberty gains additional strength when applied to liberty in the concern of religion." The house should therefore "remov[e] every species of religious, as well as civil, bondage." Finally, the Hanover memorial raised pragmatic arguments in favor of abolishing the establishment. "Religious establishments are highly injurious to the temporal interests of any community," it asserted. Not only were they arbitrary and "inconsistent with [the] equal liberty" of its citizens, "establishments greatly retard population, and consequently the progress of arts, sciences, and manufactories."[27]

Pro-establishment forces were initially caught off guard by the onslaught of memorials from dissenters, but they filed a handful of petitions seeking relief for an embattled Anglican Church that had suffered as a consequence of the war. A short petition from Methodists, who were still in communion with the Church of England, asserted that they "conceive[d] that very bad consequences will arise from abolishing the Establishment," although they did not elaborate on what those would be.[28] A lengthier petition from Anglican clergy claimed they were legally entitled to continued support based on existing laws guaranteeing them income security and tenure: "It would be inconsistent with justice either to deprive the present incumbents of any right or profits they hold or enjoy." But the clergy also asserted that disestablishment was unnecessary and harmful to society. They downplayed the injustice of the establishment, touting the "mild and tolerating spirit of the church established," and how the church had afforded "all Christian charity and benevolence . . . [toward] dissenters of every denomination" and had "shown no disposition to restrain them in the exercise of their religion." Finally, the Anglican petition asserted that virtue and salutary Christian doctrines "can best be taught and preserved in the purity of an established church." An established church also promoted civil stability; placing all denominations on the same level would produce competition and discord, the petition argued perversely, resulting in "confusion [and] civil commotions." As a pro-establishment writer added in a letter to the *Virginia Gazette*, "No government can be well regulated which turns every religious order, uncontrolled, loose on society."[29]

Although lacking in numbers and likely in popular support, the pro-establishment petitioners had a distinct advantage. House Speaker Edmund

Pendleton—an ardent churchman and member of the Committee on Religion—had appointed other traditionalist Anglicans to the committee. As Jefferson later wrote, "Although the majority of our citizens were dissenters . . . a majority of the Legislature were churchmen. . . . Our greatest opponents were Mr. Pendleton and Robert Carter Nichols, honest men but zealous churchmen." Jefferson and Madison were simply outnumbered. The committee debated the petitions throughout October and into November. Jefferson drafted a handful of resolutions—to abolish the authority of English laws punishing heresy and blasphemy and to disestablish the Anglican Church. The preamble that accompanied the latter resolution, contained in fragmentary notes, provided

> for restoring to the Citizens of this Comm'w. the right of maintaining their religious opinions, & of worshipping god in their own way; for releasing them from all legal obligations to frequent churches or other places of worship, and for exempting them from contributions for the support of any religious society independant of their good will, & for discontinuing the establishment of the church of England by law, & taking away the privilege & pre-eminence of one religious sect over another, and thereby establish[ing] . . . equal rights among all.

The operative part then resolved "that the several laws establishing the sd. Church of England, giving peculiar privileges to it's ministers, & levying for the support thereof contributions on the people independent of their good will ought to be repealed." The purpose of the resolution, he wrote, was to discontinue the religious establishment and guarantee that "no preeminence may be allowed to any one Religious sect over another." Anticipating likely resistance, Jefferson's resolution provided that Anglican clergy could continue to hold previously seized glebes for life and that parishes could retain all property that they had received through *private* donations, the implication being that Anglican parishes would not be entitled to retain property obtained through forced assessments. Here was Jefferson's second effort at disestablishment.[30]

The committee did not adopt Jefferson's resolutions, and after apparently contentious debate the matter was referred to the House of Delegates acting as a committee of the whole in mid-November. What resulted was a compromise that provided some relief but kept the establishment alive though still in distress. Dissenters were relieved from making forced contributions to the established church or to their own religious societies; the laws providing clerical support were suspended, though clergy were entitled to any monies in arrears; Anglican churches retained their existing property including church buildings and glebe lands; and the legislature retained authority to regulate the public worship of religious societies, which potentially extended not only to Anglican churches but also to those of religious dissenters. Jefferson would later write that the proceedings over disestablishment that autumn "brought on the severest contests in which I have ever been engaged."[31]

The law of December 9, 1776, did advance religious freedom in some respects. Besides exempting dissenters from paying a religious tax, the law declared that any existing law "which renders criminal the maintaining any opinions in matters of religion, forbearing to [attend] church, or the exercising any mode of worship whatsoever, or which provides punishments for the same," would "be of no validity or force" in the state. But the law had left the future of the establishment unresolved. The law stated that dissenters were exempt from supporting "the said church, as it *now is* or *may hereafter be established*," indicating its ongoing status, and the statute acknowledged the continuing authority of the vestries. The contentious issues of solemnizing marriages and administering poor relief—both functions exercised solely by Anglicans—remained sore spots for dissenters. And while leaving a permanent suspension of a religious tax for the "discussion and determination of a future assembly," the law proposed the concept of a *general* assessment to benefit all Protestant denominations in its stead, also to be considered by a future assembly. The house wanted to be clear that by reaching this compromise, "nothing in this act contained shall be construed to affect or influence the said question of a general assessment, or voluntary contributions, in any respect whatever." In future contests, therefore, the question would be whether all dissenting denominations—in particular, Presbyterians and Lutherans—would oppose a general religious assessment to which they would also benefit. While much of Virginia's establishment was inoperable by the end of 1776, it was far from dead.[32]

Based on Jefferson's and Madison's writings, it appears that the latter did not actively participate in either drafting or debating the various proposals to reform Virginia's religious laws, including those maintaining the religious establishment. As mentioned, Madison acknowledged his deferential role as a novice legislator that autumn, and both men later dated the start of their friendship and political collaboration to 1779. Jefferson too noted Madison's limited role that session, stating that his age and inexperience, "concurring with his extreme modesty, prevented his venturing himself in debate." There is little doubt, however, whether Madison supported Jefferson's resolutions in the committee, based on his earlier amendments to the Declaration of Rights where he initially sought disestablishment. Whether Madison took a more active role supporting Jefferson's actions that fall is unknown (although, as with article 16, Madison was adept at working behind the scenes). But it is likely that Jefferson came away from that "severest contest" with the knowledge that Madison shared a similar perspective about church-state matters and was an ally on whom Jefferson could rely for the battles that lay ahead.[33]

The First Interregnum

Despite the efforts of the Virginia Assembly to craft a compromise that maintained the legal status of the establishment while exempting dissenters from paying a religious tax (and suspending it for Anglican communicants), the uncertainty surrounding Virginia's establishment generated dissatisfaction among those on both sides of the issue. No sooner had the law of December 9 been enacted than pro- and antiestablishment forces renewed their campaigns through petitions and newspaper editorials. In March 1777, the *Virginia Gazette* published a public statement from the General Baptist Association, "The Sentiments of Baptists with Regard to a General Assessment on the People of Virginia." In it, the Baptists declared that although "we are happy to find the progress of liberty so far advanced" with the new law, "there is yet an undetermined point," that being the law's reservation of a future general assessment. "We believe that preachers should only be supported by voluntary contributions from the people, and that a general assessment (however harmless, yea useful some may conceive it to be), is pregnant with various evils, [and] destructive to the rights and privileges of religious society," wrote the Baptists. "The consequence of this is, that those that the State employs in its service, it has the right to regulate and dictate to; it may judge and determine *who* shall preach, *when* they shall preach, and *what* they must preach." When that occurs, the Baptists warned, then "farewell to the last article of the bill of rights! Farewell to 'the free exercise of religion' if civil rulers go so far out of their sphere as to take the care and management of religious affairs upon them."[34]

The Baptist statement was followed in April by a petition to the General Assembly from the Hanover Presbytery. It also praised the new law as "inspir[ing] us with greater confidence in our Legislature" by "exempting dissenters from all levies, taxes, and impositions whatsoever towards supporting the church of England." Echoing the Baptist statement but using more Lockean terms, the Presbyterian petition asserted that the authority of civil governments was limited to temporal matters—"the concerns of religion are beyond the limits of civil control"—leaving "the duty which we owe our Creator, and the manner of discharging it," to the direction of "reason and conviction." The petition then informed the assembly that Presbyterians had no interest in benefiting from a general assessment: "If the Legislature has any rightful authority over the ministers of the gospel in the exercise of their sacred office, and it is their duty to levy a maintenance for them as such; then it will follow that they may revive the old establishment in it former form; or ordain a new one for any sect they think proper." Again echoing the Baptists, the petition asserted this would give the state the power to determine "who shall preach, [and] what they shall preach." The "consequences [of this] are so plain as not to be denied, and they are entirely subversive of religious liberty."[35]

Taken together, the Baptists and Presbyterians viewed article 16 and the law of December 9, 1776, as making important advances in the cause of religious freedom, though being incomplete. The establishment still existed and the privileges the Anglican Church and its clergy enjoyed continued, absent the religious tax, which could be reinstated at any time. Anglicans still controlled the all-important vestries and the ability to perform marriages. Despite statutory language decrying the concept of religious *toleration*, Baptists and Presbyterians remained in a second-class status, a fact of which they were keenly aware. As such, they refused to be lulled into accepting what they perceived as half a loaf instead of securing full religious equality. And importantly, both bodies opposed a non-preferential assessment for the support of religion; any religious tax, even one distributed equally to all religions, exceeded civil authority and violated rights of conscience.

Pro-establishment forces saw matters differently. Most Anglican clergy and laity, particularly vestrymen, believed that the new laws had more than adequately accommodated the religious dissenters at a significant cost to the Anglican Church and to the social benefits that accrued from an establishment. The war with Britain had considerably disrupted the operations of the Anglican Church in America, effectively severing the relationship with the church back in England. Clergy in America had to choose between their ordination oaths of loyalty to the Crown and the episcopacy or to the patriot cause supported by most of their parishioners. "The attachment of some few of the clergy to the cause of the King subjected the Church itself to suspicion," Bishop William Meade later wrote, "and gave further occasion to its enemies to seek its destruction." Approximately 20 percent of Anglican clergy either fled Virginia or retired during the war, with many more seeking to remain neutral or hide their true loyalties. Meade's figures were higher, with him estimating that the number of Anglican clergy in Virginia declined from ninety-one before the war to twenty-eight afterward. And with the religious tax suspended, many clergy and their parishes were in dire financial straits. In the years from 1777 to 1784, therefore, support remained for restoring the establishment, or at least for providing some relief through a general assessment.[36]

During these years, pro-establishment letters and petitions took two approaches. Those taking the high road highlighted the advantages provided by an established church, particularly during a time of social disruption. One letter in the *Virginia Gazette* emphasized the burden the church experienced recruiting and ordaining clergy, which then hampered its ability to advance order, decency, and morality. The Anglican Church provided a salutary public worship that was "not only the most decent, but the most rational and useful." The author disclaimed any desire to return to an exclusive establishment, though he did not discuss the alternative of a general assessment.[37] A petition from Caroline County took a similar high tone, endorsing exempting dissenters from a religious tax based on "principles of justice and propriety, and favorable to religious liberty." Still, the petitioners asserted that publicly supported worship was "productive of effects the most beneficial to society," that is, "to preserve public peace, order, and decency, without prescribing a mode or form of worship to any." The petitioners asked the assembly to institute a tax, "defrayed by an equal contribution of all men," to support the building and repairing of churches and the salary of clergy, "leaving it to the payer . . . to direct the appropriation of his quota to the use of that church, or its ministers, under such regulations as may be thought best."[38]

Other pro-establishment letters and petitions took a less conciliatory approach, disputing dissenter claims of persecution and blaming them for the decline in public morality and the distress of the Anglican Church. One letter in the *Virginia Gazette* warned that disestablishment would bring about the leveling of all sects: "Recent experience has taught, that some particular sects hold principles not only incompatible with prosperity, but even the very existence of established governments." In seeking an exemption from taxation and regulation, dissenters were selfishly subordinating the common good. "The sectaries are mistaken, then, when they suppose they are taxed for the support of a foreign church; they only contribute to the support of government; for no government can be well regulated which turns every religious order, uncontrolled, loose on society."[39] A petition from Cumberland County picked up on the threats of social disorder represented by unrestrained religious dissenters. The petitioners were "greatly alarmed at the progress which some of the dissenters . . . are daily making in various parts of this county by persuading the ignorant and unwary to embrace their erroneous tenets." Those tenets were "not only opposite to the doctrines of true Christianity," asserted the petition, "but subversive to the morals of people and destructive to the peace of families." That concern for ensuring the "peace of families" had an ulterior motive, however, for the petitioners expressed alarm that dissenting ministers had engaged in "nightly meetings with slaves . . . without the consent of their masters." These unregulated actions "tend[ed] to alienate the affection of slaves from their masters" and had "produced very bad consequences." The Cumberland petitioners asked for legislation to ensure that "nightly meetings may be prohibited," and that "those only who, after a due examination of their morals, shall be found worthy may be authorized to preach," and then "only in such public meeting houses as it may be thought proper to license for the purpose."[40]

Another petition, this one from Mecklenburg County, evinced similar disdain for the dissenters and their social standing. The petition criticized "the undue means taken to overthrow the Established church, by imposing upon the credulity of the vulgar and engaging infants to sign petitions handed about by dissenters." In particular, the petition chastised dissenters for conditioning their support for the Revolution by encouraging their followers to enlist in the militia only on a suspension of the religious tax and licensing restrictions.[41] The petitioners were not wrong on the facts. As John Ragosta has covered extensively, dissenters tied the cause of religious freedom to that of civil freedom, insisting that Virginia's political leaders lessen the burdens dissenters experienced in order to maximize their support for the war. Baptists in particular readily acknowledged the connection; as one Baptist minister wrote, "There was a necessity for a unanimity among all ranks, sects, and denominations" behind the patriot cause. If "an establishment [should] survive our revolution, and religious tyranny raise its banner in our infant country, it would leave us to the sore reflection: What have we been struggling for?"[42] The Mecklenburg petition charged that the dissenters were opportunists for "withhold[ing] their concurrence in the common cause until their particular requests are granted." It lampooned the idea that denying "a competent number of ministers of the gospel [their] fixed salaries is the most likely means to make men unanimous in the defense of liberty." On the contrary, "An established church in any State, under proper limitations and restrictions and founded on the warranty of the Holy Scripture, is one of the great bulwarks of liberty, the cement of society, the bond of unity, and an asylum for the persecuted."[43]

Throughout 1777 and 1778, the pro- and antiestablishment forces submitted petitions to the House Committee on Religion, but the body declined to act one way or the other. Maintaining the status quo was the best way of not alienating either side during wartime. Consistent with that approach, during both legislative sessions the assembly extended the suspension of the religious tax for clerical salaries. In 1778, the house drafted a bill to authorize dissenting clergy to perform marriages, but even though the bill survived two readings, it was voted down. That failure led the Baptist Association to file a petition in 1780 asking the assembly to rectify that injustice as it involved a matter "so tender a Nature and matter of Importance." In a rare instance of responsiveness, that autumn the assembly passed a law authorizing "any minister of any society or congregation of Christians" to perform marriages and recognizing those marriages "heretofore celebrated by dissenting ministers." But overall, when it came to addressing the various outstanding church-state issues in the years between 1777 and 1784, the assembly "appeared as a master of indecision, ordering bills to be drafted, debating them at length, and them postponing or rejecting them."[44]

Madison was not reelected to the assembly in 1777, so he was unable to participate in considering the various religious petitions. In 1778, however, the assembly elected him to the Council of State under the administration of Governor Patrick Henry, a position he continued to hold when

Jefferson succeeded Henry in June 1779.[45] In contrast, Jefferson served in the House of Delegates from 1777 to 1779, leading the monumental task of revising Virginia's laws. That Jefferson was frustrated with the assembly's inability or unwillingness to address the outstanding religious issues can be assumed, as it was during this period that he wrote his seminal work on religious freedom, the Bill for Establishing Religious Freedom.

The Bill for Establishing Religious Freedom

At some point during the 1777 legislative session Jefferson wrote a draft of what would become his Bill for Establishing Religious Freedom, which was introduced in the Virginia Assembly in 1779 (bill no. 82) and finally enacted into law (in modified form) in 1786. He wrote his bill to address limitations contained in the Virginia Declaration of Rights, which, while guaranteeing the "free exercise of religion," had not secured disestablishment. The bill also likely arose out of the frustrations he had encountered during the previous legislative session that had produced the compromise law of December 9, 1776, and had tabled the more contentious issues for a later time. The Virginia Statute is one of Jefferson's leading statements about religious freedom, and he was so proud of the work that he had it listed on his grave obelisk as one of his three greatest accomplishments (along with being author of the Declaration of Independence and founder of the University of Virginia). The statute is considered a seminal founding document concerning religious freedom and separation of church and state, with historian Bernard Bailyn praising it as "the most important document in American history, bar none." Expressing a more qualified sentiment, Thomas Buckley has asserted that the "Virginia Statute offers the preeminent statement of the American faith as Jefferson defined it." As a result, Jefferson's work has been closely scrutinized and subjected to multiple interpretations.[46]

Jefferson's bill, as well as the ultimate statute, has a lengthy preamble that contains the philosophical rationale for religious freedom, followed by a shorter operative clause which declares that "no man shall be compelled to frequent or support any relig[i]ous Worship place or Ministry whatsoever, nor shall be enforced, restrained, molested, or burthened in his body or goods, nor shall otherwise suffer on account of his religious opinions or belief, but that all men shall be free to profess, and by argument to maintain their opinions in matters of religion, and that the same shall in no wise diminish, enlarge, or affect their civil capacities."[47] On its own, the operative clause reflects aspects of Jefferson's political theology: that it was wrong to compel a person to attend or support any religion, even their own, and that people should be able to hold and express their opinions free from persecution or the loss of political standing or civil privileges.

The bill's preamble is where Jefferson's rationale for religious freedom is most evident. Although the bill and final statute contain language likely designed to appeal to a wider and more religiously conventional audience— "Almighty God," "Lord," and "holy author of our religion"—Jefferson's draft "is a lyric to reason and religious freedom," in the words of John Ragosta.[48] As several scholars have noted, the contents and arguments of the preamble rely extensively on Jefferson's reading of John Locke. The deity identified in the draft is one who works through "reason alone"—the god of nature of the Enlightenment—not a god who makes god's will known through revelation or church doctrine. "God hath created the mind free," Jefferson wrote, thereby enabling people to acquire knowledge of God and other matters through the "influence [of] reason alone" and "the evidence proposed to their minds" (i.e., empiricism). Here, Jefferson paraphrased Locke's statement in his *Letter on Toleration* that "true and saving religion consists in the inward persuasion of the mind" as facilitated by reason, a phrase Jefferson had excerpted in his "Notes on Religion." Because God had "chose[n] not to propagate [religious belief] by coercions on either [the] body or mind," then civil and ecclesiastical officials, "being themselves but fallible and uninspired men," lacked authority to do so.[49]

With those prepositions, Jefferson turned to the arguments supporting full religious freedom and equality and the disestablishment of religion. Picking up on the previous point—and again following Locke—Jefferson argued that "the opinions of men are not the object of civil government, nor under its jurisdiction," meaning that religion and government operated in separate spheres. Not only did civil officials lack all authority over religious opinions, to allow "the civil Magistrate to intrude his powers into the field of opinion, and to restrain the profession or propagation of principles on supposition of their ill tendency, is a dangerous fallacy, which at once destroys all religious liberty," if for no other reason than the magistrate will always "make his own opinions the rule of judgment, and approve or condemn the sentiments of others only as they shall square with, or differ from his own." And because civil magistrates lacked authority over religious opinions, it

followed that "our civil rights have no dependance on our religious opinions. . . . Therefore the proscribing any citizen as unworthy the publick
confidence, by laying upon him an incapacity of being called to offices of
trust and emolument, unless he profess or renounce this or that religious
opinion, is depriving him injuriously of those privileges and advantages to
which, in common with his fellow citizens he has a natural right." Religious
freedom and the privileges it afforded were accordingly based on natural
rights, neither granted nor constrained by civil authorities.[50]

These preceding principles led to the heart of the bill's preamble: "That
to compel a man to furnish contributions of money for the propagation of
opinions which he disbelieves and abhors, is sinful and tyrannical: That even
the forcing him to support this or that teacher of his own religious persuasion, is depriving him of the comfortable liberty of giving his contributions
to the particular pastor whose morals he would make his pattern, and whose
powers he feels most persuasive to righteousness."[51] Thus, to force a person
to support the religion of another constituted a "sin" against God's grant of
free inquiry, was "tyrannical" through the usurpation of authority that magistrates did not possess, and was coercive and violated the freedom of conscience to arrive at one's own conception of god, or not to do so at all. Here
was the concise argument for disestablishment: religious opinions were not
a concern of the state or subject to its authority, establishments were fallible
and counter to the will of God and to free inquiry, they tended to exclude
some citizens of their natural rights and privileges, and they were coercive of
both body and mind.[52] And Jefferson's final argument for religious freedom
in his bill was that "truth is great and will prevail if left to herself; that she is
the proper and sufficient antagonist to errour, and has nothing to fear from
the conflict, unless by human interposition." This last argument also paraphrased Locke, down to the feminization of the concept of truth as Locke
had done in his *Letter.*[53] Besides making a comprehensive argument on behalf
of religious freedom and disestablishment, the bill was a precedent-breaking
piece of legislation, something never having been proposed before in human
history. As Merrill D. Peterson and Robert C. Vaughan wrote, "The Virginia Statute for Religious Freedom became the cornerstone of the unique
American tradition of religious freedom and separation of church and state.
It served as a model for other American states, both old and new."[54]

A handful of historians have attempted to recast Jefferson's bill as expressing more conventional religious ideas. Seizing on the religious terms noted

above, these commentators have asserted that Jefferson "argued from an essentially theological position to [support] freedom of religion" and "the measure presupposed a belief in God." These claims minimize the rationalistic influences behind Jefferson's conception of religious freedom by asserting that he likely read the various Baptist petitions which raised theological arguments for religious freedom when writing the bill; they also seek to cabin the more sweeping implications of the statute's separationist language. The statute, "which presumed a creator who was involved in human affairs, fell short of advocating an absolute rule that civil government and religion may never interact in a cooperative manner," writes one critic. Based on this "narrow construction," the bill "was simply a further exploration of the free exercise guarantee enshrined in the Virginia Declaration of Rights."[55]

These critiques focus on seeming inconsistencies in Jefferson's draft without examining the bill as a whole. Jefferson's limited use of conventional religious terms—again, likely included to appeal to a wider audience—does not counteract the bill's overarching rationalist argument for religious freedom. In fact, the final clause of the bill, retained in the statute, declared that "the rights hereby asserted are of the natural rights of mankind," and that any future efforts to repeal the law would "be an infringement of natural right."[56] If the bill "presupposed a belief in God," it was the god of the Enlightenment who had "created the mind free" to pursue where reason and experience took one, not the traditional Christian God. To impose such limitations on the bill runs counter to Jefferson's clear intent. Discussing the bill in his *Autobiography* years later, Jefferson celebrated the absence of a reference to Jesus, remarking that its coverage protected "the Jew and the Gentile, the Christian and Mahometan, the Hindoo, and Infidel of every denomination."[57]

Moreover, to characterize the bill as simply a repackaging of the principles contained in the Declaration of Rights begs the question of why Jefferson thought it necessary to draft an additional law. As discussed, Jefferson, Madison, and religious dissenters criticized the declaration because it did not achieve either disestablishment or sect equity. More was needed to realize full religious freedom. And finally, the fact that Jefferson possessed and likely read the dissenters' petitions for religious liberty does not turn the bill into a religiously inspired document. As already noted, the Presbyterian petitions relied on a combination of theological and rationalist arguments for religious freedom, and the Baptist petition of December 1776 that Jefferson possessed also raised natural-rights arguments for greater freedom, stating that "it is contrary to the Principles of Reason and Justice that any should be compelled to contribute to the Maintenance of a Church with which their Consciences will not permit them to join." Because religious figures used natural-rights arguments widely in justifying the Revolution and the rights of the colonists, the rationalist orientation of the bill was unlikely to offend most people, a point Jefferson knew.[58]

Jefferson's bill no. 82 was introduced in the house in June 1779, shortly after he assumed the office of governor. The delay is likely attributable to its being part of the general revision of the laws that took several years to complete. Political calculations may also have played a role, as by mid-1779 Edmund Pendleton and Robert Carter Nichols were no longer serving in the House of Delegates. Even so, the bill's introduction was met with mixed reaction. This was not Jefferson's first attempt at legislative disestablishment, and delegates were likely wary of dealing with (or of having to avoid dealing with) the religion issue.[59] Faced with a direct assault on the establishment, pro-establishment forces rallied against Jefferson's bill. Writing in the *Virginia Gazette,* "A Social Christian" attacked the bill for its effort to "discontinue all publick religious worship and to tolerate the propagation of Atheism." In the bill's long preamble, the author charged, "we have the principles of a Deist."[60] Another author, an "Eastern Layman," writing in a different edition of the *Gazette,* panned Jefferson's "humble attempt" at reducing society "to an imaginary state of uncorrupted nature." "That the opinions of men are not the objects of civil government, is dogma," wrote the Eastern Layman, but, "as we are taught to believe in the enacting clause, that all men should be free to profess, and by argument to maintain their opinions in matters of religion, without any controul of the civil magistrate, *as to the manner and limits of their religious exercises,* is a concession, to which, it will be difficult to reconcile the peaceful citizen, who has always regarded social tranquility as one of the first objects of any civil institution."[61] Petitions expressing similar sentiments were submitted to the Virginia House when it reconvened in October, all but dooming the bill's fate. Several called on the delegates to consider the alternative of a general assessment as had been suggested three years earlier.[62]

Notably, while Jefferson's bill appeared to motivate the opposition, it failed to stimulate support among religious dissenters. The Presbyterians remained silent about the bill, indicating a growing division between the more separationist Scots-Irish Presbyterians in the valley and the more accommodating Presbyterians in the east, with some of the latter openly considering a form of rapprochement with the Anglicans. The Baptists, in turn, passed a resolution of support but did not mount a petition drive as before, with their memorial of October 16 to the assembly concentrating on the right to solemnize marriages. Lacking support, Jefferson's bill was tabled indefinitely.[63]

Opposition to Jefferson's bill spurred conservatives into proposing a counter piece of legislation, titled "A Bill Concerning Religion," based on article 33 of the South Carolina Constitution adopted a year earlier. As in Virginia, colonial South Carolina had established the Church of England, which included an exclusive religious assessment. In drafting its constitution in 1778, the issue of maintaining the establishment had become contentious, with Presbyterian minister William Tennent leading the opposition against instituting even a general assessment. In a compromise, the South Carolina legislature enacted a "symbolic" establishment that declared the "Christian Protestant religion" to be established, with incorporated churches required to adhere to five articles of faith, including that "the Christian religion is the true religion" and that the Bible was of "divine inspiration." However, article 33 rejected compelled support for religion, declaring that no person was "obliged to pay towards the maintenance and support of a religious worship that he does not freely join in, or has voluntarily engaged in support."[64] The Virginia bill copied article 33 almost to the letter, declaring the "Christian Religion . . . to be the established Religion" and requiring all churches to adhere to five articles of faith, but it then provided for a general religious assessment. The bill allowed taxpayers to direct their assessments to their own churches, provided the church was an authorized religious body. If a taxpayer declined to assign their assessment, the county court would divide it among those recognized churches in the county.[65]

Initially, the bill had considerable support, with several petitions praying for its adoption. As a petition from Lunenburg proclaimed, the signatories were "of opinion that the Christian religion, free from errors of popery, and a general contribution to the support thereof, ought to be established from the principle of public utility." But opponents recognized the bill would represent a significant retreat from article 16 of the Declaration of Rights, with "A Friend of Liberty" writing that he was "adverse to the establishment of christianity, and to all impositions on people for its support. . . . Let us leave to men to judge for themselves; to believe in one or more Gods, as seems best to them." Even though the bill survived two readings, it too was tabled indefinitely. Possibly exhausted over the controversy, the Virginia Assembly then formally repealed the earlier law authorizing a tax for ministers rather than suspending it for another year. Although additional petitions regarding Virginia's church-state arrangement would be filed in the succeeding years—chiefly from Baptists seeking redress from the vestry and marriage laws—the assessment controversy laid relatively dormant until the end of the war in 1783.[66]

The Second Interregnum

Jefferson's Bill for Establishing Religious Freedom was not the only measure that he drafted touching on religious matters during his three years in the assembly. He chaired the committee in charge of revising Virginia's colonial laws, which under his leadership proposed some 126 bills. Four of those bills, drafted or rewritten by Jefferson with the assistance of George Wythe and Edmund Pendleton between 1777 and 1779, proposed the following: preserving all the property "of the Church Heretofore by Law Established," "punishing dissenters of religious worship and Sabbath breakers," nullifying marriages "prohibited by the Levitical Law," and "appointing days of public fasting and thanksgiving." Some commentators have pointed to the religiously accommodating thrust of these bills, introduced in the Virginia House in 1785 by Madison (contemporaneous to his drafting the *Memorial and Remonstrance*), to argue that neither Jefferson nor Madison were as separationist about church-state matters as they have been portrayed or that they were at least inconsistent in their application of that principle.[67]

That understandings of church-state relations were fluid and unfolding during this time is certainly true, and in their long public careers Jefferson and Madison may have undertaken actions that they later regretted or that did not strictly adhere to separationism in hindsight. As is addressed in later chapters, as presidents Jefferson approved of a treaty with a Native American tribe that included financing of a Christian mission while Madison issued four prayer proclamations during the War of 1812, actions Madison later regretted.[68] Nonetheless, cherry-picking seemingly historical inconsistencies, particularly when not viewed in their context, obscures the overall records of Jefferson and Madison.[69] First, as chair of a committee with pro-establishment members, Jefferson and his colleagues

were tasked with revising *existing* laws enacted during the colonial establishment, which technically still controlled in the late 1770s. The bills reflected cautious revisions, and sometimes improvements, that would have
been expected at a time when the ongoing status of Virginia's establishment
was uncertain. The bill to preserve the property holdings of the Anglican Church—a matter of deep concern for pro-establishment delegates—
merely protected the status quo property interests of the church at a time
that it had lost its tax subsidies and was consistent with the compromise
law of December 9, 1776. It also *advanced* disestablishment by disentangling the property interests of the church from those of the state. The marriage bill was one of several efforts to address the ongoing controversy over
the authority to grant marriages and expanded its availability by allowing common-law couples to obtain marriage licenses upon a declaration
in front of witnesses. Despite the bill's use of the term "Levitical Law"—
added by Edmund Pendleton, according to John Ragosta—the bill omitted
any requirement that marriages be conducted under any ecclesiastical authority, a clear benefit for religious dissenters. The bill for appointing days
of public fasting and thanksgiving reauthorized a longstanding colonial
custom that remained popular throughout the nation, particularly during
the Revolutionary War. Jefferson and Madison likely acceded to the bill
in order to appease the more conventionally religious delegates. And the
bill for "punishing dissenters of religious worship and Sabbath breakers"
protected the religious worship services of all denominations, addressing
a problem that dissenters had experienced at the hands of Anglican clerks
and vestry officials. Consistent with laws in all the other states—and laws
that continued well into the nineteenth century—the bill prohibited unnecessary labor or trade on Sundays, a prohibition that benefited slaves,
servants, and apprentices. Significantly, it omitted previous requirements
of church attendance. Like the marriage bill's term "Levitical Law," the use
of the word "Sabbath" reflected the common nomenclature of the time
when religious discourse was ubiquitous. More important, however, the
Sunday law—which was the only bill to be enacted—is consistent with Jefferson's and Madison's "lifelong commitment to protecting the citizenry's
right to express peacefully religious beliefs and opinions," as one critic duly
acknowledges. Seen in their contexts, these proposed bills *advanced* the
cause of religious freedom and equality, which would have appealed to Jefferson and Madison. Still, when compared to the Declaration of Rights,

Jefferson's Bill for Establishing Religious Freedom, and Madison's *Memorial and Remonstrance,* these bills were "not only not particularly memorable, but [were] in fact soon forgotten."[70]

The more significant proposed laws that Jefferson drafted during this time—at least the ones that provide greater insight into Jefferson's views about church-state relations—were his proposals for establishing a system of public education and for reforming the College of William and Mary. In 1779, Jefferson drafted a bill to create free public schools for all children—both boys and girls—with a series of advanced grammar schools for those children who exceled academically. In contrast to the religiously based education common in private academies and through tutors, Jefferson proposed a curriculum focused on secular subjects—reading, writing, "common arithmetick," history, and classical languages—taught to facilitate free inquiry and reason, rather than to indoctrinate. Writing around the same time in his *Notes on the State of Virginia,* Jefferson remarked, "Reason and persuasion are the only practicable instruments. To make way for these, free enquiry must be indulged." To further that goal, he recommended against "putting the Bible and Testament into the hands of the children, at an age when their judgments are not sufficiently matured for religious enquiries." Jefferson's vision of a secular public education system was pathbreaking for the time. Madison introduced Jefferson's education bill in 1786, but the assembly did not enact a version of it until 1796.[71]

At the same time, Jefferson drafted a bill to reform the administration and curriculum of the College of William and Mary, which he felt was declining academically. A chief cause of that decline, Jefferson believed, was the sectarian character of the college, which was controlled by the Anglican Church and run by Anglican clergy, with both factors standing in the way of modernizing the curriculum. Writing in his *Autobiography,* Jefferson noted how the professors had to adhere to the church's thirty-nine articles of faith and that students were required to attend Anglican catechism. He also believed that continuing the college as an Anglican institution would alarm dissenters of the "ascendancy [of] the Anglican sect" while serving as an additional impediment to disestablishment. Jefferson wanted to transform the college into a public university with a secular orientation; as a first step, he proposed abolishing the professorship in divinity.[72] Jefferson was stymied in this undertaking too, but his two efforts at education reform had a clear thrust of disentangling education from religion and resting its foundation on reason and free inquiry. These setbacks later served as the impetus for his late-in-life undertaking of founding the University of Virginia.[73]

Before the war concluded, the southern colonies became the site of military action with the British occupying Charleston, South Carolina, in 1780 and its forces then moving into North Carolina and Virginia. In response to the crisis, Governor Jefferson issued a proclamation calling for a day of thanksgiving and prayer, an apparent lapse that separationist critics have also seized upon.[74] A closer examination reveals that Jefferson issued the proclamation pursuant to a recommendation from the Continental Congress. In contrast to Congress's resolution with its embellished religious rhetoric—"our gracious Redeemer" and "heirs of his eternal glory"—likely written by John Witherspoon, Jefferson's proclamation was perfunctory, merely recommending that the "good people" and ministers of Virginia engage in prayers to Almighty God at a critical juncture of the war. (As a point of reference, in 1774, while serving as a member of the House of Burgesses, Jefferson had supported a similar resolution calling for a day of fasting, humiliation, and prayer in support of the Boston patriots. In that earlier episode, Jefferson noted in his *Autobiography*, he and other delegates had "cooked up" the resolution for political purposes: to "arous[e] our people from their lethargy" and to embarrass Virginia's royal governor, who promptly dissolved the House of Burgesses for its insubordination.) Thus, there is little to suggest that Jefferson's war proclamation represented a change in his perspective about church-state separation.[75]

As further evidence that Jefferson had not wavered from his commitment to religious freedom, during that same period he penned his *Notes on the State of Virginia* with its strong language affirming religious liberty and freedom of conscience. And in his final year as governor (1781), as British forces were marching across Virginia, Jefferson issued a revealing proclamation inviting the Hessian auxiliary troops to desert. In addition to offering a bounty of fifty acres of land and two cows, Jefferson promised they would "be protected in the free exercise of their respective religions, and be invested with . . . [all] the benefits of civil and religious freedom." Jefferson apparently believed that the state's prospect of greater religious freedom represented an attractive inducement to the Catholic and Lutheran Hessians.[76]

Finally, in 1783, before leaving for France to assume the duties as minister from the United States, Jefferson made his third attempt at disestablishing religion in Virginia. Contained in a draft of a new constitution for the state, Jefferson included a provision that would have forbidden the assembly "to abridge the civil rights of any person on account of his religious belief; to restrain him from professing and supporting that belief, or to compel him to contributions" to any religion. Going a step beyond his earlier proposals, Jefferson included a provision that would have made "ministers of the gospel" ineligible to serve in the assembly.[77] As he later explained to an acquaintance, "The clergy are excluded, because, if admitted into the legislature at all, the probability is that they would form it's majority. For they are dispersed through every county in the state, they have influence with the people, and great opportunities of persuading them to elect them into the legislature." With the real possibility that Virginia might reinstate a religious establishment, Jefferson still feared the power of an organized clergy and their potential impact on republican institutions and religious freedoms. The clergy, "tho shattered, is still formidable, still forms a *corps,* and is still actuated by the *esprit de corps,*" he continued. "The nature of that spirit has been severely felt by mankind, and has filled the history of ten or twelve centuries with too many atrocities not to merit a proscription from meddling with government."[78] Commenting on Jefferson's draft, Madison urged his friend to strike the provision disqualifying clergy from public service. "Does not the exclusion of Ministers of the Gospel as such violate a fundamental principle of liberty by punishing a religious profession with the privation of a civil right?" Madison asked. "Does it not violate another article of the plan itself which exempts religion from the cognizance of Civil power?" Jefferson acceded to his friend's suggestion, but the episode indicates Jefferson's lifelong anticlerical leanings. This was but one of several instances where Madison or Jefferson would influence the other's thinking about the contours of religious freedom.[79]

FIVE

The First Collaboration

Virginia Disestablishment, Part 2

Between 1779 and 1783, there was little progress toward resolving Virginia's religious situation. This was due in no small part to the British Army's invasion of the South and its gradual march into Virginia, a threat that consumed the attention of public officials. For part of that time Jefferson served as the wartime governor and Madison was a delegate to the Confederation Congress in Philadelphia, duties that limited their attention on religious matters. In contrast to those lean years, however, 1784 to 1786 became one of the more transformative periods in American church-state history. Virginia's legislative assembly came close to enacting a new tax assessment for the support of religion, only to experience a reversal of fortune resulting in the enactment of Jefferson's Bill for Establishing Religious Freedom. Madison, with Jefferson's encouragement from afar, was at the forefront of that battle.

The General Assessment Battle

With the war finally concluded in late 1783, people's attention turned to matters of governance and reconstituting civil society. The status of Virginia's establishment had been in limbo since 1776, and people renewed calls on the assembly to resolve the issue. The initial overtures came from pro-establishment forces, those who had been directly affected by the suspension of assessments since the war. On November 15, 1783, the assembly received a petition from Lunenburg County calling for a "just, equitable, and adequate contribution for the support of the Christian Churches." The sixty signatories related how, "with pain and regret, [they had] seen the propagation of the Gospel die away in many parts of the country" and had witnessed the growth of "indifference and impiety" from the absence of an establishment. To arrest this trend, the petitioners prayed "to see the reformed Christian religion supported and maintained by a general and equal contribution of the whole State that is upon the most equitable footing that is possible to place it." To further allay concerns that they sought to resume the previous establishment, the petitioners asserted that "we would have no sect or Denomination of Christians privileged to encroach upon the rights of another."[1] A similar petition from Amherst County, filed later that month, also expressed concern about the "Vice and Immorality, and Lewdness and Prophanity" that had arisen since the decline of support for the establishment. Declaring they were "duly Apprehensive about the Fatal Consequences of these Things," they called on the assembly to "restore the Public Worship of God" through an assessment.[2]

Pro-establishment petitions continued to be filed into the new year, with all of them recounting the theme of moral declension. In May, a petition from Warwick County lamented "the present neglected state of religion and morality," while it asserted that "a general assessment would greatly contribute to restore and propagate the Holy Christian religion." A petition that fall from Isle of Wight County made similar points, "praying that an act may pass to compel everyone to contribute something, in proportion to his property, to the support of religion."[3] Although these petitioners, most assuredly from Episcopalian vestrymen and communicants, chiefly sought a resumption of public support for their churches, they, like earlier petitioners, reflected a widely held belief that piety and virtue were in decline, which would put the new republic at risk. George Mason, the author of the Declaration of Rights, shared that common view. Writing to Patrick Henry in May 1783, Mason raised the prospect of "whether our Independence shall prove a Blessing or a Curse." If one were to predict the nation's "future from the Past, the Prospect is not promising," Mason wrote. "Justice & Virtue are the vital Principles of republican Government; but among us, a Depravity of Manners & Morals prevails." Like many Virginians, Mason believed that a leading cause for this trend was the lack of public support of religion and the destitute state of the Episcopal Church, which had lost almost half of its clergy and seen dozens of parishes close. Restoring financial support of the Christian religion, now through a general assessment, was the right and equitable solution to address this problem. Mason implored Henry in his capacity as legislative leader to enact laws that strictly adhered "to the Distinctions between Right & Wrong" and "restore[d] that Confidence and Reverence in the People."[4]

George Mason was not outlier; in fact, he represented the dominant perspective that had existed within Western Christianity for 1,400 years, one that was shared by establishmentarians and dissenters alike: that social order required a strong religious influence, if not a shared system of belief, and that religion was a matter of public interest. Historians Thomas Buckley and Lance Banning speculated that many Virginians desired a resolution of the religion issue and were willing to consider an equitable funding system that included limitations on the state's ability to interfere in ecclesiastical matters or regulate doctrine. As Banning observed, "In the eighteenth century, almost no one doubted that good conduct rested on religion, and a general assessment that would free a citizen to designate which church would get his taxes seemed to many a fair and liberal way to secure morality without which no republic could endure."[5] Many leaders and supporters of the new United States not only accepted this premise; as students of history, they believed that republics, more than any other system of government, required a moral foundation and a virtuous citizenry—otherwise, the new nation would go the way of earlier republics and collapse from within. Patrick Henry shared this perspective, as did many Virginia legislators. Dissenters too, such as the Hanover Presbytery, agreed that "society could not easily exist" without "the great fundamental principles of all religion."[6]

As expected, the Episcopal clergy weighed in on the issue of an assessment. Although their petition made comparable arguments, the clergy did not simply seek a resumption of financial support; the newly constituted Protestant Episcopal Church also petitioned that it be allowed to legally incorporate in order to be free from government regulation of its operations and property. Episcopalians wanted legal independence from the state; the petition prayed that "all acts which direct modes of faith and worship and enjoin the observance of certain days be repealed," and that all the church buildings, glebe lands, and all other properties "heretofore belonging to the Established church, may be forever secured to them by law." Although they supported an assessment to be shared by all recognized Protestant denominations, the Episcopalians did not want to relinquish their previously privileged status, particularly the property they had acquired under the exclusive establishment. Whether they realized it at the time, the Episcopalians' apparent overreaching would ultimately doom the general assessment. Madison skillfully exploited their ongoing quest for privilege to undermine support for any type of tax support for religion.[7]

By mid-1784, public sentiment appeared to be squarely behind establishing some form of a general assessment. Writing to Madison at the time, Richard Henry Lee—serving as Virginia delegate to the Confederation Congress—expressed satisfaction that the legislature was considering a general assessment. "Refiners may weave as fine a web of reason as they please, but the experience of all times shows Religion to be the guardian of morals," Lee wrote. One would "be a very inattentive observer in our Country, who does not see that avarice is accomplishing the destruction of religion, for want of a legal obligation to contribute something to its support," he insisted. Like many others, Lee saw no inconsistency between principles of religious freedom, affirmed in the state's Declaration of Rights, and the public support of religion on equitable and "liberal" terms. The declaration, "it seems to me, rather contends against forcing modes of faith and forms of worship, than against compelling contribution for the support of religion in general."[8]

Surprisingly, the new round of petitions seeking an assessment did not initially spark a groundswell of opposition from dissenters. In May 1784, the Baptist Association filed a petition with the House of Delegates that complained about the privileges enjoyed by the Episcopalians, restating their argument that they considered the "vestry and marriage acts as unequal and oppressive." Although the Baptists prayed that "perfect and equal religious freedom may be established," the memorial was strangely silent on the matter of an assessment. Even after the assessment bill gained momentum in the house that fall, the Baptists continued to focus on the inequalities of the vestry and marriage laws.[9]

In contrast to the Baptists, the Presbyterians were not of one mind going into 1784. Since submitting a strong memorial in 1777 condemning any form of a general assessment as "plainly subversive of religious liberty," a division had arisen between those Presbyterians residing in the Tidewater region and the Scots-Irish Presbyterians of the Blue Ridge and Shenandoah Valley. The leadership of the Hanover Presbytery was centered around Hampden-Sydney College in the southeastern part of the state. These Presbyterians, led by John Blair Smith, were chiefly concerned with ending the privileges of the Episcopal Church and receiving equal treatment under the laws; many were not philosophically opposed to the idea of tax support for religion, provided it was administered equitably and without regulation of church affairs. As discussed, the Hanover Presbytery had remained silent in 1779 in response to the failed Bill for Religion designed to reinstate an assessment. In May 1784, the presbytery submitted a memorial to the House of Delegates that complained about the privileges the Episcopal Church still enjoyed despite the intervening laws since 1776: its property holdings, "derived from the pockets of all religious societies, [which] was exclusively and unjustly appropriated to the benefit of one," and the vestries, "a remnant of hierarchical domination." "Such preferences, distinctions and advantages granted by the Legislature exclusively to one sect of Christians, are regarded by a great number of your constituents as glaringly unjust and dangerous." Yet, despite the express calls for financial support for religion by the pro-assessment proponents, the Presbyterian memorial did not address that issue.[10]

Then, at the beginning of the legislative session in October 1784, the Hanover Presbytery submitted a second memorial to the house, this one focusing chiefly on a proposed bill that would allow the Episcopal clergy to incorporate separately from their churches. The memorial argued that by authorizing the clergy to become "a distinct order in the community," the state would be creating an "illicit connection" between church and state with spiritual authority flowing from the latter rather than from God. Such "interference of government in religion cannot be indifferent to us," the Presbyterians asserted. Religion, "and its ministers in professional compacity, ought not be under the direction of the State." The memorial then segued to affirming the one instance where such "interference" was permissible: for "preserving of the public worship of the Deity, and the supporting of institutions for inculcating the great fundamental principles of all religion" through an equitable tax. "Should it be thought necessary at present for the Assembly to exert this right of supporting religion in general by an assessment on all the people, we would wish it to be done on the most *liberal plan.*" Such an assessment would produce a "happy influence upon the morality of its citizens . . . which is the cement of the social union . . . without which society could not easily exist."[11] As William Lee Miller noted, the Presbyterians' memorial "was by no means an unequivocal endorsement of tax support for churches" as it specified conditions for their support: that there be no attempts "to point out articles of faith . . . or to settle modes of worship, or to interfere in the internal government of religious communities." Still, it represented a dramatic change in position from 1776–1777, and it clearly annoyed Madison, who called their support for an assessment "shameful" and self-serving. As he wrote James Monroe that fall, at the same time that the Presbyterian clergy "remonstrated against any narrow principles" which would put them in a disadvantage, they "favor[ed] a more comprehensive establishment." The Presbyterians' switch in position continued to irk Madison; the following year he charged in another letter to Monroe that the Presbyterian clergy "seem as ready to set up an establishment which is to take them in as they were to pull down that which shut them out."[12]

Madison had returned to Virginia in late 1783 just as the renewed drive for a general assessment began. Since early 1780, Madison had served as a Virginia delegate to the Confederation Congress, earning a reputation as a defender of Virginia's territorial boundary claims and then as a proponent of securing the nation's financial footing and increasing the powers of the central government. He was known as a diligent and skillful legislator and was establishing himself as a national political figure. Jefferson had come to appreciate Madison's legislative talents, telling him, "*I want you* in the *Virginia Assembly* and also in *Congress* yet we cannot have *you everywhere*. We must therefore be contented to have *you where you chuse.*"[13]

During Madison's last year in Congress, Jefferson joined him in Philadelphia. Jefferson had suffered two trying years, first being charged with dereliction of his duties as governor during the British invasion of Virginia in 1781, and then experiencing the death of his beloved wife, Patty, in 1782. He had resigned himself to life as a private citizen, but at Madison's urging Congress in late 1782 designated Jefferson to be a member of the peace negotiation team in France.[14] Jefferson arrived in Philadelphia in December, but unexpected delays in sailing meant that negotiations over the Treaty of Paris were completed before he could leave. This allowed Jefferson to temporarily resume his earlier duties as a delegate in Congress. For several months in 1783, Jefferson and Madison were reunited, residing at the same boardinghouse where they no doubt engaged in extensive discussions about their common interests including securing religious freedom. Madison was back in Virginia when Jefferson finally sailed for France in June 1784, now as the new representative to succeed Benjamin Franklin. As a newly elected delegate to the Virginia House in 1784, Madison promised his friend that he would keep him informed about the legislative actions in

Richmond, including the efforts to reestablish a religious tax. People under-stood that Madison, with his significant legislative experience and previous activities on behalf of religious freedom, would be the "general" to lead the opposition to an assessment.[15]

The Virginia Assembly met in late spring 1784, and the pro-assessment petitions and those of the Baptists and Presbyterians were referred to a Committee of the Whole. The house leadership decided to consider the various religious issues together: reforming the marriage and vestry laws, the incorporation of the Episcopal clergy, and a general assessment. As a means of building support for a general assessment, or at least diffusing opposition to it, the leadership agreed to support reforms to the marriage and vestry laws, though only the former received house approval.[16] Patrick Henry succeeded in having the Committee for Religion adopt a resolution supporting a general assessment, though the matter proceeded no further. The committee also passed a resolution favoring the incorporation of the Episcopal clergy, drafting a bill that the full house debated, but like the as-sessment that matter was ordered held over until the "second Monday in November next." Summing up the session for Jefferson, who had recently arrived in Paris, Madison expressed dismay that the Committee for Religion had found an assessment "to be reasonable," though he noted with relief that "the friends of the measure did not chuse to try their strength in the House." Madison expressed greater dismay over the incorporation bill, which he called "a notable project for re-establishing their independence of the laity." "Extraordinary as such a project was, it was preserved from a dishonorable death by the talents of Mr. Henry. It lies over for another Session."[17]

When the fall session convened in late October, Madison faced mul-tiple legislative challenges and knew that he was at a distinct disadvantage. Public support for some type of a religious assessment was strong, and it was favored by a majority of house delegates, who were still predomi-nately Episcopalian. In addition to Patrick Henry, the assessment's chief mover, most of Virginia's leading political figures supported a tax to benefit all Christian denominations—Richard Henry Lee, George Mason, Edmund Pendleton, Benjamin Harrison, and George Washington. As Washington told Mason, he was "not amongst the number of those who are so much alarmed at the thoughts of making people pay towards the support of that which they profess, if of the denominations of Christians."[18] And, as noted, the Presbyterians' qualified endorsement of an assessment in their October memorial not only annoyed Madison but removed a leading opponent to the measure, making its passage all the more likely.[19]

In many respects, Henry's proposal represented a significant improvement over the failed 1779 Bill for Religion. Unlike that earlier proposal, which would have formally established those Christian denominations that adhered to a set of doctrines and modes of worship, Henry's proposal abandoned those requirements and sought a middle road through an equitable distribution of funds according to a taxpayer's denominational choice, with an option of the funds to support "seminaries of learning." Henry had a long record of befriending religious dissenters, and according to Edmund Randolph, he "sympath[ized] with the history of their sufferings" against the established church. Henry saw his proposal as advancing public virtue for the benefit of the state while respecting both religious equality and religious liberty at the same time.[20]

With prospects for enacting an assessment promising, Henry moved that the house adopt a resolution to direct the drafting of a bill. A record of Henry's comments is missing, but his arguments can be gleaned from Madison's speech in opposition. As one contemporary described the scene: "The Generals on the opposite sides, were Henry & Madison. The former advocated with this usual art, the establishment of the Christian Religion in exclusion of all other Denominations."[21] Madison's speech, preserved in the form of an outline, fluctuated between rebutting Henry's arguments about the necessity of public support of religion and raising practical difficulties in applying an assessment, along with philosophical objections to the practice. Seeking to undercut Henry's chief premise, Madison responded that "the true question [is] not 'is religion necessary' but are Religious Establishments necessary for Religion?" "No," Madison responded. "Experience shews that religion [is] corrupted by Establishments." Madison disputed that the decline in morality and virtue was attributable to the lack of publicly supported religion. He noted that the same charge existed in other states that maintained establishments and argued that the explanation for moral declension lay in a host of causes, not the least of which was the social disruption of the war. He then segued to practical and philosophical considerations: "What is Xity," and who is to decide—are "courts of law to judge?" And on what basis would they decide—what is "canonical, what [is] apocryphal?" And finally, raising a natural-rights point, he insisted that "religion [is] not within the purview of civil authority."[22] Madison's comprehensive speech was no match for Henry's oratory, however; he "displayed Great Learning & Ingenuity, with all of the Powers of a close reasoner, but he was unsuccessful in the Event." On November 11, the House of Delegates approved a resolution by a vote of forty-seven to thirty-two to draft a bill to "pay a moderate tax or contribution annually for the support of the Christian religion, or some Christian church, denomination, or communion of Christians, or of some form of Christian worship." Henry was appointed to chair the drafting committee.[23]

Despite the setback, Madison did not seem overly worried, even though the Hanover Presbyterians' memorial arrived the day after the vote, indicating its support for an assessment. With matters seemingly going his way, Henry let it be known that he desired another term as Virginia's governor, a position he had held from 1781 to 1783. Henry likely believed he had secured support for his general assessment from both Episcopalians and Presbyterians, so a final vote was merely a formality. Madison eagerly supported Henry's appointment in order to get his rival out of the house, and so on November 17 the assembly unanimously chose Henry as governor. With Henry now removed, the assessment bill languished in the drafting committee. As Madison told James Monroe in late November, "The Bill for a Religious Assesst. has not been yet brought in. Mr. Henry[,] the father of the Scheme[,] is gone up to his Seat [as governor] for his family & will no more sit in the H. of Delegates, a circumstance very inauspicious to his off-spring." Madison was overly optimistic about the bill's fate, as on December 3 the committee reported the general assessment bill to the house floor.[24]

In late December, the house first considered a revised incorporation bill, one for "the incorporation of all religious societies of the christian religion"—which technically applied to any Christian body, rather than to clergy—and it passed easily. But because only Episcopalians had requested that opportunity, the house drafted a specific bill for its incorporation.[25] Madison voted for the bill, though he downplayed his true motivations for supporting incorporation. As he related to his father afterward, the incorporation bill was "the result of much altercation on the subject. In its original form it was wholly inadmissible. In its present form into which it has been trimmed, I assented to it with reluctance at the time." Madison also defended his vote in a letter to Jefferson, noting "the necessity of some sort of incorporation for the purpose of holding & managing the property of the Church could not well be denied, nor a more harmless modification of it now obtained."[26]

But Madison had ulterior reasons for supporting the incorporation bill. He correctly anticipated the Presbyterians' strenuous objection to the bill; despite initially expressing ambivalence over the concept of incorporation, the Presbyterians feared it represented a resurgence of Anglican preeminence. Reverend John Blair Smith, president of Hampden-Sydney College, had written Madison in the summer, charging that an incorporation law was "an express attempt to draw the State into an illicit connexion & commerce with [the Episcopalians], which is already the ground of that uneasiness which at present prevails thro' a great part of the State." As Madison later wrote Jefferson with an air of satisfaction, the Presbyterians had "*a jealousy of the episcopalians.* The mutual hatred of these sects has been much inflamed by the late act incorporating the latter. *I am far from* being *sorry for it.*"[27] Madison also understood—or hoped—that its passage might placate some of the pro-Episcopalian forces while giving assessment opponents more time to marshal forces against what he considered to be the more egregious measure. Madison wrote that he considered the passage of the incorporation bill "as having been so far useful as to have parried for the present the Genl. Assesst. which would otherwise have certainly been saddled upon us."[28]

The house then turned to the newly drafted Bill Establishing a Provision for Teachers of the Christian Religion, barely passing it on a preliminary reading by a vote of forty-four to forty-two. Madison spoke against the measure, repeating his earlier arguments. This time, however, Madison did not have to contend with the oratorical skills of Patrick Henry, noting that the bill's "friends are disheartened at the loss of Mr. Henry."[29] And Madison's strategy appeared to be paying off. As he had surmised, the passage of the incorporation bill had accomplished two purposes, mollifying some Episcopalian delegates who had voted for Henry's resolution and scaring wavering Presbyterians, who feared the prospects of a tax-funded *and* incorporated Episcopal Church. Madison moved that the assessment bill be tabled until the next legislative session to allow voters to consider the measure, and on Christmas Eve the house voted forty-five to thirty-eight to postpone final consideration until November 1785.[30] In a letter to James Monroe that same day, Madison noted his legislative accomplishment matter of factly, simply mentioning the delay. Writing Jefferson two weeks later, however, Madison revealed the close and contentious nature of the bill's consideration, relating how the house had initially broadened its application by substituting "religious teachers" for "Christian teachers," but then how that effort had been undone by the "pathetic zeal" of former governor Benjamin Harrison to reinsert the word "Christian." Madison believed, however, that language was to the advantage of assessment opponents, telling Jefferson that "should the bill ever pass into a law in its present form it may & will be easily eluded. It is chiefly obnoxious on account of its dishonorable principle and dangerous tendency." He hoped others would feel the same way.[31]

The *Memorial and Remonstrance*

With the incorporation bill enacted and the assessment bill tabled until the next legislative session in fall 1785, Madison possibly thought he had time to catch his breath, or at least to wait and see if reaction to the former bill might build into opposition to the latter. Madison was apparently also counting on—or hoping for—a shift in the composition of the house membership that would benefit assessment opponents.[32] As he told Monroe in April 1785, the only measure of the previous session that made "a noise thro' the Country" was the "Genl. Assessmt. The Episcopal people are generally for it, tho' I think the zeal of some of them has cooled. The laity of the other Sects are equally unanimous on the other side."[33] That sense of confidence seemed to grow, as the following month Madison again related to Monroe how assessment opponents thought "the prospect here flattering to their wishes. The printed Bill has excited great discussion and is likely to prove the sense of the Community to be in favor of the liberty now enjoyed." He noted the recent defeat of several delegates who had voted for the assessment resolution, "and not of a single one where the reverse has happened." And Madison reported with satisfaction that the Presbyterian Clergy "who were in general friends to the scheme, are already in another tone, either compelled by the laity of that sect, or alarmed at the probability of further interferences of the Legislature, if they once begin to dictate in matters of Religion."[34] He struck a more cautious tone in a letter to Jefferson, however, relating on one hand that the assessment bill "has produced some fermentation below the Mountains and a violent one beyond them." Nonetheless, he predicted that "the contest at the next Session on this question will be a warm and precarious one."[35]

If Madison felt comfortable with rolling the dice with the fall legislative session, others did not. Apparently, Madison needed to be encouraged to enter the fray ahead of the session and not leave matters to chance. In April, George Nicholas, a legislative ally and opponent of the assessment, wrote Madison urging him to take a more proactive stance.[36] Nicholas was concerned that Madison had apparently told Nicholas's brother that opponents to the assessment "should remain silent." "I fear this would be construed into an assent especially to the law for establishing a certain provision for the clergy," Nicholas wrote. He then proceeded to remind Madison of how an assessment-leaning House of Delegates might interpret silence: "The Assembly only postponed the passing of it that they might know whether it was disagreeable to the people, I think they may justly conclude that all are for it who do not say to the contrary. A majority of the counties are in favor of the measure but I believe a great majority of the people against it; but if this majority should not appear by petition the fact will be denied." Nicholas then pleaded with Madison to draft a memorial to circulate throughout those counties dominated by dissenters. "By discovering an exact uniformity of sentiment in a majority of the country it would certainly deter the majority of the Assembly from proceeding," he believed. "If you think with me that it will be proper to say something to the Assembly will you commit it to paper. I wish this because, I know you are most capable of doing it properly and because it will be most likely to be generally adopted."[37]

The fact that Madison needed to be encouraged to draft the *Memorial and Remonstrance* could raise questions about his belief in its necessity or even his commitment to the principles contained therein. That view would be short-sighted, however, because if Madison was anything, he was a master legislative strategist, and as his correspondence makes clear he was closely following the popular reactions to the proposed assessment bill throughout the spring and summer of 1785. He sensed correctly that the incorporation act had spooked the Tidewater Presbyterians while it had strengthened the resolve of their Blue Ridge brethren to oppose any religious tax. Madison likely preferred to allow the Presbyterians and Baptists to take the lead in building opposition through their meetings and by circulating petitions. Whether Madison already had decided to draft his own memorial before he received Nicholas's plea is unknown, as no response to Nicholas's letter exists (although Madison later acknowledged to Jefferson that he wrote the *Memorial* "at the *insistence of some of* [the bill's] *adversaries*"). Regardless, possibly assessing that the time was ripe, Madison wrote his *Memorial and Remonstrance* in June, quickly sending a copy to a relieved Nicholas, who made multiple copies to circulate in the rural counties where people "will readily join in the measure." Nicholas happily reported back to Madison in July that "one hundred and fifty of our most respectable freeholders signed it in a day."[38]

Madison penned the *Memorial* anonymously, not publicly acknowledging his authorship until much later, though it was a poorly kept secret.[39] The *Memorial* raised fifteen arguments against religious establishments, making three essential points. The first was jurisdictional, an argument he had raised during the floor debates, affirming that religious and civil entities operated in separate spheres and exercised distinct authority. "In matters of religion," Madison wrote, "no man's right is abridged by the institution of Civil Society and that Religion is wholly exempt from its cognizance." The assessment bill falsely implied that "the Civil Magistrate is a competent Judge of Religious Truth, or that he may employ Religion as an engine of Civil policy." The first proposition, Madison insisted, was "an arrogant pretension" while the second was "an unhallowed perversion of the means of salvation." "If Religion be not within the cognizance of the Civil Government," he asked rhetorically, "how can its legal establishment be necessary to Civil Government?" Madison's second point was that religious establishments violated notions of religious equality and a society based on "equal conditions." Here, he did not distinguish between exclusive and multiple establishments; all forms of religious assessments violated rights of conscience and constituted a religious establishment. "Who does not see that the same authority which can establish Christianity, in exclusion of all other Religions, may establish with the same ease any particular sect of Christians, in exclusion to all other Sects?" Madison's third essential point was that religious establishments, rather than advancing Christian piety, harmed religion (as well as civil society); they were "adverse to the diffusion of the light of Christianity." Indeed, the "fruits" of legal establishments historically had led to "pride and indolence in the Clergy, ignorance and servility in the laity, [and] in both, superstition, bigotry and persecution."[40] Biographer Lance Banning described the *Memorial* as the "clearest and most eloquent enunciation of a set of fundamental principles that guided [Madison] throughout his public life."[41]

As a leading document about church-state relations, the *Memorial and Remonstrance* has been studied and dissected by friends and foes alike (as has Jefferson's famous letter to the Danbury Baptist Association).[42] Foes, or at least critics of church-state separation, have sought to downplay the

Memorial's originality and/or turn it into an affirmation of religious accommodation, not separationism. That narrative started early, with Anglican apologist Bishop William Meade insisting in the 1850s that the *Memorial* was "drawn upon the supposition of the truth of Christianity." More recently, conservative authors have asserted that Madison borrowed heavily from the religiously based memorials of the Presbyterians and Baptists, and that the principles identified in the document rest chiefly on religious ideas about liberty and government that Madison learned as a student at Princeton. According to one author, "Madison's stirring words reflect the evangelical approach to religious liberty held by Witherspoon and [the] other instructors at the College of New Jersey," while another author insists that Madison wrote the *Memorial* with the purpose to protect "lively, vital Christianity." This line of analysis seeks to downplay, or eliminate, Madison's reliance on secular and rationalist principles.[43]

This narrative, frequently ideologically driven, focuses on the *Memorial*'s use of religious rhetoric designed to appeal to a broad group of Virginians—"Creator," "Governour of the Universe," "Providence," and "Supreme Lawgiver"—and his arguments, found chiefly in the first paragraph, about the "duty of every man to render to the Creator . . . homage," and that this "duty is precedent, both in order of time and in degree of obligation, to the claims of Civil Society."[44] This language not only indicates that Madison believed in the sovereignty of God over the state, writes one author; it is also a theological declaration that "all men stand as equals [under God,] for all are sinners, yet all may be redeemed through His sovereign power." Or as yet another author maintains, "Religious freedom for Madison was primarily to serve the cause of Christian evangelism."[45] This interpretation elevates the document's limited religious references (and simplifies them) over the primary lines of argumentation that Madison employed, which chiefly relied on natural-rights concepts. Historian Nicholas Miller is closer to the mark in observing that Madison's arguments "draw distinctly on the idea of the right of private judgment, both in its religious and Enlightenment forms."[46]

Although Madison's worldview was undoubtedly influenced by his theological studies at Princeton, the references to a deity in the *Memorial* are couched in Enlightenment terms. Rather than being an affirmation of God's sovereignty over political society—and that the primary goal of religious freedom is to promote Christian evangelism—the first paragraph of the *Memorial*, like much of the document, is a declaration of Lockean notions of natural rights. Quoting from the Declaration of Rights, the paragraph asserts that religion can be "directed only by reason and conviction," and that the right to conscience is an "unalienable" right. The second and fourth paragraphs also rely on Locke by asserting the separate "metes and bounds" of the functions of church and state and the right of equal conditions.[47] The first and second paragraphs demonstrate Madison's reliance on social-contract theory—that humans had not surrendered their conscience and religious rights upon joining civil society. This natural-rights interest was "precedent" to "the claims of Civil Society." As such, "in matters of Religion, no man's right is abridged by the institution of Civil Society and that Religion is wholly exempt from its cognizance."[48] In other places— paragraphs 3, 5, 7, 8, 11, and 15—the *Memorial* references radical Whig theory where it relates the horrors of ecclesiastical power ("spiritual tyranny" and "torrents of blood have been spilled") and warns of the incremental threats to all liberties by acceding any authority over conscience rights to civil authorities ("take alarm at the first experiment on our liberties"). And then, several paragraphs make practical arguments designed to appeal to religious dissenters and rationalists alike (establishments deny "asylum to the persecuted" and "destroy that moderation and harmony").[49]

Finally, the *Memorial* was not simply a manifesto about the necessity of full religious freedom but also about the nature of fundamental rights generally, tying the former to other essential rights such as press, trial by jury, and voting: "The equal right of every citizen to the free exercise of his religion is held by the same tenure with all our other rights." Here, Madison was not only equating the importance of religious freedom with other rights that all former British citizens valued; he was indicating the connection between freedom of conscience and other essential rights. The various arguments contained in the *Memorial* were thus "eclectic rather than inventive," in the words of Lance Banning, but still comprehensive in their ability to appeal to evangelicals, latitudinarians, and deists alike. Nonetheless, the overarching "intellectual foundation of the Remonstrance is the philosophy of natural rights," with an overlay of Whig theories, along with arguments couched in the language of rights of private judgment that would resonate among religious dissenters.[50] Madison was apparently pleased with his composition, sending a copy of the *Memorial* to Jefferson in Paris. As he told his friend, "*I drew up the remonstrance* herewith inclosed. It has been *sent thro' the medium of confidential persons in a number of the upper county*[s] and I am told will be pretty extensively signed." Nicholas and others circulated 13 copies of the *Memorial,* and it gathered over 1,500 signatures.[51]

Madison's *Memorial* was not the only opposition petition drafted and circulated over the summer and fall of 1785. According to Rhys Isaac, between the summer and the time the Virginia Assembly reconvened in November, "an unprecedented number of petitions" were distributed and filed with the body, amounting to approximately eighty petitions, memorials, and letters against the assessment bill with only ten in favor (with a signature difference of eleven thousand to one thousand).[52] Meeting in August, the newly formed Baptist General Committee—organized to oversee the political activities of the four Baptist Associations—called for drafting another great petition. Having succeeded on reforming the marriage law, the Baptists turned their attention to the proposed assessment bill. The body adopted a resolution opposing any form of assessment, declaring that it was "repugnant to the spirit of the Gospel" for the legislature to proceed in matters of religion. The resolution relied chiefly on theological arguments: every person "ought to be left entirely free in respect to matters of religion; that the holy Author of our religion needs no such compulsive measures for the promotion of his cause; [and] that the Gospel wants not the feeble arm of man for its support." The resolution also asserted that "taxing the people for the support of the Gospel [would] be destructive to religious liberty." The Baptists circulated a series of such "spirit of the gospel" petitions throughout the state, in the end gathering close to five thousand signatures.[53]

More significant than the Baptists' action, on May 19, the Hanover Presbytery met in the valley where western Presbyterians challenged the leadership to explain their memorial of the previous October that had given qualified support for an assessment. After a discussion about whether the body "approve[s] of any kind of an assessment by the General Assembly for the support of religion," the attendees voted that the *"Presbytery are unanimously against such a measure."*[54] Later in August, the Presbyterians reconvened and drafted a memorial to that effect. In contrast to the Baptists' theologically based arguments, the Presbyterian memorial relied on a combination of religious and natural-rights arguments. Civil government possessed only the authority that the people had voluntarily ceded to it, the memorial declared, echoing Locke, and religious matters were not among those. While matters of religion and morality were important to society, it continued, "these can be promoted only by the internal conviction of the

mind and its voluntary choice, which such establishments cannot." An assessment would necessarily empower the legislature to judge the legitimacy
of religious truth, alienate otherwise "good citizens" who did not embrace the
"common faith," and cause religious dissention. Raising a complementary
theological argument, the Presbyterian memorial noted that Christianity did
not need "the intrusive hand of the civil magistrate." God did not intend for
God's religion to be "dependent on earthly governments," it declared. "And
experience has shown that this dependence, where it has been effected, has
been an injury rather than an aid." The memorial then concluded by urging the passage of Jefferson's Bill for Establishing Religious Freedom.[55] All
in all, the memorial was a dramatic switch from the one of October of the
previous year. Madison, who had seen indications of a retreat among the
Presbyterians in the spring, wrote Jefferson a week following the issuance of
the new memorial. "The opposition to the general assessment gains ground,"
he happily announced. "The presbyterian clergy have at length espoused the
side of the opposition, being moved either by *a fear of their laity* or *a jealousy
of the episcopalians.*"[56]

The numerous memorials and petitions opposing the assessment bill did
the trick. When the assembly convened in Richmond in November, the
"table was loaded with petitions & remonstrances from all parts against the
interposition of the Legislature in matters of Religion," Madison related to
Jefferson, such that the assessment bill was "crushed under" their weight.
With some satisfaction, Madison claimed that the "steps taken throughout
the Country to defeat the Genl. Assessment, had produced all the effect that
could have been wished."[57] The house tabled the assessment bill, and taking
advantage of the momentum, Madison brought up Jefferson's Bill for Establishing Religious Freedom in December. Madison successfully fought off
efforts by conservatives to amend the bill's preamble by adding the words
"Jesus Christ" before the phrase "holy author of our religion." He was less
successful, however, in preserving the preamble intact, as the state senate insisted on altering some of Jefferson's rationalist language, omitting his
opening phrase that "the opinions and belief of men depend not on their
own will, but follow involuntarily the evidence proposed to their minds."
The senate also omitted his statement that God chose to extend his religion
"by its influence on reason alone," and his declaration that "the opinions
of men are not the object of civil government, nor under its jurisdiction."
All of these phrases contained decidedly Enlightenment natural-rights

meanings that some of the delegates apparently did not share. Madison, the strategist, decided not to fight it out, as "it was getting late in the Session and the House growing thin," and he "thought [it] better to agree to than to run further risks" of failure. In his January 1786 letter to Jefferson, Madison downplayed the changes as "one or two alterations" that "did not affect the substance though they somewhat defaced the composition." As he noted, "The enacting clauses past without a single alteration." He was correct in a sense, as most of Jefferson's soaring language remained intact.[58]

After receiving the good news, Jefferson had his bill printed and circulated in Paris, in its *original* form, telling Madison that the statute "has been received with infinite approbation in Europe & propagated with enthusiasm." With pride, Jefferson related that the statute had been translated into French and Italian and was to be published in the "new Encyclopedie." Sharing the credit for the accomplishment with Madison, Jefferson boasted that "it is honorable for us to have produced the first legislature who has had the courage to declare that the reason of man may be trusted with the formation of his own opinions."[59] As great an achievement as Jefferson's statute was, it cannot be viewed in isolation; Lance Banning correctly observed that Madison's "magnificent 'Memorial' [has] assumed a rightful place beside his friend's great statute among the documentary foundations of the libertarian tradition."[60]

Jefferson's statute and Madison's *Memorial* must thus be viewed in tandem and in conjunction with the decade-long struggle to disestablish religion and achieve religious equality in the state. The result was a condition of religious freedom unparalleled in human history. Regardless of the immediate impact of the Virginia disestablishment experience on legislation in other states, its achievement did not go unnoticed as the Virginia statute would become an important referent in public discussions about church-state relations for years to come. It became the standard by which all other measures would be judged. Possibly more than any other of his accomplishments, the statute became, in John Ragosta's words, "Jefferson's Legacy [and] America's Creed."[61]

SIX

The Second Collaboration

The Constitution

The Virginia struggle for disestablishment, and James Madison's and Thomas Jefferson's leading roles in that episode, have taken on special significance because of its purported tie to the enactment of the religion clauses of the First Amendment of the US Constitution. In his *Everson v. Board of Education* majority opinion, Justice Hugo Black asserted that "the provisions of the First Amendment, in the drafting and adoption of which Madison and Jefferson played such leading roles, had the same objective and were intended to provide the same protection against governmental intrusion on religious liberty as the Virginia statute." Employing more succinct language, Justice Wiley Rutledge simply declared that "the [First] Amendment was the direct culmination" of the Virginia Statute for Establishing Religious Freedom.[1] Others have disputed that connection and the contention that the experience of one state out of thirteen influenced the drafting of the religion clauses. After all, the argument goes, the majority of members of the First Congress who debated and voted on the free exercise and establishment clauses did not hail from Virginia and were likely swayed by the experiences in their own states. According to this argument, evidence supporting the impact of the Virginia statute and Madison's *Memorial and Remonstrance* on other members of Congress is less than clear.[2]

Although both points are worth considering, the position promoted by Justices Black and Rutledge and their scholarly supporters is not without merit; by dispatching colonial America's most entrenched and repressive religious establishment and replacing it with the nation's most progressive statement about religious equality, the Virginia statute became the standard by which all other measures would be judged. And while the final text of the religion clauses was the product of Congress, not one man, no man had a greater impact on that text than James Madison.[3]

This book does not ultimately need to resolve the debate over the impact of Virginia's disestablishment on the First Amendment, because when it comes to the perspectives of Madison and Jefferson, it is indisputable that *they* saw the principles of religious freedom advanced by the Virginia statute and the First Amendment as interrelated and mutually reinforcing.[4] It would be impossible, and historically inaccurate, to assign a consensus understanding about the scope or purposes of the First Amendment to the members of the First Congress, though some general agreement likely existed. At the same time, however, it was Madison who wrote the initial drafts of the proposed religious amendments, defended them in the debates, and then prevailed in the House-Senate conference that decided the ultimate language of the amendment. Accordingly, the meanings of the free exercise and no establishment principles in that amendment likely reflect Madison's understandings of religious freedom, as reinforced by his collaborator Jefferson, more than of any other person involved in their creation.[5]

Admittedly, Jefferson's collaboration in constructing the religion clauses is less pronounced than with the disestablishment episode in Virginia, where Jefferson took on a prominent role for a decade before residing in Paris during its culmination. Jefferson's impact on the First Amendment was indirect as he was in France throughout the drafting of the Constitution and the Bill of Rights. Yet, after ten years of working together on religious freedom issues, among so many others, Jefferson's and Madison's ideas about the subject were intertwined; Madison could hardly have disassociated his views about religious freedom and conscience rights from those of his friend even if he had wanted to do so. And despite the distance and time lag in correspondence, Jefferson and Madison kept in regular contact throughout the leadup to and the passage of the Bill of Rights, and Jefferson maintained an active letter-writing campaign with others hoping to influence amendments to the Constitution. Thus, efforts to dismiss Jefferson's relevance regarding the First Amendment—as Justice William Rehnquist remarked, he "was of course in France at the time"—ring hollow.[6]

All of that said, Virginia's disestablishment experience was atypical among the states, though no state experience was "typical."[7] Because the church-state settlements in the other states impacted the attitudes of members of the First Congress, it is necessary to consider those events briefly before turning to those on the federal level. Also influencing attitudes and likely informing contemporary understandings of role of the religion clauses was the inclusion of article 6, clause 3, in the Constitution—the provision prohibiting "religious tests" for federal officeholding—so that too merits consideration before examining the drafting of the First Amendment.

State Disestablishment and Religious Settlements

In disestablishing in 1786, Virginia was one of the last states to address its church-state arrangement. With the Continental Congress recommending in May 1776 that the colonies reorganize as independent states, various legislatures began writing constitutions, with a handful enacting revised constitutions after the conclusion of the war. Most of the new states took the opportunity to address, if not adjust, their colonial church-state arrangements. Because each colony/state had its own unique church-state history and dynamic, each approached the enterprise somewhat differently, producing a variety of results.[8]

As addressed in chapter 1, in 1776 nine of thirteen states maintained some form of a religious establishment, which included forced tax support for one or more legally approved denominations, legal privileges and duties for recognized clergy, religious tests for officeholding, voting or civic participation, and property-holding privileges for official churches. By the time Virginia enacted Jefferson's bill, that ratio had been reversed with assessments and many legal privileges being banned in ten or eleven of the states (depending on how one considers the situation in the future state of Vermont). Going into the drafting of the First Amendment, three categories of church-state arrangements existed: those states that had prohibited religious assessments and most privileges, those that sought unsuccessfully to maintain some form of an establishment, and those New England states that retained their purportedly nonexclusive establishments.[9]

North Carolina was the first state to take decisive action. Unlike its neighbors to the north and south, North Carolina's Anglican establishment had never operated effectively, even in its Tidewater region. Dissenters—Baptists, Presbyterians, Quakers, and Moravians—dominated the interior, and the delegates to the state constitutional convention quickly abolished all authority for a general assessment by declaring that there "shall be no establishment of any religious church or denomination . . . in preference to any other." In order to avoid any misunderstanding that such language permitted a multiple establishment, the article also provided that "neither shall any person . . . be compelled to attend any place of worship contrary to his own faith or judgment, nor be obliged to pay for . . . the building of any house of worship, or the maintenance of any minister or ministry," constituting one of the earlier state "no compelled support" clauses.[10] New York became the second state to abolish an existing establishment, though not until 1777 due to the presence of British occupying forces that delayed the holding of a convention. When it finally convened in April, the convention adopted a provision that annulled all existing laws that shored up the earlier establishment, stating that those "parts thereof, as may be construed to establish or maintain any particular denomination of Christians or their ministers . . . hereby are abrogated and rejected." An earlier draft of that article had specifically forbidden the establishment of the Church of England, indicating that many delegates still resented the earlier machinations of the Anglican Church in that colony (another provision railed against "the bigotry and ambition of weak and wicked priests" who perpetuated "spiritual oppression and intolerance"). In the end, however, the delegates settled on the broader phrase "any particular denomination of Christians." Finally, referencing "the benevolent principles of rational liberty," the constitution guaranteed "the free exercise and enjoyment of religious profession and worship without discrimination or preference."[11]

In disestablishing, North Carolina and New York joined Pennsylvania, Delaware, and New Jersey in prohibiting religious assessments. Even though tax support for religion had not existed in those colonies, the constitutions of Pennsylvania, Delaware, and New Jersey all included provisions that guaranteed disestablishment, if for no other reason than to forestall any such moves in the future.[12] The Pennsylvania Constitution of 1776 provided that no person could "be compelled to attend any religious worship, or erect or support any place of worship, or maintain any minister, contrary to, or against, his own free will and consent." Emphasizing the total lack of governmental authority over religious matters, the article continued that no civil official "can or ought to be vested in . . . any power whatever, that shall in any case interfere with, or in any manner controul, the right of conscience in the free exercise of religious worship." The revised constitution of 1790 reaffirmed those two provisions, adding a third stating that "no preference shall ever be given, by law, to any religious establishments or modes of worship," thus reinforcing Pennsylvania's strong stance on church-state matters.[13]

As in Pennsylvania, the constitutions of Delaware and New Jersey firmly embraced disestablishment. Delaware's revolutionary constitution of 1776 was succinct, providing that "there shall be no establishment of any one religious sect in the State in preference to another." Constitutional revisions in 1792 expanded on that language, declaring that no person could "be compelled to attend any religious worship, to contribute to the erection or support of any place of worship, or to the maintenance of any ministry." In addition, the provision affirmed that "no power shall . . . be vested in or assumed by any magistrate . . . [to] interfere with, or in any manner control, the rights of conscience, in the free exercise of religious worship."[14] New Jersey's constitution of 1776 was detailed from the beginning. Similar to Delaware, it declared that "there shall be no establishment of any one religious sect in [this State] in preference to another," and like Pennsylvania, it contained a "no compelled support of religion" clause. Clarifying the scope of the latter clause, the constitution provided that no person shall "ever be obliged to pay tithes, taxes, or any other rates, for the purpose of building or repairing any other church or churches, place or places of worship, or for the maintenance of any minister or ministry, contrary to what he believes to be right, or has deliberately or voluntarily engaged himself to perform."[15]

Each of the constitutions employed "nonpreferential" language, that is, prohibiting the establishment of "one religious sect . . . in preference to another." This phrasing has led some commentators to argue that the prevailing perspective regarding disestablishment during the founding period was to prevent the government from preferring a particular religion but not to bar assistance to all religions equally.[16] There are several reasons not to place too much significance on the antipreferential language in these constitutions. Exclusive religious establishments, as had operated in the southern colonies, were considered the greater evil; after all, the revolutionaries were overthrowing the British government with its established church, which openly professed its preferred status, a claim that threatened all states. The immediate goal was to keep a preferential establishment from reoccurring in any state or at a national level. For states to memorialize opposition to preferential establishments did not necessarily translate into support for non-preferential ones. Opponents of non-preferential establishments also used such terminology out of habit and because they feared that any multiple establishment would inevitably favor one denominations over others, as occurred in New England. Even James Madison occasionally employed preferential language, despite opposing exclusive and non-preferential establishments alike. Two years after leading the opposition to Patrick Henry's nonexclusive general assessment in Virginia, Madison remarked that "fortunately for this commonwealth, a majority of the people are decidedly against any exclusive establishment—I believe it to be so in the other states." According to historian Thomas Curry, participants in the various disestablishment controversies "used the concept in diverse and loose ways, without much debate or without forming in their minds a clear distinction between an exclusive and a non-exclusive establishment." Finally, because the colonies of Pennsylvania, Delaware, and New Jersey had not maintained nonexclusive establishments through tax support, it is counterintuitive that they would now reserve that possibility as states.[17]

In contrast to the five above-mentioned states, the legislatures of Georgia, Maryland, and South Carolina struggled with whether and how much to disestablish. As in Virginia, the Anglican establishments had become essentially inoperable during the Revolution, a consequence of the transition from colonial to state governments. Many Americans also viewed the Anglican Church unfavorably due to its close association with the British government. Still, with their long tradition of religious establishments, southern states were hesitant to fully disestablish, with the initial constitutions of Georgia, Maryland, and South Carolina creating ostensibly multiple establishments. Georgia's 1777 constitution guaranteed the free exercise of religion and declared that no person, "unless by consent, [shall] support any teacher or teachers [of religion] except those of their own profession." Although couched in voluntary language, this allowed for a general assessment. Not until 1785 did the assembly enact a law for "the regular establishment and support of the public duties of Religion." The statute's preamble declared that the "regular establishment and support [of Christianity] is among the most important objects of Legislature determination," and it further provided that every county with at least thirty families could select a minister to receive the assessment. This law apparently never went into effect. A new constitution in 1789 reaffirmed that no person was "obliged to contribute to support any religious profession but their own," again potentially allowing for a general assessment, though one never occurred. Finally, in 1798 Georgia's third constitution clarified the uncertainty, declaring that no person shall "ever be obliged to pay tiths, taxes, or any other rate, for the building or repairing [of] any place of worship, or for the maintenance of any minister or ministry."[18]

The Maryland Constitution of 1776 also reflected uncertainty over how to reorder its church-state arrangement, and it included three provisions that touched on the matter. Article 33 initially proclaimed equal religious liberty to all professors of Christianity and provided that no person "ought . . . to be compelled to frequent or maintain, or contribute, unless under contract, to maintain any particular place of worship, or of any particular ministry," language that on its own appeared to prohibit a religious assessment though potentially authorizing churches to legally enforce financial obligations. The next sentence then inconsistently authorized the legislature to "lay a general and equal tax, for the support of the Christian religion," which allowed each taxpayer to assign their assessment to a "particular place of worship or minister, or for the benefit of the poor of his own denomination." This created a multiple establishment, similar to what ostensibly existed in New England. But as in Georgia, no religious assessment ever went into effect. Despite the constitutional framework for an establishment, Maryland voters rejected a proposed tax in 1785, forestalling any assessment. In 1810, the state formally repealed the dead-letter provision in article 33.[19]

South Carolina's colonial Anglican establishment had been the healthiest after Virginia's, and pro-establishment forces proposed a general assessment. As in Virginia, Presbyterian leaders considered supporting the idea but feared a general assessment would favor the Episcopalians and reinforce their privileged status. Leading the opposition, Presbyterian minister William Tennent declared that "to establish all denominations by law and to pay them equally was absurd and impossible" because some denominations would always be advantaged. Aside from the impracticality of a general assessment, Tennent also believed that "religious establishments interfere with the rights of private judgment and conscience" and amounted to "the legislature's taking the conscience of men into their own hands, and taxing them at [its] discretion."[20] The result in the 1778 constitution was a compromise. Article 38 initially declared that the "Christian Protestant religion" was deemed, "constituted and declared to be, the established religion of this State." To control which Protestant churches could claim the status of being "established," the article required their incorporation, which would be granted on their subscription to five doctrines of faith:

1st. That there is one eternal God, and a future state of rewards and punishments.

2nd. That God is publicly to be worshipped.

3nd. That the Christian religion is the true religion.

4th. That the holy scriptures of the Old and New Testaments are of divine inspiration, and are the rule of faith and practice.

5th. That it is lawful and the duty of every man being thereunto called by those that govern, to bear witness to the truth.

Finally, the constitution provided that only people and religious societies "who acknowledge[d] that there is one God, and a future state of rewards and punishments . . . shall be freely tolerated" or eligible for public office.[21]

On its face, South Carolina's article 38 appeared to create a multiple establishment, yet its language was chiefly declarative. Despite its buildup, the article concluded by providing that "no person shall, by law, be obliged to pay towards the maintenance and support of a religious worship that he does not freely join in, or has not voluntarily engaged to support." By omitting a mechanism for enforcing that "freely joined" obligation, and by substituting notions of voluntary support in lieu of forced taxation, the 1778 constitution prohibited a religious assessment. As one commentator has noted, South Carolina's "establishment" amounted to "a method of incorporating churches, and no church received public tax support."[22]

In New England, New Hampshire and Massachusetts took a different track. New Hampshire responded immediately to Congress's call to form a government, becoming the first state to draft a constitution. Its constitution of 1776 was concise, chiefly declaring the state's independence while leaving its religious assessment unaddressed. Once independence was secured, the New Hampshire legislature enacted a more comprehensive constitution in 1784, which provided that "morality and piety, rightly grounded on evangelical principles, will give the best and greatest security to the government, and . . . the knowledge of these, is most likely to be propagated through a society by the institution of public worship of the Deity, and public instruction in morality and religion." This provision affirmed New Hampshire's system of multiple establishments in which each town would "make adequate provision" through a general assessment "for the support and maintenance of public protestant teachers of piety, religion, and morality." Dissenters could designate their taxes for their own ministers, provided their churches were incorporated by the state; noncooperative dissenters were forced to pay for the majority denomination, usually the Congregational Church.[23]

Retaining Massachusetts's putative multiple establishment proved to be more contentious. The Great Awakening had spurred the growth of religious dissenters in the colony, particularly Baptists. Prior to 1773, Baptists had focused their efforts on obtaining exemptions under the colony's assessment system for their clergy, meetinghouses, and members. In that year, however, Baptist leader Isaac Backus shifted tactics to seek a repeal of the assessment system outright.[24] Now, as the Massachusetts Assembly considered drafting a constitution in 1778, Backus renewed his calls to abolish the assessment system, rather than simply reform it. Writing in a pamphlet entitled *Government and Liberty Described and Ecclesiastical Tyranny Exposed* (1778), Backus charged that claims of equality under the state's nonexclusive assessment were illusive; the system distributed tax monies only to "orthodox" ministers and government-recognized churches, thereby "impower[ing] the majority to judge for the rest about spiritual guides, which naturally causes envying and strife." "How can liberty of conscience be rightly enjoyed, till this iniquity is removed," Backus asked. His attack initiated a vigorous pamphlet war between pro- and anti-assessment forces that lasted for two years through the drafting and ratification of Massachusetts's constitution in 1780, a controversy that led John Adams to remark how a "whole company of earthly hosts hath debated these heavenly things with an hellish intensity."[25]

Adams experienced the intensity of the debate firsthand, as the convention assigned him the task of writing the initial draft of the constitution. As submitted for ratification, the constitution contained several provisions regarding religion. Article 2 of the Declaration of Rights declared the "duty" of all people "publicly" "to worship the SUPREME BEING," but then guaranteed the liberty of "worshipping God in the manner and season most agreeable to the dictates of his own conscience." The next article reinforced that affirmation by guaranteeing that every Christian denomination would have equal "protection of the law" and that "no subordination of any one sect or denomination to another shall ever be established by law." Those two strong statements on behalf of religious freedom were then undercut by the initial section of article 3. That article began by asserting that "the good order and preservation of civil government, essentially depend upon piety, religion and morality." That goal was to be accomplished "by the institution of the public worship of God, and of public instructions in piety, religion and morality." The article then provided that "the legislature shall, from time to time, authorize and require, the several towns, parishes, precincts, and other bodies politic, or religious societies, to make suitable provision, at their own expense, for the institution of the public worship of God, and for the support and maintenance of public Protestant teachers of piety, religion and morality, in all cases where such provision shall not be made voluntarily."[26] An additional provision in article 3 instituted a multiple establishment by allowing tax monies to "be uniformly applied to the support of the public teacher of [one's] own religious sect or denomination," provided there was a dissenting church within the parish; otherwise, the assessment was to "be paid towards the support of the teacher or teachers of the parish," who were to be elected by a majority of town residents. Article 3 thus not only constitutionalized Massachusetts's prior general assessment system that benefited the Congregational Church; it represented a step backward by removing the ability of dissenters to obtain exemptions from paying any assessment, now requiring that the taxes be paid to one's own church or, if not affiliated, to the minister selected by a town majority.[27]

According to one historian, article 3 "was perhaps the most controversial one in the whole constitution." Adams understood this, as he wisely declined to draft that article, which was done by a committee. Voters considered each article of the constitution separately, with article 3 receiving only 58 percent approval, short of the two-thirds required for ratification. Nonetheless, the constitutional convention declared that the entire constitution had been approved, and it went into effect on October 25, 1780. As Adams remarked at the time, "We might as soon expect a change in the solar system as to expect they would give up on their establishment."[28]

The remaining New England "state" to establish a new constitution was Vermont, which drafted constitutions in 1777 and 1786 before being admitted to the union in 1791. The religious provisions of both constitutions had more in common with those of Georgia and Maryland than its neighboring states in that they contained contradictory language as to whether Vermont maintained a legally sanctioned establishment. The 1777 constitution initially affirmed the "natural and unalienable right [of people] to worship . . .

according to the dictates of their own consciences and understanding," then continued that "no man ought, or of right can be compelled to attend any religious worship, or erect or support any place of worship, or maintain any minister, contrary to the dictates of his conscience." Together, these two clauses appeared to forbid any religious assessment and to guarantee disestablishment. However, the same article also declared that every denomination should observe the Sabbath "and keep it up, and support, some sort of religious worship, which to them shall seem most agreeable to the revealed word of God." Town officials interpreted this provision as authorizing them to continue to assess religious taxes. In 1783, the legislature enacted a law that clarified how towns were to collect assessments and how religious dissenters could obtain exemption certificates. Then, in 1786, with statehood in sight, the Vermont legislature revised the 1777 constitution, removing language in article 3 to "support" religious worship. The new constitution also omitted a previous clause limiting civil rights to "profess[ors] of the protestant religion." These revisions again appeared to forbid compelled religious assessments and repudiated legal preferences for Protestants. The following year, however, in a general revision of the laws, the legislature retained the 1783 law authorizing religious assessments, thereby allowing Congregationalist-majority towns to collect taxes over the objection of Baptists and other dissenters. Complaints that the assessment law was inconsistent with the 1786 constitutional revisions proved unsuccessful; even though the Council of Censors twice found the 1783 law was repugnant to the Declaration of Rights, the Federalist-Congregationalist-controlled legislature failed to act. Not until 1807, with the ascent of the Republican Party in Vermont and an increase in dissenters, did the state legislature abolish all legal authority for collecting assessments. Vermont's "unconstitutional" establishment finally came to an end.[29]

Not every state addressed its church-state arrangement during the Confederation period. Neither Connecticut nor Rhode Island accepted Congress's invitation to draft a constitution, preferring to operate under their colonial charters into the nineteenth century. That meant that their preexisting church-state arrangements remained intact: Connecticut with its intrenched Congregationalist establishment, and Rhode Island without one (absent its requirement that officeholders be Protestants). Altogether, in the eleven years between declaring independence from Great Britain and the convening of the Constitutional Convention, a significant shift took place in church-state arrangements, possibly reflecting a gradual evolution in attitudes. Religious assessments were now only secure or operative in four of fourteen states. Disestablishment was the trend at the state level, one that continued to unfold in the 1790s as Georgia modified its constitution and the new states of Kentucky and Tennessee disestablished outright. That said, full disestablishment was a work in progress as religious disabilities existed in the majority of states, even those without assessments systems—most commonly, religious requirements for public offices and some civic duties. Only in Virginia, New York, and Vermont had such disabilities been removed by the time of the Constitutional Convention.[30]

The Constitutional Convention

The variety of church-state arrangements in the 1780s exemplified the larger political situation of the decade. The United States under the Articles of Confederation was essentially a loose alliance of thirteen autonomous republics. The Articles, ratified in 1781, created a weak central government endowed with war and foreign affairs powers but lacking authority over other important attributes of governance such as regulating commerce, monetary policy, and taxation. Each state had one vote in Congress, regardless of population, and it took a supermajority of nine states to approve significant legislative matters. In the years following Yorktown, the states steadily gained power and experience at the expense of the central government. They developed their own taxing systems, printed their own money, established rules regarding credit and property ownership—with several creating their own policies on debt relief—and regulated commerce, sometimes at the expense of their neighbors. In the process, "They also developed more distrust and rivalry" among each other.[31]

Madison had begun to recognize the deficiencies in the Articles while serving as a Virginia delegate to Congress from 1780 to 1783. During that time, he focused on how to strengthen the confederacy and the powers of the central government rather than replace it. Specifically, he sought to stabilize the confederacy's revenue stream and assume responsibility for war debts. Achieving some uniformity over regulating commerce was also of immediate concern. Not until after he had returned to Virginia did Madison begin to consider whether more extensive reforms were necessary.[32] In August 1785, in the midst of orchestrating the campaign to defeat the proposed general assessment, Madison wrote a lengthy letter to James Monroe on the deficiencies of the confederacy and of possible solutions. In the absence of any unified trade policy, Great Britain "has shut against us the channels without which our trade with her must be a losing one; and she has consequently the triumph, as we have the chagrin, of seeing accomplished her prophetic threats," he wrote. Considering "the question whether the power of regulating trade . . . ought to be vested in Congress," Madison continued, "it appears to me not to admit of a doubt, but that it should be decided in the affirmative. If it be necessary to regulate trade at all, it surely is necessary to lodge the power, where trade can be regulated with effect," in Congress. But before such a system could be put in place, "for the U. S. they must be out of debt." He then asked rhetorically, "What is to be done. . . . How is this harmony to be obtained?" Reveling his thinking, Madison insisted that "if Congress as they are now constituted, can not be trusted with the power of digesting and enforcing this opinion, let them be otherwise constituted."[33]

By 1786, the situation had only worsened, and many Americans believed that the Confederation was about to collapse. The United States was "fast verging to anarchy & confusion!" George Washington exclaimed in November of that year. Congress could not raise tax revenue or pay its debts, and the limited powers the states had been willing to confer on Congress were proving to be illusive. According to historian Michael Klarman, "A decade's worth of failed efforts at securing incremental reform within the framework of the Articles had convinced many political leaders of the need to pursue more fundamental change." As Washington wrote to Madison in late 1786, "Thirteen Sovereignties pulling against each other, and all tugging at the fœderal head, will soon bring ruin on the whole." "Without some alteration in our political creed, the superstructure we have been seven years raising at the expence of much blood and treasure, must fall." Expressing similar concern, Congressman Rufus King of Massachusetts wrote John Adams that "the united States are in the utmost confusion, and that the Union is nearly dissolved." King identified the same causes as had Madison: "That there exists a criminal neglect in several of the states in their most important Duties to the confederacy cannot be denied. . . . Our Finances are not on that firm basis, . . . [and] our commerce is almost ruined." Echoing Washington, King observed that "the People generally through[out] the confederacy remark that we are at a crisis."[34]

The ongoing "crisis" only confirmed Madison's conclusion about the appropriate course of action. Writing to Monroe in March 1786, Madison remarked that the "question of policy" was "whether it will be better to correct the vices of the Confederation, by recommendation gradually as it moves along, or by a [constitutional] Convention." Previous "efforts for bringing about a correction thro' the medium of Congress have miscarried," Madison insisted. "If all on whom the correction of these vices depends were well informed and well disposed, the mode would be of little moment. But as we have both ignorance and iniquity to control . . . let a Convention then be tried."[35]

During the October 1785 session of the Virginia Assembly, a then-wavering Madison had promoted a resolution to increase the Confederation Congress's commerce powers. The assembly had rejected Madison's request but then authorized the calling of a convention of states which met in Annapolis in September 1786. Ostensibly, the Annapolis Convention was only to recommend reforms over commerce. However, the commissioners, representing just five states, quickly reached a conclusion "that was completely predictable before they ever met. It was that national agreement on commerce issues could not be separated from agreement on other major unresolved Confederation issues," including taxing authority. The convention disbanded in three days, recommending to the states to hold a convention in Philadelphia in May 1787. Madison, who had represented Virginia at Annapolis, later wrote to Jefferson that the recommendation for a convention had "been well received" by the Virginia Assembly. "Indeed the evidence of dangerous defects in the Confederation has at length proselyted the most obstinate adversaries to a reform." He anticipated that the Virginia delegation would include George Washington, Governor Edmund Randolph, and, unfortunately to Madison, Patrick Henry.[36]

The following spring, Madison kept Jefferson apprised of the preparations for the Constitutional Convention through a series of letters. With some relief, he informed Jefferson that Henry had withdrawn as a delegate and that they would be joined by George Wythe and George Mason.[37] In another letter, he took a moment to relate an action of the Virginia Assembly that he knew would interest his friend: the repeal of the incorporation act for the Episcopal Church, based on continuing opposition from religious dissenters. Madison failed to tell Jefferson that he had ghostwritten a petition seeking the repeal on behalf of some disgruntled Episcopalian laypeople who believed the act had benefited the clergy at the expense of parishioners. Even though Madison had supported the incorporation act in 1784, it had served its purpose of undermining support for the assessment bill, so Madison had no qualms in seeking its repeal two years later.[38]

Back to preparing for the convention, Madison laid out his plans for a new form of national government, which became known as the "Virginia Plan": an executive and judicial department in addition to Congress, proportional representation in Congress, "the positive power of regulating trade and sundry other matters in which uniformity is proper," and the power to "negative *in all cases whatsoever*" any state laws that conflicted with national authority. Finally, Madison called for ratification of a new constitution to be "by the people themselves" rather than by state legislatures. "What may be the result of this political experiment cannot be foreseen," Madison mused to Jefferson, but "the difficulties which present themselves are on one side almost sufficient to dismay the most sanguine. . . . Suffice it to say that they are at present marked by symptoms which are truly alarming, which have tainted the faith of the most orthodox republicans, and which challenge from the votaries of liberty every concession in favor of stable Government not infringing fundamental principles, as the only security against an opposite extreme of our present situation."[39]

The months leading up to the Philadelphia convention were some of the more intellectually creative of Madison's political career, a period when he refined not only his ideas about a national government but also how its structure could reinforce republican theory and individual rights. He prepared two memoranda that he would later draw from in his comments at the Philadelphia and Virginia ratifying conventions, as well as in the Federalist Papers. The first, prepared in the spring of 1786, *Notes on Ancient and Modern Confederacies,* listed the various historical attempts at creating republics and the reasons for their failures. He wrote the second, *Vices of the Political System of the United States,* approximately a year later while he was drafting the Virginia Plan and in the wake of Shays's Rebellion.[40] Although Madison saw an existential threat to the future of the American republic arising from the structural deficiencies of the Articles, the Confederation represented a symptom of a larger, endemic disease. The structural deficiencies of the Articles were traceable to deficiencies that existed in the states. Madison's chief concern was the unrestrained power of majorities in state legislatures to pass laws that violated the rights of individuals and

THE CONSTITUTION   125

minorities, including those in neighboring states. "The evils issuing from
these sources," Madison wrote Jefferson after the convention, "contributed
more to that uneasiness which produced the Convention, and prepared the
public mind for a general reform, than those which accrued to our national
character and interest from the inadequacy of the Confederation to its immediate objects." This represented an evolution in Madison's thinking—the
threats to the nation's survival lay not merely with the structural flaws of
the Articles but also with the tendency of states to place their parochial
interests above those of the nation.[41]

Of the twelve vices listed in the memoranda, the longest was titled "Injustice of Law of the States," which addressed the problems of factions and
popular majorities. A "more fatal if not more frequent cause [beyond self-
serving political leaders] lies among the people themselves," who were divided into "different interests and factions": "creditors or debtors—Rich or
poor—merchants or manufacturers—members of different religious sects."
Some of these factions were natural and unavoidable—for example, the rich
and poor—and unlikely to act beyond self-interest, which led Madison to
pose the question, "Will Religion the only remaining motive be a sufficient
restraint?" Here, Madison revealed his doubts about the ameliorating effect
of religion on the body politic. Religious interests and factions were some of
the more intractable forms. When "religion is kindled into enthusiasm, its
force [is] like that of other passions." Although enthusiasm may "only [be]
a temporary state of religion, . . . while it lasts [it] will hardly be seen with
pleasure at the helm of Government. Besides as religion in its coolest state,
is not infallible, it may become a motive to oppression as well as a restraint
from injustice." In the end, "The great desideratum in Government is such a
modification of the Sovereignty as will render it sufficiently neutral between
the different interests and factions, to controul one part of the Society from
invading the rights of another, and at the same time sufficiently controuled
itself, from setting up an interest adverse to that of the whole Society."[42]
Madison would repeat his concerns about religious factions and his doubts
about religion's positive influences on republican government in his Federalist nos. 10 and 51; as he wrote in the former, "Neither moral nor religious
motives can be relied on as an adequate control."[43]

Madison arrived in Philadelphia in early May 1787, three weeks before the
start of the convention, in order to prepare for the deliberations. Expectations about Madison's leadership were high; as Rufus King wrote to Elbridge

Gerry, "I hope you will be at leisure to attend the Convention. Madison is here. I presume he will be preparing himself for the Convention. . . . He professes great Expectations as to the good Effect of the Measure."[44] The Convention convened on May 25, and on the 29th, Edmund Randolph, leader of the Virginia delegation, introduced the Virginia Plan, which proposed a new constitutional structure to replace the Articles of Confederation.[45] For the next three and a half months the delegates debated the appropriate structure and powers of the national government and how those matters related to the sovereignty and authority of the states. Agreement was not a foregone conclusion; neither was success. In a letter to Jefferson early in the proceedings, Madison listed those delegates in attendance—a distinguished group that Jefferson drolly called "an assembly of demigods"—but then informed his friend that he could provide no further details due to a pledge of secrecy. Madison was cautiously optimistic, telling Jefferson that the "whole Community is big with expectation." And then, with his penchant for understatement, Madison wrote that "there can be no doubt but that the result will in some way or other have a powerful effect on our destiny."[46]

Religion, church-state arrangements, or religious freedom and rights of conscience were not among the topics under consideration. The purpose of the convention was to devise a national government with limited powers that would address the shortcomings of the Articles while still preserving the sovereignty of the states. It was a practical exercise in what was practicable; while philosophical matters came up—particularly surrounding theories of republicanism—metaphysical considerations were absent. Benjamin Franklin's famous proposal to introduce daily prayers, suggested at a time of deliberative impasse, caught many delegates off guard, and the matter was tabled without a vote. However, two proposals touched on religion, one tangentially and the other more directly. Late in the proceedings, George Mason moved the convention to draft a bill of rights, expressing the belief that a declaration to limit infringements on individual rights should exist at the national level as it did in the various states. Coming from Mason, any listing of rights would undoubtedly have included rights of conscience and religious exercise. Although Elbridge Gerry seconded Mason's proposal, other delegates argued that a bill of rights was unnecessary because the Constitution did not repeal or otherwise affect existing state declarations of rights. The convention unanimously voted down the motion, meaning that

Madison and the other delegates from Virginia out-voted Mason, a move that would later cause Madison much consternation.[47]

The second proposal directly implicated rights of conscience and church-state relations. Also arising late in the convention proceedings, Charles Pinckney of South Carolina proposed language that "no religious test or qualification shall ever be annexed to any oath of office under the authority of the U.S." The only recorded response to the proposal came from Roger Sherman of Connecticut, who "thought it unnecessary" considering "the prevailing liberality being a sufficient security against such tests." Gouverneur Morris and Charles Cotesworth Pinckney supported the proposal in unrecorded statements, and the convention then approved the motion, with the North Carolina delegation voting "no" and the Maryland and Connecticut delegations divided on the matter.[48] The brevity of the debate over whether to exclude a religious test at the national level apparently surprised some of the delegates. Maryland's Luther Martin, reporting later to his state legislature, wrote that the proposal "was adopted by a great majority of the convention, and without much debate." Expressing sarcasm if not derision, Martin stated that "there were some members *so unfashionable* as to think that a *belief of the existence of a Deity,* and of a *state of future rewards and punishments* would be some security for the good conduct of our rulers."[49] There is no record as to what motivated Charles Pinckney to propose a ban on religious tests or whether Madison influenced the proposal. Pinckney and Madison were federalist allies during the convention, with the former seeking to gain the latter's favor, so it is probable that Pinckney had secured Madison's support for the proposal beforehand. Whether Madison as a legislative leader and a delegate representing one of the two states that prohibited religious tests—unlike Pinckney's South Carolina—had a greater hand in Pinckney's proposal than is commonly understood is speculative, though Madison was known for using surrogates to introduce legislative matters. Regardless, he would later defend what became article 6, clause 3, in letters and debates.[50]

Roger Sherman's statement about "the prevailing liberality" regarding such tests was a considerable overstatement. Religious prerequisites for public officeholding and participating in civic affairs had long existed in the colonies, as it had in Europe. People commonly accepted the premise that church affiliation and swearing an oath or belief in essential Christian

tenets—the Trinity, Jesus's redemptive mission, the authenticity of scripture, and of accountability upon death—helped to ensure the public's virtue. Although rarely acknowledged publicly, religious tests also ensured the
dominance of established Christianity and maintained the privileged status
of its adherents. As discussed, only New York and Virginia instituted no
religious qualifications, with Jefferson's Statute for Establishing Religious
Freedom providing that "all men shall be free to profess, and by argument
to maintain, their opinion in matters of religion, and that the same shall in
no wise diminish, enlarge, or affect their civil capabilities." But even New
York's lack of a religious test was qualified by constitutional language requiring that future immigrants renounce allegiance to any foreign prince,
"ecclesiastical as well as civil," a not-too-subtle reference to the papacy. And
in 1788, at the urging of John Jay, the New York legislature enacted a law
incorporating that exclusion into the required oath for public officeholders,
effectively barring Catholics from positions of public trust.[51]

The general acceptance of religious tests did not come without detractors. British Whig authors of the mid-eighteenth century had railed against
religious tests, and the decision of states to maintain modified requirements
in their new constitutions faced criticism. Before the convention met, influential figures including Benjamin Franklin, Benjamin Rush, Richard Price,
and Noah Webster condemned the enactment of test oaths and called on
states to liberalize or abolish them entirely. In a 1787 pamphlet, Webster
railed against all religious tests, calling them "a badge of folly, borrowed from
the dark ages of bigotry." Webster prayed that a revised test oath in Pennsylvania would be "a prelude to wiser measures; people are just awakening
from delusion. The time will come (and may the day be near!) when all
test laws . . . will be proscribed from this land of freedom."[52] And during
the convention, Jewish leaders from Philadelphia petitioned the delegates to
enact the proposed ban and then extend it to prohibit states from enforcing
requirements that excluded Jews from the privilege of officeholding.[53]

Historians have disagreed over the meaning and significance of article 6,
clause 3, particularly because it was supported by delegates from states that
maintained their own religious tests. This contradiction suggests, according to some scholars, that many members of the founding generation did
not view a religious test—particularly liberalized tests requiring simply a
belief in God—as being inconsistent with religious liberty or disestablishment. One way to explain this discontinuity is to view article 6 as chiefly a

mechanism to protect federalism—that is, that the delegates sought to ensure national unity and interstate comity by prohibiting the federal government from interfering with the religious preferences of any state. Thus,
for those who advance this interpretation, "the Constitution does not even
address the church-state problem, much less solve it, comprehensively or
haphazardly."[54]

Federalism concerns likely motivated some delegates to support article 6. Neither the Second Continental Congress nor the Confederation
Congress had imposed a religious test on its members, likely because any
restriction would have alienated some states from participating in the body
and state legislatures would have viewed it as interfering with their authority
to determine the qualifications of their delegates. So, on one level, the Constitution simply continued that existing practice. But even if federalism
played a role in the enactment of the clause—as it possibly did with the
religion clauses—that fact does not diminish the significance of the article,
which represented "a bold departure from the prevailing practices in Europe, as well as in most of the states." Religious tests were one of the primary tools that maintained religious establishments; article 6 was an initial
step toward ensuring there would be no national establishment of religion.
Because of the prevailing practice in the states, it is difficult to see the omission of a religious test as an oversight. James E. Wood argued that the prohibition on religious tests "represented a major achievement for the future
course of church-state relations in America" by affirming "the concept of
the new Republic as a secular state." According to Wood and others, the
ban was an early application of the impulse of church-state separation. And
as addressed below, during the ratification debates, detractors of the new
Constitution viewed the test ban as a troubling departure from their parochial understandings of church-state relations. Contemporaries did not
perceive it merely as an affirmation of federalism principles.[55]

The Debate over the No Religious Test Clause

The public commentary and records of the state ratification debates of the
Constitution indicate that many people—chiefly Antifederalists—viewed
the no religious test clause with alarm and understood that it represented a
new ordering of church-state relations. Despite the clause being relatively
uncontroversial during the Constitutional Convention, article 6 became

one of the more contentious issues during the ratification debates. Antifederalists decried the immediate effect of the test ban and its broader implications. Colonel William Jones at the Massachusetts convention summed up the perspective of many, stating that he "thought that the rulers ought to believe in God or Christ . . . a person could not be a good man without being a good Christian." As another Antifederalist declared, "When a man has no regard to God and his laws nor any belief of a future state, he will have less regard to the laws of men." On a more basic level, opponents complained that the ban was "dangerous and impolitic" because it would allow for "a Papist, a Mohomatan, a Deist, yea an Atheist at the helm of Government."[56]

In addition to those immediate objections, Antifederalists appreciated the larger meaning of the ban on religious tests. The essayist "Samuel," writing in the *Boston Independent Chronicle*, charged that the effect of the oath clause was that "all religion is expressly rejected, from the Constitution." No nation had ever disassociated itself from God and religion. "Was there ever any State or kingdom, that could subsist, without adopting some system of religion?" A contributor to the *Virginia Independent Chronicle* concurred: "The most approved and wisest legislatures in all ages, in order to give efficacy to their civil institutions, have found it necessary to call in the aid of religion; and in no form of government whatever has the influence of religious principles been found so requisite as in that of a republic." And, as if to finish that last thought, Charles Turner of Massachusetts argued "that without the prevalence of Christian piety and morals, the best republican Constitution can never save us from slavery and ruin." The ban on religious tests, combined with the absence of any acknowledgment of God's overarching providence, indicated the Constitution's "cold indifference towards religion."[57]

Federalists readily defended the Constitution's ban on religious tests, with Samuel Spencer at the North Carolina convention arguing that tests were ineffective in barring unscrupulous politicians while they "would exclude from offices conscientious and truly religious people, though equally capable as others." Article 6, Spencer asserted, "leaves religion on the solid foundation of its own inherent validity, without any connection to temporal authority."[58] In addition to raising practical arguments, Federalists addressed the Antifederalists' charge about the Constitution's irreligious foundation, with several embracing the secular nature of the new national government. Future Supreme Court chief justice Oliver Ellsworth, writing as "A Landholder" in the *Connecticut Courant*, responded to criticism that the Constitution lacked a religious foundation. Rather than shirking from the charge, Ellsworth claimed that this presented "the true principle by which this question ought to be determined." Emphasizing the *civil* nature of the government, Ellsworth asserted that the "business of civil government is to protect the citizen in his rights, to defend the community from hostile powers, and to promote the general welfare." Civil government had no jurisdiction over religious matters and "no business to meddle with the private opinions of the people."[59]

Other Federalists went beyond Ellsworth's measured, Lockean response, willingly embracing the Constitution's irreligious character. Pennsylvania writer "Aristocrotis" disputed claims of religion's beneficial effect on civil society, charging that religion "is certainly attended with dangerous consequences to government" and had "been the cause of millions being slaughtered." Holding little back, Aristocrotis insisted that "the Christian religion . . . is of all others the most unfavorable to a government founded upon nature: because it pretends to be of a supernatural divine religion, and therefore sets itself above nature." Adopting a similar tone, New England writer "Elihu" stated, "The time has been when nations could be kept in awe with stories of God's sitting with legislatures and dictating laws. . . . But the light of philosophy has arisen in these latter days. . . . Mankind is no longer deluded with fable." He praised the Constitution, writing that "the most brilliant circumstance in honour of the framers [was] their avoiding all appearance of craft" by banning a religious test. "They come to us in the plain language of common sense, and propose to our understanding a system of government, as the invention of mere human wisdom; no deity comes down to dictate it, not even a god appears in a dream to propose any part of it."[60]

Finally, Federalist defenders also argued that "the exclusion of [religious] tests will strongly tend to establish religious freedom." Zachariah Johnston at the Virginia convention insisted that the "diversity of opinions and variety of sects in the United States have justly been reckoned a great security with respect to religious liberty. . . . This is a principle which secures religious liberty most firmly." And in North Carolina, James Iredell, another future Supreme Court justice, remarked, "I consider the clause under consideration as one of the strongest proofs that could be adduced, that it was the intention of those who formed this system to establish a general religious liberty in America."[61] The Federalists' vigorous defense of article 6 indicates that they saw the ban as helping to usher in a new era of religious freedom. Even though Madison did not directly address the test ban in his various remarks at the Virginia Ratifying Convention, he defended it in private correspondence. In a letter to Jefferson following the convention that described the contents of the Constitution in detail, Madison commented on the ban, remarking that "the inefficacy of this restraint on individuals is well known," in that history had shown that officials, "acting on oath [with] the strongest of religious ties, . . . join without remorse in acts against which their consciences would revolt."[62]

Although Madison and most Federalists would have disputed that the test ban and lack of a religious acknowledgment revealed the Constitution's "general disregard of religion," those omissions did indicate that the foundation for the new government rested on the will of the people and not some higher power. Considered in that light, writes Stephen Botein, "whatever may be said about American political culture in that period, it cannot be denied that the Constitution was a perfectly secular text—if, by that term, nothing more or less is signified that the absence of manifest religious content." The Constitution, which Madison was responsible for more than anyone else, can accurately be described as a "godless" document, not in the sense of being hostile to religion but of having an areligious character, which was as Madison and Jefferson intended.[63]

⟨⊙ SEVEN ⊙⟩

The Second Collaboration

The Bill of Rights

T he extent of Madison's involvement in the enactment of the no religious test clause is unclear. As noted, it is unlikely that Charles Pinckney introduced the provision without Madison's advanced knowledge and approval, and Madison defended the clause in later writings. Moreover, Virginia, not Pinckney's South Carolina, was one of only two states that had abolished religious tests by law. While one can speculate as to whether Madison had a greater hand in the measure than the record reflects, there is no uncertainty about Madison's leading role in the enactment of the religion clauses of the First Amendment to the Constitution. The only question is the degree to which the meaning of the clauses reflects Madison's own "spacious conception" of church-state relations.[1]

Ratification and the Drive for a Bill of Rights

The Antifederalists' attack on article 6, clause 3, was but one of many complaints they lodged against the proposed Constitution; chiefly, they feared that several provisions of the Constitution—the taxing and spending clauses, the necessary and proper clause, the treaty power, and the supremacy clause, among others—would enhance federal power at the expense of state sovereignty and authority. Others feared that with the lack of a bill of rights, Congress and federal officials would trample on individual rights. "There is no barrier to the power of the foederal constitution," wrote the essayist "Denatus." "We ought to have a bill of rights, to save us from oppression." Of particular concern for many people were rights of conscience and the free exercise of religion.[2]

In that vein, Pennsylvania writer "An Old Whig" wrote in 1788 that throughout the "history of mankind," authorities had infringed "upon the liberties of the people, and none have been more frequently successful in the attempt, than those who have covered their ambitious designs under the garb of a fiery zeal for religious orthodoxy." "We ought therefore [have] a bill of rights to secure, in the first place by the most express stipulation, the sacred rights of conscience."[3] Other writers raised similar concerns. "Respecting *liberty of conscience*," wrote "Philadelphiensis," "in the new constitution no provision is made for securing to these peaceable citizens their religious liberties."[4] In addition to ensuring protection for religious exercise and liberty of conscience, Antifederalists called for a provision preventing religious preferences through an establishment. If a majority in Congress thought "fit to establish a form of religion . . . with all the pains and penalties which . . . are annexed to the establishment of a national church," asked An Old Whig, "what is there in the proposed constitution to hinder their doing so?"[5]

Federalists responded to general calls for a bill of rights with several arguments. Alexander Hamilton asserted in Federalist no. 84 that a bill of rights, which historically served to prevent overreaching by a monarch, was unnecessary in a government "professedly founded upon the power of the people, and executed by their immediate representatives and servants." Because republican government was a manifestation of popular will, "the people surrender nothing; and as they retain every thing they have no need of particular reservations." A bill of rights also had less utility in "a Constitution like that under consideration, which is merely intended to regulate the general political interests of the nation, than to a constitution which has the regulation of every species of personal and private concerns." Based on this last reason, Hamilton argued that a bill of rights "are not only unnecessary in the proposed Constitution, but would even be dangerous. They would contain various exceptions to powers not granted; and, on this very account, would afford a colorable pretext to claim more than were granted." There was an "absurdity," Hamilton insisted, "of providing against the abuse of an authority which was not given."[6] Hamilton's argument that there were protections inherent in the Constitution's structure, however, did little to forestall Antifederalist calls for amendments, either to reform the document or to serve as a means for its outright defeat.

Concerns about the security of conscience rights came up in the various state ratifying conventions. At the New York convention, Thomas Tredwell bemoaned that "I would have wished also that sufficient caution had been used to secure to us our religious liberties, and to have prevented the general government from tyrannizing over our consciences by a religious establishment." In the North Carolina convention, Baptist minister Henry Abbot remarked that people "wish to know if their religious and civil liberties be secured under this system, or whether the general government may not make laws infringing their religious liberties."[7] The standard reply from Federalist delegates was that because the Constitution provided only limited, enumerated powers, the national government had no authority over religious matters. "Is there any power given to Congress in matters of religion?" asked James Iredell in response to Abbot. "Can they pass a single act to impair our religious liberties?" If Congress attempted to do so, he continued, "it would be an act which they are not authorized to pass."[8] Iredell's lawyerly response offered little comfort for Antifederalists, who argued that Congress might exercise powers beyond those enumerated. "Deliberator" warned in Philadelphia's *Freeman's Journal* that "Congress may, if they shall think it for the 'general welfare,' establish uniformity in religion throughout the United States. Such establishments have been thought necessary, and have accordingly taken place in almost all the other countries in the world, and will, no doubt, be thought equally necessary in this." These criticisms of religious establishments—provided they were all sincere—further demonstrate the revolutionary era's impulse toward disestablishment.[9]

Coming out of the Constitutional Convention, Madison shared the Federalist view about a national bill of rights. "Can the general government exercise any power not delegated?" Madison asked during the Virginia convention. "If an enumeration be made of our rights, will it not be implied, that every thing omitted, is given to the general government?"[10] Madison also believed that "experience proves the inefficacy of a bill of rights on those occasions when its controul is most needed." In a letter to Jefferson, he called bills of rights "parchment barriers" that had been subjected to "repeated violations . . . by overbearing majorities in every State." Using an example that was of particular interest to both men, Madison continued,

> In Virginia I have seen the bill of rights violated in every instance where
> it has been opposed to a popular current. Notwithstanding the explicit

provision contained in that instrument for the rights of Conscience it is well known that a religious establishment would have taken place in that State, if the legislative majority had found as they expected, a majority of the people in favor of the measure; and I am persuaded that if a majority of the people were now of one sect, the measure would still take place and on narrower ground than was then proposed.[11]

For Madison, the real threat to individual rights came not from the government but from popular majorities that would oppress minorities. The "invasion of private rights is *chiefly* to be apprehended, not from acts of Government contrary to the sense of its constituents, but from acts in which the Government is the mere instrument of the major number of the constituents." The better "security of civil rights," Madison proposed in Federalist no. 51, "must be the same as that for religious rights. It consists in the one case in the multiplicity of interests, and in the other in the multiplicity of sects."[12]

Jefferson disagreed about the inefficacy of a bill of rights. Contrary to Madison, he believed its absence represented a serious omission from the Constitution. In a letter to Madison in December 1787 after receiving a copy of the Constitution, Jefferson related his views on its contents, both pro and con. "I like the organization of the government into Legislative, Judiciary and Executive. I like the power given the Legislature to levy taxes," he wrote. "I will now add what I do not like," Jefferson continued. "First the omission of a bill of rights providing clearly and without the aid of sophisms for freedom of religion, freedom of the press, protection against standing armies, restriction against monopolies, the eternal and unremitting force of the habeas corpus laws, and trials by jury in all matters of fact triable by the laws of the land." As for the Federalist argument "that a bill of rights was not necessary because all is reserved in the case of the general government which is not given," he noted, it "might do for the Audience to whom it was addressed, but is surely gratis dictum, opposed by strong inferences from the body of the instrument." A bill of rights "is what the people are entitled to against every government on earth," he insisted, "and what no just government should refuse, or rest on inference."[13]

Smaller states—Delaware, New Jersey, Georgia, and Connecticut—were among the first to ratify the Constitution, either unanimously or by overwhelming majorities, with their delegates realizing they needed the security of a stable union. By early 1788, however, the momentum for a quick and easy ratification by nine states had stalled. In Pennsylvania in December 1787, the Federalists had to fight off an Antifederalist effort to consider proposed amendments. Then in February in the Massachusetts convention, Antifederalists proposed that amendments be adopted as a precondition for ratification. Only after promising to recommend amendments after voting on ratification were the Federalists able to prevail, and then only by a narrow vote of 187 to 168. Following the close call in Massachusetts, the New Hampshire convention adjourned when ratification appeared doubtful.[14] By spring, Madison's earlier cautious optimism about a clean ratification of the Constitution was waning, with him telling Jefferson, "the Public here continues to be much agitated by the proposed fœderal Constitution and to be attentive to little else." Jefferson did not share Madison's gloomy assessment, telling Edward Carrington that on the matter of a "bill of rights, which it is so much the interest of all to have, that I conceive it must be yielded." Jefferson believed that "the plan of Massachusets is far preferable, and will I hope be followed by those [states] who are yet to decide." Elaborating on how that should work, Jefferson told William Stephens Smith, "Were I in America, I would advocate it warmly till nine should have adopted, and then as warmly take the other side to convince the remaining four that they ought not to come into it till the declaration of rights is annexed to it." That declaration should include "the trial by jury in civil cases, freedom of religion, [and] freedom of the press," among other rights.[15]

As it so happened, when the Virginia convention convened in June 1788, eight states had ratified the Constitution—though Maryland and South Carolina had followed Massachusetts's example of recommending amendments—meaning that the vote in Virginia could determine the fate of the new government. Irrespective of that timing, all people knew that a negative vote in Virginia, the largest and most populous state and centrally located geographically, would effectively doom a union.[16] Antifederalist opposition to the Constitution was also stronger in Virginia, with several powerful politicians—Patrick Henry, George Mason, Richard Henry Lee, and James Monroe—opposing ratification. Mason and Edmund Randolph had refused to sign the Constitution based on its lack of a bill of rights. (Randolph later aligned with the Federalists, indicating that he merely desired some changes to the Constitution but would "join in its support from the necessity of the Case.") But Mason had left Philadelphia "in an exceeding ill humour,"

Madison had told Jefferson the previous fall. "He returned to Virginia with a fixed disposition to prevent the adoption of the plan if possible. He considers the want of a Bill of Rights as a fatal objection." Now with the state convention upon them, Madison related that Mason "is growing every day more bitter, and outrageous in his efforts to carry his point." Mason was being driven into an alliance with Henry, who advocated for amendments, not to improve the document but chiefly to "strike at the essence of the System. . . . Mr. Henry is the great adversary who will render the event precarious."[17]

Madison was correct. In the Virginia convention, Henry led the opposition to ratification and attacked the Constitution mercilessly, highlighting all of the document's putative flaws. Commenting on Henry's tactics, John Blair Smith wrote Madison that Henry "has descended to lower artifice & management upon the occasion than I thought him capable of. His gross, & scandalous misrepresentations of the New-Constitution, & the design of its enlightened authors awaken contempt & indignation."[18] Time and again, Henry returned to the absence of a bill of rights and the threat that represented to individual liberties. Why "is religious liberty not secured," Henry asked? He panned Madison's argument that because Congress lacked authority over religion there was nothing to fear: "There are many of our most worthy citizens who cannot go through all the labyrinths of syllogistic, argumentative deductions, when they think that the rights of conscience are invaded. This sacred right ought not to depend on constructive, logical reasoning."[19]

Madison, along with Edmund Randolph, defended the Constitution from Henry's various attacks, refuting his claims that religious liberties were in peril. Responding to Henry's argument that the enhanced powers of the national government would imply the power to regulate religion, Madison declared, "Were uniformity of religion to be introduced by this system, it would, in my opinion, be ineligible; but I have no reason to conclude, that uniformity of government will produce that of religion. . . . The government has no jurisdiction over it, [so] there is no danger to be feared on this ground." Returning to his argument about the inefficacy of a bill of rights to protect freedoms generally, Madison asked, "Is a bill of rights a security for religion? Would the bill of rights, in this state, exempt the people from paying for the support of one particular sect, if such sect were exclusively established by law? If there were a majority of one sect, a bill of rights would be a poor protection for liberty?" Instead, religious freedom "arises from that multiplicity of sects which pervades America, and which is the best and only security of religious liberty in any society." Madison also took umbrage at Henry's insinuation that he was not committed to religious liberty; without mentioning Virginia's disestablishment debate three years earlier, Madison confidently remarked that he could "appeal to my uniform conduct on this subject, that I have warmly supported religious freedom." Edmund Randolph agreed, repeating Madison's earlier argument: "The variety of sects which abounds in the United States is the best security for the freedom of religion. No part of the Constitution, even if strictly construed, will justify a conclusion that the general government can take away or impair the freedom of religion."[20] In the end, Madison and his Federalists allies were able to defeat Henry's efforts to derail the Constitution or to condition ratification on approval of antecedent amendments, but only by a close vote of eighty-nine to seventy-nine. A conditional ratification, Madison told Alexander Hamilton, would have been "considered as worse than a rejection."[21]

At the end of the Virginia proceedings the Federalist delegates conceded that the convention would *recommend* amendments to be submitted to the new Congress. As a final order of business, the convention appointed a committee to draft the amendments headed by George Wythe, with Madison among its members. The committee recommended forty proposed amendments, one of which tracked article 16 of the Declaration of Rights, providing that "all men have an equal, natural and unalienable right to the free exercise of religion according to the dictates of conscience, and that no particular religious sect or society ought to be favored or established by law in preference to others."[22] Madison considered many of the other amendments to be "highly objectionable," as he informed Hamilton, but "it was impossible to prevent this error." For Madison, this concession was the only way to ensure that amendments would remain under the control of the new Congress rather than serve as the basis for a second constitutional convention. There is no reason to believe Madison opposed the substance of Virginia's proposed amendment on religious freedom (though the non-preferential language likely represented the consensus of the committee); he was chiefly concerned about how to control the amending process once it began.[23] In a letter to Jefferson describing the outcome in Virginia and next steps, Madison included a list of several proposed amendments "from which mischeifs are apprehended. The great danger in the present crisis is that if another Convention should be soon assembled, it would terminate in discord, or in alterations of the federal system which would throw back *essential* powers into the State Legislatures."[24] This concern became a motivating factor in convincing Madison to sponsor the Bill of Rights.

Madison's Conversion to a Bill of Rights

Virginia's ratification vote of June 25, 1788, came four days after New Hampshire had become the ninth state to ratify the Constitution, a fact unknown at the time to the Virginia convention. Even though the new national government was secure, Madison was still not convinced about the efficacy of amending the Constitution, even to guarantee individual rights. Having just heard about the ultimate ratification, Jefferson wrote to Madison on July 31, 1788, seeking to sway his friend to support a bill of rights. Jefferson "rejoiced at the acceptance of our new constitution," describing it as "a good canvas, on which some strokes only want retouching." Noting the "general voice from North to South . . . for a bill of rights," Jefferson hoped it would guarantee at a minimum "trials by Jury, the right of Habeas corpus, freedom of the press & freedom of religion in all cases." Jefferson did not believe that the latter two rights should be absolute, however. A declaration that the "government will never restrain the presses from printing any thing they please, will not take away the liability of the printers for false facts printed." On a similar vein, he continued, a "declaration that religious faith shall be unpunished, does not give impunity to criminal acts dictated by religious error." Concluding with one last push, Jefferson pleaded that "a bill of rights will be formed to guard the people against the federal government, as they are already guarded against their state governments in most instances."[25]

On October 17, Madison responded to Jefferson, having received his July letter two days earlier. In his letter, Madison laid out in detail his reservations about amending the Constitution, even to protect individual liberties; at the same time, he also acknowledged that amendments were likely inevitable, particularly for a bill of rights. The letter reveals Madison's considerable thought about the matter and how those thoughts had evolved over time. Initially, speaking either defensively or because he remained intellectually persuaded by the strength of his earlier arguments, he listed reasons for opposing amendments: the Constitution granted enumerated powers only and a bill of rights would imply authority it did not have; that any listing of rights risked omitting others with the implication being that the latter did not exist, and then "some of the most essential rights, . . . rights of conscience in particular," would "not be obtained in the requisite latitude" and "would be narrowed"; that both history and experience demonstrated that bills of rights were ineffective; and that the true threat to individual freedoms came not from a popularly elected government but from majority factions, which would not be controlled by a bill of rights. Madison thus reaffirmed that he had "never thought the omission a material defect, nor been anxious to supply it even by subsequent amendment, for any other reason than that it is anxiously desired by others. . . . I have not viewed it in an important light."[26]

Madison then pivoted. Despite those reservations, he told Jefferson that "my own opinion has always been in favor of a bill of rights; provided it be so framed as not to imply powers not meant to be included in the enumeration. . . . I have favored it because I supposed it might be of use, and if properly executed could not be of disservice." Still, after making convincing arguments against the necessity of a bill of rights, Madison had to come up with reasons for their value. He provided two: that the solemn declaration of "political truths" and "fundamental maxims of free Government" might serve to "counteract the impulses of interest and passion," and that while the true danger of oppression came from "interested majorities," yet "there may be occasions on which the evil may spring from the latter sources; and on such, a bill of rights will be a good ground for an appeal to the sense of the community." Having just refuted supporting a bill of rights for political considerations, Madison did not mention his chief reason for supporting it now—to keep the amendment process from getting out of control. As for what should constitute the substance of a bill of rights, he noted that that subject "admit[s] of much discussion." He agreed with Jefferson, however, that "I am inclined to think that *absolute* restrictions in cases that are doubtful," not solely because emergencies might arise but that "restrictions however strongly marked on paper will never be regarded when opposed to the decided sense of the public." The one right he did mention, however, was that of religious freedom, but he expressed doubts that the New England states would be willing to embrace a strong guarantee.[27]

At that point in time, it is difficult to assess the degree to which Madison was committed to supporting a bill of rights out of principle (i.e., recognizing their value), or whether he simply realized they were inevitable and wanted to get in front of the effort in order to control it. Scholars have long debated the reasons for Madison's political conversion. Siding with the latter inter-pretation, Paul Finkelman argued that "the evidence suggests that Madison was converted to a bill of rights by political necessity rather than logical argument" or by the urgings of Jefferson. Scholars note that Jefferson's next letter to Madison was not until March 15, 1789, received well after Madison had already committed himself to a bill of rights. Other scholars concur that Jefferson "did not, as some have suggested, convince Madison to support a bill of rights. But he did provide Madison with ammunition to use before the new Congress."[28] Although Jefferson's influence can be overstated, he had written Madison three previous letters advocating a bill of rights as well as a handful of letters to joint acquaintances urging the same, so Jefferson's posi-tion on the matter was well known to his friend. The contents of Madison's October 17, 1788, letter suggests that some of Jefferson's arguments were be-ginning to sink in. (Later in life Jefferson believed that his urgings had had some effect, with him telling Joseph Priestley that several of the amendments were "all the hand I had in what related to the Constitution.") But it is also as likely that Madison was convinced by events he had directly experienced and the intelligence he had received about the ratification process in other states. In the end, whether Jefferson steered Madison in a particular direc-tion or merely provided conformation for Madison's evolving perspective about amendments is academic.[29]

Another factor that encouraged Madison to commit to amendments was the winter election to the new Congress. Most people, including Madison, expected that the Virginia Assembly would elect him to the Senate. But having now lost twice to James Madison in that body, an embittered Pat-rick Henry mounted a campaign to deny Madison that seat, convincing the assembly to select two Antifederalists. He then managed to redistrict Madison's potentially safe seat for the House of Representatives so that the latter had to run against James Monroe, who was a moderate Antifederal-ist.[30] Madison was in New York, serving as a delegate to the Confederation Congress—according to George Lee Turberville, sent there by "the Cloven hoof" (i.e., Henry) to get his rival out of the state. Madison was inclined not to return to Virginia to campaign for the House, but his father and political allies warned him that he could easily lose to the war hero Monroe if he did not return, particularly since Henry was circulating rumors that Madison was categorically opposed to any amendments to the Constitution. Upon returning to Orange County in January, a frustrated Madison wrote George

Washington that it had been "very industriously incalcated that I am dog-matically attached to the Constitution in every clause, syllable & letter, and therefore not a single amendment will be promoted by my vote. . . . This is the report most likely to affect the election, and most difficult to be com-bated with success, within the limited period." Madison had to convince the voters that he was sincerely committed to securing amendments.[31]

At this point in his campaign for Congress, Madison's commitment to religious freedom became a factor. The onslaught of misinformation had apparently resonated with local Baptists, who wanted a guarantee in the Constitution to protect rights of conscience. Understanding that Baptists represented an important constituency, Madison contacted John Leland and George Eve, Baptist ministers in Culpeper and Orange Counties, re-spectively, assuring them of his commitment to support a bill of rights. In early January Madison wrote Reverend Eve that it was his "sincere opinion that the Constitution ought to be revised," and that "amendments, if pur-sued with a proper moderation and in a proper mode, will be not only safe, but may serve the double purpose of satisfying the minds of well meaning opponents, and of providing additional guards in favour of liberty." Madi-son promised that the first Congress should consider "the most satisfactory provisions for all essential rights, particularly the rights of Conscience in the fullest latitude."[32] Madison then took the step of meeting with an as-sembly of Baptist ministers and a Lutheran gathering—together with James Monroe—to campaign for office. His efforts apparently did the trick. Later in the month, Madison ally Benjamin Johnson reported on a later Baptist meeting where Eve "took a very Spirited and decided Part in your favour," speaking "long on the Subject, and reminded them of the many important Services which you had rendered their Society, in particular the Act for establishing Religious Liberty, also the bill for a general Assessment, which was averted by your Particular efforts." Eve then told the crowd that "they were under Obligations to you, and had much more reason to place their Confidence in you, than Mr. Monroe." Around the same time, an anony-mous letter appeared in the *Virginia Herald* urging religious dissenters to vote for Madison, reminding them of his services in their behalf against the general assessment bill.[33]

Madison went on to defeat his friend Monroe by a vote of 1,308 to 972, no doubt with the support of the Baptists. Afterward, Leland wrote Madison to congratulate him on his victory but reminded him of his promise to support

a bill of rights: "One Thing I shall expect," Leland instructed, is "that if religious Liberty is anywise threatened, that I shall receive the earliest Intelligence." (Once Congress approved the language for the Bill of Rights, Leland
related to Madison that "the amendments had entirely satisfied the disaffected of his Sect.") It is a little ironic that Madison, as a leading advocate for
church-state separation, would engage in religious electioneering, but Madison would likely have insisted that he was only seeking to correct "erroneous
opinions" about him, "particularly, with respect to religious liberty." One
factor that cannot be overlooked in the leadup to proposing amendments to
the new Constitution was the prominence that both Jefferson and Madison
gave to including an express protection for religious freedom.[34]

The Introduction and Debate over the First Amendment

Newly elected representative Madison traveled to New York City in March
for the convening of the First Congress and the inauguration of George
Washington as president. While Madison prepared for the session, he
found time to draft Washington's First Inaugural Address, which included
a statement endorsing amendments provided they "carefully avoid[ed]
every alteration which might endanger the benefits of an united and effective
government."[35] Once in session, the new congress had the monumental task
of establishing federal departments, agencies, courts, and a revenue system,
as well as each chamber's rules of operation. Considering amendments to
the Constitution was not a high priority. As Madison told Edmund Pendleton in mid-April, the "subject of amendments has not yet been touched.
From appearances there will be no great difficulty in obtaining reasonable
ones. It will depend however entirely on the temper of the federalists." On
May 4, however, Madison notified his colleagues in the House he planned
to introduce proposed amendments at the end of the month, a deadline that
was then postponed for a week.[36] Finally, on June 8, according to the New
York *Daily Advertiser,* Madison made a "long and able speech" introducing
his promised amendments to the Constitution, seventeen in all, ranging
from protections in criminal proceedings to an express affirmation of separation of powers.[37] Three of the amendments dealt with religion. The first
(listed as Amendment Four), which would evolve into the First Amendment, was to be inserted into article 1, section 9 of the Constitution, which
limits the powers of Congress. It provided that "the civil rights of none shall

be abridged on account of religious belief or worship, nor shall any national religion be established, nor shall the full and equal rights of conscience be in any manner, or on any pretext, infringed."[38] A second provision contained in what would become the Second Amendment provided that "no person religiously scrupulous of bearing arms, shall be compelled to render military service in person." And Madison's third proposed religious amendment (listed as Amendment Five), to be inserted in article 1, section 10 (which limits the powers of the states), provided that "no State shall violate the equal rights of conscience, or the freedom of the press, or the trial by jury in criminal cases."[39] For his various proposed amendments, Madison drew on the recommendations from the state ratifying conventions, some two hundred in total, thirteen of which had advocated for rights of conscience. His Amendment Five, declaring that no state shall violate equal right of conscience, however, "came from Madison alone," according to biographer Irving Brant, and Madison considered it to be "the most valuable amendment in the whole list" in that it would restrict the power of factious majorities over minority conscience rights. (No doubt, Madison was aware of John Dickinson's earlier attempt to add to Articles of Confederation a similar restriction prohibiting state abridgments of civil rights "on account of their religious persuasions, profession or practice," an effort that failed.)[40]

In his speech, given before a Federalist-dominated House, Madison justified the need for amendments, though his statements indicated his continuing reservations about them. Madison remarked that as for the first several amendments, which "may be called a bill of rights, I will own that I never considered this provision so essential to the federal constitution, as to make it improper to ratify it, until such an amendment was added." However, he had long believed that "in a certain form and to a certain extent, such a provision was neither improper nor altogether useless." He acknowledged the various Federalist arguments against adding a bill of rights—that the federal government had limited enumerated powers (and thus posed no threat) and the danger of excluding some rights not listed—but stated that those arguments were "not conclusive to the extent which has been supposed. . . . Even if government keeps within those limits, it has certain discretionary powers." The "prescriptions in favor of liberty, ought to be levelled against that quarter where the greatest danger lies, namely, that which possesses the highest prerogative of power." A bill of rights would afford additional protection for "freedom of the press and rights of conscience, those choicest privileges of the people." And if they would "have a tendency to impress some degree of respect for them, to establish the public opinion in their favor, and rouse the attention of the whole community, it may be one mean to controul the majority from those acts to which they might be otherwise inclined." For Madison, these considerations justified amending the Constitution.[41]

A handful of critics questioned Madison's motivations for proposing amendments, with South Carolina senator Pierce Butler remarking that "I suppose it was done to keep his promise with his constituents, to move for alterations; but, if I am not mistaken he is not hearty in the cause of amendments." Butler derisively called Madison's proposals "milk-and-water amendments," telling James Iredell he would have to "wait longer for substantial amendments." Employing similarly mocking language, George Clymer charged that Madison was proposing amendments "merely [to throw] a tub to the whale" to deflect Antifederalist opposition.[42] Although Madison had at first supported a bill of rights to diffuse Antifederalist opposition to the Constitution and to forestall a second convention, he had come to accept its utility; whatever his initial hesitations and misgivings about amendments, by June he genuinely supported them in substance and "for the tranquility of the public mind, and the stability of the government." In the words of Lance Banning, "Madison would not have framed the Bill of Rights if he had not decided that the arguments in favor of the measure were, on balance, stronger than the arguments against it. His determination to disarm the critics of the Constitution was by no means the exclusive reason for his change in mind." As Madison said in concluding his remarks, "If we can make the constitution better . . . without weakening its frame, or abridging its usefulness, . . . we act the part of wise and liberal men to make such alterations as shall produce that effect."[43]

Madison had to wait on Congress to consider his proposed amendments while both houses focused on more pressing matters. Madison acknowledged the reason for the delay when he sent Jefferson a copy of his proposed amendments in late June. Everything "of a controvertible nature that might endanger" passage by Congress and the states "was studiously avoided," he wrote, which explained the omission of one of Jefferson's piques about restraining monopolies. Although Madison did not seek validation, Adrienne Koch maintained that he had offered amendments "of exactly the type Jefferson had advocated months earlier" that the latter would have approved of. In seeing Madison's proposals, Jefferson responded, "I like it as far as it goes; but I should have been for going further." Among those that Jefferson liked was protection of conscience rights against infringements from either the federal or state governments.[44]

Finally, on August 15, the House took up Madison's first religion amendment (Amendment Four), acting as a committee of the whole. The Committee on Amendments had rewritten Madison's proposal to read, "No religion shall be established by law, nor shall the equal rights of conscience be infringed." The debate over the amendment was relatively brief, with most comments directed toward stylistic changes to the language. Roger Sherman, an ardent Federalist, moved to strike the amendment, insisting that Congress lacked any authority over religious matters in the first instance. Responding to Sherman, Madison stated that one purpose of the amendment was to address the concerns of the state ratifying conventions but that he also believed Congress should be prohibited from making laws "as might infringe the rights of conscience, or establish a national religion." In a later statement, Madison added that the amendment sought to prevent any sect, or a combination of two, to "a pre-eminence . . . and establish a religion to which they would compel others to conform." Madison's remarks indicated that he was not committed to any particular phrasing, provided the principles were sustained. Elbridge Gerry of Massachusetts, an Antifederalist, objected to Madison's use of the word "national," as it implied the federal government was a national one, and he offered a substantive change to the language to read that "no religious doctrine shall be established by law." This language, if adopted, would have allowed for nonpreferential establishments at the federal level, consistent with the New England practice of multiple establishments. There is no record of Madison's objecting to Gerry's narrowing language, but the House did not approve the proposal; instead, it adopted language proposed by Samuel Livermore of New Hampshire that "congress shall make no laws touching religion, or infringing the rights of conscience." The amendment was then assigned to a committee on style, and five days later, on August 20, the House adopted a motion by Fisher Ames of Massachusetts that read, "Congress shall make no law establishing religion, or to prevent the free exercise thereof, or to infringe the rights of conscience." Irving Brant insisted that Madison authored the final language, employing the common technique of having a colleague submit a proposal to garner wider support (as Ames hailed from a state with a religious establishment).[45]

In between the votes on what would become the First Amendment, on August 17 the House considered Madison's other religion amendment restricting states from infringing on "the equal rights of conscience." In that this proposed a direct constraint on state authority, opposition was surprisingly light. Only Thomas Tucker of South Carolina voiced opposition, arguing that it would effectively alter "the constitutions of particular States." He urged that it would be "much better . . . to leave the State Governments to themselves, and not interfere with them more than we already do." Madison spoke in defense of his proposal, calling it "to be the most valuable amendment in the whole list." He reasoned if it was necessary to restrain the national government "from infringing on these essential rights, it was equally necessary that they should be secured against the State Governments." Based on his legislative battles in Virginia, Madison likely believed that the greater threat to freedom of conscience would arise at the state and local levels, where it would be easier for religious majorities to organize and oppress the minority. After Samuel Livermore recommended a slight rewording of the amendment, the House approved Madison's "most valuable amendment." There is every reason to believe Madison considered both of his amendments to be necessary and as working in tandem to protect conscience rights.[46]

From there, both amendments went to the Senate for consideration. Madison expressed concern about the fate of several amendments in the more conservative Senate, noting that "two or three contentious additions would even now frustrate the whole project."[47] Unlike in the House, there are no recorded debates in the Senate, only entries of proposals and votes contained in the Senate journal. To Madison's chagrin, the Senate moved forward with only his first religion amendment; the one prohibiting state restrictions on conscience rights was dead. On September 3, various senators offered substitutes to the House's language about establishments, most of which would have narrowed its scope: Congress shall make no law establishing "one Religious Sect or Society in preference to others," "any Religious Sect or Society," or "any particular denomination." All of these proposals would have forbidden only an exclusive establishment at the national level, implicitly authorizing a system of non-preferential support of religion. Each of the substitutes failed to pass, although the Senate agreed to strike the phrase "rights of conscience." On September 9, the Senate finally approved language providing "Congress shall make no law establishing articles of faith, or a mode of worship, or prohibiting the free exercise of religion," language still directed toward prohibiting only an exclusive establishment.[48] The House objected to the Senate's revisions of several amendments, including the religious amendment, and called for a conference committee to resolve the differences. Before the committee met, however, the Senate "recede[d]" from their proposal for the religion clauses, deferring to the House. The committee then drafted language that would become the First Amendment: "Congress shall make no law respecting an establishment of religion, or prohibiting the free exercise thereof." The author or authors of the final language are unknown, although there are reasons to believe Madison was chiefly responsible for the ultimate phrasing. First, the final language closely tracked the House proposal (also likely written by Madison) to which the Senate had already deferred. Second, Madison led the House committee delegation, and according to Brant, his fellow members "had shown no interest in the clause on religion."[49] Whether it was "a strange turn of events" that Madison had gone from being an opponent to a bill of rights, to a lukewarm supporter out of obligation, and then to being firmly committed to their success, it is undisputed that Madison guided them to completion, with his telling Edmund Pendleton that the work had been "extremely difficult and fatiguing." Yet, "without his doggedness," write two scholars, "the Bill of Rights that modern Americas venerate would never have become a part of the constitutional system." And if there were any amendments that Madison was committed to in substance, the First Amendment would be at the top of that list.[50]

Still, Madison was unable to achieve everything he had wished. His expansive proposal for the First Amendment that "the full and equal rights of conscience be in any manner, or on any pretext," not be infringed had been narrowed, first by the House Committee on Amendments and then by the Senate in striking any reference to "rights of conscience." And then his "most valuable" amendment to restrict the same authority of the states had been tabled. As he later complained to Edmund Pendleton, the Senate had struck or altered "in my opinion at the most salutary articles." In an oblique reference to the Virginia disestablishment struggle, Madison remarked that the "difficulty of uniting the minds of men accustomed to think and act differently can only be conceived by those who have witnessed it." It likely goes too far to declare that "Madison had failed," and that "the First Amendment resolved nothing," as one scholar insists. But nevertheless, Madison had to be satisfied with what he had been able to achieve.[51]

Ever since the Supreme Court aligned the meaning of the religion clauses with the Madisonian-Jeffersonian perspective on church-state matters, commentators and critics have examined and dissected the record surrounding their enactment, focusing particularly on the meager debate in the House, to divine a contemporary understanding of the words "no law respecting an establishment of religion or prohibiting the free exercise thereof." They have also considered the larger context of 1789, with religious establishments operating in four states and with most states maintaining religious tests for officeholding, to decipher the function of the religion clauses under the nation's system of federalism. This inquiry has taken on an urgency over the last several decades with the ascendency of an "original meaning" or "historical understandings" analysis of constitutional text. The questions are whether the Madisonian-Jeffersonian perspective on church-state matters was representative of prevailing attitudes, on the vanguard, or an outlier. This debate has also asked whether any consensus understanding existed about essential values of church-state ordering, whether that was possible, or even whether that should matter. The number of scholarly and popular works on this subject are too numerous to list, and as noted, the focus of this book is not to relitigate this debate.[52]

That said, critics have raised several arguments about how to interpret the language of the First Amendment. The first argument, again, is that Jefferson and Madison were outliers in their perspectives toward church-state matters—attitudes that a majority of members of Congress, some of whom hailed from states with religious establishments, did not share. Therefore, it is historically inaccurate to graft a Madisonian-Jeffersonian perspective onto the religion clauses. A second argument, in tension with the first's premise, is that Madison did not attempt to achieve his vision of church and state through the clauses—that based on his statements during the debate, he sought only to prevent the establishment of a preferential "national" religion. The third argument is that because of the variety of church-state arrangements at the time of the founding, and their fluid nature, it is impossible to divine a common or consensus understanding to their meaning. And the fourth, related argument is that because of the lack of a consensus understanding, the drafters of the religion clauses simply sought to maintain a status quo by depriving the federal government of any authority to affect church-state relationships in the states.[53]

To respond briefly to these critiques, it is true that Jefferson and Madison were on the vanguard when it came to their comprehensive views of liberty of conscience, religious free exercise, and non-establishment of religion. But as previous chapters of this book have documented, they were not alone, having numerous allies in their quest—James Monroe, George Wythe, George Nicholas, Edmund Randolph, and John Leland, among others—who shared many of their views. To be sure, most members of the First Congress had not read (or even heard of) Madison's *Memorial and Remonstrance* or would have known of his authorship (though Jefferson's Statute for Religious Freedom and his *Notes on the State of Virginia* were more widely available). Yet fellow congressmen were aware of Madison's involvement in Virginia's disestablishment and his church-state commitments—as well as his affiliation with Jefferson—so they would have appreciated what Madison was seeking to achieve through his amendment. Many members likely did not share Madison's broad vision, but in the end they voted for a measure largely drafted by him.[54]

Second, some critics have argued that Madison's use of the term "national" indicates that he only opposed creating an official national church, such that he accepted forms of government support for religion generally.[55] His original proposal stated that no "national religion shall be established," and in the House debate Madison stated, "He believed the people feared one sect might obtain a pre-eminence, or two combine together and establish a religion to which they would compel others to conform; he thought the word national was introduced, it would point the amendment directly to the object it was intended to prevent." The problem with interpreting Madison's comments to mean that he opposed only preferential aid to religion and not a non-preferential establishment at the national level is that it contradicts his record in securing Virginia's Statute for Establishing Religious Freedom and his later writings such as his Detached Memoranda (1820?) in which he reaffirmed his separationist views. At the time, Madison still doubted the efficacy of a bill of rights, and his remarks clearly indicate that he was trying to address the concerns of those who desired a guarantee at the national level: "The word national was inserted . . . [to] satisfy the minds of honorable gentlemen" and the requirements of "some of the state conventions," he explained. The one point upon which all the legislators agreed was in the inequity of an establishment that preferred one sect over others, so Madison knew that argument would appeal to even reticent members from New England. But a prohibition on preferential establishments did not represent the extent of Madison's views. Also, at this stage, his proposed amendment to restrict states from invading rights of conscience was still in play, so the word "national" was used to emphasize the scope of *this* amendment. (And, based on his writings and statements during the Virginia disestablishment struggle, Madison clearly believed that any form of a religious assessment would also violate "equal rights of conscience.") Finally, Madison proposed that the amendment, like others, be inserted into the appropriate existing article of the Constitution—here, in article 1, section 9, which limits the authority of Congress—so the word "national" indicated a limitation on Congress's legislative authority, which was over national matters. In the end, the words "national religion" were struck, with the House approving "no law establishing religion," and the ultimate language being "no law respecting an establishment of religion," both phrases more reflective of Madison's true perspective.[56]

Third, as commentators have observed, members of Congress came from states with a variety of church-state histories, with many of them professing alternative views about church-state intermixing. This factor, they insist, makes it impossible to arrive at any consensus understanding of the religion clauses, particularly one that reflects the Madisonian-Jeffersonian perspective.[57] That fact is undoubtedly true, as one needs only to examine the brief comments and Senate proposals to see a variety of linguistic suggestions for the First Amendment. But this argument implies that it is necessary to identify a consensus understanding of the religion clauses before one can divine a purpose or meaning. This is one of the central flaws with an originalist approach: that some consensus meaning or understanding of a constitutional provision or right existed and can be accurately determined. Donald L. Drakeman is correct that the lowest denominator point of agreement was that there should not be a preferential religion established on the national level—a point Madison recognized and exploited in his remarks. But this does not mean there were no other views on which a significant number generally agreed; again, at this point the amendment's language still prohibited infringements on rights of conscience, which many people interpreted to bar coerced taxation even under a non-preferential system.[58]

Finally, some commentators have insisted that because of this purported lack of consensus, the establishment clause has no substantive meaning—that it represents only a jurisdictional rule that prevents the national government from interfering with state religious arrangements, including the establishments that operated in four states and putatively existed in two more. According to one scholar, the various congressmen "simply could not have agreed on a general principle of governing the relationship of religion and government." Rather, "What united the representatives of all the states . . . was a much more narrow purpose: to make it plain that Congress was not to legislate on the subject of religion, thereby leaving the matter of church-state relations to the individual states." Justice Clarence Thomas has endorsed this interpretation, writing that the "text and history of the Establishment Clause strongly suggest that it is a federalism provision intended to prevent Congress from interfering with state establishments [of religion]."[59]

While it is undisputed that the Bill of Rights was designed to bar federal encroachments on individual and state's rights, and therefore reflects a federalism impulse, there is little support in the record that the majority of congressmen were concerned about *protecting* state religious establishments through the establishment clause. The events that had transpired in the states indicates that by 1789 people increasingly opposed religious establishments; moreover, New England officials were reticent to acknowledge that their assessment systems constituted the same.[60] Only two representatives offered comments during the House debate that arguably raised concerns around federalism. Benjamin Huntington of Connecticut worried that the proposed language—"no religion shall be established by law"—could be interpreted to bar federal courts from enforcing financial obligations to "support of ministers, or building of places of worship." In an earlier comment, Peter Sylvester of New York said he "apprehended that [the proposed language] was liable to a construction different from what had been made by the committee, he feared it might be thought to have a tendency to abolish religion altogether." Sylvester's phrase "abolish religion" could refer to abolishing state religious establishments.[61]

Of the two remarks, only Huntington mentioned a state establishment. But even his comment focused on ensuring that federal courts give full faith and credit to state legal obligations, and it did not express a greater fear that Congress possessed implied authority under the necessary and proper clause to interfere with state establishments. Sylvester, in contrast, hailed from a state without an establishment, so his comment about "abolish[ing] religion altogether" probably meant something other than protecting exist-ing state establishments. More likely, Sylvester was concerned that overly broad language could be interpreted to forbid government practices such as thanksgiving proclamations or church incorporations and was therefore antireligious.[62]

Finally, Samuel Livermore of New Hampshire offered language "that congress shall make no laws touching religion," which some commenta-tors have interpreted as intending to prevent the federal government from "touching" existing state religious establishments. But Livermore's statement is also ambiguous—he was offering his state convention's recommendation—and it fails to mention any jurisdictional concern. In that the House mem-bers already understood that the amendment applied only to the national government, no one would have assumed that its language would somehow authorize Congress to regulate existing state establishments (again, Mad-ison's other amendment prohibiting state restrictions on conscience rights was still alive). As Drakeman sardonically concludes, "To support such a bold interpretation of the federalism approach, one needs to posit that clever pro-establishment legislators hoodwinked Madison and others in Congress into thinking that the First Amendment contained restrictions on federal church-state interactions when, in fact, it not only protected established churches in the states but also left Congress free to establish a church at the national level."[63]

In the final analysis, what can be derived from the House debates and Senate deliberations is that the legislators ultimately rejected proposed lan-guage that would have limited the scope of the establishment clause. Both chambers rejected proposals to define an establishment as prohibiting a "national religion" or as favoring one denomination or sect, one "mode of worship," or particular "articles of faith." Undoubtedly, the various legis-lators did not agree on the meaning of a "law respecting an establishment of religion," either in the sense of what constituted an "establishment" or a law "respecting" one, but it is significant that they settled on arguably the broadest language proposed in either the House or Senate. While Madison may not be solely responsible for that phrasing, it reflects his influence and perspective about church and state, a perspective that was no doubt fash-ioned by his collaboration with Jefferson.[64]

EIGHT

The Washington and Adams Presidencies

T he first four presidencies of the United States (1789–1817) encompassed one of the more dynamic and transformative periods in the nation's history. The founders' experiment in republicanism faced numerous challenges and reconceptualizations. Although everyone professed fealty to republicanism, significant disagreements existed over what that meant and how to apply those principles through the policies and operations of government. Demographic shifts arising from a dramatic growth in population and geographical expansion also placed pressures on the society, and external and internal threats to the new government caused many to wonder whether the nation could survive. In the late 1780s, the political leadership had faced a host of issues related to organizing and sustaining the new government that required their full attention. Those issues persisted into the 1790s, but then the political establishment had to deal with the effects of the French Revolution, internal discontent exemplified by the Whiskey Rebellion, and the advent of political partisanship, resulting in a time of uncertainty that has been called the "crisis years."[1]

Religion, and notions of religious freedom, were important and recurring themes during this period; however, they were not as prominent as they had been during the late colonial and founding periods. In a like manner, religious issues held less immediacy for Jefferson and Madison, considering all of the matters of governance that took on a priority before and during their presidencies. Even so, religious issues rose to the forefront in several contexts, issues that caught the attention of Jefferson and Madison (among others) and affected developing conceptions of religious freedom.[2]

The Washington Presidency

Thomas Jefferson returned to the United States from Paris in November 1789, retreating to Monticello to contemplate George Washington's offer to become secretary of state. Just after Christmas, Madison traveled to Monticello where the two friends were reunited.[3] Despite their extensive correspondence, the two men had much to discuss, not the least of which was the unfolding revolution in France, the initial outbursts Jefferson had observed. His five years in France had made a deep impression on Jefferson in several ways, including informing his views about religion. Jefferson had relished his interactions with the French intelligentsia, most of whom espoused rationalist ideas and held deistic beliefs. Although it is unclear how much those associations influenced Jefferson's own views, the sensibilities of his French acquaintances no doubt reinforced Jefferson's ideas about rational religion.[4] As he had advised his nephew Peter Carr in 1787, "Fix reason firmly in [your mind's] seat, and call to her tribunal every fact, every opinion. Question with boldness even the existence of a god; because, if there be one, he must more approve the homage of reason, than that of blindfolded fear." Nothing he encountered in France caused him to reconsider his ideas about religion. Shortly before leaving France in September 1789, Jefferson witnessed the early stages of the revolution, advising the Marquis de Lafayette on drafting a declaration of rights and on how to form a republican government based on principles of reason.[5] As Alexander Hamilton later derisively described Jefferson, "He came from France in the moment of a fermentation" where "he drank deeply of the French Philosophy, in Religion, in Science, [and] in politics."[6]

A second experience involved Jefferson's observations about the role of the Catholic Church in French society, which only reinforced his anticlericalism. Traveling throughout France, Jefferson was shocked at the conditions of the landless "labouring poor," as he informed Madison, telling another acquaintance that he found "the general fate of humanity here most deplorable." Everywhere, Jefferson witnessed "ignorance, superstition, poverty and oppression of body and mind in every form . . . so firmly settled on the mass of the people." While he attributed the inequities to the aristocracy, he also condemned the wealth and influence of the Catholic hierarchy, which he believed kept people in ignorance by perpetuating religious superstitions. In France, he told Madison, for "so many ages . . . the human mind has been held in vassalage by kings, priests and nobles." The laboring poor were "suffering under physical and moral oppression" and had been "loaded with misery by kings, nobles and priests, and by them alone."[7] These experiences did nothing to disabuse Jefferson's commitment to rational religion or his disdain for clerical power and privilege. Over the next decade, his close association with French rationalism and deism, and his unwavering support for French republicanism, would invite harsh criticism from political opponents.

Joining the Washington administration, Jefferson's sights turned to matters of governance and managing foreign affairs. He was joined in the cabinet by Alexander Hamilton, the ambitious secretary of the treasury, and by Madison in an unofficial capacity. Initially, the three men worked together despite their ideological differences—differences over finances and foreign alliances that would shortly break out into open political warfare. Although all three men advised Washington about a host of matters, the president initially relied more heavily on Madison; according to Adrienne Koch, in 1789 and early 1790, "Madison enjoyed a singularly cordial relationship with President Washington," preparing numerous documents for the latter.[8] Madison drafted Washington's First Inaugural Address, though one can assume that most of its religious rhetoric—offering "fervent supplications to that Almighty Being . . . who presides in the Councils of Nations, and whose providential aids can supply every human defect," and "homage to the Great Author of every public and private good"—came from Washington's hand.[9] Washington was adept in employing vague, deific terms that demonstrated religious fealty and did not offend the religiously orthodox or heterodox alike. With his latitudinarian and deistic leanings, Washington showed little interest in religious doctrinalism, and his experience leading the Continental Army had committed him to religious pluralism. Writing to Lafayette in 1787, Washington wished the marquis success in his reform "plan of toleration in religeous matters" in France. "Being no bigot myself to any mode of worship," Washington continued, "I am disposed to endulge the professors of Christianity in the church, that road to heaven which to them shall seem the most direct plainest easiest and least liable to exception."[10]

Washington's religious beliefs were his own—heterodox in substance but conventional in practice—though one can speculate how much his ideas about religious freedom were influenced by observing the long disestablishment struggle in Virginia. Initially, Washington was not "alarmed at the thoughts of making people pay towards the support of that [religion] they profess," but he shortly opposed the assessment based on pragmatic considerations, expressing his desire that "an assessment had never been agitated" and that "[Patrick Henry's] Bill could die an easy death." Washington had worried that religious controversies would "rankle, & perhaps convulse the State."[11] Now, as the chief magistrate of an even more religiously diverse nation, Washington preached respect for and inclusion of all faiths, but not solely on grounds of social expediency. In the fragmentary writings prepared for his inaugural address, or perhaps for his first address to Congress, Washington mused philosophically about the inherent values of religious freedom and liberty of conscience. Sprinkled between unused deific references, Washington expressed "a belief that intellectual light will spring up in the dark corners of the earth; that freedom of enquiry will produce liberality of conduct." In acknowledging his personal desire to seek the "approbation in Heaven" through his public service, he asked, "[should I] set up my judgment as the standard of perfection? And shall I arrogantly pronounce that whosoever differs from me, must discern the subject through a distorting medium, or be influenced by some nefarious design? The mind is so formed in different persons as to contemplate the same object in different points of view. Hence originates the difference on questions of the greatest import, both human & divine." Later in the fragments, Washington again expressed doubt about the ability of civil authorities to divine god's will and then to apply it in an uncorrupted manner. He noted the "folly or perverseness in short-sighted mortals" who sought to enforce religious conformity. Even "the best Institutions may be abused by human depravity" and in other "instances be made subservient to the vilest of purposes." Expressing reservations similar to Madison's about the efficacy of a bill of rights, Washington worried "that no compact among men (however provident in its construction & sacred in its ratification) can be pronounced everlasting and inviolable."[12] Historian Paul Boller noted that Washington's "pluralistic view of human perceptions sounds very much like Jefferson." Boller speculated that "Washington's musings on the eve of his inauguration are so Jeffersonian in spirit that one cannot help wondering whether his association with Jefferson had something to do with the clear-cut enunciation of his views on religious liberty that he made while he was president." In some respects, Washington's sentiments about human nature sound more

Madisonian, which would make more sense considering their closer contact throughout the second half of the 1780s.[13]

Shortly after his inauguration, Washington undertook the task of responding to the mountain of congratulatory letters he had received. The theme that runs through many of his letters is one of religious humility and the value of toleration and respect for a diversity of religious views. As he told the United Baptists of Virginia, his office would never "be so administered as to render the liberty of conscience insecure," and he promised "that no one would be more zealous than myself to establish effectual barriers against the horrors of spiritual tyranny, and every species of religious persecution."[14]

Washington's most significant reply was to the Jewish community in Newport, Rhode Island. The initiating letter coincided with Washington's trip to Rhode Island in August 1790. In it, the leaders of the synagogue noted how Jews, "deprived as we heretofore have been of the invaluable rights of free Citizens," expressed their gratitude for "the Blessings of civil and religious liberty which we enjoy under an equal and benign administration." Washington responded in kind with memorable language: "All possess alike liberty of conscience and immunities of citizenship. It is now no more that toleration is spoken of, as if it was by the indulgence of one class of people, that another enjoyed the exercise of their inherent natural rights. For happily the Government of the United States, which gives to bigotry no sanction, to persecution no assistance [and] requires only that they who live under its protection should demean themselves as good citizens, in giving it on all occasions their effectual support."[15] Aware of the prejudice that Jews had experienced and were still encountering in the new nation, Washington's language was far from perfunctory, embracing notions of full religious liberty and equal status of religion under the law. Commentators have declared Washington's statement to be one of the "most outstanding expressions on religious liberty and equality in America."[16]

One other reply is worth mentioning as it demonstrates Washington's understanding about the separation of church and state. In October 1789, Presbyteries from New England, representing Presbyterian congregations, wrote Washington a congratulatory letter that also praised Washington's leadership and affirmed the "interpositions of divine providence" on the new government. The Presbyterians, however, set out specific hopes, if not expectations, about the new administration's orientation. After declaring Washington's election to be a sign of God's providential workings, the letter expressed desire that "under the nurturing hand of a Ruler of such virtues . . . that virtue and religion will revive and flourish—that infidelity and the vices ever attendant in its train, will be banished [from] every polite circle." That the Presbyterians were entreating Washington to enforce religious norms became clearer in a later paragraph: "Our unceasing prayers to the *great Sovereign of all* nations, shall be that your important life, and all your singular talents may be the special care of an indulgent Providence for many years to come; that your administration may be continued to your country, under the peculiar smiles of Heaven, long enough to advance the interests of learning to the zenith [and] to chace ignorance, bigotry, and immorality off the stage—to restore true virtue, and the religion of *Jesus* to their deserved throne in our land." Despite praising Washington and the new government, the Presbyterians expressed one regret. In commending the Constitution's lack of a religious test for officeholding—"that grand engine of persecution in every tyrant's hand"—the Presbyterians stated that "we should not have been alone in rejoicing to have seen some Explicit acknowledgement of the *only true God and Jesus Christ, whom he hath sent* inserted some where in the *Magna Charta* of our country." Apparently, the Presbyterians would have preferred an express acknowledgment of God's sovereignty in the Constitution but would be satisfied if Washington administered his government consistent with that idea.[17]

In Washington's carefully worded reply, he commended the Presbyterians for believing in God's "inspiration of our public-councils with wisdom and firmness" in drafting and ratifying the Constitution. He asserted, however, that public officials, while "devoted to the pious purposes of religion, desire their accomplishment by such means as advance the temporal happiness of their fellow-men." Here, Washington was distinguishing separate spheres of authority—temporal versus spiritual—to be exercised by distinct entities—civil or religious—a point he then clarified by suggesting that the "guidance of the ministers of the gospel" was "perhaps, more properly committed" to its own realm: "to instruct the ignorant, and to reclaim the devious." In contrast, if we allowed government to perform its separate civil functions, "we may confidently expect" as a consequence "the advancement of true religion, and the completion of our happiness." As to the Presbyterians' point about the absence of a deific affirmation in the

Constitution, Washington replied, "I am persuaded, you will permit me to observe that the path of true piety is so plain as to require but little political direction. To this consideration we ought to ascribe the absence of any regulation, respecting religion, from the Magna-Charta of our country."[18]

By this point in his public career, Washington was adept at drafting responses that validated people's sentiments without necessarily endorsing their perspectives. Whether Washington conferred with Madison in his replies to the religious groups is unknown, but the contents of Washington's letters indicate that he shared several of Madison's and Jefferson's more important views about church-state matters. Because of Washington's prominence, and the fact that his letters, with their affirmations of religious respect and pluralism, were publicized, Paul Boller is correct that "Washington unquestionably deserves major credit, along with Jefferson and Madison, for establishing the ideals of religious liberty and freedom of conscience . . . firmly in the American tradition."[19]

Washington's understanding of church-state matters, like many people of his generation, evolved over time. By modern standards, his actions do not always appear to be consistent. At the same time that he was drafting his letters to the various denominations, Washington issued the first of his two proclamations calling for a day of prayer and thanksgiving. In September 1789, the House of Representatives enacted a resolution, at the urging of evangelical congressman Elias Boudinot, calling on the president to issue such a proclamation. Apparently, Washington had already been considering issuing one on his own. He had broached the idea earlier with Madison in a confidential letter seeking advice on a range of matters including judicial appointments, sending ambassadors, and "a day for thanksgiving." Madison did not respond in a letter though he may have advised the president privately.[20] Washington's Thanksgiving Proclamation of October 3 called for "a day of public thanksgiving and prayer to be observed by acknowledging with grateful hearts the many signal favors of Almighty God" in the successful formation of the new government. Even though the proclamation contained deific language—declaring the "favorable interpositions of his Providence" and beseeching "the great Lord and Ruler of Nations . . . to pardon our national and other transgressions"—the document differed from earlier wartime proclamations by its absence of Christian references and by not calling on individuals to admit their own transgressions. The proclamation also called for thanks for "the civil and religious liberty for which we are blessed," possibly an indication of Madison's influence at the time.[21]

By late 1790, however, Washington had moved from Madison's counsel to that of Alexander Hamilton, due in part to the president's siding with Hamilton's policies regarding public debt and the creation of a national bank. Madison also disagreed with Hamilton's policies that used federal authority to encourage manufacturing and economic development in ways that Madison felt threatened individualistic republican values. In 1791, Madison and Jefferson encouraged the former's old Princeton classmate Philip Freneau to establish the *National Gazette* in which Madison contributed essays critical of Hamilton's far-reaching policies.[22] In one telling essay written in March 1792, "Property," Madison promoted an expansive liberal conception of private property rights that the government should respect and protect. A person not only had a property interest in their physical possessions and labor; there was a greater property interest in "his opinions and the free communication of them," and a "peculiar value in his religious opinions, and in the profession and practice dictated by them." Paraphrasing Locke, Madison insisted that "government is instituted to protect property of every sort" but that it falls short of that duty where it, "however scrupulously guarding the [physical] possessions of individuals, does not protect them in the enjoyment and communication of their opinions, in which they have an equal, and in the estimation of some, a more valuable property" interest. This was of particular concern "where a man's religious rights are violated by penalties, or fettered by tests, or taxed by a hierarchy. Conscience is the most sacred of all property," Madison insisted, and while the right to physical possessions "depend[ed] in part on positive law, the exercise of [conscience] [was] a natural and unalienable right." The implication of Madison's essay was clear: in promoting policies that compromised individual economic rights, Hamilton also threatened people's rights of conscience, which were more sacred: "Where an excess of power prevails, property of no sort is duly respected. No man is safe in his opinions, his person, his faculties, or his possessions." The essay demonstrates Madison's ongoing commitment to protecting conscience rights and his belief that the regulation of those rights lay outside the authority of government.[23]

One area where Hamilton's influence can be seen is in Washington's later religious pronouncements, which became more sectarian and politically partisan. In January 1795, Washington issued his second Thanksgiving

Proclamation, this one drafted by Hamilton. This proclamation differed from the first in that it employed more politically and religiously charged language. The proclamation made two condemning references to the "late insurrection" (i.e., the Whiskey Rebellion), asking people to pray for "liberty with order." And unlike his first proclamation, this one urged personal supplication to God, "recommend[ing] to all Religious Societies and Denominations and to all persons whomsoever" to "render their sincere and hearty thanks to the great ruler of Nations for the manifold and signal mercies," and "to beseech the kind author of these blessings . . . to diffuse and establish habits of sobriety, order, morality, and piety" among the people. Secretary of State Edmund Randolph reviewed Hamilton's drafts of the proclamation, suggesting several changes to tone down its rhetoric. Randolph succeeded in striking a phrase asking people "to bow down before the Majesty of the Almighty to acknowlege our numerous obligations to him." In a marginal comment regarding the draft's political content, Randolph wrote, "This proclamation ought to savour as much as possible of religion; and not too much of having a political object." Hamilton responded caustically with his own marginal note: "A proclamation by a government which is a national Act naturaly embraces objects which are political." The text was not otherwise changed. As one Republican-leaning minister complained after the appointed day, "The Clergy are now the Tools of the Federalists, and Thanksgiving Sermons are in the order of the Day."[24] Later, in an 1812 letter to Benjamin Rush, John Adams confirmed Hamilton's conscious efforts to politicize religion, noting sarcastically how "the pious and virtuous Hamilton, in 1790 began to teach our Nation Christianity, and to commission his Followers to cry down Jefferson and Madison as Atheists, in league with The French Nation, who were all Atheists." One can surmise that the shift in the tone of Washington's religious statements was a direct result of Madison's displacement as a primary advisor.[25]

The increasing politicization of religion was on display when Washington attended thanksgiving services at Christ Church in Philadelphia on February 19, 1795, where he heard a sermon by Episcopal bishop William White. Addressing Washington from the pulpit, White affirmed that "since your elevation to the seat of supreme Executive authority, you have, in your official capacity, on all fit occasions, directed the public attention to the Being and the Providence of God: And this implies a sense, as well of the relation, which nations, in their collective capacities, bear to him, their

Supreme Ruler, . . . [in] the execution of the trusts committed to them."
White asserted that as Washington had "embraced all the civil interests of
the American people, [he] has not overlooked the relation which they all
bear, to the great truths of religion and of morals." In a veiled reference to
the Jeffersonian view of church-state matters, White remarked that "the
relation which I have asserted of religion to civil policy, is well known to
be considered as chimerical by some; while it is contemplated by others,
as involved in whatever relates to the prosperity of the commonwealth."
The government practice of promoting religion and morals, White noted
in another jab at Jefferson, was "in contrarity to a theory, that sets open the
flood-gates of immorality." White praised Washington for his "consistency
of practice" in "having upheld the interests of religion and of virtue." In typical fashion, Washington did not comment on White's characterizations.[26]

Historian Michael I. Meyerson has observed that "Washington's Farewell
Address was written in the same politically charged environment." As with
his Thanksgiving Proclamations, Washington's Farewell Address has long
been a favorite of religious conservatives (and more recently of conservative
Supreme Court justices) for drawing parallels between religion and good
government.[27] In it, Washington wrote, "Of all the dispositions and habits
which lead to political prosperity, Religion and morality are indispensable
supports." So, "let us with caution indulge the supposition, that morality can
be maintained without religion. Whatever may be conceded to the influence
of refined education on minds of peculiar structure—reason & experience
both forbid us to expect that National morality can prevail in exclusion of
religious principle. . . . [It] is substantially true, that virtue or morality is
a necessary spring of popular government. The rule indeed extends with
more or less force to every species of free Government."[28] Again, Hamilton
had a hand in the product. In May 1796, Washington approached Hamilton
to revise a draft address that Madison had prepared for Washington when
he considered resigning in 1792. Hamilton made significant modifications to
Madison's address to bring it up to date and "to render this act *importantly*
and *lastingly* useful." That usefulness included adding specific references to
religion and morality that were absent from Madison's draft or in Washington's notes. Washington struck a handful of Hamilton's more religious
statements, including a sentence that asserted that government required "the
aid of a generally received and divinely authoritative Religion," a statement
too sectarian for Washington's taste. But overall, Washington accepted most

of Hamilton's revisions, including the above-quoted declarations about religion and morality.[29]

Washington's willingness to employ religious rhetoric but in a careful manner is demonstrated by an episode on his last full day as president. On March 3, 1797, a handful of Protestant ministers of Philadelphia, including Bishop William White and Presbyterian Ashbel Green, wrote Washington a letter of gratitude thanking him for his service and for the numerous acknowledgments that he had "given to [Christ's] holy religion." Washington had been "an edifying example of a civil ruler [by] always acknowledging the superintendence of divine providence in the affairs of men, & confirming that example by the powerful recommendation of religion & morality as the firmest basis of social happiness."[30] According to notes of a conversation between Benjamin Rush and Jefferson, Green had told Rush that the purpose of their letter was "to force [Washington] at length to declare publicly whether he was a Christian or not," based on their observations that he had "never on any occasion said a word to the public which shewed a belief in the Xn. Religion." Washington skillfully avoided the trap; while reaffirming his belief that "*Religion & Morality* are the essential pillars of Civic society," he declared his "unspeakable pleasure" over the "harmony & Brotherly love which characterizes the Clergy of different denominations." Jefferson remarked that by declining to give the ministers the affirmation of Christianity they desired, "the old fox was too cunning for them."[31]

Throughout his public career, Washington sought to diffuse religious prejudice and conflict, and even though his personal beliefs were heterodox for the times, he believed strongly in the importance of piety and morality for American society. Religious institutions—churches—played an essential role in fostering that piety and morality, and Washington regularly attended services, though he declined to take communion. He had few reservations about employing religious language in his public declarations, but he strove to make them religiously inclusive and nonsectarian in content. Yet, despite his disdain for religious conflict and the politicization of religion, his vision for church-state relations would be tested in the decades ahead.[32]

The Religious Impact of the French Revolution

Washington's tenure as president coincided with the main current of the French Revolution and several of its more dramatic phases.[33] Thomas

Jefferson was not the only American to celebrate the storming of the Bastille and the creation of the French Republic. Initially, Americans of all perspectives, including orthodox clergy, embraced the revolution and the new French Republic as an extension of republican principles to Europe. The revolution heralded "THE ERA OF FREEDOM—OF UNIVERSAL LIBERTY!" declared the New York *Gazette of the United States* in July 1789. Although the *Gazette* was destined to become a mouthpiece of the Federalist Party, in another story it effused that "the revolution in France is one of the most glorious objects that can arrest the attention of mankind. To see a great people springing into freedom, light, and happiness at once from the depressions of Despotism and Bigotry, is something so novel . . . that the whole world contemplates the scene with wonder, with rapture, and applause."[34] Expressing similar sentiments, Congregational minister Enos Hitchcock insisted that Americans should "warmly wish success to the great principles of the French revolution—principles founded on the equal liberty of all men, and the empire of the laws." Even after the beheading of King Louis XVI and the advent of the Reign of Terror in 1793, many Americans assigned the excesses to the French people's "inexperience . . . in the science of free government, and [being] unprepared for the enjoyment of it by a previous course of [republican] education." Observers also forgave the revolutionaries' confiscation of church property and their anticlerical rhetoric and actions (including the execution of priests). French anticlericalism was "less to be wondered at, when we consider, in how unamiable and disgusting a point of view it has been there exhibited, under the hierarchy of Rome," wrote Jedidiah Morse. Once "peace and a free government shall be established, the effusions of the Holy Spirit [will bring about] a glorious revival and prevalence of pure, unadulterated Christianity."[35]

According to historian Gary B. Nash, it was not until 1794 that Federalists and orthodox clergy began to turn against the French cause, but only after the violence was no longer explainable and the anticlericalism assumed a more generic attack against Christianity. Writing in 1794, Noah Webster stated that "when the revolution in France was announced in America, [my] heart exulted with joy; [I] felt nearly the same interest in success, as [I] did in the establishment of American independence. This joy has been much allayed by the sanguinary proceedings of the Jacobins, their atheistical attacks on christianity." Webster distinguished the actions of the First Assembly in seizing property of the Catholic hierarchy from the Second Assembly, controlled by Jacobins, which had engaged in "an inveterate war with christianity," including the abolition of the Sabbath and the Christian calendar. According to Webster, the French had "established, not deism only, but atheism and materialism."[36]

Webster's statement about atheism revealed the chief explanation for the American clergy's turn against the French Revolution. By the mid-1790s, orthodox ministers had grown increasingly alarmed by the rise of deism and infidelity in the United States. Deism was neither a distinct nor succinctly defined belief system, though it promoted several common ideas such as the rejection of orthodox Christian doctrines, a belief in a passive and noninterventionist creator, a denial of the divinity of Jesus, a skepticism about biblical miracles, and frequently a disdain for the authority of clergy. Deism was not new to America—British deism had arisen in the early 1700s—and many of the colonial intellectual elite held deistic leanings, though they generally kept those beliefs private. Deistic thought began to make inroads among the common folk during the American Revolution with its disruption of religion and peoples' encounters with British and French soldiers. Then, in 1784 Revolutionary War hero Ethan Allen published his deistic critique of Christian orthodoxy, *Reason the Only Oracle of Man,* which according to historian Christopher Grasso "was read more than its paltry sales might indicate, discussed more than it was read, and treated with clerical contempt more than it was refuted." Allen's book presaged a flood of deistic literature from Europe in the late 1780s and early 1790s that facilitated the formation of Democratic Societies and free-thought clubs.[37]

Then in 1794, coinciding with the increasing anticlericalism in France, Thomas Paine published his unforgiving critique of orthodox Christianity, *The Age of Reason.* It asserted that the church fathers were "Christian Mythologists" who misled the laity and that the Bible was nothing but "a history of the grossest vices and a collection of the most paltry and contemptable tales." Paine wrote on behalf of the "true Deist" and dedicated his book to "my fellow citizens of the United States of America." *The Age of Reason* was immensely popular in America, particularly among Democratic Societies, freethought clubs, and college students, going through seventeen editions by 1796.[38] Lyman Beecher, a future leader of orthodox Calvinism, wrote that while attending Yale College in 1795, "most students were skepti-cal. . . . That was the day of the infidelity of the Tom Paine school." Accord-ing to Gary Nash, "Everywhere Paine was read." This challenge presented by deism caused considerable consternation among orthodox clergy, who tied it to the growing popularity of democratic impulses.[39]

By the mid-1790s, orthodox clergy and the Federalist press were in full attack mode over the perceived threats presented by the domestic alliance of deism and republicanism. Writing in Philadelphia's *Porcupine's Gazette* in 1798, "Americus" railed that a "system that excludes a God from the moral government of the world, and denies his retributive justice, both here and hereafter, necessarily removes every restraint from the malignant passions, and sanctions all the evils that power can inflict."[40] Among clergy, Yale Col-lege president Timothy Dwight became the leading critic of deism. In a 1797 pamphlet *The Nature and Danger of Infidel Philosophy*, Dwight launched a broad attack on the century's rationalist philosophers: Shaftesbury, Vol-taire, Bolingbroke, Hume, and Rousseau, among others. Deism was "but the first step of Reason out of Superstition (i.e., out of Revealed Religion). No person remains a Deist," Dwight maintained, but turns to atheism. He expanded on that theme the following year in another pamphlet, *The Duty of Americans, at the Present Crisis*, where he charged that European infidelity was being imported into America through the Bavarian Illuminati, a secret society bent on destroying Christianity. Through their Masonic connec-tions in America, the Illuminati were "inundat[ing] [America] with books replete with infidelity, irreligion, immorality, and obscenity." Their ultimate goal was "the overthrow of religion, government, and human society civil and domestic."[41] For the panicked orthodox clergy, the effects of infidelity on the culture were everywhere. "Have not infidelity, and all manner of loose principles, and immoral practices, abounded in all parts of the land, since the revolution," asked Congregationalist minister John Smalley. "Has not the worship of God been neglected; his day and name been prophaned, his laws transgressed, and his gospel despised and rejected, of late years, more than ever."[42]

The domestic reaction to the French Revolution helped precipitate the rise of American political partisanship: the Hamiltonian Federalists and the Jeffersonian Republicans. For Federalists, the connection between deism and Jeffersonian republicanism was an easy one to make. Throughout the decade, Republican newspapers such as Philadelphia's *National Gazette*,

General Advertiser, and *Aurora* defended the republican ideals of the French Revolution and its rationalist philosophy. Jefferson, as leader of the Republicans, would have come under attack from Federalists regardless, but his experience in France, his support for Paine, and his actions and writings promoting religious tolerance made him an easy target.[43]

In the fall of 1796, Washington formally announced he would not run for reelection. Jefferson, who had retired from public life in 1793, showed little interest in seeking the presidency, but as he told Edward Rutledge, "My name however was again brought forward, without consultation or expectation on my part." Apparently, Madison worked behind the scenes to garner support for Jefferson without consulting his friend until the end. Six weeks before the election, Madison wrote James Monroe that "I have not seen Jefferson and have thought it best to present him no opportunity of protesting to his friend against being embarked in the contest."[44]

Whether Jefferson would challenge John Adams for the presidency was the worst kept secret, and the Federalist press attacked Jefferson for his Francophilia and his heterodox beliefs.[45] The *Gazette of the United States* highlighted Jefferson's association with atheists in France and with Tom Paine, "that antichristian writer." It quoted from Jefferson's *Notes on the State of Virginia* where he had written that "it does me no injury for my neighbor to say there are twenty gods or no god; it neither picks my pocket nor breaks my leg." Should we "be most shocked at the *levity* or *impiety* of these remarks?" asked the *Gazette.* "Do I receive no injury, as a member of society, if I am surrounded by atheists . . . on whom there are none of those religious and sacred ties, which refrain mankind from the perpetuation of crimes?" The newspaper also criticized Jefferson's efforts to disestablish religion in Virginia while it panned his Statute for Establishing Religious Freedom: "He has proved his religious freedom, or rather, his freedom from religion, by his conduct, and his opinions. . . . Who ever saw him in a place of worship?"[46] In response, the Republican press defended Jefferson as a "steadfast friend to the Rights of the People" and "a republican in principle and manners," accusing Adams of being a monarchist and "an advocate for hereditary power and distinctions." But the Republican press stayed away from rebutting charges about Jefferson's religious faith, preferring to emphasize his commitment to freedom of conscience. In the end, Jefferson lost a close election to Adams, receiving sixty-eight electoral votes to Adams's seventy-one. After the election, Jefferson wrote that his name had received "so much of eulogy and of abuse" that "in truth I did not know myself under the pens either of my friends or foes." Madison had to convince his reticent friend to accept the position of vice president, as was provided under the Constitution at the time for the runner-up to the presidency. "Your acceptance of a share in the administration . . . will lessen the evil of such an ostensible protest by this Country against Republicanism," Madison wrote.[47]

The Adams Presidency

Jefferson's tenure as vice president got off to a rocky start, as only two months into the administration he faced criticism for a letter he had written to a friend, Philip Mazzei, during the controversy over the Jay Treaty the previous year. In the letter, Jefferson had unloaded his frustration over how "an Anglican, monarchical and aristocratical party has sprung up" with designs to displace "that noble love of liberty and republican government." These "apostates" to republicanism "who ha[d] gone over to these heresies" had once been "Samsons in the field and Solomons in the council, but who ha[d] [now] had their heads shorn by the harlot England." Jefferson had Hamilton in mind as one apostate, but the reference to Samson and Solomon was taken—likely accurately—to refer to a pliable Washington.[48] Federalist newspapers denounced Jefferson for his duplicity and lack of respect for the revered Washington, with the *Gazette of the United States* chastising Jefferson for making "abominable falsehoods" about the ex-president. Adams and Federalists took the affair as confirmation that Jefferson was more committed to his radical ideology than to the interests of the nation.[49]

Jefferson's pejorative use of the word "Anglican" in the Mazzei letter was not a reference to the Episcopal Church but indicated his view that the pro-British Federalists favored policies of religious privilege and greater church-state intermixing—after all, the stronghold of the Federalists was the New England states with their Congregationalist establishments. He also sensed that Federalists would be willing to use religious issues for political gain. He was shortly proved to be correct.

By early 1798, relations between the US and French governments had deteriorated over France's refusal to respect American neutrality in its war with Great Britain. After Adams conferred with his cabinet over possible solutions, Secretary of War James McHenry, a Hamilton protégé, wrote to Hamilton for suggestions. Hamilton, now a private citizen but titular head of the Federalist Party, offered several recommendations including having Adams designate a day of humiliation and prayer: "Let the President recommend a day to be observed as a day of fasting humiliation & prayer. On religious ground this is very proper—On political, it is very expedient. The Government will be very unwise, if it does not make the most of the religious prepossessions of our people—opposing the honest enthusiasm of Religious Opinion to the phrenzy of Political fanaticism."[50] Hamilton had not deviated from his willingness to use religion to advance political ends. He proceeded to write other Federalist officials who were close to Adams—Massachusetts senator Theodore Sedgwick and Secretary of State Timothy Pickering—making a similar recommendation; as he told the former, Adams should "call to his aid the force of religious Ideas by a day of fasting humiliation & prayer. This will be in my opinion no less proper in a political than in a Religious View. We must oppose to political fanaticism [i.e., Republican opposition] [with] religious zeal."[51] Pickering responded that Adams had already "determined to recommend the observance of a general fast" before receiving Hamilton's letter. Whether true or not, Adams issued his first proclamation a week after Pickering received Hamilton's letter, so it is doubtful that Hamilton's recommendations had not been communicated to the president. But because Adams detested Hamilton—and vice versa—it was unlikely that the president would have acknowledged he had been influenced by Hamilton to issue a proclamation. As Adams wrote many years later, he "wanted no admonition from Mr. Hamilton to institute a national fast." Seeking to justify issuing the proclamation by distinguishing his own sincere motives from Hamilton's political ones, Adams declared that he "despised and detested [Hamilton's] letter" because he thought that "there is nothing upon this earth more sublime and affecting, than the idea of a great nation all on their knees at once before their God, acknowledging their faults and imploring his blessing and protection." In Adams's mind, "When most, if not all the religious sects in the nation hold such fasts among themselves, I never could see the force of the objections against making them, on great and extraordinary occasions, national."[52]

Adams was also responding to Republican criticism that his two Fast Proclamations (of March 23, 1798, and March 6, 1799) were overtly political and sectarian. In preparing the proclamations, Adams turned to Bishop

William White and Reverend Ashbel Green, both chaplains of Congress and critics of Washington's nonsectarian piety, to write the drafts. By making Fast Day proclamations rather than calling for a day of thanksgiving as Washington had done, Adams was relying on a New England tradition of having people cease their temporal activities and spend their day in prayer, seeking forgiveness for their transgressions against God. Following that practice, both proclamations urged all citizens to abstain "from their secular occupations, [and] devote the time to the sacred duties of religion" through "solemn humiliation, fasting and prayer." Adams implored his audience to "acknowledge before God the manifold Sins and Transgressions with which we are justly chargeable as Individuals and as a Nation" and to ask for his redemptive forgiveness. Also, in contrast to Washington's modest use of inclusive deific language, Adams's proclamations called clearly on a Christian god: "the great Mediator and Redeemer," a departure that Madison criticized as "present[ing] not only the grossest contradictions to the maxims measures & language of his predecessor, and the real principles & interests of his Constituents, but to himself." And both proclamations tied their necessity to political concerns—the first to "the unfriendly Disposition, Conduct and Demands of a foreign power," and the second, issued after the Federalist-controlled Congress had enacted the Sedition Act, asking God to "withhold us from unreasonable discontent—from disunion, faction, [and] sedition."[53]

Federalist-leaning clergy responded dutifully to Adams's call, delivering sermons that condemned Republicans while connecting them and Thomas Jefferson to French infidelity. In his Fast Day sermon, Congregationalist minister Nathanael Emmons called for uniform "submission to civil authority" because "the laws and measures of the government were calculated to promote the general good." In a reference to Republican opposition, Emmons declared that to "rise up against the government, or disobey the laws of the land" undermines the "submission which [people] owe to civil rulers." "A seditious and disorganizing spirit is extremely contagious," he warned, and "the most peaceable and virtuous citizens are liable to fall victims to the fury and revenge of lawless and ungovernable rebels."[54] Similarly, Jedidiah Morse used his Fast Day sermon to describe the threats of the Illuminati in America. In a less-than-veiled reference to Jefferson, Morse remarked, "And it is well known that some men, high in office, have expressed sentiments in accordant to the principles and views of this society."[55]

Republicans and their aligned clergy generally declined to comply with Adams's proclamations. The Philadelphia *Aurora* wrote on May 9, 1798, that it refused to cease operations on that day: "Because there is nothing in the constitution giving [the government] authority to proclaim fasts . . . because prayer, fasting, and humiliation are matters of religion and conscience, with which government has nothing to do . . . and Because we consider a connection between state and church affairs as dangerous to religious and political freedom and that, therefore, every approach towards it should be discouraged."[56] The *Aurora*'s declaration rang with Jeffersonian-Madisonian sentiments, but Federalist clergy generally disregarded Republicans' church-state arguments. In his 1798 Fast Day sermon, Morse condemned Republican criticisms of the proclamation: "But that we should have men among us, so lost to every principle of religion, morality, and even to common decency, as to reprobate the measure; as to contemn the authority who recommended it, and to denounce it as hypocritical, and designed to effect sinister purposes, is indeed alarming." Morse sought to turn the table by claiming that Republicans were the ones threatening church-state relations by criticizing orthodox clergy. "And what have [the clergy] done to provoke this hostility?" he panned. "Why they have '*preached politics!*'"[57]

In the charged partisan atmosphere, the fast proclamations became proxies for the deep political divisions that were manifested through issues such as the quasi-war with France and the Alien and Sedition Acts. "Party passions are indeed high," Jefferson remarked at the time. "Nobody has more reason to know it than myself." Prior to the day designated by the first proclamation, Adams reported that he received three anonymous letters revealing plots to burn Philadelphia. The two letters that survive asserted that there was "a vile plot" initiated by "Frenchmen," not only "to set fire to several different parts of this City" but to "Massacre man, Woman & Child." One of the letters urged Adams to "look that grandest of all grand Villains. That traitor to his country—that infernal Scoundrel Jefferson—he has too much hand in the Conspiracy." Jefferson dismissed the claims as "idle stories," though he told Madison that "many weak people [had] packed their most valuable moveables to be ready for transportation" in response to the threats.[58]

On the evening of May 9, 1798, the day designated for the first Fast Day observation, competing mobs gathered outside the State House and Adams's residence in Philadelphia, with Republicans wearing French tricolored cockades and Federalists wearing the pro-British black cockades.

Depending on whose account, either "a fray ensued," in Jefferson's words, or a "great riot happened," as one Federalist reported. Adams exclaimed that there were "multitudinous assemblies . . . before my door" that night that were "kept in order only . . . by a military patrol." Other accounts reported that the "federal mob were by far more numerous, more noisy, and more apparently dangerous." The militia disbursed the Republican rioters but "no attempt was made by the magistrate to reduce [the Federalists] to quiet." (A mob of men wearing black cockades also attacked the home of the editor of the *Aurora* that evening, apparently for its audacity to publish on the Fast Day.) Republican and Federalist leaders alike were aghast by the melee though they disagreed on whom to blame. "The scenes of yesterday should be a warning," wrote the *Aurora*. "The President of the United States has publicly denounced the freedom of opinion," and "endeavors are [being made] to silence the freedom of opinions and the freedom of the press."[59] In contrast, Adams, in a written address to the citizens of Hartford, Connecticut, the following day, claimed that "the designs of foreign hostility and the views of domestic treachery are now fully disclosed." He questioned whether "the moderation, dignity, and wisdom of government have awed into silence the clamors of faction, and palsied the thousand tongues of calumny." Later, Adams would refer to the Fast Day riot as an act of "terrorism," scolding Jefferson that "no doubt you was fast asleep in philosophical Tranquility, when ten thousand People, and perhaps many more, were parading the Streets of Philadelphia, on the Evening of my Fast Day" in a "Phrenezy." Madison remarked that Adams's protestations "form[ed] the most grotesque scene in the tragicomedy acting by the Governt." Still, Adams believed that firmer action was necessary.[60]

Whether the 1798 Fast Day riot was a factor, that summer Congress enacted a series of laws penalizing immigrants and criminalizing seditious publications against the government, commonly known as the Alien and Sedition Acts. The first laws, the Naturalization Act and the Aliens Friends Act, extended the time of residence for citizenship from five to fourteen years and authorized the president to expel, without a hearing, any noncitizens the president believed "dangerous to the peace and safety" of the nation. (President Donald Trump relied on the same legal authority to deny entry to foreigners from Muslim countries in 2017–18.)[61] While still a member of Congress in 1795, Madison had resisted earlier Federalist efforts to lengthen the residence for naturalization, in the process chastising a fellow member for making anti-Catholic statements about immigrants. In that incident, Madison remarked that he "did not approve the ridicule attempted to be thrown out on the Roman Catholics," while asserting that "in their religion, there was nothing inconsistent with the purest republicanism."[62] Regarding the alien exclusion law, Jefferson called it "a most detestable thing" designed to undermine all relations with France, whereas Madison described it as a "monster that must forever disgrace its parents."[63]

It was the Sedition Act that caused the greatest consternation among Republicans, including Jefferson and Madison. The law made it illegal to "write, print, utter, or publish . . . any false, scandalous, [or] malicious writing" against the US government or the president (though conveniently not the vice president), thereby muzzling Republican opposition. Jefferson wrote Madison that the sedition law, "among other enormities, undertakes to make printing certain matters criminal, though one of the amendments to the constitution has so expressly taken religion, printing presses &c. out of their coercion." Jefferson and Madison believed that the Sedition Act directly infringed on rights of conscience as protected under the Constitution, substantiating Madison's concern about the ineffectiveness of "parchment barriers." The laws were "so palpably in the teeth of the constitution as to shew [the Federalists] mean to pay no respect to it."[64] Jefferson's and Madison's outrage over the Sedition Act was so great that it led them to draft, respectively, the Kentucky and Virginia Resolutions, which asserted the authority of state legislatures to nullify or defy unconstitutional federal laws. Jefferson's Kentucky Resolutions, drafted first, affirmed, among other things, that "no power over the freedom of religion, freedom of speech, or freedom of the press [was] delegated to the US by the constitution." Madison's Virginia Resolutions similarly charged that "among other essential rights, the liberty of conscience and of the press cannot be cancelled, abridged, restrained or modified by any authority of the United States." Both resolutions emphasized that by infringing on political conscience, "the freedom of religious opinions and exercises" were also at stake. And both expressed concern about the precedent established by such a law; in the words of Jefferson, "insomuch that whatever violates either throws down the sanctuary which covers the others," such that the authority to outlaw political "libels, falsehood and defamation" would apply "equally with heresy & false religion." Both men predicted that the Federalist Party's overreach in enacting the Alien and Sedition Acts would haunt the party and John

Adams. At the time, however, republicanism and conscience rights were under assault, an onslaught Jefferson referred to as "the reign of witches." The conflict over the Sedition Act, including the conviction and imprisonment of a handful of Republican publishers, would lay the groundwork for the first truly partisan presidential election in 1800.[65]

NINE

The Jefferson and Madison Presidencies

T he events of the 1790s set the stage for the bitterly fought presidential election of 1800. This time, there was no suspense whether
Jefferson would challenge Adams for the office. Partisanship ran
high, with Federalists and Republicans alike asserting that the very survival
of the nation turned on the outcome.[1] Partisans on both sides attacked the
opposing candidate's character and distorted his political stances. Adams
was "a lover of monarchy" and "would make a very good king," critics
sneered, proceeding to rename him "His Rotundity." If Adams were to be
reelected, warned the *Aurora*, people would need to "prepare themselves
for the calm of despotism" and "the destruction of their liberties."[2] Jefferson,
in contrast, was portrayed as a disciple of Voltaire and Robespierre and
friend of Paine, ready to import the horrors of the French Revolution to
America. Federalists labeled Jefferson and Republicans "Jacobins," who in
every country "are destitute of religion and morality," the *Connecticut Courant* wrote. "Our own [Republicans] are as depraved, and they only will
await an opportunity, to be as cruel and abandoned, as those in France."
If Jefferson was elected, the *Courant* continued, "there is scarcely a possibility that we shall escape a *Civil War*." Federalists also resurrected the
Mazzei letter to remind voters of Jefferson's disrespect for the recently de-
ceased Washington and demonstrate his lack of temperament to be president. According to one estimate, the number of pamphlets distributed by
opponents and supporters of Jefferson exceeded one hundred, with several opposition tracts going through multiple printings. Although many of
the pamphlets were spontaneous, Federalist activists corresponded among

themselves through "a very extensive and coordinated effort," sharing the most damning charges and embarrassing tidbits.[3]

A popular topic for Federalist propagandists was Jefferson's religion, as it fit neatly with allegations about his Francophilia and radical political views; as Alexander Hamilton summed up the connection, Jefferson was "an *Atheist* in Religion and a *Fanatic* in politics."[4] Federalist pamphleteers labeled Jefferson a "deist," an "infidel," and an "atheist" who disputed the scriptures and whose election would invite God's wrath on the nation. He would erect temples for expounding on *The Age of Reason* and "endow colleges and professors for the propagation of deism and anarchy."[5]

Pamphleteers eagerly used Jefferson's own writings against him. Their favorite source was his *Notes on the State of Virginia,* where he had disputed the authenticity of miracles and famously declared that "it does me no injury for my neighbour to say there are twenty gods, or no god." "Ponder well this paragraph," wrote Presbyterian minister John M. Mason in his widely circulated *The Voice of Warning to Christians.* "Ten thousand impieties and mischiefs lurk in its womb." Jefferson's indifference to whether there were twenty gods or no god demonstrated his "disregard to the religion of Jesus Christ" and proved him to be "a confirmed infidel" who promoted "the morality of devils." Mason warned his readers that "[a] crisis of no common magnitude awaits our country" if Jefferson were elected, through the rise in immorality and the ensuing wrath of God.[6] Another widely circulated pamphlet was Presbyterian William Linn's *Serious Considerations on the Election of a President,* which also quoted extensively from Jefferson's *Notes.* Linn charged that Jefferson's "disbelief of the Holy Scriptures, . . . his rejection of the Christian Religion and open profession of Deism" disqualified him from the presidency. He was "a true infidel, . . . being directly opposite to divine revelation." The effect of his election would be "to destroy religion, introduce immorality, and loosen all the bonds of society." Summing up the allegations, Noah Webster insisted that Jefferson and his Republican followers were "a set of unprincipled and abandoned democrats, deists, atheists, adulterers, and profligate men" who would "lead down the people to destruction!"[7]

Federalist clergy across the nation went to their pulpits to condemn Jefferson and the Republicans. Nineteenth-century Jefferson biographer Henry S. Randall related that "in more than half the pulpits in New England [Jefferson] was publicly . . . stigmatized in 'sermons' preached on Sunday, as an 'atheist' or 'French infidel,' and the people were exhorted . . . [if] they valued their own safety and religious freedom, to vote against so impious a wretch." Reverend James Abercrombie, the successor to William White at Philadelphia's Christ Church, told his congregation to "beware of ever placing at the Head of Civil Society a man who is not an avowed Christian and an exemplary believer in the Holy Religion." Parishioners reputedly reacted to the sermons by hiding copies of the Bible in anticipation of a Republican victory and subsequent purge.[8]

The Federalist press fueled many of the incendiary charges. The press had already dissected Jefferson's *Notes* during the 1796 election, criticizing his rationalist French leanings. Now, the *Gazette of the United States* labeled Jefferson a "howling Atheist" for his reputed indifference to religion as revealed in the *Notes*. The *Gazette* ran the same prominent advertisement for successive weeks throughout the fall of 1800: "The Grand Question" presented by the election was whether voters would choose "GOD—AND A RELIGIOUS PRESIDENT; Or impiously declare for JEFFERSON—AND NO GOD!!!"[9] And the *New-England Palladium* charged with similar hyperbole: "Should the infidel Jefferson be elected to the Presidency, the *seal of death* is that moment set on our holy religion, our churches will be prostrated, and some infamous prostitute, under the title of the Goddess of Reason, will preside in the Sanctuaries now devoted to the worship of the Most High."[10] The *Gazette* encouraged ministers to attack Jefferson, chastising those "*lukewarm Clergy,* who have not yet come forward, at a time when the Christian Religion is so much threatened. . . . Will a Christian minister pause one moment to what side he will take? Will he forsake his Religion and his Saviour . . . and by his silence forward the election of an Infidel?"[11]

Republican newspapers and pamphleteers fought back against the Federalists' charges; this time, however, they vigorously defended Jefferson's religious character. Not only was Jefferson neither an atheist nor a deist, he was "a *real christian,*" "an excellent Christian," and an "adorer of our God." "Grotius," the pseudonym of future senator and New York governor DeWitt Clinton, strongly defended Jefferson's *Notes* and other writings, asserting that they "abound with just and elevated ideas of the Deity and his attributes."[12] Other Republican pamphleteers agreed that his *Notes* "not only declare the excellence of a Deity and religion—not only acknowledge the heavenly attributes of the Almighty, but inculcate the belief of a particular superintending providence, tenets which are peculiarly applicable to the serious Christian only." Abraham Bishop asserted that Jefferson, "in his writings, has spoken reverently of the Christian religion, and has for years supported at his own expense a preacher of the gospel." He was "a man of unquestionable morality both in theory and practice."[13] In return, Republicans charged Federalists and orthodox clergy with hypocrisy for ignoring the deistic inclinations of fellow Federalists, in particular Hamilton's favored presidential candidate, General Charles Cotesworth Pinckney. "Mr. Pinckney is a deist!!!" exclaimed "Marcus Brutus," and "Mr. Jefferson is at least as good a Christian as Mr. Adams, and in all probability a much better one."[14]

Significantly, the controversy over Jefferson's religious beliefs and his advocacy for religious freedom initiated a far-reaching debate about the latter topic. Federalists asserted that his defense of religious freedom, most clearly represented in his Statute for Establishing Religious Freedom, demonstrated his "disregard for religion." Jefferson was "an enemy to all religious establishments," decried the Gazette of the United State, as if that was a fault. "That so very important an assertion should not rest in doubt." In another edition, the Gazette complained that the "condition of Church and State in America is such as to fill every considerate mind with the most unhappy sensations." The problem lay in the "vanity and fastitidousness" of those who drafted the First Amendment (i.e., Madison), which "preclude[s] any connection [between church and state]." A "strict and indissoluble alliance of religion to government has been ordained in the nature of things," an order that was "likely to perish" with Jefferson's election. The Gazette warned voters that "here, Sir, Jacobinism is triumphant, and unless a different tempter shall soon shew itself, it will soon trample underfoot all order, law, property, as it has done [to] religion."[15]

Orthodox clergy also attacked Jefferson's stance on church and state. John Mason bemoaned that the "Federal Constitution makes no acknowledgment of that God who gave us our national existence." Because of that omission, and based on the sentiments contained in his statute, Jefferson would fulfill "his favorite wish, to see a government administered without any religious principle." William Linn agreed: if Jefferson were elected, he would maintain "a government in which no religious opinions were held, and where the security for property and social order rested entirely upon the force of laws."[16]

Republicans again did not shirk from the Federalists' charges, this time about the ordering of church-state relationships. Rather, Republican pamphleteers embraced the Jeffersonian-Madisonian perspective. Clinton praised Jefferson for his unyielding advocacy for disestablishment and religious freedom. "The boundaries between civil power and liberty in religious matters are clearly marked and determined," Clinton asserted. "For if the magistrate be possessed of a power to restrain and punish any principles relating to religion, . . . [then] religious liberty is entirely at an end." He called for drawing a firm "line" between the two entities. Another pamphleteer maintained that "more than half of our present troubles, as a nation, have originated from the religious establishments in the [New England] States, and want of due obedience to our constitution and laws, as to religious freedom." In contrast, Virginia "has enjoyed peace and liberty without conspiracies of bigotry and spiritual tyranny for twenty years," due to Jefferson's influence. The author called for "put[ting] an end to persecutions, jealousies, rancors and delusions, resulting from the union of church and state, by political establishments."[17] The *Aurora* also praised Jefferson's stance on church and state, noting that "toleration in religion, complete and perfect, was not known . . . before our revolution." Jefferson was largely responsible for this change, the *Aurora* asserted. He was "the author and mover of those laws which put down the [state] church [in Virginia] and abolished tythes." In contrast, "The New England states alone support intolerance." The *Aurora* called on Adams to renounce the "union of old Whig and old Tories, of church and state" in Massachusetts and "do as Mr. Jefferson did" by supporting disestablishment.[18]

An exceptionally strong defense of Jefferson's church-state views appeared in a pamphlet written by New York lawyer Tunis Wortman. Like his fellow Republicans, Wortman defended Jefferson's religious beliefs, calling him "a christian" and "a republican" worthy of public office. Wortman also embraced disestablishment and church-state separation: "Religion and government are equally necessary, but their interests should be kept separate and distinct. No legitimate connection can ever subsist between them. Upon no plan, no system, can they become united, without endangering the purity and usefulness of both—the church will corrupt the state, and the state pollute the church. Christianity becomes no longer the religion of God—it becomes the religion of temporal craft and expediency and policy." Wortman insisted that "the establishment of Christianity, is incompatible with civil freedom." Even formal disestablishment was insufficient. He charged his readers that it "is your duty, as christians, to maintain the purity and independence of the church, to keep religion separate from politics, to prevent an union between the church and the state, and to preserve your clergy from temptation, corruption, and reproach." He called on Christians "to keep things sacred from intermingling with things prophane, to maintain religion separate and apart from the powers of the world." For Wortman, separationism was essential for maintaining religious freedom: "The inevitable consequence of an union of the church with the state, will be the mutual destruction of both."[19] All in all, the religious debate of the 1800 election demonstrated that the Jeffersonian-Madisonian ideas about freedom of conscience and church-state separation had made inroads into the larger culture. Federalists believed their model of church-state relations was under assault, while Republicans felt their conception was ascendent.[20]

Jefferson withstood the assault on his religious character and won the election. He remained silent throughout the ordeal, writing James Monroe during the campaign that it had "been so impossible to contradict all of their lies, that I have determined to contradict none; for while I should be engaged with one, they would publish twenty new ones." The accusations still stung, with Jefferson remarking that "as to the calumny of atheism, I am so broken to calumnies of every kind." Based on the 1796 election, however, the attacks were not unexpected, with Jefferson noting that the New England states would "be the last to come over, on account of the dominion of the clergy, who had got a smell of union between church & state."[21] Following the election, Jefferson exclaimed to Joseph Priestley, "What an effort, my dear Sir, of bigotry in Politics & Religion have we gone through." He also told Benjamin Rush that his religious opinions had been "the cause of their printing lying pamphlets against me, forging conversations for me . . . which are absolute falsehoods without a circumstance of truth to rest on." The attacks by the clergy, however, had simply reconfirmed his beliefs, "for I have sworn upon the altar of God, eternal hostility against every form of tyranny over the mind of man."[22]

The extent to which the religious aspect to the election affected the outcome is an open question, though its impact was not insignificant. At least Adams thought it constituted a significant factor, later telling Rush that the "National Fast, recommended by me turned me out of Office." "A general Suspicion prevailed that the Presbyterian Church was ambitious and aimed at an Establishment as a National Church. I was represented as a Presbyterian and at the head of this political and ecclesiastical Project. The Secret

Whisper ran through them all the Sects 'Let Us have Jefferson Madison, Burr, any body, whether they be Philosophers, Deist or even Atheists, rather than a Presbyterian President.'" Adams refused to acknowledge that his Federalist supporters shared much of the blame for politicizing religious matters. By the time he wrote Rush in 1812, however, Adams admitted that his Fast Day proclamations had been a mistake and had inflamed religious dissension. He acknowledged that hatred of religious establishments was "at the Bottom of the Unpopularity of national Fasts and Thanksgivings." As he concluded, "Nothing is more dreaded than the National Government meddling with Religion."[23]

The Jefferson Presidency

Jefferson's election as president was not secure until the House of Representatives voted to break the electoral college tie between Jefferson and his putative running mate, Aaron Burr (with Alexander Hamilton urging Federalist representatives to vote for Jefferson as the lesser of two evils).[24] Jefferson faced the daunting task of uniting the nation after a bruising election fueled by partisanship. In his inaugural address of March 4, 1801, he adopted a conciliatory tone, emphasizing that "every difference of opinion is not a difference of principle." As he famously declared, "We are all republicans; we are all federalists." Maintaining that theme of unity, Jefferson wrote that Americans were "enlightened by a benign religion, professed indeed and practised in various forms, yet all of them inculcating honesty, truth, temperance, gratitude and the love of man, acknowledging and adoring an overruling providence." With its passing reference to providence, the statement celebrated the values of religious pluralism and nonsectarianism. He called on Congress to encourage "the diffusion of information, and arraignment of all abuses at the bar of the public reason," including "freedom of religion [and] freedom of the press." These "principles form[ed] the bright constellation" making the United States "the world's best hope."[25]

All those values were high on Jefferson's list. Despite asking people to "unite with one heart and one mind," Jefferson reminded his audience that even in a representative government which operated through majority rule, "that will, to be rightful, must be reasonable; that the minority possess their equal rights, which equal laws must protect, and to violate would be oppression." And in a reference to not only the progress of religious freedom but also the trials of the previous decade, Jefferson remarked, "Let us reflect that having banished from our land that religious intolerance under which mankind so long bled and suffered, we have yet gained little if we countenance a political intolerance, as despotic, as wicked, and capable of as bitter and bloody persecutions."[26]

In a possible move to diffuse persistent concerns about his religious faith, Jefferson concluded his address with a nondenominational benedictory similar to those given by George Washington: "May that infinite power, which rules the destinies of the universe, lead our councils to what is best, and give them a favorable issue for your peace and prosperity." As with his two deific references in the Declaration of Independence, the conclusion employed a rationalist pseudonym for God; however, Jefferson was not averse to employing deific language. In his Second Inaugural Address, Jefferson noted "the goodness of that Being" who favored the nation with "pleasing circumstances," while affirming "the large measure of thankfulness we owe for His bounty." But Jefferson's religious affirmations stopped considerably short of those of Adams and even Washington. And though expressing "thankfulness" to God, Jefferson declined to issue thanksgiving proclamations during his administration.[27]

Despite offering an olive branch in his First Inaugural Address, Jefferson remained embittered about the slanders and misrepresentations he had experienced at the hands of the Federalist press and orthodox clergy. The attacks from the latter only cemented his anticlerical leanings. Within three weeks of his conciliatory inaugural address, Jefferson referred to the clergy as "barbarians" who "live[d] by mystery & charlatanerie" to maintain their power. A week later, Jefferson wrote Massachusetts Republican leader Elbridge Gerry a lengthy letter complaining how the clergy—"the ravenous crew"—"live by the zeal they can kindle, & the schisms they can create." The clergy had used "their lying faculties beyond their ordinary state, to reagitate the public mind" against "the mild and simple principles of the Christian philosophy." Jefferson thought it no wonder that the people of New England had "drunk deeper of the delusion, & [were] therefore slower in recovering from it. The aegis of government & the temples of religion & of justice have all been prostituted" by the clergy, "toll[ing] us back to the times when we burnt witches." And in August 1801, Jefferson complained to his attorney general, Levi Lincoln, about the "heaping of abuse on me personally" from the "monarchical federalists" and the "Clerical paper" (the

New-England Palladium). "From the clergy I expect no mercy," Jefferson wrote. Anyone who espoused principles of rational, primitive Christianity "must expect the extreme of their wrath."[28]

Letter to the Danbury Baptists

In early 1802, Jefferson decided to make a public statement about his views on church and state. The opportunity presented itself through a letter he received from a group of Connecticut Baptists following his election. At the time, Connecticut maintained the most oppressive religious establishment where Baptists and other dissenters were at the mercy of the Congregationalist Standing Order for exemptions from religious assessments. In October 1801, elders from the Danbury Baptist Association, representing some twenty-six churches, wrote Jefferson congratulating him on his election to "the chief Magistracy of the United States," which "America's God has raised you up to fill," and commending him for his commitment to religious freedom. The Baptists complained, however, that in Connecticut, "religion is considered as the first object of Legislation," and that they enjoyed religious privileges only "as favors granted, and not as inalienable rights." They pleaded to Jefferson for an expression of support for their dilemma.[29]

Jefferson realized that a letter could provide a venue to correct the misrepresentations expressed during the campaign about his commitment to religious freedom and to strengthen an alliance with an important political constituency. He sent a draft of his response to his attorney general, Levi Lincoln, with an accompanying note stating that he saw the opportunity "by way of answering, of sowing useful truths and principles among the people, which might germinate and become rooted among their political tenets." One truth was to condemn "the alliance between church and state." Jefferson told Lincoln that he also wanted to explain to his critics "why I do not proclaim fastings & thanksgivings, as my predecessors did." Jefferson was still wincing over the attacks on his religious beliefs by the orthodox clergy—which were ongoing—so he saw a response as a way to strike back at his detractors. As Jefferson continued to Lincoln, "I know it will give great offense to the New England clergy; but the advocate for religious freedom is to expect neither peace nor forgiveness from them."[30] Finally, Jefferson hoped that writing the Baptists might encourage Connecticut Republicans to put aside their suspicions of evangelicals and work together on common goals. That tactic apparently worked as afterward, Republican newspapers endorsed the Baptist petition drive for an exemption and helped form a coalition to work on eventual disestablishment.[31]

Lincoln responded favorably but advised Jefferson to remove the criticism of fast and thanksgiving proclamations, which were highly favored in New England, even among religious dissenters. Jefferson also shared a copy of his draft with the other New Englander in his cabinet, Postmaster General Gideon Granger. Granger was more enthusiastic about Jefferson's reply, praising it as a "declaration of Truths which are in fact felt by a great Majority of New England, & publicly acknowledged by near half of the People of Connecticut." He was also less concerned about possible negative reactions, writing that the letter would "undoubtedly give great Offence to the established Clergy of New England while it will delight the Dissenters." But it was worth giving "a temporary Spasm among the Established Religionists . . . because it will 'germinate among the People' and in time fix 'their political Tenets.'" Granger urged that not "a Sentence [be] changed, or a Sentiment [be] expressed [less] equivocally."[32] Jefferson followed Lincoln's recommendation by removing the passage about religious proclamations but otherwise retained what Granger praised. His letter to the Danbury Baptists stated,

> Believing with you that religion is a matter which lies solely between man and his God, that he owes account to none other for his faith or his worship, that the legislative powers of government reach actions only, and not opinions, I contemplate with sovereign reverence that act of the whole American people which declared that their legislature should "make no law respecting an establishment of religion, or prohibiting the free exercise thereof," thus building a wall of separation between Church and State. Adhering to this expression of the supreme will of the nation in behalf of the rights of conscience, I shall see with sincere satisfaction the progress of those sentiments which tend to restore to man all his natural rights, convinced he has no natural right in opposition to his social duties.[33]

Jefferson's brief response made four essential points: first, that religious convictions were personal matters between people and God, such that one's religious obligations flowed only to their conception of god; second, affirming the sentiment in the Baptists' letter, that rights of conscience were inalienable, natural rights, not granted by civil government; third, that religious and civil authorities operated in distinct spheres, such that government lacked jurisdiction over religious matters; and last, that all of these principles were furthered by the separation of church and state, a reinforcing concept best represented through the symbolism of a wall. Jefferson's use of the wall metaphor was not novel. The idea of a wall or barrier separating religious and civil realms reached back to medieval times and through the Reformation, and the phrase likely sprung to Jefferson's mind based on his reading from a variety of authors including the Anglican apologist Richard Hooker and the Whig propagandist James Burgh, the latter having called for building "an impenetrable wall of separation between things sacred and civil. . . . The less the church had state had to do with one another, it would be better for both."[34]

Jefferson hoped his letter would "sow . . . useful truths & principles" that would "germinate and become rooted" as a political tenet, but that goal would take another two decades in Connecticut. Still, New England newspapers reprinted the letter, so he initially succeeded in reaching a larger audience. The Boston *Independent Chronicle* reported that "the Danbury Baptist Association has addressed the President of the United States, and have confirmed from his lips, their favorite truth—that 'religion is a matter which lies solely between a man and his God.'"[35] After the initial attention given to the letter, however, it was largely forgotten. In 1854, Congress commissioned a collection of Jefferson's letters, which included a copy of the Danbury letter. Its publication there may have served as the source for a reference to the wall metaphor by future attorney general Jeremiah S. Black in an 1856 address on "Religious Liberty." Without identifying either Jefferson or the Danbury letter as the source, Black remarked that the founders had intended "to have a *State without religion,* and a *Church without politics.* . . . For that reason they built up a wall of complete and perfect partition between the two." Whether Black's speech served as the basis for the Supreme Court's first use of the Danbury letter two decades later in the case of *Reynolds v. United States* (1879) is unclear. However, in that decision Chief Justice Morrison Waite identified Jefferson's authorship, asserting that the letter was "an authoritative declaration of the scope and effect of the [First] amendment." Waite's reference to the letter thus placed it in the public domain where it became available for future use. Ironically, even though the phrase came to encapsulate Jefferson's stance on religious freedom, there is no record that he ever used the metaphor again.[36]

Ever since the Supreme Court pronounced the constitutional significance of Jefferson's Danbury letter, jurists, politicians, scholars, and popular writers have dissected its meaning and influence. Separationist-leaning jurists and scholars have embraced the wall concept and the church-state principles contained in the letter. First Amendment scholar Leonard W. Levy wrote that the wall metaphor represented Jefferson's "powerful convictions on the subject of establishment and religious freedom. . . . [But] the wall is not just a metaphor. It has constitutional existence."[37] In contrast, those who have sought to dismantle Jefferson's wall have adopted several lines of attack. One approach, examined below, has been to highlight inconsistencies between the letter's declaration and those actions Jefferson undertook that were less than separationist: permitting the new Capitol building to be used for religious services and approving a treaty with an Indian tribe that included money for a Catholic mission.[38] Another critique has focused on the specific language in the letter, arguing that in using the word "church" rather than "religion," Jefferson opposed an alliance between ecclesiastical institutions and the government but not connections between the state and religion.[39] This latter critique falls short; while it is true that Jefferson expressed greater concern about the tyranny of ecclesiastical institutions and government control over the same, he was also using common nomenclature—"church and state"—rather than imposing a limitation by those words. Jefferson's body of work demonstrates a lifelong concern about the intermixing of religion and government on multiple levels, not solely institutionally.[40]

A final critique claims that Jefferson was not sincere about the sentiments expressed in the letter—that he had ulterior motives for sending his reply, which undermine its principles. After all, in his notes to Lincoln and Granger, Jefferson expressed hope that his reply would "give great offense to the New England clergy." This comment, considered in light of Jefferson's other anticlerical statements, has led critics to assert that the Danbury letter says less about Jefferson's true sentiments and that his "principal motive in writing the Danbury letter was to mount a political counterattack against his Federalist enemies." Professor Edwin Corwin raised this charge following the *Everson* decision, asserting that the Danbury letter "was not improbably motivated by an impish desire to heave a brick at the Congregationalist-Federalist hierarchy of Connecticut, whose leading members had denounced him two years before as an 'infidel' and 'atheist.'"

In essence, the Danbury letter was not a principled statement of his beliefs but an opportunistic broadside on political opponents.[41]

Like the other critiques, this one also falls short of the mark. That Jefferson may have had several reasons for writing the letter is undoubtedly true. But for this critique to be convincing, it would need to show that the letter's sentiments were inconsistent with Jefferson's previous writings and actions on the subject. His *Notes on the State of Virginia* and Statute for Establishing Religious Freedom—along with the host of personal correspondence already considered—belie the claim that his reply was not a principled statement about church-state relations. To be certain, the reply was written within a political context—to counter entrenched clerical resistance to efforts of Baptists and other dissenters to attain religious equality. But most of Jefferson's and Madison's writings on religion and government occurred in a political context; "once church and state are entangled, as they were in Connecticut," writes Michael Meyerson, "any discussion of religion is necessarily political."[42] Thomas E. Buckley agreed that Jefferson was "expressing his own deeply held convictions about the church-state relationship" while he was "condemn[ing] the Federalist position and welcome[ing] his new-found Baptist allies into the Republican fold." That Jefferson's motives for writing the Danbury letter were intertwined does not make his declaration insincere.[43]

As noted, critics of the principles enunciated in the Danbury letter have pointed to actions that Jefferson took while president that reputedly contradicted the letter's separationist sentiments. One action was that Jefferson occasionally attended worship services that were regularly held in the new Capitol building, the implication being that Jefferson did not oppose using government-owned structures for religious activities and that he willingly attended those services—according to one critic, Jefferson's "attendance at church services in the House was, then, his way of offering symbolic support for religious faith and for its beneficent role in republican government." In fact, critics note that only two days after sending his reply to the Danbury Baptists, Jefferson attended a service in the House chamber to hear a sermon by his Baptist ally Reverend John Leland.[44]

This is a curious critique, as its promoters readily acknowledge that as president, Jefferson had no control over the uses of the Capitol building, which was managed by Congress, so he had no authority to prevent its religious uses. This critique also minimizes the fact that in 1801, Washington

City had few permanent structures—the Capitol, the White House, and the War and Treasury building constituting the bulk—with the first church sanctuary not constructed until 1807. The Capitol was the primary building capable of holding a large audience, and most government officials attended worship services there. Jefferson occasionally attended services in the Capitol out of convenience and depending on the nature of the event (Jefferson also occasionally attended services at the Episcopal Christ Church parish, which were held in a tobacco barn). It exaggerates matters, however, to assert that this practice indicated that Jefferson endorsed government and religious intermixing or that it contradicted his separationist sentiments. Since the founding period, government buildings—such as public schools—have been used for religious activities and in 1993, the Supreme Court ruled that it did *not* violate the establishment clause to allow religious uses of government buildings.[45]

A possibly more significant contradiction between principle and practice involved a treaty between the US government and the Kaskaskia Indian tribe that Jefferson submitted to Congress in 1803. The tribe agreed to cede a significant tract of land in what would become Illinois in exchange for an annuity of $1,000 of general support plus a $100 annuity for seven years for "the support of a priest" of the Catholic Church (with an additional one-time grant of $300 to erect a church building). Separationist critic Robert Cord insists that the monetary provisions indicate that Jefferson did not oppose government financial assistance to religion on a nondiscriminatory basis or the government's collaboration with religious institutions.[46]

The critique about the treaty with the Kaskaskia Indians demonstrates the problem with extracting a particular event out of its larger context to prove what appears to be a contradiction under today's standards. The complex and disheartening history of the relationship between the European settlers to North American and the continent's Indigenous peoples is beyond the scope of this study, but from the 1600s to the early twentieth century, white Americans tied the "civilizing" of Indians to their conversion to Christianity.[47] All of the colonial governments supported converting American Natives to Christianity as a means of subduing and assimilating the Indigenous peoples, a practice continued by the new national government. The Second Continental Congress directed that Indian agents should "instruct [Natives] in the Christian religion," and in 1785 the Confederation Congress provided a land grant to Moravians for the purpose of "civilizing the Indians and promoting Christianity." In George Washington's reply to the Moravians, he praised their efforts "to civilize and Christianize the Savages of the Wilderness," and during his first administration, Secretary of War Henry Knox proposed appointing missionaries "of excellent moral character" among the Indians to instruct them in matters of religion, farming, and husbandry. In 1796, Congress enacted a law providing a land grant to the Moravians for the purpose of "propagating the Gospel among the Heathen." Government support of religious groups to instruct Indians in Christian morals and to train them in industry was a common practice.[48]

Jefferson, as a person of his time, accepted many of the assumptions about the need to bring "civilization" to Native Americans. Jefferson wrote extensively about America's Indigenous peoples in his *Notes on the State of Virginia*, and unlike many contemporaries, he believed that Indians were not inferior but were "on a level with Whites in the same uncultivated state." As he wrote a French acquaintance, "I believe the Indian then to be in body and mind equal to the whiteman." Indians were proto-republicans who had lived in a state of nature, a situation that could no longer coexist within contemporary American society. Therefore, they had to be taught reading, writing, and self-sufficiency skills. Writing in 1805, Jefferson declared that our "humanity enjoins us to teach them agriculture & the domestic arts; to encourage them to that industry which alone can enable them to maintain their place in existence, & to prepare them in time for that state of society, which to bodily comforts adds the improvement of the mind & morals." In two letters written to Quaker and Methodist missionaries at the end of his presidency, Jefferson commended their emphasis on teaching mathematics, writing, and the "habits of industry" rather than concentrating on religious indoctrination, praising the missionaries for having "begun at the right end for civilising these people" by "prepar[ing] their minds for the first elements of science, & afterwards for moral & religious instruction. To begin with the last has ever ended either in effecting nothing, or ingrafting bigotry on ignorance."[49]

Thus, Jefferson's goal was to bring education and habits of industry to Native Americans, not to convert them, particularly through government financial support. Almost exclusively, however, the means of accomplishing that former goal was through religious missions and societies. That said, the treaty with the Kaskaskia Indians was not written under Jefferson's direction but was negotiated by territorial governor William Henry Harrison, who was responsible for its various provisions. The Kaskaskia had had an earlier relationship with French trappers and priests, and many had converted to Catholicism. The provision for financial support for a priest and a church building was thus a negotiated condition, two among several, and the treaty expressly provided that the stipend for the priest was for him to perform "the duties of his office, and also to instruct as many of their children as possible, in the rudiments of literature," the latter being a goal of which Jefferson approved. Finally, Jefferson submitted the Kaskaskia treaty to the Senate along with treaty requests for thirteen other Indian tribes, suggesting his involvement was chiefly ministerial. Based on the foregoing context, it is difficult to see that the Kaskaskia treaty with its funding provision represents a significant contradiction from Jefferson's overall stance on church-state matters.[50]

Jefferson was likely focused on the beneficial results of the treaty rather than on its contents. Prior to the ratification of the treaty, Jefferson shared a draft of his third annual address to Congress with Madison where he discussed the Kaskaskia treaty. In a memorandum to Jefferson, Madison recommended "omit[ing] the detail of the stipulated considerations, and particularly, that of the Roman Catholic Pastor. The jealousy of some may see in it a principle, not according with the exemption of Religion from Civil power." Jefferson, who apparently had not thought it through, agreed with Madison and deleted the details, substituting more general language about how the treaty would provide "our patronage and protection, and give them certain annual aids in money, in implements of agriculture, and other articles of their choice." Whether that change indicates that Jefferson agreed there was a potential conflict is uncertain; he may simply have thought it better to follow Madison's advice that "in the Indian Treaty [the provision] will be less noticed than in a President's Speech."[51]

Jefferson's "Religious Pilgrimage"

Throughout his two terms as president, Jefferson was consumed with matters of statecraft and had few opportunities to speak or write about religious matters on a public level. In his Second Inaugural Address, however, he responded to criticism about his refusal to issue prayer or thanksgiving proclamations. Jefferson wrote that "in matters of Religion, I have considered that it's free exercise is placed by the constitution independant of the powers of the general government. I have therefore undertaken, on no occasion, to prescribe the religious exercises suited to it." Religious pronouncements were to be left, he continued, "as the constitution found them, under the direction & discipline of the state or church authorities acknowledged by the several religious societies."[52] By distinguishing the authority of the "general government"—that is, the federal government—from that of the states, his statement could be taken to indicate that he did not oppose official acknowledgments of religion but merely felt that he was constrained by the establishment clause's restriction on the federal government. Possible support for this interpretation is found in Jefferson's endorsement of religious proclamations during the 1770s. Also, near the end of his administration, Jefferson responded to a letter from Presbyterian minister Samuel Miller, who, on behalf of a group of New York clergy, requested that he issue a proclamation for a day of "Fasting, Humiliation and Prayer" or, alternatively, merely "*recommend* such a public observance."[53] Jefferson replied graciously that he did "not think myself authorised to comply with [the request]":

> I consider the government of the US as interdicted by the constitution from intermedling with religious institutions, their doctrines, discipline, or exercises. This results not only from the provision that no law shall be made respecting the establishment, or free exercise, of religion, but from that also which reserves to the states the powers not delegated to the US [i.e., the Tenth Amendment]. Certainly no power to prescribe any religious exercise, or to assume authority in religious discipline, has been delegated to the general government. It must then rest with the states, as far as it can be in any human authority.[54]

This statement, distinguishing the powers of the federal government from those of the states and acknowledging that the establishment clause restricted federal matters only, might reinforce an interpretation that Jefferson's opposition to religious proclamations was qualified, and that he viewed the First Amendment chiefly as a jurisdictional provision.[55]

That Jefferson, Madison, and their contemporaries understood that the First Amendment—like other provisions of the Bill of Rights—only restricted powers of the federal government is uncontested. They recognized that states could engage in certain religious functions to the extent permitted by their state constitutions and laws. This acknowledgment, however, is not an endorsement of state practices—their work in disestablishing

Virginia and Madison's failed constitutional amendment to restrict state infringements on rights of conscience belies such an interpretation. In the same reply to Reverend Miller, Jefferson explained why he could not—or would not—merely *recommend* an observance. In addition to stating that he lacked that authority, he expressed concern that even an informal recommendation might still carry "some degree of proscription perhaps in public opinion." Speaking more generally, he declared, "I do not believe it is for the interest of religion to invite the civil magistrate to direct it's exercises, its discipline or its doctrines." Here, Jefferson was likely responding to Miller's statement that it was "possible that your views of the subject might forbid you to take such a step as that which is proposed, under any circumstances." Seen in that context, Jefferson was communicating that he did not think it was appropriate, "under any circumstances," for a public official to issue a proclamation. The address and letter were also consistent with Jefferson's practice of not revealing his religious views to the general public and his desire to avoid additional scrutiny of them by religious conservatives. Emphasizing jurisdictional rationales for refusing to make religious pronouncements was a convenient way to deflect the issue.[56]

Jefferson's presidency came at a crucial time in his personal life as he was reevaluating the relationship between his religious beliefs and Christianity. Jefferson's "religious pilgrimage" had begun a decade earlier, shortly after advising his nephew to "question with boldness even the existence of a god."[57] In July 1789, he had written Richard Price, the liberal London minister whom he had met while serving as minister to France, about recommending readings into Socinianism (the forerunner to Unitarianism). Price responded by sending Jefferson several pamphlets by Dr. Joseph Priestley, the scientist and leader of British Unitarianism.[58] That introduction led Jefferson to read Priestley's *An History of the Corruptions of Christianity* sometime after 1793. Priestley wrote that Jesus had been a great moral teacher but had made no claims to being divine. Early church leaders had corrupted Jesus's simple message by introducing false doctrines like the Virgin Birth, substitutional atonement, original sin, and the Trinity as a way to awe the heathens and maintain power over the laity. Priestley insisted that Unitarianism represented the original and purest form of Christianity. Priestley's work was an epiphany for Jefferson, as it persuaded him that he could be a Christian despite rejecting the Trinity and other church doctrines. Priestley had not gone as far as Jefferson in his heterodoxy, with the former asserting that God had chosen Jesus for a divine mission and endowed him with powers to perform miracles, actions that Jefferson believed contradicted laws of nature.[59] But those differences did not prevent Jefferson from embracing the core of Priestley's thesis, which he described as "establish[ing] the groundwork of my view of this subject" and serving "as the basis of my own faith." Decades later, Jefferson told John Adams that he had read Priestley's *Corruptions of Christianity* "over and over again." In 1794, Priestley fled from Britain to Philadelphia to escape persecution; there he met Jefferson and the two established a friendship that lasted until Priestley's death in 1804.[60]

Priestley's writings did not change the substance of Jefferson's beliefs; they merely allowed Jefferson to place them within the framework of a broad form of Christian Unitarianism. By reinforcing Jefferson's doubts about Jesus's divinity and core church doctrines, Priestley also allowed Jefferson to embrace Jesus as a great moral teacher. Writing to Priestley in 1803, Jefferson asserted that Jesus's "system of morality was the most benevolent & sublime probably that has been ever taught," calling him "the most eloquent and sublime character that ever has been exhibited to man." In another letter written at the same time, Jefferson declared that "the moral precepts of Jesus, [are] more pure, correct, & sublime than those of the antient philosophers," and that "the morality of Jesus, as taught by himself & freed from the corruptions of later times, is far superior."[61]

Jefferson's renewed acceptance of Christianity, with a Unitarian thrust and emphasis on Jesus's moral mission, led him to contemplate whether there could be a unifying form of moralistic, rational Christianity on which all people of good faith could agree. These explorations were encouraged by his friend Dr. Benjamin Rush, the Philadelphia physician and social reformer. Although Rush held more conventional religious beliefs about Jesus's divine mission and substitutional atonement, he agreed with Jefferson on identifying the essential and purer precepts of Christianity, with an emphasis on virtue and morality. Still, Rush sought to elicit from a reticent Jefferson some clearer declaration of his beliefs, fearing that the accusations of deism, if not infidelity, might be true. Writing Jefferson during the 1800 election, Rush recollected "with pleasure the many delightful hours we have spent together" in discussion and reminded him that "you promised when we parted . . . to send me your religious Creed." Jefferson replied that "I promised you a letter on Christianity, which I have not forgotten," but that he was distracted by other matters (i.e., the election) so he needed "much more time necessary" to prepare a response. As a preview, however, he told Rush that he had "a view of the subject which ought to displease neither the rational Christian or Deist."[62]

Jefferson's promised response came three years later, but not until after he had read Joseph Priestley's new pamphlet *Socrates and Jesus Compared* (1803), where the latter argued for the superior moral quality of revealed religion over natural religion. Jefferson was again persuaded by Priestley's compelling arguments, as well as his conclusion about the superiority of Jesus's system of morality, though Jefferson felt he would "omit the question of his divinity & even of his inspiration." He was also impressed by Priestley's comparative method for discussing religion, which he then applied in his long-delayed reply to Rush.[63] Writing Rush on April 21, 1803, Jefferson related that his beliefs reflected "a life of enquiry & reflection" and were "very different from that Anti-Christian system, imputed to me by those who know nothing of my opinions." Jefferson repeated his opposition to "the corruptions of Christianity" perpetrated by the church fathers "but not to the genuine precepts of Jesus himself. I am a Christian, in the only sense in which he wished any one to be; sincerely attached to his doctrines, in preference to all others; ascribing to himself every human excellence, & believing he never claimed any other (i.e., his divinity)." Jefferson then attached "a Syllabus, or Outline, of such an Estimate of the comparative merits of Christianity" where he identified those core elements he accepted: Jesus's superior moral mission, Unitarianism, and the possibility of "the doctrine of a future state." Jefferson also shared copies of his syllabus with Madison, Priestley, and a handful of his closest cabinet advisors, cautioning all of them, including Rush, not to share its contents as he was "averse to the communication of my religious tenets to the public." He emphasized that "it behoves every man, who values liberty of conscience for himself, to resist invasions of it in the case of others," particularly when it involved "questions of faith, which the laws have left between god & himself."[64] Rush responded almost immediately to Jefferson's letter, writing that he had read his "creed with great attention, and was much pleased to find you are by no means so heterodox as you have been supposed to be by your enemies." However, Rush, like Priestley, expressed disappointment over Jefferson's refusal to acknowledge "the character and mission of the Author of our Religion," with Priestley "express[ing] some surprise" that Jefferson continued to "be of the opinion, that Jesus never laid claim to a divine mission." There is no record of Madison's having responded to seeing the syllabus, possibly because its contents were of no surprise to him.[65]

Jefferson resisted another overture from Rush, that being to modify his position on the relationship between religion and government. In his letter to Rush in the midst of the 1800 election, Jefferson had railed against his clerical attackers, charging that they possessed the "very favorite hope of obtaining an establishment of a particular form of Christianity thro' the US." As "every sect believes it's own form the true one," he reminded Rush, "every one perhaps hoped for it's own" privileged position vis-à-vis the government.[66] Rush responded that he agreed "in your wishes to keep religion and government independant of each Other," though rather than highlighting the threats of organized religion to civil government, Rush emphasized the opposite: that "Christianity disdains to receive Support from human Governments." In contrast to Jefferson's view that republican government was the fulfillment of secular natural-rights impulses, the millennialist Rush believed that Christianity and republicanism were intertwined. "I have always considered Christianity as the *strong ground* of Republicanism," Rush wrote Jefferson. For Rush, the future success and glory of the United States depended on this relationship: "It is only necessary for Republicanism to ally itself to the christian Religion, to overturn all the corrupted political and religious institutions in the World."[67] Rush's proselytizing efforts met with limited success; while Jefferson never accepted Rush's belief in the indispensability of Christianity for republican government, the president did acknowledge that Christianity, "when divested of the rags in which they have inveloped it, and brought to the original purity & simplicity of it's benevolent institutor, is a religion of all others most friendly to liberty, science, & the freest expansions of the human mind." In essence, religion and government were not interdependent, but a pure form of Christianity could be consistent with and supportive of republican values.[68]

The Madison Presidency

As with Jefferson, James Madison's presidency provided few opportunities to act on religious matters. Even Madison's private pen remained silent on religious topics. His two inaugural addresses were generally devoid of religious allusions. In the conclusion of his first address, however, Madison acknowledged the "guidance of that Almighty Being whose power regulates the destiny of nations, whose blessings have been so conspicuously dispensed to this rising Republic" and to whom deserves "our devout gratitude." Earlier in the address, Madison announced his commitment as president "to avoid the slightest interference with the rights of conscience, or the functions of religion so wisely exempted from civil jurisdiction," thus reaffirming his long-held priorities. His Second Inaugural Address concentrated on the war with Great Britain and made only the passing claim that the American cause was "stamped with that justice, which invites the smiles of heaven on the means of conducting it to a successful termination." With the address given during a time of war, it remarkably made no appeal to God to interpose on the nation's behalf.[69]

Madison's handful of actions as president concerning religious matters stand in contrast to each other. First, on one side, Madison issued four prayer proclamations during the War of 1812, all at the behest of Congress. At least initially, doubt existed whether Madison would comply with Congress's request. In late spring of 1812, the General Assembly of the Presbyterian Church considered petitioning Madison to proclaim a national fast day but voted it down, not out of opposition to the idea but because they believed their petition would not be successful. On the same day that the House of Representatives voted for war, Benjamin Rush railed in a letter to John Adams, "Are we not the Only nation in the world, France excepted, . . . that has ever dared to go to war without imploring supernatural aid, either by prayers, or Sacrifices?"[70] A month later, however, on July 9, Madison issued the first of four religious proclamations—one for each year of the war. They are remarkable, not just because they came from Madison but also for the language he employed. All four proclamations contain highly religious allusions to God—"Almighty God," "Sovereign of the Universe," "Benefactor of mankind," "Holy and Omniscient Being," "Beneficent Parent," "Heavenly Benefactor," "Divine Author," and "Great Disposer of events"—and all but the last called on people to confess their sins and transgressions against God and ask for his forgiveness. In many respects, Madison's proclamations were as religiously charged as those of John Adams that had received so much criticism. As a result, conservative commentators have long cited Madison's proclamations as evidence that he was not as committed to church-state separation as has been portrayed or that the proclamations represented a serious lapse of principle. Others have suggested that

Madison's proclamations reveal he was willing to use religious discourse for reasons of political expediency, understanding its power during times of national crisis.[71]

That Madison faced significant political pressure to issue the proclamations may provide a simple explanation for his actions. This does not explain why Madison used such religiously charged language, though it is possible that once he had reconciled issuing the proclamations he borrowed from his Calvinist training at Princeton. After leaving office, Madison sought to put the best face on it by explaining to a friend that he was "always careful to make the Proclamations absolutely indiscriminate, and merely recommendatory; or rather mere *designations* of a day, on which all who thought proper might *unite* in consecrating it to religious purposes, according to their own faith & forms."[72] His second proclamation appears to support that rationale, as it contained a phrase that he was merely "recommending to all, who shall be piously disposed to unite their hearts and voices." It continued with the affirmation that "those who join in it are guided only by their free choice, by the impulse of their hearts and the dictates of their consciences" and "freed from all coercive edicts." Possibly realizing the tension between his long-held commitments and issuing a religious proclamation, Madison included a plea for the former, condemning "that unhallowed connexion with the powers of this world, which corrupts religion into an instrument or an usurper of the policy of the state, and, making no appeal but to reason, to the heart and to the conscience." The apparent contradictions, however, provide little clarity.[73]

In another writing around the time of the above letter, however, Madison repudiated his "recommendation" rationale and condemned all official religious proclamations. In his Detached Memoranda, likely compiled in the early 1820s, Madison wrote that official religious proclamations, though "recommendations only, . . . imply a religious agency, making no part of the trust delegated to political rulers. . . . An *advisory* Govt. is a contradiction in terms." Another concern with religious proclamations, Madison continued, was that they "seem [to] imply and certainly nourish the erronious idea of a *national* religion." He understood that religious proclamations would inevitably favor "the faith of certain Xn sects." The "practice if not strictly guarded [against], naturally terminates in a conformity to the creed of the majority and of a single sect." Finally, recalling Alexander Hamilton's brutal honesty about the practice, Madison argued that government use of religious discourse resulted in its "subserviency to political views; to the scandal of religion, as well as the increase of party animosities." In the end, Madison completely rejected the practice of religious proclamations, and he regretted having participated in it.[74]

One other incident during Madison's presidency is also best explained as a lapse in his otherwise steadfast commitment to religious equality. In 1815, Madison recalled the US diplomatic consul to Tunis, one of the Barbary States, for the minister's failure to secure the secret release of American prisoners in Algiers and for irregularities in his financial accounts. Concerned that disclosing the actual reasons for the dismissal might cause embarrassment, Madison and Secretary of State James Monroe concocted a rationale that the consul, Mordecai Manuel Noah, was being recalled because he was Jewish. In writing to Monroe on April 24, Madison suggested that "in recalling Noah, it may be well to rest the measure pretty much on the ascertained prejudices of the Turks against his Religion, and its having become public that he was a Jew, a circumstance which if was understood at the time of his appt might be withheld."[75] Three years later, in attempting to clear his name over the incident, Noah wrote Madison seeking clarification of the reasons for his dismissal. He noted that the rationale in his recall letter on file in the State Department "refers Solely to my religion, an objection, that I am persuaded you cannot feel, nor authorize others to feel." Noah assured Madison "that no injury arose in Barbary to the public Service from my religion as relating to myself." Madison's reply to Noah was less than forthcoming; rather than answering Noah's inquiry directly, Madison responded that "it is certain that your religious profession was well known at the time you received your Commission; and that in itself it could not be a motive for your recall." Possibly seeking to save face, Madison asserted that he "ever regarded the freedom of religious opinions & worship as equally belonging to every sect, & the secure enjoyment of it as the best human provision for bringing all either into the same way of thinking, or into that mutual charity which is the only proper substitute." Nothing more came of the incident, other than some possible embarrassment for Madison.[76]

On the other side, Madison twice had the opportunity as president to interpret the meaning of the Constitution's establishment clause. In February 1811, Madison vetoed two pieces of congressional legislation that he believed violated that clause. The first instance involved a bill authorizing the incorporation of an Episcopal church in Alexandria, Virginia, which was then part of the District of Columbia, and the second instance concerned a federal land grant to a Baptist church in the Mississippi Territory. The second veto is more understandable than the first, though both reveal a strict application of church-state separation. Regarding the land grant, Madison wrote in his veto message that an "appropriation of funds of the United States, for the use and support of Religious Societies" constituted a "law respecting a religious establishment," even though Congress made similar grants to other private entities. The other veto provides even greater insight into his separationist perspective. Madison objected on two grounds, the first being that incorporation would establish "sundry rules and proceedings relative purely to the organization and polity of the Church" affecting "the principles and cannons, by which Churches of that denomination govern themselves," and thus making it "a religious establishment by law." He also believed that the incorporation would have given the church certain authority—"a legal force and sanction"—that it could then enforce legally. Incorporation would authorize the church to engage in quasi-public functions including providing "for the support of the poor and the education of poor children," which Madison interpreted as "giving to religious societies as such a legal agency in carrying into effect a public and civil duty." Congress was effectively awarding civil authority to a religious society, which, he wrote, violated "the essential distinction between civil and religious functions." Here was a practical example of a violation of the separate spheres of religious and civil authority.[77] Finally, in 1816, Madison used a "pocket veto" to kill legislation that would have exempted Bible societies from paying duties on the importation of stereotype plates for printing Bibles. Later, Madison would refer to this action as indicating "precedent" for the meaning of *"the separation between Religion & Govt. in the Constitution."*[78]

In December 1816, Madison delivered his final annual message to Congress. Washington, DC, was still rebuilding from the British sacking of the city two years earlier. With the war over and the prospect of "tranquility and prosperity at home," Madison had reason to be upbeat. After an obligatory acknowledgment of providence, Madison urged Congress to continue with a program of national development: "a comprehensive system of roads and Canals," the creation of a national university, and the establishment of a department of justice under the attorney general, among other things. He closed by commending the character of the American people, "in their

devotion to true liberty, and to the constitution which is its palladium."
This was exhibited by "a Government, pursuing the public good . . . which
watches over the purity of elections, the freedom of speech and of the press,
the trial by Jury, and the equal interdict against enchroachments and com-
pacts, between religion and the State." With all the issues and concerns
that his administration had had to address and still lay ahead, matters of
church and state remained a priority for Madison. Although his actions as
president revealed some inconsistencies about his approach to church and
state, he would clarify any doubt about his views through his writings in
retirement.[79]

TEN

Retirement

B y the time of James Madison's retirement in 1817, the United States
was a very different place from where it had been in 1776. Geographically, the nation now extended to the spine of the Rocky
Mountains (or, as some claimed, to the Pacific Ocean). The original thirteen states had expanded to eighteen, with an additional five organized
territories knocking on the door of statehood. In those forty years, the nation's population had more than doubled. With the end of the War of 1812
and the conclusion of the Napoleonic Wars in 1815, the nation was finally
territorially secure and able to turn its full attention to internal matters,
several of which Madison had mentioned in his final address to Congress:
expanding the nation's infrastructure and developing its natural resources.
"In 1815 for the first time Americans ceased to doubt the path they were to
follow," wrote Henry Adams in his monumental *History of the United States
during the Administration of Thomas Jefferson and James Madison.* "Not only
was the unity of the nation established, but its probable divergence from
older societies was also well defined. . . . As far as politics supplied a test,
the national character had already diverged from any foreign type." Adams
insisted that "the American, in his political character, is a new variety of
man," and the South and West were giving "to society a character more
aggressively American than had been known before."[1]

The revolutionary generation was also passing away, along with much
of its institutional memory. Commiserating with John Adams in 1812, Jefferson looked back "in remembrance of our old friends and fellow laborers,
who have fallen before us." He noted that of the signers of the Declaration

of Independence, not more than a handful were still alive in the northern states whereas, "on this side [of the Potomac River], myself alone" lives. Similarly, only eleven delegates to the Constitutional Convention were alive in 1815, with just two, Madison and Rufus King, still engaged in public matters. The revolutionary impulse was over, and some old republicans—Jefferson and Madison included—feared that the republican impulse was also waning, or at least moving in uncharted directions. A republicanism committed to Enlightenment principles, an idea on which Jefferson, Madison, and many other founders had rested their hope, was "modified or perverted" by 1815, according to historian Gordon S. Wood. By that date, the republic was establishing its own identity: not one that embraced Enlightenment rationalism but one that fostered the world's most evangelically Christian culture.[2]

During his presidency, Jefferson had not anticipated (or had refused to recognize) that the religious complexion of the nation was shifting, moving away from a rational Christianity that he thought represented the inevitable future of American religion.[3] However, two impulses were already underway when he assumed the presidency that impacted popular religious attitudes: the decline in deistic thought and the rise of evangelicalism.

The Demise of Deism

The conservative counterreaction to American deistic thought was more successful than Jefferson and other rational theists anticipated. Thomas Paine's *Age of Reason* had experienced a meteoric life in America, reaching new heights of popularity only to plummet to the ground under a weathering onslaught by orthodox clergy and their Federalist allies. By the early years of the nineteenth century, the excesses of the French Revolution and its association with atheism had all but discredited American deism. One may have assumed that Jefferson's election in 1800 would have been a boon for deists, but as discussed, his Republican surrogates worked assiduously to disassociate him from charges of infidelity. Without Jefferson's open embrace, deism had no prominent defenders or apologists.[4]

In the new century, orthodox clergy kept up their attacks on "infidelity," despite its decreasing challenge to traditional Christianity. Picking up where he had left off in his *Voice of Warning* (1798), Yale's Timothy Dwight in 1816 warned that people were again becoming complacent about the "propagators of infidelity and vice." Writing around the same time, Dwight's former student Lyman Beecher urged people to adhere to orthodox Christianity, otherwise there would be another "brood of infidels, and heretics, and profligates" who would "assail, as they have done [before], our most sacred institutions." Beecher railed against nineteenth-century skepticism with intensity, delivering a series of public lectures on "Political Atheism, and Kindred Subjects." He asserted skepticism was an "epidemic" "sweep[ing] over the world." The "polluted page of infidelity everywhere" was "an organized effort against our civil and religious institutions." While the threat was due to the lingering effects of French atheism, it was also associated with "lax observance of the sabbath, a loose morality," and the false claims of Socinianism and rational Christianity. Skepticism, or freethought, would witness a mild resurgence in the late 1820s through the efforts of figures such as Frances Wright and Robert Dale Owen and the workingman's reform movement; however, it never represented a significant challenge to orthodox and evangelical Christianity. By the time of Madison's retirement, publicly associating oneself with rational religion was no longer fashionable.[5]

Revivals, Reform, and Evangelicalism

The phenomenal growth in evangelical Protestantism in the new century represented the second religious development that neither Jefferson nor Madison fully anticipated. Even though the revivals of the First Great Awakening were essentially spent by the 1740s, remnants of the evangelical impulse had persisted within American religion throughout the revolutionary era, perpetuated by Separate Baptists and Methodists after 1780. A new round of revivals broke out in the late 1790s, fueled in part by frontier expansion and demographic dislocation, and then exploded with the advent of camp meetings at Cane Ridge, Kentucky, in 1801. The revivals spread like a wildfire throughout the Ohio River Valley and then back into the South, New York, and New England. Baptists and Methodists were the greatest beneficiaries of what became known as the Second Great Awakening, which quickly surpassed its namesake in its impact on American society; both denominations gained over ten thousand new members in the Ohio Valley between 1800 and 1803. Presbyterian leaders, despite their evangelical orientation, approached the revivals hesitantly as they were frequently led by untrained clergy; as a result, the denomination experienced defections leading to the formation of the Cumberland Presbyterian Church and the Stone-Campbell "Christian movement," which became the Disciples of Christ Church. Before long, however, the evangelical impulse made inroads into orthodox Calvinism (Presbyterians and Congregationalists) and even among some Episcopalians.[6]

The revivals of the Second Great Awakening had more staying power than those of the First Great Awakening, lasting into the 1830s, becoming institutionalized under the direction of evangelists like Charles G. Finney. By then, the evangelical impulse dominated Protestantism and would continue to expand its influence on American culture throughout the remainder of the century. Writing in 1844, evangelical commentator Robert Baird claimed that 2.5 million Americans were active members of an evangelical church while another 12 million were under the influence of some evangelical body. Baird's questionable figures meant that there were approximately 14. 5 million evangelicals out of a national population of 17.5 million. As significant as the numbers, the growth of evangelical membership represented an increasing unity among Protestants over basic doctrine, Baird asserted, such that all evangelicals could be viewed "as branches of one great body, even [as] the entire visible church of Christ in this land." One goal of evangelicals was to create a godly society in America that would lay the groundwork for the second coming of Jesus Christ.[7]

Coinciding with the Second Great Awakening, and feeding off its momentum, was the nation's first moral reform movement. Despite the revivals' emphasis on personal salvation, orthodox Calvinists—chiefly Presbyterians and Congregationalists, who approached the "new measures" cautiously—retained their belief in a collective accountability before God. Agreeing with their evangelical brethren about the need to create a godly society, orthodox Protestants were unwilling to leave God's kingdom to chance, particularly considering the disruptions and temptations associated with an expanding frontier. They called for forming moral reform or "benevolent" societies to address various social ills and to bring people to Christ. Leading the charge was Lyman Beecher, who asserted that "irreligion hath become in all parts of our land, alarmingly prevalent." Beecher provided a list of problems: "The name of God is blasphemed; the bible is denounced; the sabbath is profaned; the public worship of God is neglected; intemperance hath destroyed its thousands . . . while luxury, with its diversified evils, with a rapidity unparalleled, is spreading in every direction." To address this moral declension,

Beecher advocated enacting stricter sumptuary laws, but he acknowledged that with disestablishment there were limits to the government's enforcement of moral conduct. To supplement behavioral laws, Beecher called for creating moral reform societies that would use persuasion and shame to reform people and hence society; their purpose was "to promote vigilance, to hold up the connection between vice and misery, to give correctness and efficacy to public opinion, and to strengthen the sinews of the law." In "a free government," Beecher insisted, "moral suasion and coercion must be united."[8]

Protestants answered Beecher's call, creating by 1830 the American Bible Society, the American Sunday School Union, the American Tract Society, the American Temperance Society, and the General Union for the Promotion of the Christian Sabbath, among others. The transformative effect of the evangelical impulse and the moral reform movement on American society is hard to overstate. Religious historian Robert T. Handy once observed that "in many ways, the middle third of the nineteenth century was more of a 'Protestant Age' than was the colonial period with its established churches." Mark A. Noll has noted with irony that "by the early nineteenth century, evangelicalism was the unofficially established religion in a nation that had forsworn religious establishments."[9] Thus, in the nineteenth century the evangelical perspective, with its goal of making America into a "Christian nation," became the counterpoise to the Jeffersonian-Madisonian idea of separation of church and state. By midcentury, evangelicals would embrace a modified view of church-state separation, one that prohibited the public funding of Catholic parochial schools but otherwise did not stand in the way of "nonsectarian" Protestant influences in the nation's institutions, particularly its public schools. Neither official disestablishment nor a "one-way" separationism could block an unofficial "moral establishment" of evangelical Protestantism.[10]

Jefferson and Evangelicalism

This "counterrevolution of evangelical religion," according to Edwin Gaustad, "threatened the entire ideology of the Enlightenment. It revived enthusiasm . . . [and] encouraged emotion to place a check on Reason, rather than the other way around." Evangelicalism also emphasized an uncritical biblical literalism that honored the supernatural aspects of scripture: the immaculate conception, the miracles, the atonement and resurrection, and the Trinity. All of this was anathema to Jeffersonian rationalism. Although Jefferson continued to believe that "truth will prevail over fanaticism," as he told Unitarian minister Jared Sparks in 1820, the upsurge in evangelicalism represented a challenge to Jefferson's hopes for rational Christianity and his views about church and state. Based on his earlier experiences with orthodox clergy, Jefferson already deplored much about sectarian religion; the growing influence of sectarian evangelicalism on the culture only provided him with more frustration.[11]

Jefferson could have found some common ground with evangelicals based on their insistence on personal liberty and the right of private judgment, their devotion to morality, and their embrace of republicanism. In correspondence, Jefferson distinguished evangelical groups by their commitment to the last value: "The Baptists are sound republicans and zealous supporters of their government," he noted in a letter to Thomas Cooper. "The Methodists are republican mostly, satisfied with their government meddling with nothing but the concerns of their own calling." Presbyterians, however, were "violent, ambitious of power, and intolerant in politics as in religion."[12] On another level, Jefferson also concurred with some proponents of "primitive" Christianity—such as the Disciples of Christ—who wanted to return to the uncorrupted essentials of Christianity. But Jefferson clearly parted from evangelicals who went beyond preaching voluntary commitment to morality to employing forms of compulsion.[13]

Jefferson's belief in the individual freedom of the mind put him at odds with the *evangelistic* activities of evangelicals; as he said on more than one occasion, "our particular principles of religion are a subject of accountability to our god alone. I enquire after no man's, and trouble none with mine."[14] Because of his ongoing reputation as an infidel or religious skeptic, Jefferson was frequently the object of evangelizing efforts. Throughout retirement Jefferson received unsolicited letters from well-meaning strangers and acquaintances with evangelical leanings encouraging him to be "born again." Over a decade, Jefferson received a series of letters from an anonymous writer using the pseudonym "Goodwill" or "A Friend to the Christian Religion," who claimed to have visited Monticello. Goodwill's letters needled Jefferson that his lack of faith put his immortal soul at risk: "Thousands of times," Goodwill wrote, he had "addressed the Almighty Sovereign in your behalf; praying, thro Jesus Christ, our Divine Advocate, that you may be brought to embrace & enjoy, that holy religion. . . . Remember, Dear Sir, that your time on earth is short. '*Now is the accepted time; now is the day of Salvation.*'" In a letter in late 1818 or early 1819, Goodwill sinisterly remarked how after their last encounter, Jefferson appeared to be "declining fast! you had the appearance of a person hastening to the tomb!" Goodwill's advice to Jefferson was to "go frequently on your knees in secret, and pray to the GOD who made you . . . till you know by happy experience, the Joys of Religion."[15] A similar overture came in 1814 from Miles King, a Methodist evangelist who wrote a rambling missive to convince Jefferson of "the infinite Merit of Jesus Christ!!" and to procure "the salvation of your precious and immortal soul!" No doubt, Jefferson was offended by Goodwill's and King's assumptions about his infidelity and the latter's attack on rationalism—that "reason, the handmaid of religion [must] become subordinate to sublimer revelation"—but he tactfully replied to King that so long as disputes existed over religious doctrines, "our reason at last must ultimately decide, as it is the only oracle which god has given us to determine between what really comes from him, & the phantasms of a disordered or deluded imagination," the last phrase being a not-too-subtle quip about religious enthusiasm.[16]

These experiences validated Jefferson's reticence to make public his views about religion, though at the same time this hesitation fueled speculation about his beliefs. One related incident was particularly frustrating for Jefferson. In January 1816, Jefferson wrote to his longtime friend Charles Thomson, who had served with Jefferson in the Continental Congress and then the Confederation Congress. Thomson had been a protégé of Benjamin Franklin and had recently published a new translation and commentary on the Bible, which Jefferson complimented. Jefferson then related that he had written "a wee little book" several years earlier, titled the *Philosophy of Jesus,* which he described as "a paradigma of his doctrines, made by cutting the texts out of the book, and arranging them on the pages of a blank book, in a certain order of time or subject." The excerpts related to Jesus's moral and ethical teachings and, Jefferson declared, represented "proof that I am a *real Christian,* that is to say, a disciple of the doctrines of Jesus." The *Philosophy of Jesus,* prepared in 1804, had been an expansion of Jefferson's syllabus from the year before.[17]

Thomson responded in May, noting with pleasure Jefferson's declaration that he considered himself to be a "real Christian." Thomson was eight-six years old and had suffered a stroke, however, and for several months he did not recall having replied to Jefferson or that he had shown Jefferson's letter to several Philadelphia acquaintances. He later apologized to Jefferson that he had shared the letter with the best of intentions to refute "the slanderous charges bandied about respecting your infidelity and disbelief."[18] Thomson's breach of Jefferson's confidence fueled speculation that the former president had had a conversion experience, producing another round of inquiring correspondence. "It is in general circulation, & a current opinion & belief, that you have avowed yourself a perfect believer in the Christian Religion & that you believe in the Divinity of Our saviour," wrote Joseph Delaplaine in November 1816. "I can say that the Religious world in this quarter, are daily congratulating each other, on what they call, your happy change of Religious belief."[19] An old family friend, Margret Bayard Smith, also wrote Jefferson to confirm rumors that he had made "a profession of faith." Smith rejoiced that "Bible societies, Sunday schools, & various charitable institutions have been form'd, which . . . owe their existence to a zeal for religion which pervades all ranks of society." She related that it would please her and other "zealous Christians . . . to see the name of one of the greatest of Statesmen & Philosophers enrol'd among that of Christians!" Jefferson brusquely denied that his religious views had changed—"a change from what?" he replied indignantly. "I never told my own religion, nor scrutinised that of another," Jefferson informed Smith. And in a rebuke of evangelistic methods, he affirmed that "I never attempted to make a convert, nor wished to change another's creed. I have ever judged of the religion of others by their lives."[20]

In his letters to close friends, Jefferson was more open about his views of evangelicalism. In 1812, Jefferson and John Adams resumed their correspondence after a decade-long hiatus caused by the bitter 1800 election. They wrote extensively about religious matters, usually on a philosophical or historical level. Even though Adams did not share all of Jefferson's heterodox beliefs, he similarly rejected trinitarianism and eschewed dogma and doctrinalism. Adams and Jefferson were "unmistakable vestiges of the vanished Age of Enlightenment," wrote Lester J. Cappon, and "the upsurge of the evangelistic spirit in the early nineteenth century were matters of serious concern to Adams and Jefferson, who felt that freedom of the mind must be maintained at all cost."[21] In 1816, Adams wrote sarcastically that "we have now, it Seems, a National Bible Society to propagate King James's Bible, through all Nations. Would it not be better, to apply these pious Subscriptions, to purify Christendom from the Corruptions of Christianity; than to propagate those Corruptions in Europe Asia, Africa and America!"

Jefferson concurred with Adams's sentiment, responding that his books on speculative theology were "more valuable than [what] the Chinese will [receive] from our bible-societies. These Incendiaries [i.e., reform societies], finding that the days of fire and faggot are over in the Atlantic hemisphere, are now preparing to put the torch to the Asiatic regions."[22] A year later Jefferson celebrated the dismantling of the religious establishment in Connecticut, hoping that it represented "the last retreat of Monkish darkness, bigotry, and abhorrence of those advances of the mind which had carried the other states a century ahead of them." "Oh! Lord!" Adams snapped back, "Do you think that a Protestant Popedom is annihilated in America?" Adams pointed to the ongoing religious disruptions caused by the revivals in the mid-Atlantic region. "What a mercy it is, that these People cannot whip and crop, and pillory and roast, as yet in the U.S.? If they could they would." Adams disputed the effectiveness of the Madisonian tonic for sectarianism: "The multitude and diversity of them, you will Say, is our Security against them all. God grant it." Rather, because "the Presbyterians and Methodists are [by] far the most numerous," he wrote, they were "the most likely to unite" and oppress other sects.[23]

Jefferson's view of evangelicalism was colored by his long-running antipathy toward orthodox clergy, whom he called "mountebanks," "cannibals," "pseudo-Christians," and "false shepherds"—people who engaged in "priestcraft" for their own power and wealth. They were men "of pious whining, hypocritical canting, lying & slandering," Jefferson declared.[24] As he informed Reverend Charles Clay, the rector of his home church in Charlottesville and a friend, "I abuse the priests indeed, who have so much abused the pure and holy doctrines of their master, and who have laid me under no obligations of reticence as to the tricks of their trade. The genuine system of Jesus, and the artificial structures they have erected to make him the instrument of wealth, power, and preeminence to themselves."[25] Writing another acquaintance, Jefferson famously declared that "there would never have been an infidel, if there had never been a priest."[26] Jefferson criticized Presbyterian clergy in particular, calling them the "loudest, the most intolerant of all sects, the most tyrannical, and ambitious."[27]

This anticlericalism easily transferred to evangelical clergy as the line that distinguished evangelicalism and orthodoxy began to blur, and when evangelicals adopted similar methods to impose their religiosity on society and to constrict free inquiry. Early on, Jefferson appeared receptive to

Bible distribution initiatives, contributing fifty dollars to the Bible Society of Virginia in 1813, remarking that "there never was a more pure & sublime system of morality delivered to man than is to be found in the four evangelists."[28] His opinion about the agenda of reform societies soured over time. In an anonymous essay published in the Richmond Inquirer in January 1816, Jefferson attacked a Lyman Beecher–established society "for the education of *pious* young men for the ministry" that was sending "missionaries" to Virginia to evangelize its residents. The society was "now looking to the flesh-pots of the South, and aiming at foothold there by their missionary teachers; they have lately come forward boldly with their plan to establish '*a qualified religious instructor* over every thousand souls in the United States'; and they seem to consider none as qualified, but their own sect." Jefferson warned that this represented an "immediate, universal, vigorous and systematic effort made to evangelize the nation, to see that there is a bible for every family, a school for every district, and a qualified (i.e. Presbyterian) pastor for every thousand souls; that newspapers, tracts, magazines, must be employed, the press be made to groan, and every pulpit in the land to sound its trumpet long and loud." For Jefferson, the evangelical agenda threatened to reinvigorate religious persecution and to inhibit "those who wish to enjoy freedom of opinion."[29] In a letter several years later, Jefferson again criticized the activities of missionary and Bible societies, in part for their fundraising tactics for overseas ministries. "I do not know that it is a duty to disturb by missionaries the religion and peace of other countries," he commented.[30]

Jefferson's hostility toward evangelical clergy and their followers was most pronounced in his decade-long correspondence with Thomas Cooper. Cooper was a lawyer, natural scientist, and intellectual who Jefferson unsuccessfully recruited to teach at his new University of Virginia. Cooper had been a protégé of Joseph Priestley, having fled with him from Britain to Pennsylvania in 1794 to escape persecution for his heretical religious beliefs. In 1800, Cooper had been prosecuted under the Sedition Act for publishing a pamphlet critical of John Adams. Cooper and Jefferson shared many interests, including similar perspectives about religion and politics, and the two maintained a lively and candid correspondence.[31]

Throughout his scholarly career, Cooper was assailed by conservative clergy for his heretical religious beliefs, attacks that scuttled his faculty appointment at the University of Virginia (discussed below). Like Jefferson, however, Cooper's disdain of evangelicalism transcended his bitterness toward the clergy to include their followers. In 1819, Cooper secured a professorship at the College of South Carolina in Columbia, and he and Jefferson exchanged views about the revivals and religious activities taking place in both of their states, with their remarks evincing scorn for evangelical beliefs accompanied with a little misogyny. In a July 4, 1820, letter, Jefferson jokingly called evangelical clergy "half rogues" and their members "half dupes." Responding eight days later, Cooper scolded Jefferson for underestimating the threat: "I feel gloomy at the persevering, determined, unwearied march of religious intolerance among us. The clergy daily acquire more strength: they insinuate themselves among the females of the families, whose [husbands] will not bend to their sway, & they exercise compleat controul over the ignorant every where." Suggesting that other motives were in play, Cooper charged that "the bible and missionary societies, and the clerical propagandists, raise (chiefly from the females) at least a million and a half of dollars annually."[32] In a subsequent letter describing his experience while living in Pennsylvania, Cooper criticized "the predominant influence of the Presbyterian preachers, over the women particularly, whom they tempt out to nightly Sermons & prayer meetings." He noted contemptuously that "these religious parties occupy *every* evening, and the meeting houses are crowded with women, while the taverns are equally crowded with their husbands." Yet, Cooper stated that he "greatly fear[ed] [the evangelists] will succeed" in creating a church establishment. "The people not aware of the frauds committed, are the gross dupes of missionary societies, bible societies, and theological seminaries; and every head of a family of a religious town, or in any way connected with that sect, must submit to the power these persons have acquired, by making the females of the families which they are permitted to enter, the engines of their influence over the male part. I foresee another night of superstition, not far behind the inquisition."[33]

Jefferson agreed with Cooper's critique, remarking that "the atmosphere of our country is unquestionably charged with a threatening cloud of fanaticism, lighter in some parts, denser in others, but too heavy in all." He related that in Richmond, "there is much fanaticism, but chiefly among the women: they have their night meetings, and praying-parties, where attended by their priests, and sometimes a hen-pecked husband, they pour forth the effusions of their love to Jesus in terms as amatory and carnal as their modesty would permit them to use to a more earthly lover." In contrast to Richmond, Jefferson declared that a high degree of religious harmony existed among the sects in Charlottesville, but chiefly because no denomination held the upper hand. In places "where presbyterianism prevails undividedly, [however,] their ambition and tyranny would tolerate no rival if they had power." Cooper concurred that the Presbyterians represented the greatest threat to religious freedom and free inquiry: "They are a systematic and persevering sect, and while they have the address to cajole the people out of their money, their power will increase." But Presbyterian machinations aside, Cooper expressed concern about how "to stem this tide of fanaticism." Methodists too addressed the passions of "the more ignorant fanatics," and they "will keep fast hold of the multitude; more especially from the erotic language of their devotional poetry." Cooper worried about the anti-intellectualism of evangelicalism, particularly its "effect on the female part of the sectarians, who are not affected by mere argument or sound reasoning."[34]

One could easily dismiss the comments in Jefferson's and Cooper's correspondence as intellectual snobbery laced with misogynistic biases. But both men expressed sincere concerns about the challenge that evangelicalism, its clergy, and the moral reform societies presented to rational religion and free inquiry, as well as to the boundaries separating church and state that appeared to be under assault. Jefferson believed that "in every country and in every age, the priest has been hostile to liberty."[35] He feared that the rise of sectarianism would lead to religious competition and conflict, that claims of doctrinal unity among evangelicals would "erect the standard of uniformity" to be imposed on others, that evangelical intolerance would promote censorship of heretical opinions, and that some evangelicals—Presbyterians in particular—demonstrated little hesitation in enlisting the law to accomplish their goal of religious conformity.[36] Confirming Jefferson's fears was the fact that conservative clergy attacked his Statute for Establishing Religious Freedom as an impediment to their goals. Evangelical historian Robert Baird, for one, while giving lip-service to church-state separation, ridiculed the statute, writing that it gave Jefferson "great satisfaction, not because it embodied principles of eternal justice, but because by putting all religious sects on an equality, it seemed to degrade Christianity," a result "that made the arch-infidel chuckle with satisfaction." Such attacks reinforced Jefferson's belief that for "freedom of religion, guaranteed to us by law *in theory,* . . . [to] ever rise *in practice* under the overbearing inquisition of public opinion, truth [must] prevail over fanaticism."[37]

Madison and Evangelicalism

Unlike Jefferson, Madison expressed little concern in his private correspondence about the rise of evangelicalism. In an 1819 letter that described the current religious situation in Virginia, Madison offered a rosier picture, noting that the populace was evenly divided among Presbyterians, Baptists, Methodists, and Episcopalians who coexisted in relative harmony due to disestablishment and the inability of one faction to dominate the others. Although he alluded to the "zeal" and lack of "qualifications of the Preachers . . . among the new Sects" as their "greatest deficiency," Madison was overall complimentary of evangelicals, commending "the purity of their lives" and their religious devotion. Those positive attributes were not by happenstance, however; Madison believed that "the number, the industry, and the morality of the priesthood & the devotion of the people have been manifestly increased by the total separation of the Church from the State."[38] Thus, even though Madison was not particularly devout or observant himself, he took a laissez-faire approach to religious enthusiasm, provided there was no prospect that various sects could combine to impose their will on others. If "new sects arise with absurd opinions or overheated imaginations," he wrote, "the proper remedies lie in time, for-bearance, and example." As for Madison's view of the activities of moral reform societies, one salient piece of evidence might be his 1816 pocket veto of a congressional bill that would have exempted Bible societies from paying duties, but that action likely reflected his adherence to constitutional principle rather than indicating disfavor with their evangelistic activities. Among the handful of negative statements on record, Madison in 1822 called evangelical reform groups "repulsive Sects," and in 1826 he referred to evangelical clergy as "divines of more zeal than discretion," the latter criticism likely reflecting Madison's own rationalist leanings.[39]

There are several explanations for Madison's more accepting view of the rise in evangelicalism. Aside from their different personalities, Madison demonstrated little interest in theological speculations whereas Jefferson was frequently consumed by them, in no small part because of the attacks he had received from conservative clergy. Madison's writings extending back to his *Memorial and Remonstrance* and the Federalist essays also demonstrate that he strongly believed the solution for diffusing religious conflict and controversy was to maintain a diversity among religious sects that would keep all of them in check—that "rival sects with equal rights [will] exercise mutual censorships in favor of good morals." Finally, as addressed in previous chapters, Jefferson's and Madison's earlier experiences with religious groups differed. Whereas Jefferson's disdain for Presbyterian clergy and their theology increased over time, Madison had a relatively favorable experience with Presbyterianism while at Princeton and he had worked patiently with the fickle Hanover Presbytery during the Virginia disestablishment struggle. During that time, Madison served as a trustee for the Presbyterian Hampden-Sydney College where his younger brother William attended. And based on his experience with religious dissenters in the 1770s, Madison developed a lifelong admiration for Baptists, with him remarking how their struggle for religious freedom "obtained for him a lasting place in favour of that particular sect." Whatever his reasons, Madison ended up being more tolerant of religious enthusiasm than Jefferson, even though he apparently also found it theologically and culturally disagreeable.[40]

One episode in 1822 illustrates the different ways Jefferson and Madison approached the growing influence of evangelicalism in society. On February 16, Jedidiah Morse sent identical letters to Jefferson, Madison, and John Adams, informing them that as former presidents they had been selected as honorary board members of his new reform society, the American Society for Promoting the Civilization and General Improvement of the Indian Tribes. In the 1790s, Morse had been a prominent Federalist orthodox minister who had attacked deism and French infidelity. He resigned from the pulpit of the prestigious First Congregational Church in Charlestown, Massachusetts, in 1819 to devote himself to "civilizing" Indigenous Americans. His reform society differed from others in that he solicited membership from public officials and clergy—with representatives from both groups comprising its board of directors—and he planned for the society to collaborate closely with the government on Indian affairs. The society's constitution and annual report declared its goal of extending the "blessings derived from out common Christianity" to the Indian tribes, while working in concert with government agencies to achieve those ends. In his letters to Jefferson, Madison, and Adams, Morse claimed that the society' actions would merely continue with the measures "which were pursued during your administration in reference to the Indian tribes in our country," which had provided limited funding for religious missions.[41]

Upon receiving the solicitation, Jefferson wrote Madison an exasperated letter, declaring, "I disapprove the proposition altogether." Jefferson stated that while he "acknowledge[d] the right of voluntary associations for laudable purposes and in moderate numbers," Morse's proposal crossed the line by enlisting government collaboration in its religious activities. The proposal would establish terrible precedent, he noted, and would be one step removed from turning "the government itself into an instrument to be wielded by themselves [i.e., the society] and for purposes directed by themselves." Untroubled, Madison replied that the "project appears to me to be rather [more] ostentatious than dangerous." Madison restated his belief that an exercise of religious authority was unlikely where the groups were "too numerous, too heterogeneous, and too much dispersed to concentrate their views in any covert or illicit object." Even though clergy would likely control the society and "might be most naturally distrusted [as] are themselves made up of such repulsive Sects . . . they are not likely to form a noxious confederacy, especially with ecclesiastical views."[42] Madison wrote Morse a polite letter declining membership without mentioning his concerns over the proposal. John Adams's reply to Morse was more direct, in his typical fashion, stating that "I have great doubts of the propriety of a voluntary Association, for such purposes," those being the involvement of government officials and the employment of government authority in its activities. "As I cannot approve the Institution, I must decline the honour," Adams wrote.[43]

In contrast, Jefferson wrote Morse a lengthy reply, raising many of the concerns he had related to Madison. In a lecturing tone, Jefferson disclaimed the intermixing of government and religious functions; he noted that the society would be dominated by clergy, which raised the potential that they would command the powers of the US government. "Is it that there is no danger that a new authority, marching independently along side of the government, in the same line, and to the same object, may not produce collision, may not thwart & obstruct the operations of the government, or wrest the object entirely from their hands?" he asked. If approved, Jefferson added, how many other societies would "spring up" to "take the government out of it's constitutional hands." He stated that he would "not undertake to draw the line of demarcation between private associations of laudable views" and those that "jeopardise the march of regular government. Yet such a line does exist." Jefferson believed the proposal "is, in it's magnitude of dangerous example." In no place in his reply did Jefferson use language of church and state or mention the First Amendment, but given the context—a religious association seeking to work in concert with the government while employing official authority for religious ends—his meaning was clear. His reply also indicated that he still believed in a separation between secular and religious functions, here using the term "line" in place of "wall."[44]

Madison's reticence to make gratuitous attacks on evangelicals or their belief system did not mean his views about ecclesiastical power and its effects on republican institutions had waned in his later years. He dismissed Morse's proposed society primarily as being impractical and unlikely to form a "noxious confederacy." Otherwise, his concerns had grown, possibly spurred by the shifting religious winds of the early antebellum period. As he warned in a letter to an acquaintance, any "coalition between Government & Religion" would have a "corrupting influence on both the parties."[45]

Sometime after leaving office, likely around 1820, Madison wrote a memorandum to himself as part of undertaking the laborious task of organizing his public and private papers. The thirty-page manuscript, known as Madison's Detached Memoranda, discusses sundry topics and events but contains nine pages under the heading "Monopolies. Perpetuities. Corporations. Ecclesiastical Endowments" that consider religious matters. In it, Madison laid out his most comprehensive discussion about church-state relations since writing the Memorial and Remonstrance some thirty-five years earlier.[46]

Madison began his essay about church-state matters at an unusual place—not with issues related to protecting conscience rights or preventing tax support for religion but with a warning that "the danger of silent accumulations and encroachments by Ecclesiastical Bodies have not sufficiently engaged attention in the U.S." This concern was manifested in two interrelated ways, "the indefinite accumulation of property" and wealth by religious bodies, and "the capacity of holding it in perpetuity by ecclesiastical corporations." Madison strongly believed that the "growing wealth acquired by them never fails to be a source of abuses," while legal incorporation facilitated their indefinite ownership of property. (In 1785, Madison had supported the legal incorporation of religious bodies in Virginia as part of a tactical ploy and he later worked for the law's repeal.) Madison referenced his 1811 vetoes of the land grant to a Mississippi Baptist church and of the incorporation of an Episcopal church as examples of him acting on both concerns, writing that "strongly guarded as the separation between Religion and Government in the Constitution of the United States [is] the danger of encroachment by Ecclesiastical Bodies." Whether that concern over ecclesiastical encroachment also included the recent growth of evangelical moral reform societies he did not say.[47]

From there, Madison addressed other widely accepted practices he believed violated church-state separation. Chaplains in Congress were "a palpable violation of equal rights, as well as of Constitutional principles," Madison charged, which "forbids everything like an establishment of a national religion." Chaplaincies would always favor the dominant denominations to the exclusion of minority sects, and they violated the principle of voluntary support of religion with "ministers of religion [being] paid by the entire nation." Madison questioned the constitutionality of chaplains for the military as well, though he gave allowance for naval chaplains when ships were at sea. Tax exemptions for houses of worship also violated constitutional principles in Madison's mind. Finally, Madison provided a lengthy discussion about the impropriety of religious proclamations, a practice that he regretted having undertaken as president. Proclamations "seem to imply and certainly nourish the erroneous idea of a *national* religion." They promote the idea of "a union of all to form one nation under one Government in acts of devotion to God." Madison believed that even a nonsectarian proclamation "naturally terminates in a conformity to the creed of the majority and a single sect." But even beyond the inevitable problem of sect preference, civil government simply lacked the authority to issue religious proclamations, which "imply a religious agency" that is "no part of the trust delegated to political rulers."[48]

Informing these illustrative examples were broader constitutional principles. Madison referred to the example of the Virginia Statute for Establishing Religious Freedom, which he called "a *true* standard of Religious liberty: *its principle [being] the great* barrier against usurpations on the rights of conscience." In more than one place, Madison wrote that religious freedom was not secure without maintaining a "separation between the authority of human laws, and the natural rights of Man." For true religious freedom to exist, it was necessary to distinguish between "what relates to the freedom of the mind and its allegiance to its maker, [and] what belongs to the legitimate objects of political & civil institutions." Written as it was after a long public career engaged in advocating for religious freedom, Madison's Memorandum confirms that he had grown only more certain about the importance of church-state separation for maintaining religious equality and republican government.[49]

Jefferson's Later Years

During his presidency, Jefferson wrote little about church-state matters, his Danbury Baptist letter and his 1808 letter to Reverend Samuel Miller representing the chief exceptions. In his last months in office, however, he responded to addresses by two Baptist associations commending his public service. Jefferson utilized his replies to both associations to publicly reaffirm his commitment to religious freedom and church-state separation. To the Baltimore Baptist Association, Jefferson recalled that in their "early struggles for liberty, religious freedom could not fail to become a primary object." He expressed hope that people's "recollection of our former vassalage in religion and civil government" would "unite the zeal of every heart" to "preserve that independence in both" spheres.[50] To the Baptists of Chesterfield, Virginia, he affirmed that "in reviewing the history of the times through which we have past, no portion of it gives [me] greater satisfaction, on reflection, than that which presents the efforts of the friends of religious freedom, & the success with which they were crowned." "We have solved, by fair experiment, the great & interesting question whether freedom of religion is compatible with order in government and obedience to the laws; & we have experienced the quiet as well as the comfort which results from leaving every one to profess freely & openly those principles of religion which are the inductions of his own reason, & the serious convictions of his own enquiries."[51] These commitments would continue throughout the remainder of his life. His later writings, however, reflected a mix of optimism and pragmatism. Much had been accomplished, but true freedom of inquiry and a "perfect separation" frequently remained elusive.

Retiring from public life provided Jefferson with greater opportunity to resume his considerations about religion generally and Christianity in particular. This final page in his life would be fruitful for him, enabling him to address religious matters through two different mediums. One was through writing a second "book," *The Life and Morals of Jesus of Nazareth*—popularly called the "Jefferson Bible"—compiled after 1819. A second involved a practical application of Jefferson's religious views, the founding of the University of Virginia as a secular institution of higher learning. It would be in this last endeavor that Jefferson and Madison had their final collaboration in the cause of free inquiry and religious freedom.

The "Jefferson Bible"

In late 1819 or early 1820, seventy-seven-year-old Jefferson prepared a work he entitled *The Life and Morals of Jesus of Nazareth*, which was a compilation of textural extracts from the New Testament gospels. Jefferson gathered testaments in Greek, Latin, French, and English and cut out those passages from the gospels he believed provided an accurate and uncorrupted account of Jesus's life and moral teachings. He then arranged them in corresponding columns that were glued onto blank paper, which he had bound into book form. The excerpts contained in *The Life and Morals of Jesus* represented those parts of the Bible that reaffirmed Jefferson's religious beliefs—references to the Immaculate Conception, miracles, angels, the Resurrection, atonement, and other supernatural accounts were left on the cutting-room floor. Jefferson compiled *The Life and Morals of Jesus* for his personal use—in fact, his family was unaware of the book, which was not rediscovered until long after his death. That could mean the work had little or no impact on the development of American religious freedom. But in that the book represented the culmination of Jefferson's beliefs about rational Christianity and coincided with his organizing the University of Virginia as a secular institution, the book's creation and content are relevant to this discussion.[52]

The Life and Morals of Jesus found its impetus in the same considerations that motivated Jefferson to write his "Syllabus or Outline" in 1803. The syllabus had merely been an outline of Jefferson's personal beliefs about rational Christianity. Although he had no desire to publicize his religious beliefs—instructing the recipients of the syllabus to keep it private—he wanted a book to be written that corresponded to his beliefs and promoted his aspirational view of a unifying rational Christianity. In April 1803, Jefferson encouraged Joseph Priestley to write a book that emphasized Jesus's moral mission—to "take up the subject on a more extensive scale." To Jefferson's initial disappointment, Priestley declined the invitation to write the book but then in December he agreed to undertake the task. A grateful Jefferson wrote back on January 29, 1804, informing Priestley that he had already ordered several New Testaments anticipating writing the book himself but was relieved that "I shall now get the thing done by better hands." Unfortunately, Priestley died on February 6 before receiving Jefferson's letter or completing the book that Jefferson desired.[53]

Jefferson received his testaments two days before Priestley's death, so after receiving that news he decided to go ahead with the project himself. Rather than writing a critical analysis of relevant biblical passages, Jefferson compiled a list of those passages from the gospels that he believed contained the authentic moral teachings of Jesus, "selecting only those whose style and spirit proved them genuine." He then "cut out the morsels of morality, and past[ed] them on the leaves of a book." Jefferson felt confident about his ability to distinguish those passages that represented the true teachings of Jesus from the false doctrines that had been added by the Bible's authors, later describing the effort as "easily distinguishable as diamonds in a dunghill." The resulting document, some "46 pages of pure and unsophisticated doctrines," was the aforementioned "The Philosophy of Jesus," also called his "Extracts."[54]

Feeling confident about his effort, Jefferson wrote Benjamin Rush in August 1804, offering to send him a copy of "The Philosophy of Jesus" for his comments. Jefferson considered his pamphlet to be an extension of the syllabus he had sent Rush the year before, essentially "as containing the exemplification of what I advanced in [the] former letter." Jefferson likely anticipated a cordial response from Rush similar to what he had received regarding his syllabus; at that time, Rush had complimented Jefferson's "long & patient investigation of that Subject" but noted they had to "agree, to disagree." Now, in a brusque reply, Rush told Jefferson he was not interested in reading "The Philosophy of Jesus" "unless it advances it to divinity, and renders his *death* as well as his *life*, necessary for the restoration of mankind." Otherwise, "I shall not accord with its Author." Rush's rebuff disappointed Jefferson, so he did not forward his pamphlet. Rush's response also likely caused Jefferson to consider whether his "wee little book" needed more work and was not ready for publication. As he confided in a friend several years later, the pamphlet "was too hastily done . . . being the work of one or two evenings only" while he was "overwhelmed with other business" as president. Jefferson put aside his plans of a more extensive study of Jesus's moral ministry, keeping "The Philosophy of Jesus" for personal devotional use. Unfortunately, no copy of the pamphlet has survived, though in the 1980s a team of scholars reconstructed a likely facsimile of the document.[55]

Jefferson never gave up on his quest for a book that would highlight the genuine moral teachings of Jesus and separate them from the mysteries and other false doctrines that had perverted Christianity and distracted its followers from Jesus's true ministry. In his correspondence during retirement, Jefferson referred occasionally to "The Philosophy of Jesus" and to the need for a more comprehensive work. In an 1813 letter to John Adams, Jefferson solicited his fellow rationalist for moral support for a work that would discard all "corrupt maxims" contained in the Bible, "reduc[ing] our volume to the simple evangelists, select, even from them, the very words only of Jesus." There "will be found remaining the most sublime and benevolent code of morals which has ever been offered to man." He informed Adams that he had already "performed this operation for my own use," but something more extensive was needed. As he told another friend, "If I had time I would add to my little book the Greek, Latin and French texts, in columns side by side."[56]

Jefferson hoped he had found a possible author for such a book in Francis Adrian Van der Kemp, an immigrant Dutch scholar. Van der Kemp had contacted Jefferson in 1816 after reading his syllabus (which Adams had shared with Van der Kemp without Jefferson's permission). Jefferson solicited Van der Kemp, a former Unitarian minister, to take up the task, and the two exchanged a series of letters about the project. Unbeknownst to Jefferson, Van der Kemp had a reputation for not completing his scholarly undertakings, and the latter never followed through with his promise.[57] The impetus for Jefferson to finally write a monograph himself came in 1819 from William Short, his former secretary while in Paris, after the two exchanged letters where Jefferson wrote at length about his syllabus, his extracts, and his continuing desire for a book that emphasized Jesus's role as a great moral reformer. Short acknowledged Jefferson's hesitation to undertake the project but flattered him that "I know nothing which could be more [agreeable to you] & at the same time more useful to others." Referring to the syllabus in a subsequent letter, Short continued with the compliments, writing that "your view of the subject as relative to the Christian system is the most satisfactory that I have met with." Sometime following those exchanges, likely in the summer of 1820, Jefferson completed *The Life and Morals of Jesus.*[58]

In the end, *The Life and Morals of Jesus* was not the book Jefferson had encouraged others to write and that he thought was necessary to correct the mischaracterizations of Jesus's moral mission and refute Christian orthodoxy. The book met his own needs, and he decided to keep it for his private use; some twelve years after leaving public office, he still abjured the prospect of his religious beliefs being publicly scrutinized. The book, however, reaffirmed to him the correctness of his views about rational Christianity, which he them readily shared with his circle of friends and correspondents.[59]

Jefferson's Later Correspondence

Many of Jefferson's later musings about religion and its relation to civil society are found in his active correspondence with John Adams. As noted, the two former presidents frequently exchanged ideas about religious matters, mostly on an esoteric level. In the privacy that their letter-writing provided, both men were outspoken about their personal religious views. As Adams famously closed one letter, "I have more to Say, upon this Subject of Religion."[60] One recurring topic was the ongoing repression of free inquiry that existed in parts of the country, perpetuated chiefly by religious figures. In 1821, Jefferson remarked that "this country, which has given to the world the example of physical liberty, owes to it that of moral emancipation also, for, as yet, it is but nominal with us." Sadly, he noted, "the inquisition of public opinion overwhelms in practice the freedom [of conscience] asserted by the laws." Adams agreed, writing in January 1825 that "we boast that we are so of Liberty of Conscience on all subjects and of the right of free inquiry and private judgment; . . . yet how far are we from these exalted privileges in fact." He noted that blasphemy was still a crime not only in Europe but also throughout much of America. Beyond infringing on rights of conscience, Adams believed such restraints were unnecessary, as "the substance and essence of Christianity as I understand it is eternal and unchangeable and will bear examination forever." Adams, like Jefferson, "condemned the Christian world for conveying the impression that Christianity would not bear examination and criticism."[61]

In their frank discussions about religion, Jefferson and Adams condemned "priestcraft," disputed miracles and doctrines such as the Virgin Birth and Trinity as being untenable to rational people, and otherwise questioned the historical accuracy of the Bible, all positions that would have invited criticism if made public. Both men agreed that clergy had invented the idea of the Trinity to enhance their spiritual and temporal authority. It was "too late in the day for men of sincerity to pretend they believe in the Platonic mysticisms that three are one, & one is three; & yet the one is not three, and the three are not one," Jefferson wrote in 1813. The doctrine "constitutes the craft, the power and the profit of the priests. Sweep away their gossamer fabrics of factitious religion, and they would catch no more flies." In order to extract "the pure principles which he taught, we should have to strip off the artificial vestments in which they have been muffled by priests." Not only were such doctrines false and counter to Jesus's true ministry, but they were used to suppress freedom of inquiry. Jefferson looked forward to the day when the country would completely "put down the aristocracy of the clergy, and restore . . . to the citizen the freedom of the mind."[62]

One of Jefferson's last letters to Adams contains what is possibly the closest profession of Jefferson's faith. In a March 10, 1823, letter, Adams in jest wished Jefferson to live so long "until you shall become as perfect a calvinst as I am in one particular." The pun goaded Jefferson into a long reply, with him damning Calvin as "a dæmon of malignant spirit" for perpetuating false doctrines that corrupted the purity and simplicity of Christianity. On the contrary, he wrote, "I hold (without appeal to revelation) that when we take a view of the Universe, in it's parts general or particular, it is impossible for the human mind not to percieve and feel a conviction of design, consummate skill, and indefinite power in every atom of it's composition." It was impossible, he continued, "for the human mind not to believe that there is, in all this, design, cause and effect, up to an ultimate cause, a fabricator of all things from matter and motion, their preserver and regulator while permitted to exist in their present forms, and their regenerator into new and other forms." For Jefferson, nature's order sufficed as proof of "an intelligent and powerful Agent." The expositors of incomprehensive doctrines were the enemies of Christianity. Jefferson told Adams that they must "hope that the dawn of reason and freedom of thought in these United States will do away all this artificial scaffolding, and restore to us the primitive and genuine doctrines of this the most venerated reformer of human errors." He hoped that they might live to see that day, but if not, then "may we meet there again, in Congress, with our antient Colleagues, and recieve with them the seal of approbation 'Well done, good and faithful servants.'" In many respects, the letter represents the culmination of Jefferson's "spiritual pilgrimage," demonstrating confidence in his beliefs about a benevolent god who is discoverable through empiricism rather than revelation, and in an afterlife.[63]

Jefferson's correspondence with other acquaintances also contains the recurrent themes about the simplicity of pure Christianity, the corruptions of it by clergy, and how the activities of the latter threatened free inquiry and religious freedom.[64] Like Madison, Jefferson clearly saw the greater threat to religious freedom as coming from the clergy, empowered by their followers—their "willing dupes & drudges"—rather than from the government: "For although we have freedom of religious opinion by law, we are yet under the inquisition of public opinion."[65] That "loathsome combination of church and state" would likely occur only through the instigation of clergy.[66] Jefferson believed that the early uniting of church and state had also brought about the early church's rejection of primitive Christianity. The unity of God was not "ousted from the Christian creed by the force of reason, but by the sword of civil government wielded at the will of the fanatic Athanasius" (the instigator of the doctrine of the Trinity). Jefferson looked forward to the full "freedom of religious opinion, and it's eternal divorce from the civil authority."[67] Finally, rising sectarianism also caused Jefferson concern; he expressed dismay that Christianity had been "split into so many thousands of sects . . . who are disputing, anathematising, and where the laws permit, burning and torturing one another for abstraction[s] which no one of them understand, and which are indeed beyond the comprehension of the human mind." Jefferson believed "that, in heaven, God [knows] no distinctions, but consider[s] all good men as his children, and as brethren of the same family." Anyone "who steadily observes those moral precepts in which all religions concur, will never be questioned, at the gates of heaven, as to the dogmas in which they all differ." Sectarianism, Jefferson insisted, perpetuated religious intolerance, obfuscated basic Christian moral teachings, and undermined his goal of unifying Christianity under Unitarian and rationalistic principles. In the end, Jefferson believed he was one of the few "real Christians."[68]

The Final Collaboration

The University of Virginia

I n retirement, Thomas Jefferson's and James Madison's long and fruitful collaboration had one more chapter to write: creating a secular
university committed to free inquiry. For Jefferson in particular, but
also for Madison, this last collaboration would give them much satisfaction,
in no small part because it promised to be an enduring legacy on behalf of
religious freedom and republicanism. Even after the opening of the University of Virginia in 1825 and Jefferson's death the following year, the effects
of Jefferson's and Madison's collaboration on behalf of religious freedom
continued through the final efforts of Madison, who lived long enough to
see their ideas about church-state relations severely challenged.

"The Hobby of My Old Age"

No undertaking during Jefferson's retirement consumed as much of his attention and passion as did the founding of the University of Virginia. For
Jefferson, it was such a significant event that he engraved the accomplishment on his gravestone obelisk alongside two other two achievements—
the Declaration of Independence and the Statute for Establishing Religious
Freedom. In many respects, it represents one of Jefferson's and Madison's
more enduring legacies in the advance of American religious freedom.
For Jefferson, creating a university committed to free inquiry and rational
thought was the culmination of his lifelong commitment to freedom of conscience. The acquisition of knowledge, guided by reason and freed from the
constraints of hobbling doctrines, religious or otherwise, was essential for

the progress of republican society. Autocratic governments had exploited people's ignorance to keep them in vassalage to "kings, priests, and nobles," he wrote in 1786. Jefferson had implored his former professor George Wythe to "preach, my dear Sir, a crusade against ignorance" and "establish and improve the law for educating the common people." Later in retirement, Jefferson remained committed to these goals: "Enlighten the people generally, and tyranny and oppressions of body & mind will vanish like evil spirits at the dawn of day."[1]

Jefferson's lifelong crusade for expanding educational opportunities reflected his own valuation of learning and his unyielding belief that an educated populace was essential for the operation of republican governance. As he wrote to Madison from Paris in 1787, "I hope the education of the common people will be attended to; convinced that on their good sense we may rely with the most security for the preservation of a due degree of liberty." Writing some thirty years later to Joseph C. Cabell, a Virginia state senator who would become his indispensable ally in establishing the university, Jefferson reaffirmed the same sentiment: "There are two subjects indeed which I shall claim a right to further as long as I breathe, the public education and the subdivision of the counties into wards [for greater local governance, in part, for operating public schools]. I consider the continuance of republican government as absolutely hanging on these two hooks."[2] Jefferson also believed that education was an essential leveler in society for dismantling the "artificial aristocracy founded on wealth and birth" and for replacing it with "the natural aristocracy," which he "consider[ed] as the most precious gift of nature, for the instruction, the trusts, and government of society." Popular education was the means of achieving these goals.[3]

In 1779, Jefferson had drafted a bill in the Virginia Assembly for "the More General Diffusion of Knowledge." In it, he laid out a three-tiered plan for public education in the new state. At the initial level would be primary schools ("hundred schools") in every ward where young children, both boys and girls, could receive three years of free instruction in reading, writing, and basic arithmetic. Those boys who excelled would then go on to grammar schools, sometimes referred to as colleges, where they would receive up to six years of a classical education, including foreign languages. Finally, the top graduates of the grammar schools would be able to matriculate to the College of William and Mary for three years of free university education. Although Jefferson's bill did not expressly address the status of religious instruction, it was clear that he envisioned a secular-based curriculum for the primary and grammar schools: a "liberal education."[4] Jefferson elaborated on his plan in his *Notes on the State of Virginia* two years after drafting the bill, writing that "reason and free enquiry are the only effectual agents against error. . . . Instead therefore of putting the Bible and Testament in the hands of the children, at an age when their judgments are not sufficiently matured for religious enquiries, their memories may be stored with the most useful facts from Grecian, Roman, European, and American history." This was a bold departure from all existing schooling in early America where few people questioned whether religious instruction should be part of an educational program, the only issue being how pervasive it should be.[5]

As for the College of William and Mary, Jefferson had equally bold plans. In a separate bill that accompanied his bill for the diffusion of knowledge, Jefferson proposed amending the charter of the college to transform it from a private, Anglican college that received tax support into a publicly controlled university. Part of Jefferson's rationale for seizing control was that even though the college had been "amply endowed by the public," it had "not answered their expectation" in being a true institution of higher learning. Sectarian control and resistance to change had stifled that necessary development. Jefferson proposed adding several professorships in sciences, medicine, mathematics, and natural philosophy while abolishing the professorship of divinity. A publicly appointed board of visitors would replace those beholden to the Episcopal Church.[6] Jefferson had high hopes for his education reform bills; however, both bills languished in the assembly for years, with Madison advising Jefferson while he was in Paris that there simply was no political will to enact either measure. Finally, in 1796, the Virginia legislature enacted a watered-down law establishing Jefferson's first tier of public elementary schools.[7]

Jefferson never gave up on his desire to expand educational opportunities and improve their quality in the new nation. The pinnacle of this endeavor for Jefferson was to establish a public university committed to academic excellence and free inquiry. By 1800, however, Jefferson had abandoned that part of his plan to transform William and Mary into a public institution, now disparaging the college as "just well enough endowed to draw out the miserable existence to which a miserable constitution has doomed it." Jefferson turned his attention to creating a new state university "on a plan so broad & liberal & *modern,* as to be worth patronising with the public support, and be a temptation to the youth of other states to come, and drink of the cup of knolege." In January 1800, he solicited ideas from Joseph Priestley for a secular-based curriculum with a broad range of offerings in the sciences, medicine, mathematics, history, and fine arts. Priestley responded with a list of subjects though noting that Jefferson had failed to inquire about instruction in "the scriptures, ecclesiastical history," which was necessary "to qualify persons for commencing preachers." Priestley believed also that "every person liberally educated should have a general knowledge of Metaphysics, the theory of morals, and religion," such that a public university was obligated to offer lectures in these areas. Jefferson disagreed about any obligation to teach religion, and he feared that any such attempt would invite sectarian rivalries.[8] Jefferson's initial plans for establishing a public university were shelved with his election as president. (While serving as president, both Jefferson and Madison advocated establishing a national public university. Earlier, during his final year in Congress in 1796, Madison had spearheaded a proposal by President Washington to establish a public university in the new capital. All such efforts were to no avail.)[9]

Upon retiring from public office in 1809, Jefferson was able to return to his idea of creating a secular public university. As early as 1810, in a letter to the trustees of East Tennessee College (the forerunner of the University of Tennessee), Jefferson laid out some thoughts for the design of the campus he was envisioning for his future university.[10] The opportunity to move forward with his ideas arose in 1814 when he accepted an appointment to the board of a local secondary school, Albemarle Academy, that was being established by his nephew Peter Carr. Jefferson had grander plans for the school than his nephew, and after one failed attempt, he secured legislation to convert the academy into Central College, to be supported by a lottery, paid subscriptions, and the sale of old glebe lands. The incorporation of Central College created a Board of Visitors, which, in addition to Jefferson, included James Madison, President James Monroe, and Joseph C. Cabell, Jefferson's ally in the Virginia Senate. The board met in Charlottesville in May 1817, with the two former presidents and current president in the lead, and it purchased two hundred acres of land just west of town for a campus. Later that month, John Adams wrote Jefferson to "congratulate You and Madison and Monroe, on your noble Employment in founding a University. From Such a noble Tryumvirate, the World will expect Something very great and very new." Adams then included what became a premonition, adding, "but if it contains any thing quite original, and very excellent, I fear the prejudices are too deeply rooted to Suffer it to last long."[11]

Despite the initial fanfare, neither the status nor site of the new college was secure, as other towns vied to become the home for a state university. The location for the university, as well as a source of revenue, still needed legislative approval. In 1818, Governor James Preston appointed a commission to make recommendations for a plan and site for the state university, with the group meeting at Rockfish Gap in the Blue Ridge on August 1. Jefferson prepared a detailed report in advance setting out his vision for a university and making the case for locating it in Charlottesville. With Madison at his side, the commission unanimously adopted Jefferson's report, which in addition to stating the goals of higher education—to "develope the reasoning faculties of our youth, enlarge their minds, cultivate their morals, and instil into them the precepts of virtue & order"—set out ten separate academic departments in mathematics, languages, government, history, law, and the sciences, each to be headed by a distinguished professor. Missing in the report, and not just by omission, was a department of religion or theology. Jefferson's report explained why the university would not include a professor of divinity: it was "in favor of freedom of religion," to guard against "the jealousies of the different sects," and to "conform . . . with the principles of our constitution" (which, of course, Madison and Jefferson were responsible for). Any considerations of "the proofs of the being of a god, the creator, preserver, & supreme ruler of the universe" and their relation to morality would "be within the province of the professor of ethics." The report went on to rail against religion's stifling effect on acquiring knowledge, declaring that it promoted "the desponding view that the condition of man cannot be ameliorated," which was "the genuine fruit of the alliance between Church and State." Jefferson's report concluded that the commissioners "thought it proper," in order to follow the Virginia constitution, "to leave every sect to provide as they think fittest, the means of further instruction in their own peculiar tenets."[12] The legislature approved the report in January 1819, and the governor quickly appointed Jefferson, Madison, and Cabell to a new, seven-member Board of Visitors, which in turn appointed Jefferson rector, or chief executive officer.[13]

The legislature's approval of a university that Jefferson had envisioned was the culmination of five years of effort, but more accurately it was the realization of a lifelong goal. Jefferson believed, with some basis in fact, that the university represented a new experiment in higher education, one committed to freedom of inquiry unconstrained by orthodoxies, religious or otherwise. Most colleges were private and denominationally controlled, while other public colleges—the Universities of North Carolina, Georgia, and Tennessee, and the College of Charleston—operated under religious influences. Describing his plan to a British educator, Jefferson wrote, "This institution will be based on the illimitable freedom of the human mind. For here we are not afraid to follow truth wherever it may lead, nor to tolerate any error so long as reason is left free to combat it."[14]

This did not mean that either Jefferson or Madison considered that the university itself would be ideologically neutral or ambivalent about competing philosophies. The university would promote republicanism and rationalist thought: it would be "a Nursery of Republican patriots as well as genuine Scholars," Madison would later write.[15] In the "Principles of Government" for the university, adopted in 1825, Jefferson declared that "it is the opinion of this board" to inculcate "the general principles of liberty and the rights of man, in nature, and in society," and "to provide that none shall be inculcated which are incompatible with those on which the constitutions of this state and of the U.S. were genuinely based." As Jefferson wrote in a follow-up letter to Madison, when it came to teaching theories of government at the university, "it [is] a duty in us to lay down the principles which are to be taught." Jefferson was concerned that it was in this subject area "in which heresies may be taught," as he echoed in a letter to Joseph Cabell, and "it is our duty to guard against the dissemination of such principles among our youth, and the diffusion of that poison." Madison also worried about how to "safeguard against heretical intrusions" that might undermine the university's promotion of republicanism. So far as Jefferson and Madison were concerned, the "illimitable freedom of the human mind" promoted by the university went in one direction.[16]

Jefferson committed the remainder of his life to "the Hobby of my old age": building the university campus, developing its curriculum, and hiring a faculty. Madison worked closely with Jefferson on all of those matters, sharing the latter's bold vision for the university. Madison agreed that the faculty "should be amenable to their political as well as pedagogical perspectives," and he expressed concern over the lack of appropriate texts to promote republican values. The theorists they had studied in college, he noted—Locke

and Sydney—were adequate to inspire people to establish republican governments "but afford[ed] no aid in guarding our [existing] Republican
Charters against constructive violations." He shared Jefferson's sentiment
that "our post-revolutionary youth" took republicanism for granted, leaving
them susceptible to contrary "heretical intrusions." It was as if "they acquire
all learning in their mothers' womb, and bring it into the world ready-made.
The information of books is no longer necessary."[17] Historian James Morton
Smith, compiler of the correspondence between the two men, noted that
"every letter they exchanged in 1818 and 1819, discussed that subject," and
the operations of the university dominated their letter-writing through 1826.
Jefferson's use of the word "hobby" to describe his actions in developing the
university—the term appears frequently in his letters—clearly understates
how the matter both consumed and motivated him during his final years.[18]

Jefferson's and Madison's commitment to maintaining the secular character of the university was tested with one of their first faculty hirings. Even
before the university was formally launched, Jefferson had the Central College Board of Visitors offer Thomas Cooper a professorship in chemistry
and law, an appointment the university Board of Visitors confirmed in 1819.
Jefferson had actively corresponded with Cooper for several years, solic-
iting his ideas about how to structure the curriculum at the prospective
university. Obtaining Cooper would be a coup, Jefferson believed, as he
considered Cooper, "without a single exception," to be "the greatest man
in America in the powers of mind and in acquired information." Jefferson,
of course, was fully aware of Cooper's heretical writings and his reputation
as an intellectual pugilist. Those qualities no doubt attracted Jefferson to
Cooper, but in offering Cooper the position Jefferson's normally keen political instincts failed him.[19]

Shortly after Cooper's appointment became publicly known, evangelical
clergy launched an attack against him for being "rash, dogmatic, and pre-
emptory." Richmond Presbyterian minister John Rice led the charge. Rice
had been monitoring the planning for the University of Virginia for some
time and expressed concern over the lack of a theology department. For
Rice and other evangelicals, the omission confirmed Jefferson's heretical
reputation, and they suspected that he intended to turn the university into
a deistic or Unitarian institution. In 1818, Rice warned that "Christians of
various denominations will loudly complain, that, although they are citizens, possessing equal rights with others, . . . their opinions are disregarded,

their feelings trampled on, and their money appropriated utterly contrary to their wishes." The appointment of Cooper now confirmed evangelicals' suspicions about the university's irreligious orientation.[20]

In February 1820, Rice published an attack on Cooper in his *Virginia Evangelical and Literary Magazine* that quoted extracts of Cooper's *Memoirs of Dr. Joseph Priestley* (1806), where he had declared that a person could be a good member of society whether he believed "in one God, in three Gods, in thirty thousand Gods, or no God!" Rice called Cooper a "speculative infidel" and charged that "we cannot wish that a man who obtrudes such sentiments on the public, should have the direction of our young citizens" at the university.[21] Cooper's appointment had been delayed by a year due to university financial constraints, so he had acquired a temporary position teaching at South Carolina College. Upon reading the article, Cooper wrote Jefferson complaining about "the incessant attacks of the clergy against my *supposed* heterodoxy," though noting that "while you & Mr Madison live, & I live, I know that I shall be defended." Still, he offered to resign the appointment to prevent additional controversy. Jefferson wrote back immediately, seeking to reassure Cooper that only "a dozen or two fanatics or bigots of his sect in this state may read his Evangelical magazine." "The snarle of mr Rice issues from the spirit of *his priesthood*," Jefferson wrote, and Presbyterians in particular "are jealous of the general diffusion of science, and therefore hostile to our Seminary. . . . Not daring to attack the institution with the avowal of their real motives, they peck at you, at me."[22]

But support for Cooper among the Board of Visitors was already weak; a year earlier Madison had told Jefferson that he was "begin[ing] to be uneasy on the subject of Cooper" out of concern the appointment would embolden opponents of the university. Joseph Cabell also expressed reservations, remarking that while Cooper's "talents and acquirements are unquestioned . . . in point of manners, habits or character, he is defective."[23] After making inquiries among colleagues who were "better judges of popular feeling" and considering "the hue and cry raised from the different pulpits" over Cooper's appointment, Jefferson realized the controversy would not subside. In April 1820, he wrote Cooper that he now had "reason to apprehend that I had estimated too lightly the opposition had then pointed at yourself." It was not, as he had assumed, "the clamor of a single sect only [i.e., Presbyterians] which is raised; but all have sounded the tocsin of alarm on your appointment, as bringing into the institution principles subversive of the religion of the land, and threatening dangerous effect on the youth who may come to it." Jefferson regrettably accepted Cooper's offer to withdraw, expressing hope that Cooper might be able to join the faculty in a few years after the appointment of other professors. As Jefferson informed his Board of Visitors, he "sincerely lament[ed] that untoward circumstances have brought on us the irreparable loss of this professor, whom I have looked to as the corner stone of our edifice."[24]

The episode over Cooper left Jefferson embittered and only reconfirmed his anticlerical views. In a follow-up letter to Cooper, Jefferson denounced "the bellowings of our pulpit mountebanks." It was within this context that Jefferson referred to Presbyterian clergy as the "loudest, the most intolerant of all sects, the most tyrannical, and ambitious. . . . They pant to reestablish *by law* that holy inquisition, which they can now only infuse into *public opinion.*" Cooper concurred that the Presbyterians were "a systematic and persevering sect." He also expressed "regret [over] the storm that has been raised on my account, for it has separated me from many fond hopes and wishes." He felt "gloomy at the persevering, determined, unwearied march of religious intolerance among us."[25] Cooper faced similar attacks from Presbyterian and Baptist clergy in South Carolina, with him relating to Jefferson about their efforts to dismiss him from South Carolina College for allegedly turning it into a "seat of infidelity and tyranny."[26]

Jefferson, who still admired Cooper and regretted having accepted his resignation, later wrote Madison in January 1824, raising the prospect of rehiring Cooper at the university. "I have no hesitation in saying I should be willing myself to accept him," Jefferson implored, but he did not want to "to force him on our colleagues by a bare majority." Madison wisely counseled against the idea. Although he "lamented that at his stage of life . . . [Cooper] should experience the persecutions which torment and depress him," Madison wrote, "what is worse [is] that the spirit which persecuted him where he is, would find a co-partner here not less active in poisoning his happiness, and impairing the popularity of th[is] Institution." Madison's head prevailed over Jefferson's heart. Despite Jefferson's desires, Cooper never came to the University of Virginia, remaining at South Carolina College until 1833, eventually becoming its president while fending off ongoing attacks on his theological beliefs.[27]

Jefferson spent his remaining years developing his university, which finally opened to students in 1825. He persistently defended the secular character of the university, resisting efforts by Presbyterians and Episcopalians to exert influence over its operations and to encroach on its funding from the state.[28] As a partial concession to his religious critics and a means of deflecting charges of hostility toward religion, Jefferson agreed to allow various sects to establish their own "professorships" housed adjacent to the university, and to allow them access to the facilities and library. Jefferson and Madison believed that "by bringing the sects together, and mixing them with the mass of other students, we shall soften their asperities, liberalise and neutralise their prejudices."[29] In conjunction with this accommodation, in 1824 Jefferson solicited Madison to prepare a list of theological works for the library, "Christian as well as Pagan," remarking that with Madison's early theological training, he knew of no one "[more] capable to whom we could refer the task." Madison sent Jefferson a list containing an "intermixture of the doctrinal & controversial part of Divinity with the metaphysical & moral part," affirming that "altho' Theology was not to be taught in the University, its Library ought to contain pretty full information for such as might voluntarily seek it in that branch of Learning." Committed to freedom of conscience, neither man opposed people exercising their own private judgment about matters of religious belief.[30]

Jefferson kept up his correspondence about university matters until the end of his life, remarking to John Adams that working on his "Hobby" helped relieve the "tedium . . . [during] the hoary winter of age" while he awaited "the friendly hand of death."[31] In one of his final letters to Madison, Jefferson wrote at length about the appropriate qualifications for a professor of law and about purchasing additional books for the library. Although he knew it was unnecessary, Jefferson urged Madison to continue with their vision of a university committed to republicanism and free inquiry: "It is in our Seminary that that Vestal flame is to be kept alive." Madison replied with a note of reassurance, declaring, "You do not overrate the interest I feel in the University as the Temple through which alone lies the road to that of Liberty." After Jefferson's death, Madison reaffirmed that "the University of Virginia, as a temple dedicated to Science & Liberty, was after his retirement from the political sphere, the object nearest his heart." It bore "the stamp of his genius, and will be a noble monument of his fame."[32]

Even though their final letters contained the usual attention to shared matters of interest—politics, agriculture, the university—they included a poignant awareness that their grand collaboration was coming to an end.

As Jefferson told Madison, "The friendship which has subsisted between us, now half a century, and the harmony of our political principles and pursuits, have been sources of constant happiness to me thro' that long period." "If ever the earth has beheld a system of administration conducted with a single and steadfast eye, to the general interest and happiness of those committed to it, one which, protected by truth, can never know reproach, it is that to which our lives have been devoted. To myself, you have been a pillar of support thro' life. Take care of me when dead, and be assured that I shall leave with you my last affections."[33] Madison replied with similar affection:

> You cannot look back to the long period of our private friendship & political harmony, with more affecting recollections than I do. If they are a source of pleasure to you, what ought they not be to me? We can not be deprived of the happy consciousness of the pure devotion to the public good, with which we discharged the trusts committed to us. And I indulge a confidence that sufficient evidence will find its way to another generation, to ensure, after we are gone, whatever of justice may be witheld whilst we are here.[34]

As is well known, Jefferson died on July 4, 1826, fifty years to the day from the signing of his Declaration of Independence and on the same day that his friend and rival John Adams also passed away. People mourned the joint loss of the two statesmen while some saw the coincidental date of their deaths on the nation's fiftieth anniversary as a providential affirmation from God. The loss of Jefferson was particularly great for Madison, not simply for the passing of his political collaborator and intellectual ally but for the loss of a true friend. As Madison commiserated with Lafayette a few months afterward, "The loss of others dear to us both, shortens the list to which we belong, [but] that which we have lately sustained at Monticello is irreparable."[35]

Madison's Later Years

Madison succeeded Jefferson as rector of the University of Virginia, a duty he fulfilled for the remainder of his life, serving longer as the head of the university with students enrolled than did Jefferson. In one of his last letters to Madison, Jefferson had expressed "a comfort to leave that institution under your care, and an assurance that they will neither be spared, nor ineffectual." Madison remained true to the task, reaffirming his belief in the benefits of a liberal education in a letter to a Kentucky acquaintance concerning that state's efforts to establish its own educational system: "Learned Institutions ought to be favorite objects with every free people. They throw that light over the public mind which is the best security against crafty & dangerous encroachments on the public liberty. . . . What spectacle can be more edifying or more seasonable, than that of Liberty & Learning, each leaning on the other for their mutual & surest support?"[36]

Madison also defended the university's secular character. As two biographers note, while serving as rector he "was constantly in communication with the other, younger members of the Board of [Visitors], seeing to it that they did not convert a secular institution into one with religious affiliation." In 1828, board member Chapman Johnson wrote Madison about a potential faculty candidate for the chair in natural philosophy, William Ritchie from Britain. Johnson mentioned that there was some confusion as to whether Ritchie was also a clergyman, but even if he was, Johnson thought it should not "constitute a valid objection to his appointment." On the contrary, Johnson wrote, "it would, in our estimation, be rather a recommendation; for whilst we would guard the University, with jealousy, against all manner of agency in propagating sectarian doctrines, and would not consent that it should have any connexion with ecclesiastical affairs, we would anxiously protect it, from the injurious imputation of being a school for infidelity." Obviously, Johnson was aware of the earlier criticism of the university's secular character.[37]

Madison replied to Johnson that after having examined Ritchie's credentials, he did not believe he was a clergyman. Still, he cautioned, "I cannot but think nevertheless, that desireable as it may be that the Professors should be exemplary in a proper respect for Religion as in every thing else, it will be better to have that benefit separated from than united with the Ecclesiastical profession, in an Institution, essentially un-sectarian." Madison was concerned, based on criticisms they had weathered from Presbyterians and others, that if they appointed a clergyman to the faculty, "jealousy and discontent could not fail to be excited among the Sects not having the same advantage in [the] Institution." Madison felt he was steering a delicate course, attempting to avoid religious conflict that would undermine the university's mission.[38] As he informed another acquaintance, he maintained his position not out "of any disrespect to Religion, but of the impossibility of providing for [theological education] in a country abounding in different Sects." An additional reason for not teaching religion, Madison noted, was that the university was "an Institution created by [state] Authority and supported by a revenue, common to them all." To do otherwise would result in one person's paying for another's religious training. Here was an example of Madison's opposition to the government funding religious instruction, even while it was funding comparable instruction in secular matters.[39]

Madison defended the university's approach to religion to Edward Everett, who at that time was a professor at Harvard University during its conflict between Unitarian and Trinitarian factions. Madison empathized with "the dilemma produced at your University, by making Theological Professorships an integral part of the System." A "University with Sectarian professorships, becomes of course, a Sectarian Monopoly; with professorships of rival sects, it would be an arena of Theological Gladiators." Madison acknowledged that "without any such professorship, it must incur, for a time at least, the imputation of irreligious tendencies if not designs. The last difficulty was thought more manageable [at the University of Virginia], than either of the others." He commented on how some Virginia clergy continued "to arraign the peculiarity [of having no theology department]; but it is not improbable that they had an eye to the chance of introducing their own Creed into the Professor's Chair." Madison believed that "there seems to be no alternative but between a public University without a Theological professorship, or Sectarian Seminaries without a University." He was firmly committed to the former.[40]

In his retirement correspondence, Madison commented on his views about church-state relations only occasionally, usually during recollections about debates over disestablishment in Virginia some four decades earlier. In 1819, Madison replied to an inquiry by Philadelphia journalist Robert Walsh Jr. about the religious situation in Virginia since the Revolution. Madison responded that it had been "the universal opinion of the Century preceding the last, that Civil Govt. could not stand without the prop of a Religious establishment, and that the Christian religion itself, would perish if not supported by a legal provision for its Clergy." He declared that the disestablishment "experience of Virginia conspicuously corroborates the disproof of both opinions." Due to the resulting religious equality and system of voluntaryism, "religious instruction is now diffused throughout the Community, by preachers of every Sect with almost equal zeal," Madison noted. As a result, he told Walsh, "the industry, and the morality of the priesthood & the devotion of the people have been manifestly increased by the total separation of the Church from the State."[41]

Madison made similar boasts about the value of church-state separation in letters to other acquaintances. To New York Lutheran minister Frederick C. Schaeffer, Madison remarked that "the [religious] experience of the U.S. is a happy disproof of the error so long rooted in the unenlightened minds of well meaning Christians, as well as in the corrupt hearts of persecuting Usurpers, that without a legal incorporation of religious & civil polity, neither could be supported. A mutual independence is found most friendly to practical Religion, to social harmony, & to political prosperity."[42] And to Louisiana congressman Edward Livingston, Madison wrote that "the immunity of Religion from Civil Jurisdiction, in every case where it does not trespass on private rights or the public peace . . . has always been a favorite point with me." This statement reflected Madison's longstanding view that civil government lacked jurisdiction or agency over religious matters. Madison expressed concern, however, that "there remains in others, a strong bias towards the old error, that without some sort of alliance or coalition between Government & Religion, neither can be duly supported." Despite legal disestablishment, Madison noted, "th[is] danger can not be too carefully guarded against." And as he had expressed earlier to Robert Walsh, Madison affirmed that "Religion & Govt. will both exist in greater purity, the less they are mixed together." The solution, Madison declared, was to maintain "a perfect separation between ecclesiastical & Civil matters."[43]

Madison's continuing concern about the fragility of the gains he and Jefferson had achieved on behalf of religious freedom, and of the need for the separation of religious and civil functions to ensure it, came up in his March 1823 letter to Edward Everett. At the time, Massachusetts maintained the only remaining religious establishment, technically benefiting all recognized Protestant denominations but favoring Trinitarian and Unitarian Congregationalist churches. Madison attacked the system, remarking that "a legal establishment of Religion," even one that professed toleration, "is no security for public quiet & harmony, but rather a source itself of discord & animosity." In contrast, Madison noted, "the settled opinion [in Virginia] is that religion is essentially distinct from Civil Govt. and exempt from its cognizance; that a connexion between them is injurious to both." And, Madison continued, "no doubt exists that there is more religion among us now than there ever was before" disestablishment. "This proves rather more than that the law is not necessary to the support of Religion." Madison's occasional correspondence on the issue, considered in conjunction with his Detached Memoranda written around the same time, demonstrates that his views on church-state matters did not waver in his later years.[44]

One final letter deserves mention, as it came late in Madison's life at a time when the informal Protestant establishment was gaining ground in society. In the spring of 1833, Reverend Jasper Adams, rector of St. Michael's Episcopal Church in Charleston, South Carolina, and nephew of John Adams, sent Madison a printed version of a sermon where he maintained, in great detail, that the United States was legally a "Christian nation." Reverend Adams criticized the assertion that was "gradually gaining belief among us, that Christianity has no connexion with the law of the land, or with our civil and political institutions." That sentiment, advanced "by men distinguished for their talents, learning, and station" (a slight on Jefferson), was "in contradiction to the whole tenor of our history," Adams asserted, and "to be false in fact, and in the highest degree pernicious in its tendency, to all our most valuable institutions." The "question of great interest," therefore, was whether the founders "intend[ed] to renounce all connexion with the Christian religion," Adams asked rhetorically, or had they only intended "to disclaim all preference of one sect of Christians over another, as far as civil government was concerned; which they still retained the Christian religion as the foundation-stone of all their social, civil and political institutions?" He believed that history clearly supported the latter proposition, and his pamphlet provided examples of government recognition of Christianity. This evidence led Adams to declare, in capital letters: "THE PEOPLE OF THE UNITED STATES HAVE RETAINED THE CHRISTIAN RELIGION AS THE FOUNDATION OF THEIR CIVIL, LEGAL AND POLITICAL INSTITUTIONS." Accordingly, Adams asserted, "while all others enjoy full protection in the profession of their opinions and practice, Christianity is the established religion of the nation, its institutions and usages are sustained by legal sanctions, and many of them are incorporated with the fundamental law of the country."[45]

Adams insisted the First Amendment was not to the contrary; rather, it was simply designed to leave the religious "situation in which it found it." But he interpreted the religion clauses to impose only a one-way street; while Congress had "no commission to destroy or injure the religion of the country . . . [its] laws ought to be consistent with its principles and usages," including enforcing Christian morality. Failure to do so, he insisted, would result in "a decline of public and private morals" and the undermining of religion. (Adams also warned about the threat of "Infidelity," which thanks to "adversaries" like Jefferson and Franklin, had "put on the decorous garb of rational and philosophical enquiry.") Adams's missive, coming as it did from a scion of one of the nation's more respected political families, represented a significant public broadside on the Jefferson-Madison vision of church-state separation. (Adams's sermon was also likely directed at Jefferson protégé Thomas Cooper, whose vocal ideas about church and state had embroiled his tenure as president of South Carolina College.) In addition to sending his pamphlet to Madison, Adams sent copies to several leading public figures, including Supreme Court justices John Marshall and Joseph Story, hoping for the greatest impact. Story, a longtime nemesis of Jefferson on church-state matters, sent Adams a letter praising the sermon's contents.[46]

Madison was now eighty-three and in poor health. Nonetheless, he responded at length in a polite but resolute letter. Rather than criticizing Adams's account directly, Madison offered a measured rebuttal, drawing from his own knowledge of history. That history had taught that the best system was one where support of religion was "left to the voluntary associations & contributions of individuals." Rights of conscience, Madison insisted, are "more or less invaded by all religious Establishments." The example of Virginia, where "now more than 50 years since the legal support of Religion was withdrawn, sufficiently prove[s] that it does not need the support of Government, and it will scarcely be contended that Government has suffered by the exemption of Religion from its cognizance." Madison acknowledged that "it may not always [be] easy to trace the line of separation between the rights of religion and the Civil authority with such distinctness as to avoid collisions & doubts on unessential points." He insisted, however, that any uncertainty as to those boundaries did not justify intermixing the two entities. "The tendency to an usurpation on one side or the other, or to a corrupting coalition or alliance between them, will be best guarded against by an entire abstinence of the Government from interference in any way whatever, beyond the necessity of preserving public order and protecting each sect against the trespasses on its rights by others."[47]

Some scholars have focused on Madison's choice of words in that he used the phrase "line of separation" rather than employing Jefferson's "wall." A "line," rather than a "wall," "does not conjure up the image of . . . a clearly defined and impregnable barrier" that separates religion from government, wrote historian Sidney E. Mead. But as has previously been discussed, Madison used multiple terms to describe the concept of church-state separation. Other language in his reply—decrying "the interference of Government in *any* form" in religion and calling for its "entire abstinence"—indicates that Madison was not retreating from his stance on church-state matters.[48]

Madison's long public career reveals a striking consistency in his approach to religious freedom, the rights of conscience, and the separation of church and state. A handful of discrepancies, such as prayer proclamations, cannot tarnish his monumental contributions or writings about these matters. Biographer Ralph Ketcham insisted that "there is no principle in Madison's wide range of private opinions and long public career to which he held with greater vigor and tenacity than this one of religious liberty." That included an "unwavering . . . support for complete separation of church and state." And considering his role in crafting Virginia's Declaration of Rights, the Statute for Establishing Religious Freedom, and the First Amendment, there can be little doubt that "Madison was prouder of his forward role in support of freedom of religion . . . than he was of any other accomplishment." But Madison was humble about his accomplishments until the end of his life, frequently giving credit to his collaboration with Jefferson. In one of his final letters, Madison thanked George Tucker for dedicating his book *The Life of Thomas Jefferson* to him, remarking about his good fortune of having had such a long association with one "whose principles of liberty and political career mine have been so extensively congenial."[49]

James Madison died on June 28, 1836, and was buried at his home at Montpelier, Virginia. A grave marker simply designates him as "Father of the Constitution" and "Fourth President of the United States." It could say so much more about his many contributions on behalf of the nation, particularly in the cause of religious freedom.[50]

TWELVE

The Legacy

T homas Jefferson's and James Madison's contributions in further-ance of American religious freedom are unmatched by any other figures of the founding period, or by any person since. As Edwin Gaustad remarked, "No collaboration had more significance for America's history, or for religious liberty, than the one that kept this potent team knit tightly together for a half century."[1] Their contributions influenced popular conceptions about rights of conscience, religious freedom, and the church-state jurisprudence of the nation's courts for close to two hundred years. Even though their expansive views of religious freedom and church-state separation have fallen into disfavor among judicial and religious conser-vatives in recent decades, their understandings still represent the begin-ning point for any discussion about these issues and are the standards by which all competing schemas are measured.[2] As much as critics have tried to marginalize Jefferson's and Madison's influence and relevance, the fact is their contributions cannot be ignored; despite the criticism, Jefferson and Madison "have remained the spiritual fathers of American religious lib-erty." More than any other figures, they deserve the title as the inventors of American religious freedom.[3]

Constructing Jefferson's Legacy

Consideration of their legacy, including an evaluation of the American ideas of religious freedom and church-state separation, began almost immedi-ately upon Jefferson's death. In 1829, his grandson and namesake Thomas

Jefferson Randolph published Jefferson's *Memoirs*, which were a compilation of his *Autobiography*, letters, notes, and miscellaneous papers. For the
first time, the public was able to read some of Jefferson's private correspondence where he revealed his opinions about a range of matters including his
religious inclinations. However, it was his "Anas"—a collection of anecdotes
and reflections chiefly about political opponents (e.g., "[Alexander] Hamilton was not only a monarchist, but for a monarchy bottomed on corruption")—that was most explosive and provided fodder for his critics. "Have
you seen Mr. Jefferson's Works?" Supreme Court justice Joseph Story exclaimed to an acquaintance. "If not, sit down at once and read his fourth
volume. It is the most precious mélange of all sorts of scandals you ever
read. . . . His attacks on Christianity are *a mode de Voltaire*; and singularly
bold, and mischievous."[4]

Randolph's collection of Jefferson's writings was followed in 1837 by
the first biography of Jefferson, written by George Tucker, which offered a
sympathetic portrait of the former president. Tucker's biography, *The Life
of Thomas Jefferson*, extensively discussed the disestablishment episode in
Virginia and Jefferson's leading role in it, praising "the celebrated act of religious freedom drawn by Mr. Jefferson" as leading to the "entire freedom
of religion in the United States." Tucker also related Madison's role in the
enterprise, describing his *Memorial and Remonstrance* as "exhibiting the
same candid, dispassionate, and forceful reasoning, which have ever characterized the productions of his pen." According to Tucker, the *Memorial*
convinced all doubters of the merits of disestablishment. Without using the
term "separation of church and state," Tucker defended the wisdom of the
Jeffersonian-Madisonian model of church-state relations, borrowing arguments from the *Memorial* to commend the voluntary support of religion,
which he insisted had given rise to public piety.[5]

Accounts of Jefferson's life and his role in securing religious freedom appeared at a crucial time. Even before Andrew Jackson's election as president
in 1828, he was reconstituting the Jeffersonian Republican coalition into the
Democratic Party, whose leaders eagerly claimed Jefferson as their titular
founder. In so doing, they embraced Jeffersonian conceptions of church-
state separation.[6] Between 1828 and 1830, a national controversy broke out
over the issue of Sunday mail delivery. Disregard for Sabbath observance
was a leading pique of moral reformers like Lyman Beecher, and following
Jackson's election the General Union for the Promotion of the Christian

Sabbath launched a petition drive to Congress seeking the repeal of a federal law that required Sunday mail delivery. Over the course of two years, approximately nine hundred petitions were forwarded to Washington, many of them mass-produced containing hundreds of signatures, arguing that Sunday mail delivery violated the "law of God," conflicted with state and local Sabbath laws, and infringed on the rights of Christian postmasters. More than one petition asserted that "the Government of the United States was formed under the influence of Christian principles."[7]

A loose coalition of Jacksonian Democrats, skeptics, and the Workingmen's Party members opposed the law's repeal, submitting their own petitions that contended a Sunday ban would invite an "abhorrent and antirepublican union of church and state." As a group of New Jersey memorialists declared, a repeal would constitute "a direct violation of the principles of the Constitution . . . the object of which would be to sustain their particular tenets or religious creeds to the exclusion of others, thereby uniting ecclesiastical and civil law."[8] Committees in both houses of Congress considered the petitions on different occasions, with each issuing reports sustaining the Sunday delivery law. Both reports were authored by Richard M. Johnson, a leading Democrat and the future vice president under Martin Van Buren. Johnson embraced the Jeffersonian model of church and state, writing that "our government is a civil, and not a religious, institution." If Congress through legislation should "define the law of God, or point out to the citizen one religious duty, it may, with equal propriety, proceed to define every part of divine revelation, and enforce every religious obligation, even to the forms and ceremonies of worship, the endowment of the church, and the support of the clergy." For these reasons, he concluded, it "is inevitable that the line cannot be too strongly drawn between church and state." In neither report did Johnson mention Jefferson or Madison by name, although Johnson intimated their influence by noting that the "framers of the Constitution recognized the eternal principle that man's relation with God is above human legislation, and his rights of conscience inalienable."[9]

The same time period witnessed a revival of religious skepticism, led by figures such as labor reformer Robert Owen, his son Robert Dale Owen, George Evans, and the infamous Frances Wright, the "Red Harlot of Infidelity." In addition to advocating workers' rights and sexual liberation, the skeptics railed against religious orthodoxy and the efforts of the moral reform societies. They praised Jefferson and his *Notes on the State of Virginia* while they embraced separation of church and state. This combination found a receptive audience among Jacksonian Democrats, artisans, and working people who resented the efforts of the benevolent societies and their Whig business allies to impose forms of social and labor control. Historians have noted that anticlericalism was strong among Jacksonians and their allies, which by the 1830s had "reached a zenith."[10]

Then, in 1832, President Jackson followed Jefferson's example by refusing to issue a prayer proclamation in the wake of the cholera epidemic that ravaged the eastern states. Jackson declared that to do so would transcend his authority as president and "disturb the security which religion now enjoys in this country in its complete separation from the political concerns of the General Government." Jackson was also prepared to veto a prayer resolution proposed by Henry Clay if it had passed Congress. "I deem it my duty to preserve this separation and to abstain from any act which may tend to an amalgamation perilous to both" church and state, he wrote. Jackson, who willingly accepted the title as the "Second Jefferson," saw himself as protecting Jefferson's vision of church-state separation.[11]

These trends and events, which relied on Jeffersonian ideas of separationism, were criticized by religious conservatives and moral reformers. The critics understood, correctly, that the Jeffersonian legacy of church-state relations represented an impediment to achieving their ideal of a Christian republic, as Jasper Adams had expressed in his 1832 sermon sent to Madison. In 1837, conservative Episcopalian minister Francis Lister Hawks wrote a blistering review of George Tucker's *Life of Thomas Jefferson* in the *New York Review* that contested Tucker's hagiographic account of Jefferson's accomplishments. Hawks committed approximately one-third of his fifty-four-page review to attacking Jefferson's religious character, selectively quoting the more damning statements from Jefferson's correspondence to show that "he entertained a hatred of Christianity, as commonly understood and received." Jefferson used his political authority to undermine religion, Hawks insisted, while he used his university to turn "gifted and unsuspecting youth" into "victim[s] of a deliberate, coldblooded, calculated design for [their] corruption" by "seeking to make young infidels by the wholesale."[12] The following year Theodore Dwight published his *The Character of Thomas Jefferson*, which also selectively used Jefferson's letters to prove the longstanding charges of his infidelity. After quoting from Jefferson's letters to Benjamin Rush, Joseph Priestley, John Adams, and William Short,

Dwight concluded that any man who "disbelieved the divine authority and inspiration of the Scriptures, . . . who denies the divinity of the Saviour . . . and who calls God a cruel and remorseless being, cannot be a Christian."[13]

Whereas both Hawks and Dwight concentrated their attacks on Jefferson's religious character, another critique published in 1838 attacked Jefferson's stance on church-state matters. That year, Whig senator Theodore Frelinghuysen wrote a lengthy missive about the dangers of the Jeffersonian approach to church-state matters. Frelinghuysen was a devout evangelical, known as "the Christian statesman" and a "man of most preserving religiosity," who was affiliated with several moral reform societies.[14] In his pamphlet *An Inquiry into the Moral and Religious Character of the American Government*, Frelinghuysen denounced the "false" theory of church-state relations being advanced by Jacksonians and their freethinking allies. "The danger of formal alliances between church and state, is [a] matter of history and well understood," Frelinghuysen wrote, "but the propriety and merit of *political irreligion*—of carrying on the business of the commonwealth professedly as 'without God in the world' . . . was never openly taught and accredited till very recent times." The person responsible for this alarming trend was obvious: "President Jefferson was the first American teacher of this sort of doctrine." The "sophistry of this reasoning" was responsible not only for the rise of immorality but also for efforts to restrict Christian influences on society: "The whole land is infected and becoming sick with the notion, that somehow there is that in the nature of our government, that calls not only for caution in regard to religion, but for a distinct jealousy against it." He urged people to distinguish the necessary influence of "ethical Christianity" from that of "ecclesiastical Christianity." "We want the government honestly *administered on christian principles, and with christian ends in view*." But "Mr. Jefferson's dogma" about church-state separation, Frelinghuysen insisted, represented "a false position."[15]

Conservative resistance to the Jeffersonian perspective about church and state continued into the following decade, even though the threats presented by organized skepticism had declined by then. As discussed in an earlier chapter, evangelical historian Robert Baird attacked Jefferson and his statute in Baird's 1844 book *Religion in the United States of America*. He condemned the statute for placing all religions on the same level, to the detriment of Christianity. This conflicted with the country's status, both culturally and legally, as a "Christian nation," Baird insisted. As for the

Constitution, Baird explained the First Amendment as simply leaving religious matters under the responsibility of the states but not as affecting any
change. The absence of a deific acknowledgment in the document also did
not trouble Baird: "The authors of that constitution never dreamed that they
were to be regarded as treating Christianity with contempt, because they
did not formally mention it as the law of the land, which it was already;
much less that it should be excluded from the government." Under Baird's
revisionist view of history and the law, rather than the government's lacking
jurisdiction over religious matters as Jefferson and Madison had insisted,
"the general government is not restrained from promoting religion."[16]

Another attack on the Jeffersonian-Madisonian conception of church-
state separation came from Tayler Lewis, a conservative theologian and
editor at *Harper's Magazine.* In an 1846 article in the *American Whig Review*
titled "Has the State a Religion?" Lewis criticized "that shallow doctrine of
the Monticello School, which some regard as . . . the last and greatest attainment of political wisdom." He noted sarcastically that according to that
doctrine, for someone "to mention the word religion in connection with
politics . . . [then] you are for [a union of] Church and State." On the contrary, Lewis argued, "the fact is, that we are, as yet, a Christian nation. . . .
We meet on the broad ground of a common professed Christianity; not in
the narrow sense of being *established* by law, but as forming the basis on
which the law itself is *established.*" Like Baird and Frelinghuysen, Lewis
was reacting less to any actual challenge to evangelical dominance than to
the ongoing resiliency of Jefferson's image, which remained popular among
Democrats, liberal intellectuals, and transcendentalists, who emerged in
the 1840s promoting the latest form of religious liberalism.[17]

One other constituency attacked Jefferson's image and his view of
church-state separation: conservative jurists.[18] Leading the charge was
Justice Joseph Story, whose appointment to the Supreme Court Jefferson
had opposed based on the former's pro-Federalist leanings while serving
in Congress. Story held similar disdain for Jefferson, for his democratic
popularism, and for his religious views, the latter of which Story believed
threatened public virtue and the nation's moral underpinnings.[19] In 1824,
two years before his death, Jefferson had written the British radical Major
John Cartwright a letter containing a legal argument disputing the maxim
that Christianity formed part of the common law. According to Jefferson,
beginning in the fourteenth and fifteenth centuries, English judges had

purposefully misconstrued the origins of the common law, infusing it with Christian doctrines and explanations, with later jurists passing on the "judiciary forgery" to future generations, producing "a conspiracy this, between Church and State!" To Jefferson, having the law enforce religious doctrines would represent the epitome of a religious establishment and a violation of rights of conscience.[20]

Without seeking his approval, Cartwright had Jefferson's letter published in a London newspaper. The letter's publication caught the attention of Edward Everett, editor of the *North American Review*, who passed it on to Justice Story. An incredulous Story replied that Jefferson's interpretation was "untenable" and that it "appears to me inconceivable how any man can doubt, that Christianity is part of the Common Law of England."[21] For some reason, however, Story refrained from issuing a public rebuttal to Jefferson until 1829 when, in his inaugural address as a professor at Harvard Law School, he declared, "One of the most beautiful boasts of our municipal jurisprudence is, that Christianity is a part of the common law, from which it seeks to sanction its rights, and by which it endeavors to regulate its doctrines. And notwithstanding the specious objections of one of our distinguished statesmen, the boast is as true as it is beautiful. There has never been a period in which the common law did not recognize Christianity as lying at its foundations."[22] Story then waited another four years to again attack Jefferson's letter to Cartwright, now identifying Jefferson by name, in a short article in *American Jurist* titled "Christianity a Part of the Common Law." In it, Story challenged Jefferson's historical analysis, calling his interpretation of the British common law "novel." Story concluded that considering the weight of legal authority, "can any man seriously doubt, that Christianity is recognized as true, as a revelation, by the law of England, that is by the common law?" Even though the thrust of Story's article was to demonstrate the influence of ecclesiastical law on the development of British civil law, and thus American common law, his purpose was greater: to refute Jefferson's claim that the legitimacy for the law and government came from secular sources and not from notions of a higher law.[23]

That Story's fundamental disagreement with Jefferson was over whether the foundations of government and the law were secular or religious became clearer in Story's *Commentaries on the Constitution of the United States*, published the same year as his *American Jurist* article. Story's *Commentaries* quickly became the most influential treatise on the meaning of the

Constitution published in the nineteenth century. It was not a dispassionate work, however, as it was "part of the New England [Whig] effort to undo Jefferson's hold on America," wrote one historian. Through his *Commentaries,* Story sought to demonstrate the superiority and authority of the law over the rampant democratic impulses of the Jacksonian era: "The *Commentaries* were ammunition for [the] shock troops of conservatism."[24]

Story's belief in the indispensability of Christianity for the maintenance of government is evident in his discussion of the Constitution's religion clauses. The section begins in a starkly different place from Madison's "no agency" approach. Disagreeing with Madison's argument that the government lacked jurisdiction over religious matters, Story asserted there was a "right and duty of the interference of government in matters of religion":

> Indeed, the right of a society or government to interfere in matters of religion will hardly be contested by any persons who believed that piety, religion, and morality are intimately connected with the well-being of the state, and indispensable in the administration of civil justice. . . . It is, indeed, difficult to conceive how any civilized society can exist without them. . . . Indeed, in a republic, there would seem to be a peculiar propriety in viewing the Christian religion as the great basis on which it must rest for its support and permanence.[25]

With those foundational assumptions announced, Story turned to the specific purpose of the religion clauses, which was to prevent the government from preferring any particular Christian denomination but otherwise to allow it "to foster and encourage the Christian religion generally as a matter of sound policy as well as of revealed truth." That authority of the "government in matters of religion" was clearly Christian-specific: "The real object of the [First] amendment was not to countenance, much less advance Mahometanism or Judaism, or infidelity, by prostrating Christianity, but to exclude all rivalry among Christian sects." Although Story's discussion did not mention the Jeffersonian-Madisonian alternative, it stood in stark contrast to it. Story did not specify how far the government could go to "foster and encourage Christianity" or how it could accomplish those ends, but having fiercely opposed abolishing the religious assessment in his home state of Massachusetts that year, it is clear he supported a non-discriminatory religious tax. The *Commentaries'* one passing reference to the Virginia model was to contrast the "duty of supporting religion" from violations of conscience. Story insisted that "the duty of supporting religion, and especially the Christian religion, is very different from the right to force the consciences of other men or to punish them for worshiping God in the manner which they believe their accountability to him requires." Although conscience rights were "beyond the just reach of any human power," Story declared, paraphrasing the Virginia Declaration of Rights, the state's encouragement of religion generally "was not incompatible with the private rights of conscience and the freedom of religion." Story's *Commentaries* represented a clear repudiation of the Jeffersonian-Madisonian model for church-state matters. For the remainder of the century, conservative jurists and religious commentators would cite Story's interpretation as authority for truncated views of church-state separation.[26]

As Merrill D. Peterson discussed in *The Jefferson Image in the American Mind,* the Jeffersonian-Madisonian model, though often contested, remained a powerful force throughout the antebellum period, if not the entire nineteenth century. The idea of church-state separation also remained resilient, however one interpreted that principle. Foreign visitors to the United States commended the concept, with Alexis de Tocqueville in his *Democracy in America* (1838) marveling over "the peaceful dominion of religion in their country" that Americans attributed "to the separation of Church and State." He remarked that he "did not meet with a single individual, of the clergy or of the laity, who was not of the same opinion upon the subject."[27] Tocqueville clearly overstated that degree of consensus, but he was not the only foreigner to comment about Americans' commitment to church-state separation, at least as an abstract principle. Hungarian statesman Louis Kossuth wrote in 1852 that while several European countries were endangered by the "direct or indirect amalgamation of Church and State, . . . of this danger, at least, the future of your country is free. [Your] institutions left no power to your government to interfere with the religion of your citizens."[28] And writing around the same time, Polish Count Adam G. De Gurowski observed that "religious liberty, the absolute separation of Church and State, has become realized in America far beyond the conception, and still more the execution, of a similar separation in any European Protestant country. This separation, and the political equality of all creeds, constitute one of the cardinal and salient traits of the American Community." All three foreigners were likely swayed by the official disestablishment that existed in the United States, which stood in contrast to those autocratic European regimes that chiefly aligned themselves with the Catholic Church. Even so, foreign writers were not simply promoting church-state separation as a counterpoise to the European religious arrangements but were documenting a perspective they had observed in the United States.[29]

Accounts of Jefferson's and Madison's contributions on behalf of religious freedom continued to appear, although more commonly regarding Jefferson's actions. In 1858, Henry S. Randall published his *Life of Thomas Jefferson*, which relied extensively on Jefferson's papers, the first biography of Jefferson since Tucker's work. Four years earlier, the Library of Congress had published a nine-volume compilation of Jefferson's writings, based on the government's purchase of his papers from Thomas Jefferson Randolph.[30] Randall's three-volume biography was a "labor of love," according to Merrill Peterson, with Randall portraying Jefferson as a great intellectual, political leader, and family man. With the entirety of Jefferson's monumental career to cover, Randall provided only a brief account of Jefferson's work toward securing religious freedom. Still, he praised those efforts, describing Jefferson's activities in the fall of 1776 while serving on the Committee on Religion as "determined" and as reflecting the same commitment to principles "as were afterwards ingrafted into his Bill for Religious Freedom." In his discussion of the disestablishment episode a decade later, however, Randall was more detached, possibly because of Jefferson's limited role from France. Nonetheless, Randall described the struggle as "tremendous," praising Madison's "consummate ability" in defeating the assessment bill through the "matchless logic" of his *Memorial,* which "made such an unanswerable appeal to the good sense of reflecting men, that everything went down before it."[31]

In the third volume, Randall defended Jefferson's efforts at establishing the University of Virginia as a *nonsectarian* institution—rather than as a *secular* one—in order to avoid religious divisiveness. He applauded Jefferson's wisdom and moderation in withdrawing Thomas Cooper's appointment to the faculty and in allowing religious groups to meet on campus, both of which demonstrated Jefferson's lack of hostility toward religion. Randall's portrayal of Jefferson's religious moderation continued in the conclusion where he considered Jefferson's beliefs. In that discussion, Jefferson emerged as a deep and sincere religious thinker, a churchgoer, a Unitarian in his theological inclinations, and someone who, according to his family, "habitually [spoke] reverently of God, the Savior, and the great truths of

Christianity." As Randall concluded, "Mr. Jefferson was a public professor of his belief in the Christian religion."[32] Despite some criticism of Randall's hagiographic account of Jefferson's life, the biography successfully secured the image of Jefferson as a great political figure and helped to transform popular views of him from being an infidel into a firm believer.[33]

Neither Tucker's nor Randall's biographies of Jefferson discussed his ideas about church-state separation as contained in his *Notes on the State of Virginia* or in his Danbury letter, the letter having been largely forgotten. As noted in an earlier chapter, however, the letter was included in the collection of Jefferson's papers prepared in 1854 at the direction of Congress. Future attorney general Jeremiah S. Black referred to the wall of separation metaphor in an 1856 speech—declaring that the founders had "built up a wall of complete and perfect partition between" church and state—after having possibly encountered the letter in Jefferson's papers. Black did not credit Jefferson for coining the phrase, however. The impetus for the Supreme Court's reference to the letter in the 1879 case of *Reynolds v. United States* likely lay in the friendship between Chief Justice Morrison Waite and the noted historian George Bancroft, who had certainly perused Jefferson's *Writings* when researching his *History of the United States*. Bancroft was an old Jacksonian Democrat and a Unitarian-Transcendentalist who commended Jefferson's and Madison's roles in disestablishing Virginia in his works. Bancroft reputedly shared the Danbury letter with Chief Justice Waite during the Court's considerations in *Reynolds*. As noted, Waite declared that Jefferson's sentiments in the letter represented the authoritative statement on the meaning of the religion clauses, which elevated Jeffersonian separationism to a position of jurisprudential prominence.[34]

Constructing Madison's Legacy

As for Madison, Henry D. Gilpin published an early series of his papers in 1841, but it only included writings related to Madison's work in the Confederation Congress and the Constitutional Convention. A more complete collection, *Letters and Other Writings of James Madison*, edited by Philip A. Fendall, appeared in 1865, which contained various letters concerning the Virginia disestablishment—chiefly those of Madison to Jefferson and Monroe—and reproduced the *Memorial and Remonstrance*, but it included nothing related to Madison's actions with respect to the First Amendment.[35]

In 1850, John Quincy Adams's posthumous *The Lives of James Madison and James Monroe* was published. Adams provided a favorable description of Madison's and Jefferson's involvement in securing disestablishment in Virginia and enacting the Statute for Establishing Religious Freedom. Emphasizing Madison's indispensable role in the affair, Adams called him "the champion of Religious Liberty." Even though Adams noted Madison's participation in the Constitutional Convention, he too curiously failed to credit Madison's involvement in drafting the First Amendment.[36]

Three later biographies of Madison provided greater detail on Madison's leading role in Virginia's disestablishment. The earliest, *History of the Life and Times of James Madison* (1859), was written by Madison's neighbor and US senator William C. Rives, and it lacked some of the detachment needed for a biography. Rives wrote that of all the "great questions . . . which affected the mind of Mr. Madison the more painfully," none was more important than "the vital question of religious freedom." He quoted from Madison's 1774 letter to William Bradford concerning the jailed Baptist preachers, describing it as demonstrating Madison's "generous indignation" over their mistreatment. Rives then segued to disagree with Madison's assessment of the religious persecution in Virginia—calling it "somewhat overcharged"—and to defend the Anglican establishment, asserting that there was a "general peace and happiness" throughout the colony "where the principle of universal and unlimited freedom of religion had existed from the first." In Rives's mind, "There was nothing in the Church of England, as existed in this [state], that was hostile to liberty." Rives also used the correspondence with Bradford to exaggerate Madison's religious devotion, suggesting that Madison maintained those early sentiments throughout his life: Madison possessed an "elevated strain of religious sentiment" and was "an enlightened believer in the truth and divine authority of the Christian system." The same perspective carried over into Rives's discussion of the disestablishment struggle of 1784–85. He praised Madison for his principled commitment to opposing the general assessment but asserted that Madison stood "almost as the solitary opponent to it." The *Memorial and Remonstrance* was a "masterly paper," Rives acknowledged, though he emphasized those sections where Madison had argued for the benefits that flowed to religion from disestablishment, not vice versa. The *Memorial* turned the tide of public opinion, Rives contended. It "cleared away every obstruction, and so smoothed the ground before it that [the] passage of [Jefferson's bill] became a matter of course." Yet, the thrust of Rives's coverage was clear: despite "the conscientious zeal of Mr. Madison in the cause of religious freedom," disestablishment had been unnecessary.[37]

Sydney Howard Gay's 1884 biography *James Madison* was more balanced than Rives's, with him affirming the significance of the disestablishment struggle in Virginia and Madison's leading role in the matter. Unlike Rives, Gay willingly acknowledged the existence of religious persecution that had motivated Madison to act. Gay praised Madison's foresight in his proposed amendments to the Declaration of Rights and his opposition to the general assessment, suggesting that Madison was ahead of his time in understanding the importance of full religious equality and its relation to disestablishment: "Madison was quick to see in [a general assessment] the possibility of religious intolerance, of compulsory uniformity enforced by civil power, and the suppression of any freedom of conscience or opinion." Gay placed the significance of the *Memorial* within this larger context, not as Rives had done as primarily to protect religion. Similar to Rives's biography, however, Gay made only a passing reference to Madison's having introduced the Bill of Rights during the First Congress, with no discussion of his role in the drafting of the First Amendment. Gay's biography, which would go through multiple editions into the twentieth century, would have a greater influence on later studies about Madison and on public attitudes toward his numerous contributions to the nation's founding, including to securing religious freedom.[38]

Gaillard Hunt's 1902 *The Life of James Madison* confirmed Gay's analysis about the importance of the Virginia disestablishment episode and of Madison's leading role in the matter. Hunt also highlighted the significance of Madison's contribution to the phrasing of the Declaration of Rights and of his failed proposal that would have effectively disestablished Virginia in 1776, thus making Jefferson's statute unnecessary. Hunt extensively discussed Madison's leadership in defeating Patrick Henry's assessment bill a decade later, crediting his "argument against the bill [as] one of the most careful and elaborate ever constructed," and calling the *Memorial* "an unanswerable protest against all religious legislation." (Like previous biographers, Hunt failed to discuss Madison's involvement in securing the First Amendment, simply noting his introduction of amendments in the First Congress.) Summing up his overall contribution, Hunt maintained that Madison was "in advance of his colleagues" in his thinking about religious freedom but that he "believed that human liberty was impossible of attainment, unless legislative interference in concerns of conscience disappeared from the face of the earth." In Hunt's view, Madison was the indispensable figure in establishing religious freedom.[39]

So, upon entering the era of the modern Supreme Court in the mid-twentieth century, the reputations of Jefferson and Madison as the leading contributors to the development of American religious freedom were already well established. It would have been difficult for any comprehensive legal consideration of that development to have ignored their contributions.

Creating the Legal Legacy

Two trends preceded the Supreme Court's 1947 embrace of the Jeffersonian-Madisonian view of church-state separation that helped ensure their legacy would be familiar to the justices. One was President Franklin Roosevelt's personal admiration of Thomas Jefferson, with Roosevelt calling himself the "new Jefferson." He and his administration consciously tied the policies of the New Deal to the ideals of Jefferson. This elevation of Jefferson's legacy reached its zenith through Roosevelt's promotion of the construction of the Jefferson Memorial in Washington, DC. Roosevelt's administration then coordinated the celebration of its opening on the two hundredth anniversary of Jefferson's birth on April 13, 1943. Governors and mayors across the nation issued proclamations commending Jefferson's bicentennial, and prominent clergy delivered sermons lionizing Jefferson's promotion of individual rights, including religious freedom: "We have occasion not only to praise the author of the Declaration of Independence," one minister asserted, but also "to hail him who waged as successful fight in the cause of religious liberty." President Roosevelt's address at the memorial's dedication declared the nation's "long overdue" debt to Jefferson for his promotion of "freedom of conscience and freedom of mind," calling him the "apostle of freedom" and alluding to how such freedoms were under assault with the ongoing war. Jefferson emerged from the celebrations as the intellectual father of the nation's democratic values: "Washington was the father of the nation," noted one orator. "Jefferson was the father of its spirit."[40]

Two months after the dedication of the Jefferson Memorial, an event several justices attended, the Court delivered its decision in *West Virginia State Board of Education v. Barnette*, striking down a state statute mandating compulsory reciting of the Pledge of Allegiance by public schoolchildren. Even though the challenge had been brought by Jehovah's Witnesses parents and children who had theological objections to swearing allegiance to civil governments, Justice Robert Jackson's majority opinion cast the conflict as an effort to "coerce uniformity of sentiment" and a threat to the "individual freedom of mind," rather than as a specific violation of religious freedom. Jackson could have referred to Jefferson as a source for a broad understanding of freedom of conscience, but he did not, leaving that task to other justices. In his concurring opinion, Justice Frank Murphy maintained the case involved the "right of freedom of thought and of religion" and chiefly imposed "a restriction on religious freedom." "Official compulsion to affirm what is contrary to one's religious beliefs is the antithesis of freedom of worship," Murphy asserted, which "was achieved in this country only after what Jefferson characterized as the 'severest contests in which I have ever been engaged.'" Murphy then cited the preamble of the Virginia statute, whose "trenchant words . . . remain unanswerable." Ironically, the larger number of references to Jefferson (along with one to Madison) appeared in the dissenting opinion of Justice Felix Frankfurter, who doubted the ability of government to accommodate all the idiosyncratic religious views held by the large number of religious groups. He acknowledged that Jefferson and Madison were among "the great exponents of religious freedom" and "were determined to remove political support from every religious establishment." However, he continued, "Jefferson and those who followed him wrote guaranties of religious freedom into our constitutions. Religious minorities as well as religious majorities were to be equal in the eyes of the political state. But Jefferson and the others also knew that minorities may disrupt society. It never would have occurred to them to write into the Constitution the subordination of the general civil authority of the state to sectarian scruples."[41] Despite their disagreement over what the principle of religious freedom required, Justices Murphy and Frankfurter agreed that Jefferson had played a prominent role in its acquisition.

The other trend that presaged the Court's 1947 *Everson v. Board of Education* decision was a new round of histories and biographies of Jefferson and Madison that began appearing after the mid-1920s. In 1925, Claude G. Bowers wrote his *Jefferson and Hamilton: The Struggle for Democracy in*

America to be followed in 1936 with *Jefferson in Power: The Death Struggle of the Federalists* In both books Bowers contrasted Jefferson's commitment to religious freedom with Hamilton's cynical manipulation of religion for political gain. The Constitution had decreed "the complete separation of Church and State," Bowers asserted. Jefferson, "more than any other single man had insisted in the separation of Church and State and had fought a successful battle on the issue in the Virginia Assembly," unfortunately failing to give Madison credit for the latter.[42] In 1938, Edward McNall Burns published *James Madison: Philosopher of the Constitution,* which concentrated on Madison's leadership in the drafting and ratification of the Constitution.[43] Then, preceding the Court's consideration of *Everson,* Bowers published *The Young Jefferson* and Adrienne Koch wrote *The Philosophy of Thomas Jefferson,* with both emphasizing the influence of Lord Bolingbroke and other Enlightenment thinkers in the formation of Jefferson's religious ideas. These new historical works helped to reinforce the public view of Jefferson's and Madison's many contributions to religious freedom and freedom of conscience.[44]

Whether the justices had read or were familiar with any of the foregoing works is uncertain. One biography that likely *did* impact the justices' thinking about Madison's contributions to establishing religious freedom (and Jefferson's by implication) was that of Irving Brant, author of the six-volume biography of Madison. Brant, an editor of the *St. Louis Star-Times* newspaper, was a longtime friend of Justice Wylie Rutledge, having known Rutledge since his time as dean of Washington University Law School and his service on the Eighth Circuit Court of Appeals, based in St. Louis. Active in Democratic circles, Brant had lobbied Franklin Roosevelt to appoint Rutledge to the Supreme Court in 1943.[45] By the time of the Court arguments in *Everson,* Brant had written his first volume on Madison and was completing his second, which covered Madison's career to the drafting of the Constitution.[46] Brant was a strong proponent of church-state separation, and his works related Madison's commitment to that principle. Brant wrote that the *Memorial and Remonstrance* "continues to stand, not merely through the years but through the centuries, as the most powerful defense of religious liberty ever written in America." And the First Amendment "was Madison's further answer, in behalf of all the American people," to achieve "the total separation between government and religion."[47] There is nothing in

Rutledge's official papers indicating that he and Brant corresponded during the opinion-writing in *Everson*—though they did afterward to commiserate on the holding—but Rutledge's research notes contain Brant's name at the top of at least one document suggesting the historian provided the justice with background material. In his dissenting opinion, Rutledge cited Brant's work in nine places, so one can surmise the impact of Brant's biography on his dissenting opinion.[48]

Incorporating the Legacy

As indicated in the introduction, in *Everson* the high court considered the constitutionality of public funding to assist religious education, whereas in *McCollum v. Board of Education* (1948) the justices confronted the issue of religious instruction in public schools. Both were core issues arising under the religion clauses, and despite the fact that both questions had long been contentious, these cases were of first instance for the Court.[49] Consequently, the justices had little precedent on which to rely in adjudicating the controversies. The handful of prior interpretations of the religion clauses had involved regulations related to suppressing Mormon polygamy as in *Reynolds*.[50] In three earlier funding cases, however, the justices had sidestepped the establishment clause question by holding that the recipient, a Catholic hospital, was not truly a religious institution (*Bradfield v. Roberts*), that the funds were not truly public monies but belonged to an Indian tribe (*Quick Bear v. Leupp*), and that the public funding benefited children, not the religious schools (*Cochran v. Louisiana State Board of Education*).[51] Thus, the justices had no prior decisions on which to rely, which invited them to turn to history for authority to resolve the controversies.

And rely on history they did. *Everson* and *McCollum* are relatively unique in that the various majority, concurring, and dissenting opinions not only referred to the same historical material; they essentially agreed on its overall significance. The opinions only parted over its application to the issues before them. In *Everson*, the justices cited Madison seventy-eight times and Jefferson thirty-four times. Both the majority and leading dissent highlighted the importance of the *Memorial and Remonstrance* and the Virginia statute. In addition, both the majority and lead dissent referred to Madison's Detached Memoranda. In *McCollum*, the justices called on Madison nine times and Jefferson fifteen. Few, if any, Supreme Court decisions have demonstrated such a high degree of agreement over controlling authority.[52]

The long association of Jefferson and Madison with the development of religious freedom may have made it inevitable that the two founders would figure into the various opinions in *Everson* and *McCollum*. But that reliance was not a foregone conclusion; circumstances made that narrative more prominent. *Everson* involved the relatively minor issue of state reimbursements for expenses parents incurred in transporting their children to private religious schools (i.e., bus fares). Although the financial benefit to the religious schools was relatively insignificant, opponents criticized such "auxiliary aid" for the precedent it set—bus fares today, tuition reimbursements tomorrow. The plaintiff, Arch Everson, a New Jersey taxpayer, challenged the reimbursement law, not as an establishment clause violation but as a due process "taking" of his taxes for a private purpose (he also raised a claim under the New Jersey Constitution). Everson prevailed in the trial court but lost on appeal, with the New Jersey Court of Errors and Appeals relying on the "child benefit" theory from *Cochran* to uphold the program.[53] On his appeal to the Supreme Court, Everson restated his takings argument and then added an establishment clause claim, almost as an afterthought. Still, his brief concentrated on the former claim, arguing that assisting private education was not a "public purpose" as required for a due process taking to be legal. The brief's establishment clause argument was perfunctory, chiefly included to demonstrate that funding religious education could not be a *public* purpose. His brief mentioned neither Jefferson, Madison, nor the Virginia disestablishment episode, though it did assert in conclusory fashion that the aid violated the separation of church and state.[54]

That left it to the briefs of Everson's three amicus curiae to develop the establishment clause claim and to provide any relevant historical context. The amicus brief of the Seventh-day Adventists and Baptists made the former argument, though in cursory fashion; only the brief by the American Civil Liberties Union (ACLU) provided both. "That separation of church and state is a fundamental American principle is manifest from history," the ACLU brief asserted. The brief tied that principle, as incorporated into the federal establishment clause, to the Virginia disestablishment experience. The brief cited Jefferson's statute and Madison's *Memorial*, melding the contents of both documents into a unitary principle that informed the drafting of the First Amendment. The section concluded with a quote from Jefferson's Danbury letter in which he asserted that the purpose of the First Amendment was "thus building a wall of separation between church and State." Here was one source for the historical justification for church-state separation that would figure so prominently in the *Everson* opinions.[55]

Even then, that reference came close to possibly not being included in the ACLU brief. While the case was pending in the New Jersey courts, the ACLU Board of Directors had directed its Committee on Academic Freedom to make a recommendation on whether the organization should continue to oppose forms of indirect aid to religious schools, or only object when the aid subsidized religious-based instruction. After heated discussion, the committee voted eleven to eight to continue with the ACLU's position opposing all forms of aid. At the risk of engaging in counterfactual history, had ACLU adopted a moderate position on auxiliary aid there might have been no reference to Jefferson and Madison in the briefing, which in turn might have affected the prominence the justices gave their works in their opinions. The amicus brief sponsored by the Catholic bishops supporting the reimbursement law also raised a historical argument but chiefly in response to the ACLU brief. It acknowledged Madison's role in drafting the First Amendment and Jefferson's wall metaphor but argued that the latter concept was for the purpose of protecting the separate civil and religious spheres, and it cautioned the justices not to "transform . . . the legitimate 'wall' into an illegitimate 'iron curtain' separating areas between which there should be free passage."[56]

In the conference following the oral arguments, the justices initially voted six to two to uphold the reimbursement law, with Catholic justice Frank Murphy abstaining. Chief Justice Fred Vinson assigned the opinion to Justice Hugo Black, who promised his colleagues he would write a narrow opinion to forestall the possibility of more significant forms of public aid to religion.[57] Two weeks later Black circulated a draft opinion among the justices; it was relatively concise and bereft of any extensive discussion of history. The draft cited a nineteenth-century church property case and several early Mormon cases but did not mention Jefferson, Madison, or the Virginia controversy. The draft concluded with a reference to the wall metaphor without acknowledging Jefferson's authorship: "The First Amendment requires a complete and permanent separation between church and state. The wall between the two must be kept high and impregnable if the historic purpose of the First Amendment is to be carried out."[58]

Justice Rutledge, one of two justices to vote no, then wrote a lengthy dissenting opinion that challenged the premises in Justice Black's draft. Rutledge related in detail the Virginia disestablishment struggle and Madison's leading role, emphasizing the significance of the *Memorial and Remonstrance* in defeating Patrick Henry's assessment bill. Rutledge quoted extensively from the *Memorial,* calling it the most sweeping and complete statement about the value of religious freedom in the nation's history—he was so enamored with it that he had the *Memorial* printed as an appendix to his opinion. From there, Rutledge segued to connecting the Virginia disestablishment episode to the drafting of the First Amendment; as he remarked, "The Remonstrance is at once the most concise and the most accurate statement of the views of the First Amendment's author concerning what is 'an establishment of religion.'" Rutledge also gave significant credit to Jefferson, praising "Virginia's great statute of religious freedom." He concluded by asserting that "all the great instruments of the Virginia struggle for religious liberty thus became warp and woof of our constitutional tradition, not simply by the course of history, but by the common unifying force of Madison's life, thought and sponsorship."[59]

Rutledge's extensive historical research and persuasive argument forced Justice Black to expand his own historical analysis, more than doubling the length of his draft in response to Rutledge. As one scholar has noted sardonically, "Justice Black's often-cited and influential historical analysis in *Everson* would never have occurred had Wiley Rutledge not first had a Founding Fathers epiphany."[60] In the end, Black agreed with Rutledge about the singular significance of the Virginia disestablishment and of Jefferson's and Madison's leading roles in achieving it. Black also concurred that the Virginia statute and the *Memorial* represented the most authoritative statements on the meaning of religious freedom, which were then incorporated into the Constitution: "The provisions of the First Amendment, in the drafting and adoption of which Madison and Jefferson played such leading roles, had the same objective and were intended to provide the same protection against governmental intrusion on religious liberty as the Virginia statute." Black simply disagreed that the neutral aid program before the Court, one designed to get schoolchildren safely to and from school, breached that "wall of separation."[61]

The following year the justices heard *McCollum,* which involved the popular practice of setting aside a period during the school day so that students could attend religious instruction conducted by religious teachers from the community ("released time"). The constitutional issue was whether the schools, by opening their facilities for outside instructors to teach devotional religion during the school day, were essentially promoting religious education. By an eight-to-one majority the justices held that they were, in violation of the establishment clause. Writing again for a Court majority, Justice Black held that the state's "tax supported public school buildings [were] used for the dissemination of religious doctrines," which also "afford[ed] sectarian groups an invaluable aid [in access to students] . . . through use of the state's compulsory public school machinery. This is not separation of Church and State." This time, Black did not discuss the Virginia disestablishment episode or mention Madison, though he did recite the wall of separation metaphor three times. Justice Frankfurter's separate opinion for himself and the other dissenters in *Everson* cited Madison and the *Memorial* three times, though he also bypassed discussing the Virginia episode, spending instead considerable space relating the development of nonsectarian public education since the founding period. Frankfurter concluded, however, by declaring that "separation means separation, not something less. Jefferson's metaphor in describing the relation between Church and State speaks of a 'wall of separation,' not of a fine line easily overstepped." Having firmly established the authority of Jefferson's and Madison's works in *Everson* thus freed the justices from needing to cite them as extensively in *McCollum.* Ironically, Justice Stanley Reed's dissenting opinion discussed Jefferson's statute, Madison's *Memorial,* and the Virginia episode in greater detail than the other opinions, but with him insisting that that authority was not relevant for the issue of religious instruction.[62]

With the two decisions, the Jeffersonian-Madisonian perspective on religious freedom and church-state separation was constitutionalized. The potentially competing views of other members of the founding period who were more religiously orthodox—John Witherspoon, Patrick Henry, John Jay, Elias Boudinot, Roger Sherman—were never considered.[63] Commentators on the two decisions, both popular and scholarly, generally accepted the justices' identification of Jefferson's and Madison's works and the Virginia episode as relevant, if not authoritative, for interpreting religious freedom and church-state separation.[64] There were a handful of voices to the contrary, but they were a minority. The narrative of Jefferson and Madison as the fathers of American religious freedom had been set in law.[65]

Perpetuating the Legacy

The image of Jefferson and Madison as the leading expositors of the meaning of the religion clauses and of the idea of American religious freedom has persisted to this day. Over the last several decades historical scholarship has worked to broaden the narrative of religious freedom in important ways, expanding on the variety of events and players (not just white men) that have contributed to its realization. Those salient events and players are also not restricted to the founding period; understandings of religious freedom and equality have unfolded over time, hopefully for the better. People such as Rabbi Isaac Wise, Lucretia Mott, Elizabeth Cady Stanton, Robert Ingersoll, Archbishop John Ireland, Reinhold Niebuhr, Father John Courtney Murray, and Malcom X have stood in the breach and challenged and expanded our perspectives. As the historical enterprise has become more inclusive, it has become more authoritative. Jefferson and Madison still matter—and their contributions were indispensable at a critical time—but the magnitude of their contribution has lessened in historical perspectives as those of others have rightly been acknowledged.[66]

This expansion has not been the case in the law, which is a much more conservative and cautious enterprise. In the law, the seminal role of Jefferson and Madison has largely remained intact, though their reputation has been tarnished in recent years. For the four decades following *McCollum,* the supremacy of the Jefferson-Madison interpretation of the religion clauses essentially went unchallenged among members of the Supreme Court and by most scholars. In the next case to affirm that interpretation, *McGowen v. Maryland* (1961), Chief Justice Earl Warren referred to Madison and the *Memorial* ten times; Jefferson got only two nods, but Warren repeated his declaration that the establishment clause "was intended to erect 'a wall of separation between Church and State.'" Warren concluded by affirming that the Virginia disestablishment episode "best reflect[ed] the long and intensive struggle for religious freedom in America" and was "particularly relevant in the search for the First Amendment's meaning."[67] In the highly contentious school prayer and Bible reading cases that followed *McGowen, Engel v. Vitale* (1962) and *Abington School District v. Schempp* (1963), the justices referred to Jefferson and Madison twelve times and forty-five times, respectively (with the justices in *Schempp* citing the *Memorial* six times). And in the 1968 case of *Flast v. Cohen*, Chief Justice Warren asserted that Madison "is generally recognized as the leading architect of the religion clauses of the First Amendment," which incorporated the sentiments of "his famous Memorial and Remonstrance Against Religious Assessments."[68] Allusions to Jefferson and Madison continued with later cases; one study of the Supreme Court's church-state cases indicated that between *McCollum* and 2009 (the publication date of the study), the justices referred to Madison 345 times and to Jefferson 253 times in their opinions; George Washington came in a distant third at 63 citations.[69] Although that trend has decreased in recent decades, liberal members of the Court continue to rely on Jefferson and Madison for authority. As recently as 2022, Justice Stephen Breyer cited both Jefferson and Madison while quoting from the Virginia statute and the *Memorial* to argue against allocating public funds for tuition at a religious school.[70]

Resistance to the Jeffersonian-Madisonian interpretation began in the 1980s, coinciding with the conservative Reagan Revolution (and likely fueled by it). The first significant attack on that narrative came from Professor Robert L. Cord in his 1982 book *Separation of Church and State: Historical Fact and Current Fiction*, which asserted that Jefferson and Madison did not represent the prevailing church-state perspective during the founding period and, inconsistently, that they were not as separationist as had been portrayed. Other conservative scholars have picked up on these themes, most notably Philip Hamburger, Vincent Phillip Muñoz, and Daniel L. Dreisbach.[71] Cord's work served as the inspiration and source of material for the first significant attack on the narrative from a sitting justice in 1985. Dissenting from a decision striking down a law authorizing "silent prayer" in public schools, Justice William Rehnquist launched into an extended broadside on Jefferson's legacy. He asserted that Jefferson's contribution to understandings of the First Amendment was insignificant at best: "Jefferson was of course in France at the time the . . . Bill of Rights were passed by Congress and ratified by the States." Rehnquist derided the Danbury letter as being simply "a short note of courtesy" and for containing "Jefferson's misleading metaphor." After documenting the purported inconsistencies in Jefferson's record, drawn from Cord's book, Rehnquist declared that "there is simply no historical foundation for the proposition that the

Framers intended to build the 'wall of separation' that was constitutional-ized in *Everson*." The metaphor was "bad history" and had "proved useless as a guide to judging," Rehnquist asserted. "It should be frankly and explic-itly abandoned."[72]

Justice Rehnquist's broadside on the Jeffersonian-Madisonian interpre-tation and on separation of church and state generally was soon picked up by other conservative justices appointed by Presidents Ronald Reagan, George H. W. Bush, George W. Bush, and Donald Trump: Justices Antonin Scalia, Clarence Thomas, Samuel Alito, Neil Gorsuch, and Brent Kava-naugh. For example, in his dissenting opinion in *McCreary County v. ACLU* (2005), where a majority struck down a Ten Commandments plaque in a county courthouse, Justice Scalia contested the relevance of Madison's *Memorial* as "written before the Federal Constitution had even been pro-posed" and as applicable only to situations involving "enforced contribu-tion[s] to religion" (though he did find the religious language in Madison's First Inaugural Address to be relevant). The judicial marginalization of the Jeffersonian-Madisonian legacy has continued to this day.[73]

A 1995 case demonstrates the Supreme Court's reconsideration of that legacy. In *Rosenberger v. University of Virginia,* the Court heard an establish-ment clause case concerning the government funding of religious speech. Ironically, the case arose at the university founded by Jefferson and Mad-ison, with the student plaintiffs challenging a policy that prohibited the university from allocating funds for student publications that promoted a particular religious belief. The university supported a wide range of stu-dent activities and publications but had refused to fund *Wide Awake* maga-zine, which advocated an evangelical perspective. By a narrow majority, the Court struck down the policy on free speech grounds as constituting view-point discrimination against religion. This holding came notwithstanding the university's argument that to fund religiously proselytizing expression would violate the establishment clause. As Justice David Souter declared in his dissenting opinion, "For the first time, [the Court] approves direct funding of core religious activities by an arm of the State."[74]

Aside from *Rosenberger's* holding representing another step in the ero-sion of Jeffersonian-Madisonian church-state separation, the case is salient for its concurring and dissenting opinions. Both Justice Clarence Thomas (in concurrence) and Justice David Souter (in dissent) anchored their op-posing positions on their readings of Madison's *Memorial and Remonstrance.*

Justice Thomas emphasized passages in the *Memorial* where Madison used language condemning preferential treatment of religion. (Thomas also relied on Madison's original proposal for the First Amendment, which would have prohibited a "national religion.") Such language, Thomas insisted, indicated that Madison would not have opposed a neutral, non-preferential funding program that benefited religion. Then, after using Madison as authority for a narrow interpretation of the establishment clause, Thomas pivoted to remark that "even if more extreme notions of the separation of church and state can be attributed to Madison . . . the views of one man do not establish the original understanding of the First Amendment." In contrast, Justice Souter emphasized other passages from the *Memorial,* along with language from Jefferson's statute, to argue that "using public funds for the direct subsidization of preaching the word is categorically forbidden under the Establishment Clause." Although Thomas attempted to have it both ways regarding the authority of Madison's views, Souter was unequivocal, declaring that "the writings of Madison, whose authority on questions about the meaning of the Establishment Clause is well settled," should determine the outcome of the case. (Unfortunately, Souter did not discuss, or was unaware of, Madison's 1833 letter to Benjamin Peers, discussed in the previous chapter, where Madison explained why the university could not support religious instruction, even though it funded instruction in comparable secular courses.)[75]

Since *Rosenberger,* conservative justices have rarely cited Madison and Jefferson, preferring to rely on events contemporaneous to the nation's founding that reputedly demonstrate a narrow understanding of church-state separation—for example, legislative chaplaincies—and on writings and proclamations by other members of the founding generation—such as Washington's Thanksgiving proclamations and his Farewell Address—to uncover a purported "original meaning" or "original understanding" of the religion clauses. More than one justice has declared that the "Establishment Clause must be interpreted 'by reference to historical practices and understandings'" at the time of the nation's founding (although Jefferson's and Madison's understandings apparently no longer count).[76] This approach led Justice John Paul Stevens to remark that "a reading of the First Amendment dependent on . . . the purported original meanings . . . would eviscerate the heart of the Establishment Clause. It would replace Jefferson's 'wall of separation' with a perverse wall of exclusion" of non-Christians.[77] In contrast, liberal justices, increasingly in a minority in church-state decisions, have persisted in affirming the authority of Jefferson and Madison for interpreting the religion clauses, not only to support their understanding of those clauses but also to reaffirm the relevance of Jefferson and Madison at a time when the Court's conservatives seek to marginalize their importance. That debate over Jefferson's and Madison's legacy continues.[78]

Conclusion

T wo questions regarding Jefferson's and Madison's contribution to American religious freedom remain to be considered. The first is the one asked in this book's introduction: "why?" Why were Jefferson and Madison so committed to advancing religious freedom and equality and then church-state separation? This is a particularly compelling question considering Jefferson's disdain for conventional religious beliefs and practices, particularly of the evangelical variety, and Madison's apparent ambivalence toward the same. For both men, the foundational principle on which all related ones were built was *free inquiry*. Each man arrived at the importance of that value through somewhat different paths, though both acquired their initial fealty to free inquiry through their college educations. For Jefferson, that occurred under the influence of the triumvirate of George Wythe, William Small, and Francis Fauquier, all of whom expressed heterodox views about religion and politics and exposed him to writers such as Shaftesbury and Bolingbroke.[1] Madison's initial embrace of free inquiry was through more conventional study under the guidance of Reverend John Witherspoon, who ensured that his pupils were exposed to a wide range of philosophical works, including radicals like David Hume. Witherspoon believed that the mind must be free to arrive at its own philosophical conclusions, an emphasis that complemented his belief in the right of private judgment concerning religious faith.[2]

Free inquiry necessarily involved the ability not simply to inquire but also to fashion and hold heterodox ideas, which was the core of freedom of conscience. Freedom of inquiry and conscience were therefore the central values that motivated both Jefferson and Madison. As Jefferson wrote in his Statute for Establishing Religious Freedom, God had "created the mind free." What William Lee Miller said about Jefferson could apply to Madison as well: "For Jefferson, religious liberty was part of that larger liberty (larger to him—larger and also smaller to many believers), freedom of the *mind*." Their understanding of freedom of religion must thus be considered in conjunction with their advocacy for a secular university; for public education, freedom of the press and other individual rights; and for Jefferson, his interest in science.[3]

Naturally, Jefferson and Madison realized that one of the more significant manifestations of freedom of inquiry was that of religious freedom. In an eighteenth-century culture imbued with religious customs, practices, and rhetoric, true freedom of conscience could not operate without religious freedom. For contemporaries such as Isaac Backus and John Leland, who espoused religious epistemologies, freedom of conscience and freedom of religion were equivalent if not interchangeable. For Jefferson and Madison, however, free inquiry and freedom of conscience were precedents; religious freedom was a subset of freedom of conscience—clearly the latter's most visible manifestation—but not its equivalent. "Free enquiry must be indulged," Jefferson wrote in his *Notes on the State of Virginia*. "Reason and free enquiry are the only effectual agents against error." Allow them to thrive and "they will [then] support the true religion, by bringing every false one to their tribunal, to the test of their investigation." Two decades later, in his Danbury letter, Jefferson affirmed that the establishment clause represented an "expression of the supreme will of the nation in behalf of the rights of conscience . . . which [will] tend to restore to man all his natural rights."[4] Madison also declared "the freedom of conscience to be a *natural and absolute* right." In his 1792 article on "Property" in the *National Gazette*, he declared that "conscience is the most sacred of all property," cherished even more than one's house, which was subject to positive law, but authority to restrict physical property "can give no title to invade a man's conscience which is more sacred than his castle." And in his proposals for religious amendments to the US Constitution, Madison used the broader term "full and equal rights of conscience" rather than the "free exercise of religion," which was substituted by the House select committee to Madison's chagrin.[5] Finally, Jefferson's and Madison's commitment to a broad conception of freedom of inquiry and conscience is demonstrated by their work establishing the University of Virginia, to create an institution "based on the illimitable freedom of the human mind."[6] Jack Rakove asserts that Jefferson's and Madison's expansive understanding of freedom of conscience represented their valuation of "individual moral authority" and personal privacy, to use modern conceptions. Thus, the protections enshrined in the religion clauses were a means to ensure these natural rights of conscience.[7]

And based on their studies and observations, the greatest impediment to true freedom of conscience, including religious freedom, was the maintenance of church establishments. The effect of ecclesiastical establishments, Madison argued in his *Memorial,* had been "to erect a spiritual tyranny" on the minds of men. Full disestablishment was a necessary prerequisite for realizing freedom of conscience, and in order to ensure the ongoing operation of both disestablishment and conscience freedom, society had to maintain a separation between the authority and activities of the church and the state.[8]

The second, related question is how should we understand Jefferson's and Madison's perspectives on religious freedom and church-state separation. To be sure, there was no unitary perspective; though Jefferson and Madison shared many ideas, their views were not in lockstep.

Some differences existed. Jefferson was more anticlerical and more critical of religious enthusiasm; he believed in the superiority of rational, liberal Christianity. Jefferson placed greater emphasis on protecting civil government from religious incursions, although in his statute he did assert the need to protect individual religious practice and choices from government compulsion—that religious opinions "are not the object of civil government, nor under its jurisdiction."[9]

Madison was more ambivalent about forms of individual religious expression and, though he also had an anticlerical streak, it was less pronounced than Jefferson's. One example of Madison's more moderate approach, and of the value of their collaboration, was when he convinced Jefferson to remove a provision in the latter's proposed constitution for Virginia that would have prohibited clergy from holding public office.[10] As revealed in his Detached Memoranda, however, Madison expressed grave concerns about the power of ecclesiastical institutions, in part through "the indefinite accumulation of property from the capacity of holding it in perpetuity." But he also worried about "the danger of encroachment by Ecclesiastical Bodies" on individual liberties in ways that threatened "the freedom of the mind." To the end, Madison remained committed to his belief that a "multiplicity of sects," in which no religious group could achieve dominance, offered the greatest protection for freedom of conscience. Although he doubted the efficacy of "parchment barriers" in the form of legal constraints to protect individual freedom, he also worked assiduously to improve the Declaration of Rights and to enact Jefferson's statute. In his Detached Memoranda, Madison called the statute the "*true* standard of Religious liberty," serving as "*the great* barrier against usurpations on the rights of conscience." Madison believed the statute came closer to that ideal than the ultimate language of the First Amendment's religion clauses.[11]

Like Jefferson, Madison believed that church-state separation was essential to ensure freedom of conscience and freedom of religion, and to protect civil government from religious incursions. But more than Jefferson, Madison also advocated separationism for how it protected religion. As he declared in his *Memorial,* religious establishments were "adverse to the diffusion of the light of Christianity." An "alliance" between government and religion would have a "corrupting influence on both parties," he told Edward Livingston, noting that "religion & government will both exist in greater purity, the less they are mixed together." And as he asserted to Robert Walsh, "The number, the industry, and the morality of the priesthood & the devotion of the people have been manifestly increased by the total separation of the Church from the State."[12] Finally, both men argued for equal standing in society regardless of religious opinions. Jefferson declared that a person's "opinions in matters of religion . . . shall in no wise diminish, enlarge, or affect their civil capacities," whereas Madison called for a condition of "equal conditions" with regard to religious affiliation. As Jack Rakove has observed, "There were thus some differences in the ways in which the sages of Monticello and Montpelier thought about religiosity. But on fundamental constitutional matters their convictions converged. . . . Both treated the free exercise of religion as a natural right that the state could not abridge. Both wanted to sever the formal legal ties between church and state. And both grasped the historical novelty of their position."[13]

With respect to the free exercise of religion, Jefferson and Madison took an expansive view about what constituted protected religious conduct. As discussed, during the drafting of the Declaration of Rights, Madison attempted to narrow the ability of authorities to restrict religious activities when they "disturb[ed] the peace, the happiness, or safety of society," arguing instead that authority should exist only where religious acts interfered with "equal liberty" of others or that "the existence of the State [is] manifestly endangered." At the same time, however, they did not go so far as to exempt religious actors from adhering to neutral public welfare laws.[14] In his Danbury letter, Jefferson asserted that rights of conscience were natural rights but that "he has no natural right in opposition to his social duties." And in his statute, Jefferson affirmed that civil government has a "rightful purpose" to "interfere when [religious] principles break out into overt acts against peace and good order." Madison too warned against granting some denominations "peculiar exemptions" from laws that would endow them "above all others with extraordinary privileges." To provide a contemporary example, both men would likely have supported enforcing neutral closure and social gathering restrictions on houses of worship—along with comparable entities—during times of a pandemic, as occurred with COVID-19 between 2020 and 2022.[15]

Jefferson and Madison also believed that threats to religious freedom and rights of conscience would arise from oppressive religious majorities. While a violation of either the establishment clause or the free exercise clause requires "state action"—in essence, the clauses represent a restraint only on official conduct, not on that of private individuals—the writings of Jefferson and Madison urge that to ensure full religious freedom and equality the government should create guardrails (i.e., take affirmative steps) that minimize the opportunity for private, religious oppression. As Madison wrote in his *Memorial,* it is "also true that the majority may trespass on the rights of the minority." Thus, "A Government will be best supported by protecting every Citizen in the enjoyment of his Religion . . . by neither invading the equal rights of any Sect, nor suffering any Sect to invade those of another."[16] So, both men would likely have approved of the nondiscrimination provisions of Title VII of the Civil Rights Act (outlawing private religious discrimination in employment) and the application of public accommodation laws to bar religiously based discriminatory actions of business that serve the general public. In Rakove's words, "The idea that free exercise claims would broadly justify exemptions from ordinary law was manifestly *not* a legacy of Revolutionary-era thinking about the realm of religious freedom."[17]

Thus, when it comes to writing about church-state matters and then acting to secure freedom of conscience, free inquiry, and religious equality, no other figures can match the record of Jefferson and Madison. The two were responsible for several of the seminal texts of American religious freedom: the Virginia Declaration of Rights, the Statute for Establishing Religious Freedom, the chapter on religion in *Notes on the State of Virginia,* the *Memorial and*

Remonstrance, the First Amendment, the Letter to the Danbury Baptist Association, and the Detached Memoranda. As Noah Feldman has remarked, "Without Madison, the bill of rights would not have been enacted." And together, Madison and Jefferson founded the first truly secular university in America. No figure or figures come close to that record of achievement.[18]

Critics will continue to insist that Jefferson and Madison were outliers in their perspectives on church and state and that most Americans held more accommodating beliefs about church-state intermixing, including other leading founders (or, conversely, that Jefferson and Madison also believed in more conventional forms of church-state intermixing than as they have traditionally been portrayed).[19] But as this book has demonstrated, these claims are highly exaggerated. The wide support for Jefferson's church-state record during the 1800 election among his defenders and the ongoing embrace of those ideas into the Jacksonian era indicates that Jefferson and Madison were not alone in their views. Vincent Phillip Muñoz is correct that "there is no single church-state position that can claim the exclusive authority of America's founding history," but the fact that there were competing views about church-state relations does not mean they all were of equal merit or influence.[20] No other political or religious figures of the time were as instrumental in creating the seminal documents and directing the events concerning religious freedom as were Jefferson and Madison, a fact that critics are forced to admit. Similarly, when it comes to informing and influencing the decisions of jurists and policymakers on church-state controversies, the works of Jefferson and Madison are unmatched. As stated, no one is more responsible for the First Amendment than Madison—for its ultimate language, if not for its very existence. "It is entirely proper to regard the religion clauses as Madison's text and Jefferson's legacy," notes Jack Rakove.[21]

The public debate over the proper relationship between church and state, and whether separationism should be a part of that arrangement, will not end soon. Neither will the scholarly and partisan debate over how much the Jeffersonian-Madisonian legacy should serve as "an" or "the" authority for resolving church-state questions. This author is under no delusion that this book has settled either of these debates. But at its core, the complaint about the Jeffersonian-Madisonian legacy, that the "[Supreme] Court . . . has never gotten the Founders right," is essentially a philosophical disagreement over the way that certain justices have interpreted the religion clauses. It is less of a disagreement over history.[22]

The Statute for Establishing Religious Freedom

[Below is the text of Jefferson's draft of his bill, with the deletions by the General Assembly shown in italics and the assembly's insertions to the statute shown within brackets.]

Well aware that the opinions and belief of men depend not on their own will, but follow involuntarily the evidence proposed to their minds; that [Whereas] Almighty God hath created the mind free, *and manifested his supreme will that free it shall remain by making it altogether insusceptible of restraint;* that all attempts to influence it by temporal punishments, or burthens, or by civil incapacitations, tend only to beget habits of hypocrisy and meanness, and are a departure from the plan of the holy author of our religion, who being lord both of body and mind, yet chose not to propagate it by coercions on either, as was in his Almighty power to do, *but to extend it by its influence on reason alone;* that the impious presumption of legislators and rulers, civil as well as ecclesiastical, who, being themselves but fallible and uninspired men, have assumed dominion over the faith of others, setting up their own opinions and modes of thinking as the only true and infallible, and as such endeavoring to impose them on others, hath established and maintained false religions over the greatest part of the world and through all time: That to compel a man to furnish contributions of money for the propagation of opinions which he disbelieves and *abhors,* is sinful and tyrannical; that even the forcing him to support this or that teacher of his own religious persuasion, is depriving him of the comfortable liberty of giving his contributions to the particular pastor whose morals he would make his pattern, and whose powers he feels most persuasive to righteousness; and is withdrawing from the ministry those temporal[ry] rewards, which proceeding from an approbation of their personal conduct, are an additional incitement to earnest and unremitting labours for the instruction of mankind; that our civil rights have no dependance on our religious opinions, any more than on our opinions in physics or geometry; that therefore the proscribing any citizen as unworthy the public confidence by laying upon him an incapacity of being called to offices of trust and emolument, unless he profess or renounce this or that religious opinion, is depriving him injuriously of those privileges and advantages to which, in common with his fellow citizens, he has a natural right; that it tends *also* [only] to corrupt the principles of that very religion it is meant to encourage, by bribing, with a monopoly of worldly honours and emoluments, those who will externally profess and conform to it; that though indeed these are criminal who do not withstand such temptation, yet neither are those innocent who lay the bait in their way; *that the opinions of men are not the object of civil government, nor under its jurisdiction;* that to suffer the civil magistrate to intrude his powers into the field of opinion and to restrain the profession or propagation of principles on supposition of their ill tendency is a dangerous fallacy, which at once destroys all religious liberty, because he being of course judge of that tendency will make his opinions the rule of judgment, and approve or condemn the sentiments of others only as they shall square with or differ from his own; that it is time enough for the rightful purposes of civil government for its officers to interfere when principles break out into overt acts against peace and good order; and finally, that truth is great and will prevail if left to herself; that she is the proper and sufficient antagonist to error, and has nothing to fear from the conflict unless by human interposition disarmed of her natural weapons, free argument and debate; errors ceasing to be dangerous when it is permitted freely to contradict them.

We the General Assembly of Virginia do enact [Be it enacted by the General Assembly] that no man shall be compelled to frequent or support any religious worship, place, or ministry whatsoever, nor shall be enforced, restrained, molested, or burthened in his body or goods, nor shall otherwise suffer, on account of his religious opinions or belief; but that all men shall be free to profess, and by argument to maintain, their opinions in matters of religion, and that the same shall in no wise diminish, enlarge, or affect their civil capacities.

And though we well know that this Assembly, elected by the people for the ordinary purposes of legislation only, have no power to restrain the acts of succeeding Assemblies, constituted with powers equal to our own, and that therefore to declare this act [to be] irrevocable would be of no effect in law; yet we are free to declare, and do declare, that the rights hereby asserted are of the natural rights of mankind, and that if any act shall be hereafter passed to repeal the present or to narrow its operation, such act will be an infringement of natural right.

Memorial and Remonstrance against Religious Assessments

To the Honorable the General Assembly of the Commonwealth of Virginia
A Memorial and Remonstrance

We the subscribers, citizens of the said Commonwealth, having taken into serious consideration, a Bill printed by order of the last Session of General Assembly, entitled "A Bill establishing a provision for Teachers of the Christian Religion," and conceiving that the same if finally armed with the sanctions of a law, will be a dangerous abuse of power, are bound as faithful members of a free State to remonstrate against it, and to declare the reasons by which we are determined. We remonstrate against the said Bill,

1. Because we hold it for a fundamental and undeniable truth, "that Religion or the duty which we owe to our Creator and the manner of discharging it, can be directed only by reason and conviction, not by force or violence" [Virginia Declaration of Rights, art. 16]. The Religion then of every man must be left to the conviction and conscience of every man; and it is the right of every man to exercise it as these may dictate. This right is in its nature an unalienable right. It is unalienable, because the opinions of men, depending only on the evidence contemplated by their own minds cannot follow the dictates of other men: It is unalienable also, because what is here a right towards men, is a duty towards the Creator. It is the duty of every man to render to the Creator such homage and such only as he believes to be acceptable to him. This duty is precedent, both in order of time and in degree of obligation, to the claims of Civil Society. Before any man can be

considered as a member of Civil Society, he must be considered as a subject of the Governour of the Universe: And if a member of Civil Society, who enters into any subordinate Association, must always do it with a reservation of his duty to the General Authority; much more must every man who becomes a member of any particular Civil Society, do it with a saving of his allegiance to the Universal Sovereign. We maintain therefore that in matters of Religion, no mans right is abridged by the institution of Civil Society and that Religion is wholly exempt from its cognizance. True it is, that no other rule exists, by which any question which may divide a Society, can be ultimately determined, but the will of the majority; but it is also true that the majority may trespass on the rights of the minority.

2. Because if Religion be exempt from the authority of the Society at large, still less can it be subject to that of the Legislative Body. The latter are but the creatures and vicegerents of the former. Their jurisdiction is both derivative and limited: it is limited with regard to the co-ordinate departments, more necessarily is it limited with regard to the constituents. The preservation of a free Government requires not merely, that the metes and bounds which separate each department of power be invariably maintained; but more especially that neither of them be suffered to overleap the great Barrier which defends the rights of the people. The Rulers who are guilty of such an encroachment, exceed the commission from which they derive their authority, and are Tyrants. The People who submit to it are governed by laws made neither by themselves nor by an authority derived from them, and are slaves.

3. Because it is proper to take alarm at the first experiment on our liberties. We hold this prudent jealousy to be the first duty of Citizens, and one of the noblest characteristics of the late Revolution. The free men of America did not wait till usurped power had strengthened itself by exercise, and entangled the question in precedents. They saw all the consequences in the principle, and they avoided the consequences by denying the principle. We revere this lesson too much soon to forget it. Who does not see that the same authority which can establish Christianity, in

exclusion of all other Religions, may establish with the same ease any particular sect of Christians, in exclusion of all other Sects? that the same authority which can force a citizen to contribute three pence only of his property for the support of any one establishment, may force him to conform to any other establishment in all cases whatsoever?

4. Because the Bill violates that equality which ought to be the basis of every law, and which is more indispensible, in proportion as the validity or expediency of any law is more liable to be impeached. If "all men are by nature equally free and independent" [Virginia Declaration of Rights, art. 1], all men are to be considered as entering into Society on equal conditions; as relinquishing no more, and therefore retaining no less, one than another, of their natural rights. Above all are they to be considered as retaining an "*equal* title to the free exercise of Religion according to the dictates of Conscience" [Virginia Declaration of Rights, art. 16]. Whilst we assert for ourselves a freedom to embrace, to profess and to observe the Religion which we believe to be of divine origin, we cannot deny an equal freedom to those whose minds have not yet yielded to the evidence which has convinced us. If this freedom be abused, it is an offence against God, not against man: To God, therefore, not to man, must an account of it be rendered. As the Bill violates equality by subjecting some to peculiar burdens, so it violates the same principle, by granting to others peculiar exemptions. Are the Quakers and Menonists the only sects who think a compulsive support of their Religions unnecessary and unwarrantable? Can their piety alone be entrusted with the care of public worship? Ought their Religions to be endowed above all others with extraordinary privileges by which proselytes may be enticed from all others? We think too favorably of the justice and good sense of these denominations to believe that they either covet preeminences over their fellow citizens or that they will be seduced by them from the common opposition to the measure.

5. Because the Bill implies either that the Civil Magistrate is a competent Judge of Religious Truth; or that he may employ Religion as an engine of Civil policy. The first is an arrogant pretension falsified by the contradictory opinions of Rulers in all ages,

and throughout the world: the second an unhallowed perversion of the means of salvation.

6. Because the establishment proposed by the Bill is not requisite for the support of the Christian Religion. To say that it is, is a contradiction to the Christian Religion itself, for every page of it disavows a dependence on the powers of this world: it is a contradiction to fact; for it is known that this Religion both existed and flourished, not only without the support of human laws, but in spite of every opposition from them, and not only during the period of miraculous aid, but long after it had been left to its own evidence and the ordinary care of Providence. Nay, it is a contradiction in terms; for a Religion not invented by human policy, must have pre-existed and been supported, before it was established by human policy. It is moreover to weaken in those who profess this Religion a pious confidence in its innate excellence and the patronage of its Author; and to foster in those who still reject it, a suspicion that its friends are too conscious of its fallacies to trust it to its own merits.

7. Because experience witnesseth that ecclesiastical establishments, instead of maintaining the purity and efficacy of Religion, have had a contrary operation. During almost fifteen centuries has the legal establishment of Christianity been on trial. What have been its fruits? More or less in all places, pride and indolence in the Clergy, ignorance and servility in the laity, in both, superstition, bigotry and persecution. Enquire of the Teachers of Christianity for the ages in which it appeared in its greatest lustre; those of every sect, point to the ages prior to its incorporation with Civil policy. Propose a restoration of this primitive State in which its Teachers depended on the voluntary rewards of their flocks, many of them predict its downfall. On which Side ought their testimony to have greatest weight, when for or when against their interest?

8. Because the establishment in question is not necessary for the support of Civil Government. If it be urged as necessary for the support of Civil Government only as it is a means of supporting Religion, and it be not necessary for the latter purpose, it cannot be necessary for the former. If Religion be not within the cognizance of Civil Government how can its legal establishment be necessary

to Civil Government? What influence in fact have ecclesiastical establishments had on Civil Society? In some instances they have been seen to erect a spiritual tyranny on the ruins of the Civil authority; in many instances they have been seen upholding the thrones of political tyranny: in no instance have they been seen the guardians of the liberties of the people. Rulers who wished to subvert the public liberty, may have found an established Clergy convenient auxiliaries. A just Government instituted to secure & perpetuate it needs them not. Such a Government will be best supported by protecting every Citizen in the enjoyment of his Religion with the same equal hand which protects his person and his property; by neither invading the equal rights of any Sect, nor suffering any Sect to invade those of another.

9. Because the proposed establishment is a departure from that generous policy, which, offering an Asylum to the persecuted and oppressed of every Nation and Religion, promised a lustre to our country, and an accession to the number of its citizens. What a melancholy mark is the Bill of sudden degeneracy? Instead of holding forth an Asylum to the persecuted, it is itself a signal of persecution. It degrades from the equal rank of Citizens all those whose opinions in Religion do not bend to those of the Legislative authority. Distant as it may be in its present form from the Inquisition, it differs from it only in degree. The one is the first step, the other the last in the career of intolerance. The magnanimous sufferer under this cruel scourge in foreign Regions, must view the Bill as a Beacon on our Coast, warning him to seek some other haven, where liberty and philanthrophy in their due extent, may offer a more certain repose from his Troubles.

10. Because it will have a like tendency to banish our Citizens. The allurements presented by other situations are every day thinning their number. To superadd a fresh motive to emigration by revoking the liberty which they now enjoy, would be the same species of folly which has dishonoured and depopulated flourishing kingdoms.

11. Because it will destroy that moderation and harmony which the forbearance of our laws to intermeddle with Religion has produced among its several sects. Torrents of blood have been spilt

in the old world, by vain attempts of the secular arm, to extinguish Religious discord, by proscribing all difference in Religious opinion. Time has at length revealed the true remedy. Every relaxation of narrow and rigorous policy, wherever it has been tried, has been found to assuage the disease. The American Theatre has exhibited proofs that equal and compleat liberty, if it does not wholly eradicate it, sufficiently destroys its malignant influence on the health and prosperity of the State. If with the salutary effects of this system under our own eyes, we begin to contract the bounds of Religious freedom, we know no name that will too severely reproach our folly. At least let warning be taken at the first fruits of the threatened innovation. The very appearance of the Bill has transformed "that Christian forbearance, love and charity" [Virginia Declaration of Rights, art. 16], which of late mutually prevailed, into animosities and jealousies, which may not soon be appeased. What mischiefs may not be dreaded, should this enemy to the public quiet be armed with the force of a law?

12. Because the policy of the Bill is adverse to the diffusion of the light of Christianity. The first wish of those who enjoy this precious gift ought to be that it may be imparted to the whole race of mankind. Compare the number of those who have as yet received it with the number still remaining under the dominion of false Religions; and how small is the former! Does the policy of the Bill tend to lessen the disproportion? No; it at once discourages those who are strangers to the light of revelation from coming into the Region of it; and countenances by example the nations who continue in darkness, in shutting out those who might convey it to them. Instead of Levelling as far as possible, every obstacle to the victorious progress of Truth, the Bill with an ignoble and unchristian timidity would circumscribe it with a wall of defence against the encroachments of error.

13. Because attempts to enforce by legal sanctions, acts obnoxious to so great a proportion of Citizens, tend to enervate the laws in general, and to slacken the bands of Society. If it be difficult to execute any law which is not generally deemed necessary or salutary, what must be the case, where it is deemed invalid and

dangerous? And what may be the effect of so striking an example of impotency in the Government, on its general authority?

14. Because a measure of such singular magnitude and delicacy ought not to be imposed, without the clearest evidence that it is called for by a majority of citizens, and no satisfactory method is yet proposed by which the voice of the majority in this case may be determined, or its influence secured. "The people of the respective counties are indeed requested to signify their opinion respecting the adoption of the Bill to the next Session of Assembly." But the representation must be made equal, before the voice either of the Representatives or of the Counties will be that of the people. Our hope is that neither of the former will, after due consideration, espouse the dangerous principle of the Bill. Should the event disappoint us, it will still leave us in full confidence, that a fair appeal to the latter will reverse the sentence against our liberties.

15. Because finally, "the equal right of every citizen to the free exercise of his Religion according to the dictates of conscience" is held by the same tenure with all our other rights. If we recur to its origin, it is equally the gift of nature; if we weigh its importance, it cannot be less dear to us; if we consult the "Declaration of those rights which pertain to the good people of Virginia, as the basis and foundation of Government," it is enumerated with equal solemnity, or rather studied emphasis. Either then, we must say, that the Will of the Legislature is the only measure of their authority; and that in the plenitude of this authority, they may sweep away all our fundamental rights; or, that they are bound to leave this particular right untouched and sacred: Either we must say, that they may controul the freedom of the press, may abolish the Trial by Jury, may swallow up the Executive and Judiciary Powers of the State; nay that they may despoil us of our very right of suffrage, and erect themselves into an independent and hereditary Assembly or, we must say, that they have no authority to enact into law the Bill under consideration. We the Subscribers say, that the General Assembly of this Commonwealth have no such authority: And that no effort may be omitted on our part against so dangerous an usurpation, we oppose to it, this remonstrance;

earnestly praying, as we are in duty bound, that the Supreme Lawgiver of the Universe, by illuminating those to whom it is addressed, may on the one hand, turn their Councils from every act which would affront his holy prerogative, or violate the trust committed to them: and on the other, guide them into every measure which may be worthy of his blessing, may redound to their own praise, and may establish more firmly the liberties, the prosperity and the happiness of the Commonwealth.

◈ NOTES ◈

INTRODUCTION

1. Jefferson Memorial, National Park Service, https://www.nps.gov/thje /index.htm. See "Jefferson's Words Carved in Panels," *New York Times,* April 14, 1943, 16.

2. Thomas Jefferson, gravestone, Monticello, https://www.monticello.org/ site/research-and-collections/jeffersons-gravestone. "Because of these," Jefferson wrote, "as testimonials that I have lived, I wish most to be re- membered." Cushing Strout notes that the excerpts from the Virginia Stat- ute on the memorial contain its less controversial passages, thus "tam[ing] the radical force of Jefferson's statute." Nonetheless, Strout agrees that "the wall's quotation eloquently illustrates the way in which Jefferson's legacy has been received." Strout, "Jeffersonian Religious Liberty and American Pluralism," in *The Virginia Statute for Religious Freedom,* ed. Merrill D. Pe- terson and Robert C. Vaughan (New York: Cambridge University Press, 1988), 201–2. See also Andrew Burstein, *Democracy's Muse* (Charlottes- ville: University of Virginia Press, 2015), 13–17.

3. Merrill D. Peterson, *The Jefferson Image in the American Mind* (Charlottes- ville: University Press of Virginia, 1998), 420–32; Annette Gordon-Reed and Peter S. Onuf, *"Most Blessed of the Patriarchs": Thomas Jefferson and the Empire of the Imagination* (New York: Liveright, 2016), 273–74; "Jef- ferson's Religious Beliefs," Monticello, https://www.monticello.org/site/ research-and-collections/jeffersons-religious-beliefs.

4. *Jefferson's Extracts from the Gospels,* ed. Dickinson W. Adams (Princeton, NJ: Princeton University Press, 1983). See also *The Adams-Jefferson Let- ters,* ed. Lester J. Cappon, (Chapel Hill: University of North Carolina Press, 1987), particularly the years between 1813 and 1818, and Edwin S. Gaustad, *Sworn on the Altar of God: A Religious Biography of Thomas Jeffer- son* (Grand Rapids, MI: Eerdmans, 1996), xiii.

5. David McCullough, *John Adams* (New York: Simon and Schuster, 2001).

6. Noah Feldman, *The Three Lives of James Madison: Genius, Partisan, President* (New York: Random House, 2017), 9. See also Jack N. Rakove, *Beyond Belief, Beyond Conscience: The Radical Significance of the Free Exercise of Religion* (New York: Oxford University Press, 2020), 67, noting the "central place that religious freedom occupied in the political thinking of Thomas Jefferson and James Madison."

7. William Linn, *Serious Considerations on the Election of a President* (New York: John Furman, 1800), 12, 20; Charles O. Lerche Jr., "Jefferson and the Election of 1800: A Case Study in the Political Smear," *William and Mary Quarterly*, 3rd series, 5 (Oct. 1948): 467–91; Frank Lambert, "'God—and a Religious President . . . [or] Jefferson and No God': Campaigning for a Voter-Imposed Religious Test in 1800," *Journal of Church and State* 39 (1997): 769–89.

8. Rakove, *Beyond Belief, Beyond Conscience*, 68–69.

9. Thomas S. Kidd, *Thomas Jefferson: A Biography of Spirit and Flesh* (New Haven, CT: Yale University Press, 2022), 40; Charles B. Sanford, *The Religious Life of Thomas Jefferson* (Charlottesville: University Press of Virginia, 1984), 173 (quotation); Royden J. Mott, "Sources of Jefferson's Ecclesiastical Views," *Church History* 3 (1934): 270; George Harmon Knoles, "The Religious Ideas of Thomas Jefferson," *Mississippi Valley Historical Review* 30 (1943): 188.

10. Lance Banning, "James Madison, the Statute for Religious Freedom, and the Crisis of Republican Convictions," in Peterson and Vaughan, *Virginia Statute for Religious Freedom*, 109–38; Ralph Ketcham, *James Madison: A Biography* (Charlottesville: University Press of Virginia, 1990), 47. In contrast, Martha Nussbaum calls Madison "a devout and curious believer." Nussbaum, *Liberty of Conscience: In Defense of America's Tradition of Religious Equality* (New York: Basic Books, 2008), 75.

11. Steven Waldman, *Founding Faith: Providence, Politics, and the Birth of Religious Freedom in America* (New York: Random House, 2008), 81, 98–99; Alf J. Mapp Jr., *The Faiths of Our Fathers: What America's Founders Really Believed* (New York: Barnes and Noble, 2006), 6–7, 47; Brooke Allen, "Jefferson the Skeptic," *Hudson Review* 59 (2006): 193–217; Fred C. Luebke, "The Origins of Thomas Jefferson's Anti-Clericalism," *Church History* 32 (1963): 344–56.

12. See Lance Banning, *Jefferson and Madison: Three Conversations from the Founding* (Madison, WI: Madison House, 1995), 127: "The long collaboration . . . of two great minds engaged with one another in the process of confronting several of the largest questions of their day."

13. Ralph L. Ketcham, "James Madison and Religion—A New Hypothesis," *Presbyterian Historical Society* 38 (June 1960): 76–77.
14. Adrienne Koch, *Jefferson and Madison: The Great Collaboration* (1950; reprint New York: Oxford University Press, 1964); Rakove, *Beyond Belief, Beyond Conscience*, 3.
15. Gaustad, *Sworn on the Altar of God*, 194–95: "No collaboration had more significance for America's history, or for religious liberty, than the one that kept this potent team knit tightly together for a half century."
16. Vincent Phillip Muñoz, *God and the Founders: Madison, Washington, and Jefferson* (New York: Cambridge University Press, 2009), 3. See also Michael W. McConnell, "The Origins and Historical Understanding of Free Exercise of Religion," *Harvard Law Review* 103 (1990): 1409–517.
17. Rakove, *Beyond Belief, Beyond Conscience*, 99.
18. Everson v. Board of Education, 330 U.S. 1, 16, 31–43 (1947).
19. McCollum v. Board of Education, 333 U.S. 203, 211, 231 (1948).
20. McGowen v. Maryland, 366 U.S. 420, 437 (1961).
21. Rosenberger v. University of Virginia, 515 U.S. 819 (1995). See Oral Argument Transcript, Shurtleff v. Boston, Jan. 18, 2022, https://www.supreme court.gov/oral_arguments/audio/2021/20-1800.
22. See Muñoz, *God and the Founders;* Robert L. Cord, *Separation of Church and State: Historical Fact and Current Fiction* (1982; reprint Grand Rapids, MI: Baker, 1988); Daniel L. Dreisbach, *Thomas Jefferson and the Wall of Separation between Church and State* (New York: NYU Press, 2002).
23. Charles B. Sanford, "The Religious Beliefs of Thomas Jefferson," and Mary-Elaine Swanson, "James Madison and the Presbyterian Idea of Man and Government," in *Religion and Political Culture in Jefferson's Virginia*, ed. Garrett Ward Sheldon and Daniel L. Dreisbach (Lanham, MD: Rowman and Littlefield, 2000), 61–91, 119–32; Joseph Loconte, "Faith and the Founding: The Influence of Religion on the Politics of James Madison," *Journal of Church and State* 40 (2003): 699–715.
24. Koch, *Jefferson and Madison;* Merrill D. Peterson, *Jefferson and Madison and the Making of Constitutions* (Charlottesville: University Press of Virginia, 1988); Andrew Burstein and Nancy Isenberg, *Madison and Jefferson* (New York: Random House, 2010); Jeff Broadwater, *Jefferson, Madison, and the Making of the Constitution* (Chapel Hill: University of North Carolina Press, 2019); Sanford, *Religious Life of Thomas Jefferson;* Gaustad, *Sworn on the Altar of God;* Kidd, *Thomas Jefferson;* Feldman, *Three Lives of James Madison.*
25. Rakove, *Beyond Belief, Beyond Conscience*, 4: "On the religion question, Jefferson and Madison marked the advanced edge of American thinking.

They may not have been the most representative commentators on this issue."

26. Rosenberger v. University of Virginia, at 871, 868 (Souter, J., dissenting).

27. Rakove, *Beyond Belief, Beyond Conscience,* 66–96.

28. See Nicholas P. Miller, *The Religious Roots of the First Amendment: Dissenting Protestants and the Separation of Church and State* (New York: Oxford University Press, 2012), 1.

29. See John A. Ragosta, *Religious Freedom: Jefferson's Legacy, America's Creed* (Charlottesville: University of Virginia Press, 2013), and Rakove, *Beyond Belief, Beyond Conscience,* 66–96 ("It is entirely proper to regard the Religion Clauses as Madison's text and Jefferson's legacy").

30. David Sehat, *The Myth of American Religious Freedom* (New York: Oxford University Press, 2011); Winnifred Fallers Sullivan, *The Impossibility of Religious Freedom* (Princeton, NJ: Princeton University Press, 2007); Finbarr Curtis, *The Production of American Religious Freedom* (New York: NYU Press, 2016); Tisa Wenger, *Religious Freedom: The Contested History of an American Ideal* (Chapel Hill: University of North Carolina Press, 2017); Steven K. Green, *Separating Church and State: A History* (Ithaca, NY: Cornell University Press, 2022).

31. See Trump v. Hawaii, 138 S.Ct. 2392 (2018).

32. McCollum v. Board of Education, at 213 (opinion of Frankfurter, J.); Steven K. Green, "'A Spacious Conception': Separationism as an Idea," *Oregon Law Review* 85 (2007): 443–80.

1. THE SETTING

1. Sidney E. Mead, *The Lively Experiment: The Shaping of Christianity in America* (New York: Harper and Row, 1976), 16–17; Chris Beneke, *Beyond Toleration: Religious Origins of American Pluralism* (New York: Oxford University Press, 2006), 17–22.

2. Thomas J. Curry, *The First Freedoms: Church and State in America to the Passage of the First Amendment* (New York: Oxford University Press, 1986), 54–77; Joel A. Nichols, "Religious Liberty in the Thirteenth Colony: Church-State Relations in Colonial and Early National Georgia," *New York Law Review* 80 (2005): 1738–51; J. William Frost, *A Perfect Freedom: Religious Liberty in Pennsylvania* (New York: Cambridge University Press, 1990), 10–28; John Webb Pratt, *Religion, Politics, and Diversity: The Church-State Theme in New York History* (Ithaca, NY: Cornell University Press, 1967), 18–48.

3. Mead, *Lively Experiment,* 22–23; Jon Butler, *Awash in a Sea of Faith: Christianizing the American People* (Cambridge, MA: Harvard University Press, 1990), 63–66, 191–93 (commenting that by 1700 a spiritual lethargy existed in many areas, even among dissenting religious groups).

4. Leonard W. Levy, *The Establishment Clause: Religion and the First Amendment* (New York: Macmillan, 1986), 1–2; Steven K. Green, *The Second Disestablishment: Church and State in Nineteenth-Century America* (New York: Oxford University Press, 2012), 24–31.

5. Beneke, *Beyond Toleration,* 34–35.

6. Rakove, *Beyond Belief, Beyond Conscience,* 56.

7. Ethan H. Shagan, *The Birth of Modern Belief* (Princeton, NJ: Princeton University Press, 2018), 207–49; James MacGregor Burns, *Fire and Light: How the Enlightenment Transformed Our World* (New York: St. Martin's Press, 2013), 3–4.

8. Sanford Kessler, "Locke's Influence on Jefferson's 'Bill for Establishing Religious Freedom,'" *Journal of Church and State* 25 (1983): 231–52; S. Gerald Sandler, "Lockean Ideas in Thomas Jefferson's Bill for Establishing Religious Freedom," *Journal of the History of Ideas* 21 (1960): 110–16; Gary Rosen, *American Compact: James Madison and the Problem of Founding* (Lawrence: University Press of Kansas, 1999), 3, 6, 10, 22–24; Donald S. Lutz, *The Origins of American Constitutionalism* (Baton Rouge: Louisiana State University Press, 1988), 143. Locke was the most commonly cited secular authority in political writings of the 1760s and 1770s.

9. John Locke, *A Letter on Toleration,* ed. Raymond Klibansky (Oxford: Clarendon Press, 1968); John Marshall, *John Locke, Toleration and Early Enlightenment Culture* (Cambridge: Cambridge University Press, 2006), 17–193; Sanford Kessler, "John Locke's Legacy of Religious Freedom," *Polity* 17 (1985): 484–503.

10. Locke, *A Letter on Toleration,* 65–69, 85; Green, *Separating Church and State,* 25–27.

11. Lutz, *Origins of American Constitutionalism,* 142–45.

12. Roger B. Oake, "Montesquieu's Religious Ideas," *Journal of the History of Ideas* 14 (1953): 548–60; Montesquieu, *Spirit of the Laws,* ed. Philip B. Kurland and Ralph Lerner (Chicago: University of Chicago Press, 1987), books 12 and 25, in The Founders' Constitution, vol. 5, amendment 1 (Religion), doc. 12, http://press-pubs.uchicago.edu/founders/documents/amendI_religions12.html; Green, *Separating Church and State,* 27–28.

13. Voltaire, *Philosophical Dictionary,* trans. Peter Gay (New York: Harcourt, Brace and World, 1962), vol 9, "rights."

14. Eugene R. Sheridan, *Jefferson and Religion* (Monticello, VA: Thomas Jefferson Memorial Foundation, 1998), 16–18.

15. Bernard Bailyn, *The Ideological Origins of the American Revolution* (Cambridge, MA: Belknap Press of Harvard University Press, 1967), 27.

16. Ibid., 35–36; Carolina Robbins, *The Eighteenth-Century Commonwealthman* (Cambridge, MA: Harvard University Press, 1961), 9–13.

17. John Trenchard, *Cato's Letters*, no. 60, Jan. 6, 1721, in *Contexts of the Constitution: A Documentary Collection on Principles of American Constitutional Law*, ed. Neil H. Cogan (New York: Foundation Press, 1999), 141.

18. Bailyn, *Ideological Origins*, 35–37.

19. Richard Price, *Observations on the Nature of Civil Liberty, the Principles of Government, and the Justice and Policy of War with America* (New York: S. Loudon, 1776), 3; Gregory I. Molivas, "Richard Price, the Debate on Free Will, and Natural Rights," *Journal of the History of Ideas* 58 (1997): 105–23; Robbins, *The Eighteenth-Century Commonwealthman*, 335–47.

20. Joseph Priestley, *Essay on the First Principles of Government; and on the Nature of Political, Civil, and Religious Liberty*, 2nd ed. (1768; London: J. Johnson, 1771), 53–55, 65, 77–78, 82; Robbins, *The Eighteenth-Century Commonwealthman*, 347–54.

21. Bailyn, *Ideological Origins*, 35.

22. Beneke, *Beyond Toleration*, 113–15.

23. Mead, *Lively Experiment*, 23–26.

24. Ibid., 29–31; David S. Lovejoy, *Religious Enthusiasm in the New World* (Cambridge, MA: Harvard University Press, 1985), 178–94; William Warren Sweet, *Revivalism in America: Its Origin, Growth and Decline* (Gloucester, MA: Peter Smith, 1965), 44–70; Thomas S. Kidd, *The Great Awakening: The Roots of Evangelical Christianity in Colonial America* (New Haven, CT: Yale University Press, 2007).

25. Beneke, *Beyond Toleration*, 49–77; Mead, *Lively Experiment*, 34–35 (quotation).

26. Elisha Williams, *The Essential Rights and Liberties of Protestants: A Reasonable Plea for the Liberty of Conscience and the Right of Private Judgment in Matters of Religion*, in *Political Sermons of the American Founding Era, 1730–1805*, ed. Ellis Sandoz (Indianapolis: Liberty Fund, 1991), 51–108, 52, 90, 92, 94–95, 97 (quotations).

27. Carl Bridenbaugh, *Mitre and Sceptre: Transatlantic Faiths, Ideas, Personalities, and Politics, 1689–1775* (New York: Oxford University Press, 1962), 25–32; Arthur Lyon Cross, *The Anglican Episcopate and the American Colonies* (Hamden, CT: Archon Books, 1964), 35–36; William M. Hogue,

"The Religious Conspiracy Theory of the American Revolution: Anglican Motive," *Church History* 45 (1976): 277–92.

28. Jonathan Mayhew, *A Discourse Concerning Unlimited Submission and Non-Resistance to the Higher Powers* (1750), in *Religion and the Coming of the American Revolution,* ed. Peter N. Carroll (Waltham, MA: Ginn-Blaisdell, 1970), 30–52; Cross, *The Anglican Episcopate and the American Colonies,* 146–60.

29. John Adams to Hezekiah Niles, Feb. 13, 1818, in John Adams, *Works,* ed. Charles Francis Adams (Boston: Little and Brown, 1850–61), 10:288; Chris Beneke, "The Critical Turn: Jonathan Mayhew, the British Empire, and the Idea of Resistance in Mid-Eighteenth-Century Boston," *Massachusetts Historical Review* 10 (2008): 23–56.

30. Pratt, *Religion, Politics, and Diversity,* 67–74.

31. William Livingston, "The Independent Reflector, No. 22," April 26, 1753, in Carroll, *Religion and the Coming of the American Revolution,* 52–60; Bridenbaugh, *Mitre and Sceptre,* 138–68.

32. William Livingston, "The Absurdity of the Civil Magistrate Interfering in Matters of Religion," *Independent Reflector,* no. 36, Aug. 2, 1753, in Carroll, *Religion and the Coming of the American Revolution,* 60–63.

33. Bridenbaugh, *Mitre and Sceptre,* 153–65; Pratt, *Religion, Politics, and Diversity,* 67–74; Madison to Theodore Sedgwick, Feb. 12, 1831, in Founders Online, National Archives, Washington, DC, https://founders.archives.gov/.

34. Cross, *The Anglican Episcopate and the American Colonies,* 165–77; William G. McLoughlin, *New England Dissent, 1630–1883: The Baptists and the Separation of Church and State* (Cambridge, MA: Harvard University Press, 1971), 1:597–98.

35. William G. McLoughlin, "Isaac Backus and the Separation of Church and State in America," *American Historical Review* 73 (1968): 1392–413.

36. John Adams to Jedidiah Morse, Dec. 2, 1815; Adams to Hezekiah Niles, Feb. 13, 1818, in Adams, *Works,* 10:185, 288; Patricia U. Bonomi, *Under the Cope of Heaven: Religion, Society, and Politics in Colonial America* (New York: Oxford University Press, 1986), 199.

37. Jon Butler, "Coercion, Miracle, Reason: Rethinking the American Experience in the Revolutionary Age," in *Religion in a Revolutionary Age,* ed. Ronald Hoffman and Peter J. Albert (Charlottesville: University Press of Virginia, 1994), 3.

38. John A. Ragosta, *Wellspring of Liberty: How Virginia's Religious Dissenters Helped Win the Revolution and Secured Religious Liberty* (New York: Oxford University Press, 2010), 13. See also Thomas E. Buckley, *Church and State in Revolutionary Virginia, 1776–1787* (Charlottesville: University

Press of Virginia, 1977); William Lee Miller, *The First Liberty: Religion and the American Republic* (New York: Knopf, 1986); Peterson and Vaughan, *Virginia Statute for Religious Freedom;* Ragosta, *Religious Freedom;* and Thomas E. Buckley, *Establishing Religious Freedom: Jefferson's Statute in Virginia* (Charlottesville: University of Virginia Press, 2013).

39. Edward L. Bond, *Damned Souls in a Tobacco Colony: Religion in Seventeenth Century Virginia* (Macon, GA: Mercer University Press, 2000), 58; Curry, *First Freedoms,* 29.

40. Perry Miller, "Religion and Society in the Early Literature of Virginia," in *Errand into the Wilderness* (Cambridge, MA: Harvard University Press, 1956), 126.

41. See "Articles, Laws, and Orders, Divine, Politique, and Martiall for the Colony of Virginia" (1611), in *The Sacred Rights of Conscience,* ed. Daniel L. Dreisbach and Mark David Hall (Indianapolis: Liberty Fund, 2009), 84–86; Bond, *Damned Souls,* 44–46, 57–58, 66–67, 83–92; George Lewis Chumbley, *Colonial Justice in Virginia* (Richmond, VA: Dietz Press, 1938), 12–13; and David Flaherty, "Law and the Enforcement of Morals in Early America," in *American Law and Constitutional Order: Historical Perspectives,* ed. Lawrence M. Friedman and Harry N. Schneiber (Cambridge, MA: Harvard University Press, 1978), 53–66.

42. "Act for the Suppression of Quakers" (1659), in Dreisbach and Hall, *Sacred Rights of Conscience,* 113–14; Frank Lambert, *Founding Fathers and the Place of Religion in America* (Princeton, NJ: Princeton University Press, 2003), 67–70; Bond, *Damned Souls,* 145–52, 160–74; Chumbley, *Colonial Justice in Virginia,* 245–48.

43. Curry, *First Freedoms,* 30; Cross, *The Anglican Episcopate and the American Colonies,* 3; Ragosta, *Religious Freedom,* 42–43; Buckley, *Church and State,* 9.

44. Buckley, *Church and State,* 10–12; Rhys Isaac, "Religion and Authority: Problems of the Anglican Establishment in Virginia in the Era of the Great Awakening and the Parson's Cause," *William and Mary Quarterly,* 3rd series, 30 (Jan. 1973): 6–7; Rhys Isaac, *The Transformation of Virginia, 1740–1790* (Chapel Hill: University of North Carolina Press, 1982), 63–65, 120–21 (quotation); Alyssa G. Penick, "The Churches of Our Government: Parishes, Property, and Power in the Colonial and Early National Chesapeake" (Ph.D. diss., University of Michigan, 2020), 64–73, 95–98, 114–15.

45. Isaac, *Transformation of Virginia,* 120.

46. Buckley, *Church and State,* 10; Joan R. Gundersen, *The Anglican Ministry in Virginia, 1723–1766* (New York: Garland, 1989), 173–74.

47. Buckley, *Church and State*, 10–11; Ragosta, *Religious Freedom*, 40–47; Ragosta, *Wellspring of Liberty*, 3, 16–19, 180–83.

48. Gundersen, *The Anglican Ministry in Virginia*, 204–15; Isaac, "Religion and Authority," 5–7; Arthur P. Scott, "The Constitutional Aspects of the 'Parson's Cause,'" *Political Science Quarterly* 31 (1916): 558–77; William Meade, *Old Churches, Ministers, and Families of Virginia* (Philadelphia: J. P. Lippencott, 1857, 1878), 1:216–25.

49. Scott, "Constitutional Aspects," 558–77; Isaac, "Religion and Authority," 16.

50. Richard Bland, "A Letter to the Clergy of Virginia, in Which the Conduct of the General-Assembly Is Vindicated, against the Reflexions Contained in a Letter to the Lords of Trade and Plantations, from the Lord Bishop of London" (1760), in Carroll, *Religion and the Coming of the American Revolution*, 64–69; Scott, "Constitutional Aspects," 562–67; Isaac, "Religion and Authority," 19–20.

51. William Henry Foote, *Sketches of Virginia* (1850; reprint Richmond, VA: John Knox Press, 1966), 84–86, 104–32; Hamilton James Eckenrode, *Separation of Church and State in Virginia: A Study in the Development of the Revolution* (Richmond, VA: Department of Archives and History, 1910), 31–32.

52. Meade, *Old Churches*, 225; Edmund Randolph, "Edmund Randolph's Essay on the Revolutionary History of Virginia" (1809), *Virginia Magazine of History and Biography* 43 (April 1953): 113–58; Curry, *First Freedoms*, 99–100; Isaac, *Transformation of Virginia*, 148–51; Buckley, *Establishing Religious Freedom*, 17–20.

53. Lewis Peyton Little, *Imprisoned Preachers and Religious Liberty in Virginia* (Lynchburg, VA: J. P. Bell, 1938), 24–25; Isaac, *Transformation of Virginia*, 149; Buckley, *Establishing Religious Freedom*, 19–21.

54. Foote, *Sketches of Virginia*, 221–307; Isaac, *Transformation of Virginia*, 151–54; Gundersen, *The Anglican Ministry in Virginia*, 178–79; Buckley, *Establishing Religious Freedom*, 22–32.

55. Isaac, *Transformation of Virginia*, 163–77; Robert B. Semple, *A History of the Rise and Progress of the Baptists in Virginia*, rev. ed. (1810; Philadelphia: American Baptist Publication Society, 1894), 11–28, 42–43; Foote, *Sketches of Virginia*, 315; Buckley, *Establishing Religious Freedom*, 39–44; Eckenrode, *Separation of Church and State*, 36–38.

56. Foote, *Sketches of Virginia*, 315; Buckley, *Church and State*, 13–14.

57. Rhys Isaac, "Evangelical Revolt: The Nature of the Baptists' Challenge to the Traditional Order in Virginia, 1765 to 1775," *William and Mary Quarterly*, 3rd series, 31, no. 3 (1974): 345–68; Isaac, *Transformation of Virginia*,

168–69; Ragosta, *Wellspring of Liberty*, 5, 26, 31; Ragosta, *Religious Freedom*, 51–55; Semple, *A History of the Rise and Progress*, 25.

58. Ragosta, *Wellspring of Liberty*, 28–31; Little, *Imprisoned Preachers*, 75.
59. Little, *Imprisoned Preachers*, 229–31; Semple, *A History of the Rise and Progress*, 27; Ragosta, *Wellspring of Liberty*, 29.
60. Semple, *A History of the Rise and Progress*, 28–32; Foote, *Sketches of Virginia*, 315–16; Little, *Imprisoned Preachers*, 265–73; Ragosta, *Wellspring of Liberty*, 32, 171–80.
61. James Madison to William Bradford, Jan. 24, 1774, in Founders Online; Ketcham, *James Madison*, 56–59.
62. Miller, *First Liberty*, 87–96; "James Madison's Autobiography," ed. Douglass Adair, *William and Mary Quarterly*, 3rd series, 2 (April 1945): 198–99; Ragosta, *Religious Freedom*, 58–60; Rhys Isaac, "'The Rage of Malice of the Old Serpent Devil': The Dissenters and the Making and Remaking of the Virginia Statute for Religious Freedom," in Peterson and Vaughan, *Virginia Statute for Religious Freedom*, 139–69.

2. THOMAS JEFFERSON'S BACKGROUND

1. Reynolds v. United States, 98 U.S. 145, 163–64 (1879); Everson v. Board of Education, 330 U.S. 13; Abington School District v. Schempp, 374 U.S. 203, 234 (1963) (Brennan, J., concurring). See also McGowen v. Maryland, at 420, 437; Rakove, *Beyond Belief, Beyond Conscience*, 2–5, 66–96; Levy, *The Establishment Clause*, 181–85.
2. Philip Hamburger, *Separation of Church and State* (Cambridge, MA: Harvard University Press, 2002), 163–80.
3. Sanford, "The Religious Beliefs of Thomas Jefferson"; Swanson, "James Madison and the Presbyterian Idea of Man and Government."
4. Daniel L. Dreisbach, "Thomas Jefferson and Bills Number 82–86 of the Revision of the Laws of Virginia, 1776–1786: New Light on the Jeffersonian Model of Church-State Relations," *North Carolina Law Review* 69 (1990): 159–211; Cord, *Separation of Church and State*, 38–39; Muñoz, *God and the Founders*, 119–95.
5. Rakove, *Beyond Belief, Beyond Conscience*, 4: "On the religion question, Jefferson and Madison marked the advanced edge of American thinking. They may not have been the most representative commentators on this issue."
6. Paul K. Conkin, "The Religious Pilgrimage of Thomas Jefferson," in *Jeffersonian Legacies*, ed. Peter S. Onuf (Charlottesville: University Press of Virginia, 1993), 19–20.

7. Lambert, *Founding Fathers and the Place of Religion in America,* 178; Edwin S. Gaustad, *Faith of Our Fathers: Religion and the New Nation* (San Francisco: Harper and Row 1987), 36–58; William D. Gould, "The Religious Opinions of Thomas Jefferson," *Mississippi Valley Historical Review* 20 (1933): 199.

8. Koch, *Jefferson and Madison,* 7; Burstein and Isenberg, *Madison and Jefferson,* xix.

9. James Morton Smith, introduction, in *The Republic of Letters: The Correspondence between Thomas Jefferson and James Madison, 1776–1826,* ed. James Morton Smith (New York: Norton, 1995), 1:1.

10. Founders Online indicates a total of 2,322 letters between the two men. Jefferson to Madison, May 3, 1826; Madison to Jefferson, May 6, 1826, in Founders Online.

11. Jefferson to Madison, Feb. 17, 1826, in Founders Online; Smith, introduction, 1:7.

12. Burstein and Isenberg, *Madison and Jefferson,* xvii; Merrill D. Peterson, *Thomas Jefferson and the New Nation* (New York: Oxford University Press, 1970), 8.

13. Madison to Samuel Harrison Smith, Nov. 2, 1826; Madison to Margaret Smith, Sept. 1830, in *Writings of James Madison,* ed. Gaillard Hunt (New York: G. P. Putnam's Sons, 1910), 9:259, 9:405.

14. Knoles, "The Religious Ideas of Thomas Jefferson," 187–204; Jefferson to John Adams, Jan. 11, 1817; Jefferson to Margaret Bayard Smith, Aug. 6, 1816, in Founders Online.

15. Sheridan, *Jefferson and Religion,* 14; Peterson, *Jefferson Image,* 303; Kidd, *Thomas Jefferson,* 3–4.

16. Peterson, *Thomas Jefferson,* 4–6, 9; Noble E. Cunningham, *In Pursuit of Reason: The Life of Thomas Jefferson* (Baton Rouge: Louisiana State University Press, 1987), 1–3.

17. Henry Wilder Foote, *Religion of Thomas Jefferson* (Boston: Beacon Press, 1963), 5–6; Conkin, "Religious Pilgrimage of Thomas Jefferson," 21; Ragosta, *Religious Freedom,* 9; Gaustad, *Sworn on the Altar of God,* 7–8.

18. Gaustad, *Sworn on the Altar of God,* 8–9; Peterson, *Thomas Jefferson,* 7–8; Kidd, *Thomas Jefferson,* 16–23; Thomas Jefferson, *Autobiography of Thomas Jefferson,* ed. Dumas Malone (New York: Capricorn Books, 1959), 20.

19. Dumas Malone, *Jefferson the Virginian* (Boston: Little, Brown, 1948), 45–46.

20. Jefferson, *Autobiography,* 20; Ragosta, *Religious Freedom,* 10–11; Gaustad, *Sworn on the Altar of God,* 8–11.

21. Jefferson to John Page, July 15, 1763, in Founders Online.

22. Jefferson to J. P. P. Derieux, July 15, 1788, in ibid.
23. Sheridan, *Jefferson and Religion*, 15. Paul K. Conkin doubts that any such crisis occurred. Conkin, "Religious Pilgrimage of Thomas Jefferson," 22–23.
24. Jefferson, *Autobiography*, 20; Jefferson to Louis H. Girardin, Jan. 15, 1815, in Founders Online.
25. Jefferson, *Autobiography*, 20–21; Jefferson to Louis H. Girardin, Jan. 15, 1815, in Founders Online; Foote, *Religion of Thomas Jefferson*, 11–13; Peterson, *Thomas Jefferson*, 12, 14–15.
26. Foote, *Religion of Thomas Jefferson*, 13; Peterson, *Thomas Jefferson*, 14; Jefferson, "Notes for the Biography of George Wythe," ca. Aug 31, 1820, in Founders Online.
27. Meade, *Old Churches*, 1:191.
28. *Jefferson's Literary Commonplace Book*, ed. Douglas J Wilson (Princeton, NJ: Princeton University Press, 1989), 5, 7–8; Douglas L. Wilson, "Jefferson and Bolingbroke: Some Notes on the Question of Influence," in Sheldon and Dreisbach, *Religion and Political Culture in Jefferson's Virginia*, 107–18.
29. Wilson, "Jefferson and Bolingbroke," 19; Allen Jayne, *Jefferson's Declaration of Independence* (Lexington: University of Kentucky Press, 1988), 19–40; Sheridan, *Jefferson and Religion*, 16–17; *Jefferson's Literary Commonplace Book*, 24–51.
30. Luebke, "Origins of Thomas Jefferson's Anti-Clericalism," 344–45; Gilbert Chinard quoted in Jayne, *Jefferson's Declaration of Independence*, 21; Adrienne Koch, *The Philosophy of Thomas Jefferson* (Gloucester, MA: Peter Smith, 1957), 10–14.
31. See, for example, Jefferson to Robert Skipwith, August 3, 1771; Jefferson to Peter Carr, August 10, 1787; Jefferson to John Garland Jefferson, June 11, 1790; Jefferson to Francis Epps, Jan. 19, 1821, in Founders Online; Conkin, "Religious Pilgrimage of Thomas Jefferson," 23; and Sheridan, *Jefferson and Religion*, 17.
32. Conkin, "Religious Pilgrimage of Thomas Jefferson," 24–25; Ragosta, *Religious Freedom*, 11–13; Randolph, "Edmund Randolph's Essay on the Revolutionary History of Virginia," 123.
33. Luebke, "Origins of Thomas Jefferson's Anti-Clericalism," 345; Conkin, "Religious Pilgrimage of Thomas Jefferson," 23–25; Sheridan, *Jefferson and Religion*, 19–20; Jefferson to Robert Skipwith, Aug. 3, 1771, in Founders Online.
34. Jefferson to Peter Carr, Aug. 10, 1787, in Founders Online; Koch, *The Philosophy of Thomas Jefferson*, 15–22.
35. Sheridan, *Jefferson and Religion*, 20.

36. Conkin, "Religious Pilgrimage of Thomas Jefferson," 24.

37. Jefferson, "Notes on Religion," Oct. 11–Dec. 9, 1776, in Founders Online.

38. Jefferson to Peter Carr, Aug. 10, 1787, in ibid.; Sheridan, *Jefferson and Religion,* 16–17.

39. Thomas Jefferson, *Notes on the State of Virginia,* ed. Daniel Waldstreicher (Boston: Bedford/St. Martins, 2002), 192–93.

40. Jefferson to Carr, Aug. 10, 1787, in Founders Online.

41. Conkin, "Religious Pilgrimage of Thomas Jefferson," 20–22; Sheridan, *Jefferson and Religion,* 15; Ragosta, *Religious Freedom,* 12–13; Gordon-Reed and Onuf, *"Most Blessed of the Patriarchs,"* 274.

42. See Thomas Jefferson Randolph to Henry S. Randall, n.d., in Henry S. Randall, *The Life of Thomas Jefferson* (New York: Derby and Jackson, 1858), 3:672; Randall, *Life of Thomas Jefferson,* 1:555; Peterson, *Thomas Jefferson,* 27.

43. Gould, "The Religious Opinions of Thomas Jefferson," 196–97; Mott, "Sources of Jefferson's Ecclesiastical Views," 270; Sanford, "The Religious Beliefs of Thomas Jefferson," 61; Kidd, *Thomas Jefferson,* 39–40.

44. Miller, *First Liberty,* 61.

45. Jefferson to Benjamin Rush, Jan. 16, 1811, in Founders Online; Jefferson, *Autobiography,* 53.

46. Jefferson's Composition Draft, June 26–July 6, 1775, in Founders Online; Thomas Paine, *Common Sense,* in *The Life and Major Writings of Thomas Paine,* ed. Philip S. Foner (1974; reprint New York: Citadel Press, 1993), 29.

47. Jefferson, "Notes on Religion."

48. Ibid.

49. Ibid.; Rakove, *Beyond Belief, Beyond Conscience,* 74–75.

50. In between these two writings, Jefferson penned a draft of his Bill for Establishing Religious Freedom. The bill is considered in a later chapter.

51. Jefferson, *Notes on the State of Virginia,* 192–93.

52. Ibid., 193–94.

53. John Fea, *Was America Founded as a Christian Nation?* (Louisville, KY: Westminster John Knox Press, 2011), 131–33; Robert G. Parkinson, "The Declaration of Independence," in *A Companion to Thomas Jefferson,* ed. Francis D. Cogliano (Oxford, UK: Wiley-Blackwell, 2012), 44–59; Julian P. Boyd, *The Declaration of Independence: The Evolution of the Text* (Princeton, NJ: Princeton University Press, 1945); Michael I. Meyerson, *Endowed by Our Creator: The Birth of Religious Freedom in America* (New Haven, CT: Yale University Press, 2012), 61–64; John Adams to Timothy Pickering, Aug. 6, 1822, in Founders Online.

54. Carl Becker, *The Declaration of Independence: A Study in the History of Political Ideas* (New York: Vintage, 1958); Robert Ginsberg, ed., *A Casebook on the Declaration of Independence* (New York: Thomas Y. Crowell, 1967); Morton White, *The Philosophy of the American Revolution* (New York: Oxford University Press, 1978); Garry Wills, *Inventing America: Jefferson's Declaration of Independence* (Garden City, NY: Doubleday, 1978); Pauline Maier, *American Scripture: Making the Declaration of Independence* (New York: Knopf, 1997); Jayne, *Jefferson's Declaration of Independence*; David Armitage, *The Declaration of Independence: A Global History* (Cambridge, MA: Harvard University Press, 2007).

55. William F. Dana, "The Declaration of Independence," *Harvard Law Review* 13 (Jan. 1900): 319–42, 337 (quotation).

56. Steven K. Green, *Inventing a Christian America: The Myth of the Religious Founding* (New York: Oxford University Press, 2015), 163, 169; Thomas Paine, *The American Crisis II*, in Foner, *Life and Major Writings of Thomas Paine*, 71; Derek H. Davis, *Religion and the Continental Congress, 1774–1789* (New York: Oxford University Press, 2002), 101–2.

57. Parkinson, "The Declaration of Independence," 51.

58. The Declaration of Independence, in Cogan, *Contexts of the Constitution*, 37–39.

59. See Thomas Jefferson's draft with Congress's editorial changes, in Cogan, *Contexts of the Constitution*, 586–90; Boyd, *The Declaration of Independence*, 19–38; Davis, *Religion and the Continental Congress*, 102; Fea, *Was America Founded as a Christian Nation?* 131–32; and Meyerson, *Endowed by Our Creator*, 62–64.

60. Fea, *Was America Founded as a Christian Nation?* 132; Thomas Jefferson, *A Summary View of the Rights of British America* (1774), in Founders Online; Jefferson to John Manners, June 12, 1817, in Founders Online; Jayne, *Jefferson's Declaration of Independence*, 132. Allen Jayne argues that though rights were endowed by a god, they were "self evident" in the sense "of evidence born of feelings or consciousness within the individual self, provided by the individual's inner sense of truth of the rights mentioned," an idea derived from his reading of Lord Kames. Jayne, *Jefferson's Declaration of Independence*, 118.

61. Fea, *Was America Founded as a Christian Nation?* 131. See Waldman, *Founding Faith*, 88–89: "This was language of the Enlightenment theology that grew up in the eighteenth century as a result not only of philosophical innovations—John Locke, David Hume, and others—but also, more important, of scientific innovations."

62. Jayne, *Jefferson's Declaration of Independence,* 39. Thus, "'Nature's God,' or the God of natural theology, natural religion, and deism, was a God whose natural laws could be discovered by reason and science, who left men free to make their own laws with their reason, and who was worthy of adoration, since He was a perfect God with subline attributes" (40).

63. Fea, *Was America Founded as a Christian Nation?* 131; Meyerson, *Endowed by Our Creator,* 62. A handful of scholars, and a host of popular writers, make more robust claims about the religious nature of the Declaration. Garrett Ward Sheldon has argued that the phrase "Laws of Nature and of Nature's God" reflects "a long tradition of Christian teachings on the place of law and government within God's order and universe." "Jefferson's words in the Declaration of Independence reflect the prevalent Calvinist Christian culture in the North American colonies." Sheldon, "The Political Theory of the Declaration of Independence," in *The Declaration of Independence: Origins and Impacts,* ed. Scott Douglas Gerber (Washington, DC: CQ Press, 2002), 23–25. Popular author Gary DeMar claims, "The Declaration is a religious document, basing its argument for rights on theological grounds," whereas Gary T. Amos boldly asserts that "every key term in the Declaration of Independence had its roots in the Bible, Christian theology, [and] the Western Christian intellectual tradition." According to Amos, the phrase "Law of Nature and of Nature's God" meant "the eternal moral law of God the Creator established over His created universe." See DeMar, *America's Christian History: The Untold Story* (Atlanta, GA: American Vision, 1995), 114, and Amos, *Defending the Declaration* (Brentwood, TN: Wolgemuth and Hyatt, 1989), 3, 35–46.

64. Green, *Inventing a Christian America,* 125–30, 163–72; Thomas S. Kidd, *Benjamin Franklin: The Religious Life of a Founding Father* (New Haven, CT: Yale University Press, 2017), 63–67; Maier, *American Scripture,* 148; Jefferson to Madison, Aug. 30, 1823, in Founders Online.

65. Jefferson to John Manners, June 12, 1817, in Founders Online.

66. Jayne, *Jefferson's Declaration of Independence,* 139–41, 148–54; Meyerson, *Endowed by Our Creator,* 61–64.

3. JAMES MADISON'S BACKGROUND

1. Ketcham, *James Madison,* 1–13; Ketcham, "Madison and Religion," 67; Irving Brant, *James Madison: The Virginia Revolutionist* (Indianapolis: Bobbs-Merrill, 1941), 51–53, 69–71; Little, *Imprisoned Preachers,* 265–73.

2. Ketcham, *James Madison*, 19–24; "James Madison's Autobiography," 197; Miller, *First Liberty*, 88; Mark Noll, *Princeton and the Republic, 1768–1819* (Princeton, NJ: Princeton University Press, 1989), 32; Meade, *Old Churches*, 2:99.

3. Noll, *Princeton and the Republic*, 16–18.

4. Ibid., 23, 17; Gideon Mailer, *John Witherspoon's American Revolution* (Chapel Hill: University of North Carolina Press, 2017); James H. Smylie, "Madison and Witherspoon: Theological Roots of American Political Thought," *Princeton University Library Chronicle* 22 (1961): 118–32; Ralph Ketcham, "Madison at Princeton," *Princeton University Library Chronicle* 28 (1966): 24–54; Ketcham, *James Madison*, 30; Burstein and Isenberg, *Madison and Jefferson*, 12; Miller, *First Liberty*, 89; Miller, *Religious Roots of the First Amendment*, 135–36.

5. Ketcham, *James Madison*, 38; Miller, *Religious Roots of the First Amendment*, 136–41; Madison to Theodore Sedgwick, Feb. 12, 1831, in Founders Online.

6. Smylie, "Madison and Witherspoon," 121.

7. Ketcham, *James Madison*, 28–33, 42–43, 46–47; Ketcham, "Madison at Princeton," 40–48.

8. Ketcham, "Madison and Religion," 68–70; Madison to Frederick Beasley, Nov. 20, 1825, in Founders Online; Ketcham, *James Madison*, 46; Smylie, "Madison and Witherspoon," 131; Garrett Ward Sheldon, *The Political Philosophy of James Madison* (Baltimore: Johns Hopkins University Press, 2001), xi–xv, 2–3.

9. Smylie, "Madison and Witherspoon," 120; "James Madison's Autobiography," 197.

10. Madison to William Bradford, Nov. 9, 1772, in Founders Online.

11. Madison's Notes on Commentary on the Bible, 1770–73, in Founders Online; William C. Rives, *History of the Life and Times of James Madison* (Boston: Little, Brown, 1859), 1:33–34; Brant, *James Madison*, 109–34; Ketcham, "Madison and Religion," 72–73; Garrett Ward Sheldon, "Religion and Politics in the Thought of James Madison," in *The Founders on God and Government*, ed. Daniel L. Dreisbach, Mark D. Hall, and Jeffry H. Morrison (Lanham, MD: Rowman and Littlefield, 2004), 88–89.

12. William Bradford to Madison, Oct. 13, 1772; Madison to Bradford, Nov. 9, 1772, in Founders Online.

13. William Bradford to Madison, Aug. 12, 1773; Madison to Bradford, June 10, Sept. 25, 1773, in ibid.

14. Madison to William Bradford, Jan. 24, 1774; Dec. 1, 1773, in ibid.

15. Madison to Frederick Beasley, Nov. 20, 1825, in ibid.
16. Mailer, *John Witherspoon's American Revolution*, 336–38.
17. Rives, *History of the Life and Times of James Madison*, 1:33; Meade, *Old Churches*, 2:99.
18. Sheldon, *Political Philosophy of James Madison*, 2–3; Sheldon, "Religion and Politics in the Thought of James Madison," 83; Swanson, "James Madison and the Presbyterian Idea of Man and Government," 119. See also Loconte, "Faith and the Founding," 699–715.
19. Nussbaum, *Liberty of Conscience*, 75.
20. Miller, *First Liberty*, 91, 93.
21. Rakove, *Beyond Belief, Beyond Conscience*, 71. Several letters touching on religious subjects are contained in *James Madison on Religious Liberty*, ed. Robert S. Alley (Buffalo, NY: Prometheus Books, 1985), 80–88.
22. Rodney A. Grunes, "James Madison and Religious Freedom," in *James Madison: Philosopher, Founder, and Statesman*, ed. John R. Vile, William D. Pederson, and Frank J. Williams (Athens: Ohio University Press, 2008), 105–32.
23. Madison to Frederick Beasley, Nov. 20, 1825, in Founders Online; Gaustad, *Faith of Our Fathers*, 56–57.
24. Meade, *Old Churches*, 2:99–100.
25. Charles Crowe, "Bishop James Madison and the Republic of Virtue," *Journal of Southern History* 30 (1964): 58–70; David L. Holmes, *The Faiths of the Founding Fathers* (New York: Oxford University Press, 2006), 96–97; Grunes, "James Madison and Religious Freedom," 107; Ketcham, *James Madison*, 47; Ketcham, "Madison and Religion," 76–77.
26. Sheldon, *Political Philosophy of James Madison*, 24; Sheldon, "Religion and Politics in the Thought of James Madison," 83–115; Loconte, "Faith and the Founding," 704–7.
27. Smylie, "Madison and Witherspoon," 120–22.
28. Loconte, "Faith and the Founding," 704–7; Sheldon, *Political Philosophy of James Madison*, 20–26; Swanson, "James Madison and the Presbyterian Idea of Man and Government," 122–23.
29. See Madison, *Vices of the Political System of the United States* (April 1787), in Founders Online, identifying three motives for achieving political office: ambition, personal interest, and public good: "Unhappily the two first are proved by experience to be most prevalent."
30. Federalist Papers, nos. 55, 10, in *The Federalist Papers*, ed. Clinton Rossiter (New York: New American Library, 1961).
31. Federalist Papers, nos. 51, 57.
32. Federalist Papers, no. 10.

33. Federalist Papers, no. 10.

34. Federalist Papers, no. 51.

35. Federalist Papers, no. 55.

36. Madison, Virginia Debates, June 20, 1788, in Founders Online; Federalist Papers, no. 57.

37. Loconte, "Faith and the Founding," 704–5; Sheldon, *Political Philosophy of James Madison*, 24; Swanson, "James Madison and the Presbyterian Idea of Man and Government," 122–23.

38. John Locke, *Two Treatises of Government*, ed. Peter Laslett (New York: New American Library, 1963), 1:10, 2:91–92; Trenchard, *Cato's Letters*, no. 60, Jan. 6, 1721, 142; Green, *Inventing a Christian America*, 95–99.

39. David Hume, "Of the Independence of Parliament," in *Essays Moral, Political, and Literary* (1742), in Founders' Constitution, vol. 1, chapter 11, doc. 4; Douglass Adair, "That Politics May Be Reduced to a Science: David Hume, James Madison, and the Tenth Federalist," *Huntington Library Quarterly* 20 (1957): 343–60; Marc M. Arkin, "'The Intractable Principle': David Hume, James Madison, Religion, and the Tenth Federalist," *American Journal of Legal History* 39 (1995): 148–76; Mark G. Spencer, "Hume and Madison on Faction," *William and Mary Quarterly*, 3rd series, 59 (2002): 869–96.

40. Adair, "That Politics May Be Reduced to Science," 343–59.

41. Spencer, "Hume and Madison on Faction," 883–88; Federalist Papers, no. 10.

42. See Madison's Federalist no. 47, with its numerous references to "the celebrated Montesquieu."

43. George M. Marsden, "America's 'Christian' Origins: Puritan New England as a Case Study," in *John Calvin: His Influence in the Western World*, ed. W. Stanford Reid (Grand Rapids, MI: Zondervan, 1982), 250–51.

44. Noll, *Princeton and the Republic*, 31–32; Miller, *Religious Roots of the First Amendment*, 137–41; Ketcham, "Madison at Princeton," 40–45; Ketcham, *James Madison*, 42–43, 48–49.

45. Miller, *First Liberty*, 90.

46. Madison to William Bradford, Dec. 1, 1773, in Founders Online; Spencer, "Hume and Madison on Faction," 889–91.

47. Madison to William Bradford, Jan. 4, 1774, in Founders Online; Feldman, *Three Lives of James Madison*, 9–11.

48. Madison to William Bradford, Jan. 4, 1774, in Founders Online.

49. Little, *Imprisoned Preachers*, 265–73; Ragosta, *Wellspring of Liberty*, 171–80; Madison to William Bradford, Jan. 4, 1774, in Founders Online.

50. William Bradford to Madison, March 4, 1774, in Founders Online.

51. Madison to William Bradford, April 1, 1774, in ibid.

52. "James Madison's Autobiography," 198–99.
53. Madison to William Bradford, April 1, 1774, in Founders Online; Feldman, *Three Lives of James Madison*, 13; Rakove, *Beyond Belief, Beyond Conscience*, 72.

4. THE FIRST COLLABORATION: VIRGINIA DISESTABLISHMENT, PART 1

1. See Buckley, *Church and State*; Ragosta, *Religious Freedom*; Miller, *First Liberty*; Levy, *The Establishment Clause*, 51–60; Lambert, *Founding Fathers and the Place of Religion in America*, 225–35; Meyerson, *Endowed by Our Creator*, 94–121; Everson v. Board of Education, 330 U.S. 16, 31–43; and McCollum v. Board of Education, at 211, 231.
2. Daniel L. Dreisbach, "Church-State Debate in the Virginia Legislature: From the Declaration of Rights to the Statute for Establishing Religious Freedom," in Sheldon and Dreisbach, *Religion and Political Culture in Jefferson's Virginia*, 154–55; Mark David Hall, "Jeffersonian Walls and Madisonian Lines: The Supreme Court's Use of History in Religion Clause Cases," *Oregon Law Review* 85 (2006): 563–614 (noting that in the previous 60 years, justices had cited Jefferson 112 times).
3. John Witte Jr., "'A Most Mild and Equitable Establishment of Religion': John Adams and the Massachusetts Experiment," *Journal of Church and State* 41 (1999): 213–52; Carl Esbeck, "Dissent and Disestablishment: The Church-State Settlement in the Early American Republic," *Brigham Young University Law Review* (2004): 1385–1584.
4. Merrill D. Peterson and Robert C. Vaughan, introduction, in Peterson and Vaughan, *Virginia Statute for Religious Freedom*, ix; W. B. Swaney, "Religious Freedom," *Virginia Law Review* 12 (1925): 635–44.
5. Curry, *First Freedoms*, 134; Rakove, *Beyond Belief, Beyond Conscience*, 66–87; Meyerson, *Endowed by Our Creator*, 113–15.
6. John Adams to Timothy Pickering, Aug. 6, 1822, in Founders Online.
7. John A. Ragosta, "The Virginia Statute for Establishing Religious Freedom," in Cogliano, *A Companion to Thomas Jefferson*, 82; Curry, *First Freedoms*, 134; Strout, "Jeffersonian Religious Liberty," 202.
8. Steven Waldman, *Sacred Liberty: America's Long, Bloody, and Ongoing Struggle for Religious Freedom* (New York: Harper One, 2019), 27–32; Forrest Church, *So Help Me God: The Founding Fathers and the First Great Battle over Church and State* (New York: Harcourt, 2007), 236–41.
9. See generally Ragosta, *Wellspring of Liberty*.
10. Miller, *First Liberty*, 43–45.

11. Peterson, *Jefferson Image,* 93, 127–29; Strout, "Jeffersonian Religious Liberty," 206–11. Jack Rakove is correct that the majority of newly entering states borrowed language from Pennsylvania's 1790 constitution rather than from Virginia's statute. Nonetheless, he acknowledges the widespread influence of the Virginia statute. Rakove, *Beyond Belief, Beyond Conscience,* 101–2.

12. Ketcham, *James Madison,* 64–65, 68–69.

13. Madison to George Mason, Dec. 27, 1827, in Founders Online; Ketcham, *James Madison,* 70–72; Buckley, *Church and State,* 19; Eckenrode, *Separation of Church and State,* 42–43.

14. "A Dissenter to the Church of England," *Virginia Gazette,* April 26, 1776, 2.

15. "Committee's Proposed Article on Religion," May 27–28, 1776, in Founders Online; Eckenrode, *Separation of Church and State,* 43–44.

16. Ketcham, *James Madison,* 72–73; Meyerson, *Endowed by Our Creator,* 68–70; Madison to George Mason, Dec. 27, 1827, in Founders Online; "James Madison's Autobiography," 199.

17. "Committee's Proposed Article on Religion"; Ragosta, *Religious Freedom,* 60–61; Ketcham, *James Madison,* 72–73; Banning, "James Madison, the Statute for Religious Freedom," 111–12.

18. "Committee's Proposed Article on Religion"; Ragosta, *Religious Freedom,* 60–61; Banning, "James Madison, the Statute for Religious Freedom," 112–13; Buckley, *Church and State,* 18–19.

19. "Committee's Proposed Article on Religion"; Meyerson, *Endowed by Our Creator,* 69.

20. "James Madison's Autobiography," 199; Ragosta, *Religious Freedom,* 61; Buckley, *Church and State,* 18–19; Banning, "James Madison, the Statute for Religious Freedom," 113.

21. Jefferson to Thomas Nelson, May 16, 1776, in Founders Online.

22. Jefferson's Third Draft of Virginia Constitution, June 13, 1776, in ibid.; Ragosta, *Religious Freedom,* 61; Buckley, *Church and State,* 19–20; Meyerson, *Endowed by Our Creator,* 70.

23. Madison to Margaret B. Smith, Sept. 1830, in Founders Online; Ketcham, *James Madison,* 75; Ragosta, *Religious Freedom,* 62–64; Eckenrode, *Separation of Church and State,* 46.

24. "Memorial of the Hanover Presbytery," Oct. 24, 1776, in Charles F. James, *Documentary History of the Struggle for Religious Liberty in Virginia* (Lynchburg, VA: J. P. Bell, 1900), 222; Baptist petition of June 20, 1776, in James, *Documentary History,* 65–66.

25. Petitions of Oct. 16, 1776, and from Prince Edward County, Oct. 11, 1776, in ibid., 68–69; Ketcham, *James Madison*, 75; Buckley, *Church and State*, 21–23.

26. James, *Documentary History*, 74.

27. "Memorial of the Hanover Presbytery," 70–73, 222–25; Foote, *Sketches of Virginia*, 323–24; Debra R. Neill, "Disestablishment of Religion in Virginia," *Virginia Magazine of History and Biography* 127 (2019): 2–41. See also "Queries on the Subject of Religious Establishments," *Virginia Gazette*, Nov. 1, 1776, 1.

28. Methodist petition, Oct. 28, 1776, in James, *Documentary History*, 75–76; Buckley, *Church and State*, 27–29.

29. Clergy petition, Nov. 8, 1776, in James, *Documentary History*, 76–77; *Virginia Gazette*, Dec. 13, 1776, 1.

30. Rough Draft of Jefferson's Resolutions for Disestablishing the Church of England, Nov. 1776, in Founders Online; Jefferson, *Autobiography*, 53.

31. Buckley, *Church and State*, 32–35; Meyerson, *Endowed by Our Creator*, 70–72; William Walter Hening, *The Statutes at Large: Being a Collection of All of the Laws of Virginia* (New York: R. and W. and G. Bartow, 1823), 9:164–67; Jefferson, *Autobiography*, 53.

32. Hening, *Statutes at Large*, 9:164–65; Buckley, *Church and State*, 34–36; Meyerson, *Endowed by Our Creator*, 71–72.

33. Madison to Samuel Harrison Smith, Nov. 2, 1826; Madison to George Mason, Dec. 27, 1827, in Founders Online; Jefferson, *Autobiography*, 55.

34. "The Sentiments of Baptists with Regard to a General Assessment on the People of Virginia," *Virginia Gazette*, March 28, 1777, 6–7.

35. Reprinted in Foote, *Sketches of Virginia*, 326–27.

36. Buckley, *Church and State*, 41–45; Ragosta, *Wellspring of Liberty*, 62–66; Meade, *Old Churches*, 1:16–17.

37. "To the Clergy and Laity of the Church Formally Established," *Virginia Gazette*, April 24, 1778, 1. In March 1777, the *Gazette* also announced the publication of a pamphlet entitled "The Necessity of an Established Church in Any State; or, An Humble Address to the Legislators of the Commonwealth of Virginia." *Virginia Gazette*, March 28, 1777, 3.

38. "A Petition of Sundry Inhabitants of the County of Caroline," May 22, 1777, in James, *Documentary History*, 90–91.

39. *Virginia Gazette*, Dec. 13, 1776, 1.

40. Cumberland County petition, May 22, 1777, in James, *Documentary History*, 84–85.

41. Mecklenburg County petition, May 29, 1777, in ibid., 86–87.

42. Ragosta, *Wellspring of Liberty*, 52–66. See also Baptist petitions of Aug. 14, 1775, and June 20, 1776, in Semple, *A History of the Rise and Progress*, 492–95, and James, *Documentary History*, 88, 218–19.

43. Mecklenburg County petition, May 29, 1777, in James, *Documentary History*, 87.

44. Baptist Association Petition, Oct. 16, 1780, in Semple, *A History of the Rise and Progress*, 496–99; Foote, *Sketches of Virginia*, 331; Buckley, *Church and State*, 44–45, 62; Ragosta, *Wellspring of Liberty*, 64–66.

45. Ketcham, *James Madison*, 77–78.

46. Bailyn quoted in Dreisbach, "Thomas Jefferson and Bills Number 82–86," 160; Thomas E. Buckley, "The Political Theology of Thomas Jefferson," in Peterson and Vaughan, *Virginia Statute for Religious Freedom*, 93; Miller, *First Liberty*, 46–73.

47. "A Bill for Establishing Religious Freedom," in Founders' Constitution, vol. 5, amendment 1 (Religion), doc. 37. See appendix A.

48. Buckley, "Political Theology of Thomas Jefferson," 93; Ragosta, "The Virginia Statute for Establishing Religious Freedom," 75.

49. "Bill for Establishing Religious Freedom"; Sandler, "Lockean Ideas," 110–16; Kessler, "Locke's Influence on Jefferson's 'Bill for Establishing Religious Freedom,'" 231–52; Miller, *First Liberty*, 51–52, 64–65.

50. "Bill for Establishing Religious Freedom"; Miller, *First Liberty*, 58–59.

51. "Bill for Establishing Religious Freedom."

52. Miller, *First Liberty*, 56–59.

53. "Bill for Establishing Religious Freedom"; Sandler, "Lockean Ideas," 115–16; Miller, *First Liberty*, 61–62.

54. Peterson and Vaughan, introduction, xi; Swaney, "Religious Freedom," 632–44.

55. Buckley, "Political Theology of Thomas Jefferson," 93; Mark A Beliles, "The Christian Communities, Religious Revivals, and Political Culture of the Central Virginia Piedmont, 1737–1813," in Sheldon and Dreisbach, *Religion and Political Culture in Jefferson's Virginia*, 21–22; Dreisbach, "Thomas Jefferson and Bills Number 82–86," 187–88; Broadwater, *Jefferson, Madison, and the Making of the Constitution*, 120–21 ("Jefferson rested freedom of conscience on a theological basis").

56. Miller, *First Liberty*, 62–64.

57. Jefferson, *Autobiography*, 58–59.

58. "Bill for Establishing Religious Freedom"; Beliles, "Christian Communities," 21; Green, *Inventing a Christian America*, 120, 167–69.

59. Buckley, *Church and State*, 46–51; Ragosta, *Religious Freedom*, 69–70.

60. *Virginia Gazette,* Sept. 11, 1779, 1; Sept. 18, 1779, 1.

61. *Virginia Gazette,* Aug. 14, 1779, 1.

62. James, *Documentary History,* 92–94.

63. Memorial of the Baptist Association, Oct. 16, 1780, in ibid., 219–21; Foote, *Sketches of Virginia,* 330–31; Buckley, *Church and State,* 50–55; Fred J. Hood, "Revolution and Religious Liberty: The Conservation of the Theocratic Concept in Virginia," *Church History* 40 (1971): 176.

64. Green, *Second Disestablishment,* 29–30, 34–35.

65. "A Bill Concerning Religion," in Dreisbach and Hall, *Sacred Rights of Conscience,* 247–49; Buckley, *Church and State,* 58–59; Green, *Second Disestablishment,* 38–39.

66. *Virginia Gazette,* Oct. 30, 1779, 2; Nov. 29, 1779, 2; "Memorial of the Baptist Association," Oct. 16, 1780, in James, *Documentary History,* 219–21; Buckley, *Church and State,* 59–61.

67. Jefferson, *Autobiography,* 58; bills reprinted in Dreisbach and Hall, *Sacred Rights of Conscience,* 251–52; Cord, *Separation of Church and State,* 216–21; Dreisbach, "Thomas Jefferson and Bills Number 82–86," 159–210.

68. See Treaty with the Kaskaskia Indians (1803); Proclamations, July 9, 1812; July 23, 1813; Nov. 16, 1814; March 4, 1815, in Dreisbach and Hall, *Sacred Rights of Conscience,* 476, 458–61; Madison, Detached Memoranda, Jan. 31, 1820, in Founders Online.

69. Green, *Second Disestablishment,* 41–42; Ragosta, *Religious Freedom,* 98–99.

70. Green, *Second Disestablishment,* 41–42; Ragosta, *Religious Freedom,* 98–99; Dreisbach, "Thomas Jefferson and Bills Number 82–86," 188–200.

71. See "A Bill for the More General Diffusion of Knowledge," bill no. 79, Monticello, https://www.monticello.org/site/research-and-collections/bill-more-general-diffusion-knowledge; Jefferson, *Notes on the State of Virginia,* 160, 146–147; Jefferson, *Autobiography,* 61; Malone, *Jefferson the Virginian,* 284; Cunningham, *In Pursuit of Reason,* 59–60; and Gordon E. Mercer, "Thomas Jefferson: A Bold Vision for American Education," *International Social Science Review* 68 (1993): 19–25.

72. "A Bill for Amending the Constitution of the College of William and Mary," bill no. 80, in Founders Online; Jefferson, *Notes on the State of Virginia,* 146; Jefferson, *Autobiography,* 61. See also Jefferson to Joseph Priestley, Jan. 27, 1800, in Founders Online, telling Priestley that the college "was at that time pretty highly Episcopal, the dissenters after a while began to apprehend some secret design of a preference to that sect."

73. Malone, *Jefferson the Virginian,* 284–85; Mark R. Wenger, "Thomas Jefferson, the College of William and Mary, and the University of Virginia," *Virginia Magazine of History and Biography* 103 (July 1995): 339–74.

74. Dreisbach, "Thomas Jefferson and Bills Number 82–86," 197; Buckley, *Church and State,* 68–69.

75. Jefferson, "Proclamation Appointing a Day of Thanksgiving and Prayer," Nov. 11, 1779, in Founders Online; *Virginia Gazette,* Nov. 12, 1779, 1; Jefferson, *Autobiography,* 24.

76. Jefferson, "Proclamation Inviting Mercenary Troops in the British Service to Desert," Feb. 2, 1781, in Founders Online.

77. Jefferson's Draft of a Constitution for Virginia, May–June 1783, in ibid.; Buckley, *Church and State,* 69–70. The draft also excluded members of the executive branch and military officers from serving.

78. Jefferson to Marquis de Chastellux, Sept. 2, 1785, in Founders Online.

79. Madison to Jefferson, Oct. 15, 1788, in ibid.

5. THE FIRST COLLABORATION: VIRGINIA DISESTABLISHMENT, PART 2

1. Petition from Lunenburg County, Nov. 15, 1783, in Virginia Memory, http://digitool1.lva.lib.va.us/.

2. Petition from Amherst County, Nov. 27, 1783, in ibid.

3. Petition from Warwick County, May 15, 1784; Petition from Isle of Wight County, Nov. 4, 1784, in James, *Documentary History,* 122, 125.

4. George Mason to Patrick Henry, May 6, 1783, in *The Papers of George Mason,* ed. Robert A. Rutland (Chapel Hill: University of North Carolina Press, 1970), 2:770; Buckley, *Church and State,* 72, 81–82.

5. Buckley, *Church and State,* 74–75; Banning, "James Madison, the Statute for Religious Freedom," 116.

6. Miller, *First Liberty,* 27–29; Thomas S. Kidd, *Patrick Henry: First among Patriots* (New York: Basic Books, 2011), 167; Presbyterian Memorial of October 1784, in James, *Documentary History,* 234–35.

7. Episcopal petition, June 4, 1784, in James, *Documentary History,* 124; Ketcham, *James Madison,* 163; Madison to James Madison Sr., Jan. 6, 1785; Madison to Jefferson, Jan. 9, 1785, in Founders Online.

8. Richard Henry Lee to Madison, Nov. 24, 1784, in Founders Online.

9. "Memorial of the Baptist Association," May 26, 1784; "Memorial of the Baptist General Committee," Nov. 11, 1784, in James, *Documentary History,* 122–23, 126.

10. "Memorial of the Presbytery of Hanover in May, 1784," in Foote, *Sketches of Virginia*, 333–34; Hood, "Revolution and Religious Liberty," 177–78.
11. Presbyterian Memorial of October 1784, in James, *Documentary History*, 231–35; Hood, "Revolution and Religious Liberty," 178–79.
12. Miller, *First Liberty*, 29–31; Buckley, *Church and State*, 94–96; Madison to James Monroe, Nov. 14, 1784; April 12, 1785, in Founders Online.
13. Jefferson to Madison, March 18, 1785, in Founders Online; Lance Banning, *The Sacred Fire of Liberty: James Madison and the Founding of the Federal Republic* (Ithaca, NY: Cornell University Press, 1995), 43.
14. Miller, *First Liberty*, 23; Koch, *Jefferson and Madison*, 4–5; Burstein and Isenberg, *Madison and Jefferson*, 89–94. See Jefferson to James Monroe, May 20, 1782, in Founders Online: "I am persuaded that having hitherto dedicated to [the state] the whole of the active and useful part of my life I shall be permitted to pass the rest in mental quiet."
15. Koch, *Jefferson and Madison*, 6–11; Ketcham, *James Madison*, 88–111, 140–41; Burstein and Isenberg, *Madison and Jefferson*, 93–98, 103; Banning, *The Sacred Fire of Liberty*, 46–47; Edmund Randolph to Jefferson, May 15, 1784, in Founders Online.
16. Ragosta, *Religious Freedom*, 78, 80.
17. Ibid., 78; Buckley, *Church and State*, 87–88; Madison to Jefferson, July 3, 1784, in Founders Online.
18. Marvin K. Singleton, "Colonial Virginia as First Amendment Matrix: Henry, Madison and Assessment Establishment," *Journal of Church and State* 8 (Aug. 1966): 344–64; Ragosta, *Religious Freedom*, 79; Washington to George Mason, Oct. 3, 1785, in Founders Online.
19. Hood, "Revolution and Religious Liberty," 171, 178; Banning, "James Madison, the Statute for Religious Freedom," 116; Ketcham, *James Madison*, 162.
20. "A Bill Establishing a Provision for Teachers of the Christian Religion" (1784), in Dreisbach and Hall, *Sacred Rights of Conscience*, 252–53; Randolph, "Edmund Randolph's Essay on the Revolutionary History of Virginia," 119; Miller, *First Liberty*, 26–27; Kidd, *Patrick Henry*, 167–68.
21. Eckenrode, *Separation of Church and State*, 85.
22. James Madison, "Notes of Speech against Assessments for Support of Religion," Nov. 1784, in Hunt, *Writings*, 88–89; Buckley, *Church and State*, 99–100.
23. Miller, *First Liberty*, 31; Eckenrode, *Separation of Church and State*, 85.
24. Madison to James Monroe, Nov. 14, 1784; Madison to Richard Henry Lee, Nov. 14, 1784; Madison to Monroe, Nov. 27, Dec. 4, 1784, in Founders Online; Kidd, *Patrick Henry*, 170–71; Buckley, *Church and State*, 101, 105.

25. Buckley, *Church and State,* 97.

26. Madison to James Madison Sr., Jan. 6, 1785; Madison to Jefferson, Jan. 9, 1985, in Founders Online.

27. Miller, *First Liberty,* 33–34; John Blair Smith to Madison, June 21, 1784; Madison to Jefferson, Aug. 20, 1785, in Founders Online.

28. Miller, *First Liberty,* 33–34; Madison to James Madison Sr., Jan. 6, 1785, in Founders Online.

29. "Madison's Notes for Debates on the General Assessment Bill [Outline B]," Dec. 23–24, 1784; Madison to James Monroe, Dec. 4, 1784, in Founders Online.

30. Banning, "James Madison, the Statute for Religious Freedom," 117; Ragosta, *Religious Freedom,* 83–85; Buckley, *Church and State,* 107–9.

31. Madison to James Monroe, Dec. 24, 1784; Madison to Jefferson, Jan. 9, 1785, in Founders Online; Irving Brant, *James Madison: The Nationalist* (Indianapolis: Bobbs-Merrill, 1948), 348.

32. Brant, *James Madison: The Nationalist,* 348–49.

33. Madison to James Monroe, April 12, 1785, in Founders Online.

34. Madison to James Monroe, May 29, 1785, in ibid.

35. Madison to Jefferson, April 27, 1785, in ibid.

36. Brant, *James Madison: The Nationalist,* 348.

37. George Nicholas to Madison, April 22, 1785, in Founders Online.

38. Ibid.; George Nicholas to Madison, July 7, 1785; Madison to Jefferson, Aug. 20, 1785, in Founders Online; Brant, *James Madison: The Nationalist,* 350.

39. See Semple, *A History of the Rise and Progress,* 52 (acknowledging Madison's authorship in 1810).

40. Madison's *Memorial and Remonstrance* was published in the *Virginia Journal,* Nov. 17, 1785, reprinted in Founders' Constitution, vol. 5, doc. 43; Curry, *First Freedoms,* 134–48; Buckley, *Church and State,* 131–36; Miller, *First Liberty,* 96–106. See appendix B.

41. Banning, *The Sacred Fire of Liberty,* 91.

42. Ibid., 91–97; Miller, *First Liberty,* 38–41, 96–106; Irving Brant, "Madison: On the Separation of Church and State," *William and Mary Quarterly,* 3rd series, 8, no. 1 (Jan. 1951): 9–11; Dreisbach, "Church-State Debate in the Virginia Legislature," 148–54.

43. Meade, *Old Churches,* 2:99; Swanson, "James Madison and the Presbyterian Idea of Man and Government," 128–30; Sheldon, *Political Philosophy of James Madison,* 33–35.

44. Madison, *Memorial and Remonstrance,* ¶ 1.

45. Swanson, "James Madison and the Presbyterian Idea of Man and Government," 129; Sheldon, "Religion and Politics in the Thought of James Madison," 97.

46. Miller, *Religious Roots of the First Amendment*, 145.

47. Madison, *Memorial and Remonstrance*, ¶¶ 2, 4; Miller, *First Liberty*, 101–3; Banning, *The Sacred Fire of Liberty*, 92–93.

48. Madison, *Memorial and Remonstrance*, ¶¶ 1, 2; Richard K. Matthews, *If Men Were Angles: James Madison and the Heartless Empire of Reason* (Lawrence: University Press of Kansas, 1995), 122–23.

49. Madison, *Memorial and Remonstrance*, ¶¶ 3, 5, 7, 8, 9, 10, 11, 13, 14, 15; Miller, *First Liberty*, 99–105.

50. Miller, *First Liberty*, 99; Banning, *The Sacred Fire of Liberty*, 94–95; Madison, *Memorial and Remonstrance*, ¶ 15.

51. Madison to Jefferson, Aug. 20, 1785, in Founders Online; Miller, *First Liberty*, 39.

52. Isaac, "'The Rage of Malice,'" 146.

53. Semple, *A History of the Rise and Progress*, 95–96; Isaac, "'The Rage of Malice,'" 150–52; Miller, *First Liberty*, 39; Ragosta, *Religious Freedom*, 85–86.

54. Foote, *Sketches of Virginia*, 340–41; Hanover Presbytery Resolution, May 19, 1785, in James, *Documentary History*, 136–37; Miller, *First Liberty*, 40.

55. Foote, *Sketches of Virginia*, 342–44; Hanover Presbytery Memorial, Aug. 13, 1785, in James, *Documentary History*, 236–40; Hood, "Revolution and Religious Liberty," 180–81; Ragosta, *Religious Freedom*, 87.

56. Madison to Jefferson, Aug. 20, 1785, in Founders Online.

57. Madison to Jefferson, Jan. 22, 1786; Madison, Detached Memoranda.

58. Compare the Bill for Establishing Religious Freedom with the "Act for Establishing Religious Freedom," in Founders' Constitution, vol. 5, docs. 37 and 44; Madison to Jefferson, Jan. 22, 1786, in Founders Online; Ragosta, *Religious Freedom*, 90–91.

59. Jefferson to Madison, Dec. 16, 1786, in Founders Online.

60. Banning, "James Madison, the Statute for Religious Freedom," 130.

61. Ragosta, *Religious Freedom*, subtitle.

6. THE SECOND COLLABORATION: THE CONSTITUTION

1. Everson v. Board of Education, 330 U.S. 13; 33–34 (Rutledge, J., dissenting): "No provision of the Constitution is more closely tied to or given

content by its generating history than the religious clause of the First Amendment. . . . The history includes not only Madison's authorship and the proceedings before the First Congress, but also the long and intensive struggle for religious freedom in America, more especially in Virginia, of which the Amendment was the direct culmination. In the documents of the times, particularly of Madison, who was leader in the Virginia struggle before he became the Amendment's sponsor, but also in the writings of Jefferson and others and in the issues which engendered them is to be found irrefutable confirmation of the Amendment's sweeping content."

2. Cord, *Separation of Church and State*, 120–21; Gerard V. Bradley, *Church-State Relationships in America* (Westport, CT: Greenwood Press, 1987), 3, 37; Mark David Hall, "Madison's Memorial and Remonstrance, Jefferson's Statute for Religious Liberty, and the Creation of the First Amendment," *American Political Thought* 3 (2014): 32–63. Hall writes, "There is little evidence to support the assertion that the documents had the significant influence on the drafters and ratifiers of the Frist Amendment as many jurists, scholars, and textbook authors have claimed" (56).

3. Levy, *The Establishment Clause*, 75–89.

4. Brant, "Madison: On the Separation of Church and State," 24.

5. Irving Brant, *James Madison: Father of the Constitution* (Indianapolis: Bobbs-Merrill, 1950), 264–75.

6. Wallace v. Jaffree, 472 U.S. 38, 92 (1985) (Rehnquist, J., dissenting); Cord, *Separation of Church and State*, 47.

7. See Curry, *First Freedoms*, 134–92.

8. Ibid.; Lutz, *Origins of American Constitutionalism*, 104–6; John Witte Jr. and Joel A. Nichols, *Religion and the American Constitutional Experiment*, 4th ed. (2000; New York: Oxford University Press, 2016), 57–62; Vincent Phillip Muñoz, "Church and State in the Founding-Era State Constitutions," *American Political Thought* 4 (2015): 1–38.

9. Esbeck, "Dissent and Disestablishment," 1385–584.

10. North Carolina Constitution of 1776, art. 34, in *The Federal and State Constitutions, Colonial Charters, and Other Organic Laws of the States, Territories, and Colonies Now or Heretofore Forming the United States of America*, ed. Francis Newton Thorpe (Washington, DC: Government Printing Office, 1909), 5:2793; Curry, *First Freedoms*, 151–52; Esbeck, "Dissent and Disestablishment," 1481–84.

11. New York Constitution of 1777, arts. 38, 35, in Thorpe, *Federal and State Constitutions*, 5:2636–37; Pratt, *Religion, Politics, and Diversity*, 82–93; Mark McGarvie, *One Nation under Law: America's Early National Struggles*

to Separate Church and State (DeKalb: Northern Illinois University Press, 2004), 109–11.

12. Carl Esbeck states that an Anglican establishment technically existed in New Jersey after 1702 but that it was inoperable. Esbeck, "Dissent and Disestablishment," 1470–71.

13. Pennsylvania Constitution of 1776; Pennsylvania Constitution of 1790, in Thorpe, *Federal and State Constitutions*, 5:3082, 3100; Curry, *First Freedoms*, 160–61; Frost, *A Perfect Freedom*, 74–78.

14. Delaware Constitution of 1776; Delaware Constitution of 1792, in Thorpe, *Federal and State Constitutions*, 1:567, 568.

15. New Jersey Constitution of 1776, in ibid., 5:2597; Curry, *First Freedoms*, 159–60.

16. See Chester James Antieau, Arthur L. Downey, and Edward C. Roberts, *Freedom from Federal Establishment: Formation and Early History of the First Amendment Religion Clauses* (Milwaukee: Bruce, 1964), 134.

17. James Madison, June 12, 1788, in *The Debates in the Several State Conventions, on the Adoption of the Federal Constitution*, ed. Jonathan Elliot (New York: Burt Franklin, 1827–88), 3:330; Curry, *First Freedoms*, 146–48, 160; Douglas Laycock, "'Nonpreferential' Aid to Religion: A False Claim about Original Intent," *William and Mary Law Review* 27 (1986): 875–923.

18. Georgia Constitution of 1777, art. 56; Georgia Constitution of 1789, art. 4, sec. 5; Georgia Constitution of 1798, art. 4, sec. 10, in Thorpe, *Federal and State Constitutions*, 2:784, 789, 800–801; Nichols, "Religious Liberty in the Thirteenth Colony," 1723–27; Curry, *First Freedoms*, 152–53.

19. Maryland Constitution of 1776, in Thorpe, *Federal and State Constitutions*, 3:1689–90; Curry, *First Freedoms*, 153–58.

20. William Tennent, *Speech on the Dissenting Petition* (Charles-Town, SC: Peter Timothy, 1777), 15–16; Green, *Second Disestablishment*, 29–30; McGarvie, *One Nation under Law*, 131–51.

21. South Carolina Constitution of 1778, in Thorpe, *Federal and State Constitutions*, 6:3255–56.

22. Ibid., 3256–57; McGarvie, *One Nation under Law*, 141–44; Curry, *First Freedoms*, 150.

23. New Hampshire Constitution of 1784, art. 6, in Thorpe, *Federal and State Constitutions*, 4:2454; Curry, *First Freedoms*, 185–88.

24. Isaac Backus, *An Appeal to the Public for Religious Liberty* (1773), in Sandoz, *Political Sermons of the American Founding Era*, 331–68; McLoughlin, "Isaac Backus and the Separation of Church and State in America," 1392–413.

25. Isaac Backus, *Government and Liberty Described and Ecclesiastical Tyranny Exposed* (Boston: Powars and Willis, 1778), 4, 13; John Adams to Edmund Jennings, Sept. 23, 1780, in *The Works of John Adams, Second President of the United States*, ed. Charles Francis Adams (Boston: Little, Brown, 1850–56), 9:509.

26. Massachusetts Constitution of 1780, arts. 2 and 3, in Thorpe, *Federal and State Constitutions*, 3:1889–90; *The Popular Sources of Political Authority: Documents on the Massachusetts Constitution of 1780*, ed. Oscar and Mary Handlin (Cambridge, MA: Belknap Press of Harvard University Press, 1966), 442–43.

27. Samuel Eliot Morison, "The Struggle over the Adoption of the Constitution of Massachusetts, 1780," *Massachusetts Historical Society Proceedings* 50 (1916–17): 353, 371; Ronald M. Peters Jr., *The Massachusetts Constitution of 1780: A Social Compact* (Amherst: University of Massachusetts Press, 1978), 33, 50–54; Jacob C. Meyer, *Church and State in Massachusetts from 1740 to 1833* (New York: Russell and Russell, 1968), 107–8.

28. "The Report of a Constitution or Form of Government for the Commonwealth of Massachusetts," Oct. 28–31, 1779, in Founders Online; Robert J. Taylor, "Construction of the Massachusetts Constitution," *Proceedings of the American Antiquarian Society* 90 (1980): 331–32; Handlin and Handlin, *Popular Sources of Political Authority*, 443; Morison, "Struggle over the Adoption," 411.

29. Vermont Constitution of 1777, chap. 3; Vermont Constitution of 1786, chap. 3, in Thorpe, *Federal and State Constitutions*, 6:3740, 3752; Curry, *First Freedoms*, 188–89; McLoughlin, *New England Dissent*, 2:795–812; Esbeck, "Dissent and Disestablishment," 1525–29.

30. Daniel L. Dreisbach, "The Constitution's Forgotten Religion Clause: Reflections on the Article VI Religious Test Ban," *Journal of Church and State* 38 (1996): 261–95; James E. Wood Jr., "'No Religious Test Shall Ever Be Required': Reflections on the Bicentennial of the Constitution," *Journal of Church and State* 29 (1987): 199–208.

31. David Brian Robertson, *The Constitution and America's Destiny* (New York: Cambridge University Press, 2005), 48–52; George William Van Cleve, *We Have Not a Government: The Articles of Confederation and the Road to the Constitution* (Chicago: University of Chicago Press, 2017), 48–113; Michael J. Klarman, *The Framers' Coup: The Making of the United States Constitution* (New York: Oxford University Press, 2016), 11–73.

32. Banning, *The Sacred Fire of Liberty*, 43–45; Van Cleve, *We Have Not a Government*, 90–94.

33. Madison to James Monroe, Aug. 7, 1785, in Founders Online; Banning, *The Sacred Fire of Liberty*, 53–55.

34. Banning, *The Sacred Fire of Liberty*, 71; Klarman, *The Framers' Coup*, 72; Washington to Madison, Nov. 5, 1786; Rufus King to John Adams, May 5, 1786, in Founders Online. Whether a crisis truly existed at the time has been the subject of much debate among historians. What is clear is that many political leaders believed it to exist. See Van Cleve, *We Have Not a Government*, 7–13, discussing the historiographical debate over the Confederation period.

35. Madison to James Monroe, March 19, 1786, in Founders Online.

36. Van Cleve, *We Have Not a Government*, 124–29; Klarman, *The Framers' Coup*, 106–10; Madison to Jefferson, Dec. 4, 1786, in Founders Online.

37. Madison to Jefferson, March 19, April 23, May 15, June 6, 1787, in Founders Online.

38. Madison to Jefferson, Feb. 15, 1787; Copy of a Protestant Episcopal Church Petition to the General Assembly of Virginia, in ibid.; Brant, *James Madison: The Nationalist*, 349, 457n14.

39. Madison to Jefferson, March 19, 1787, in Founders Online; Robertson, *The Constitution and America's Destiny*, 95–98; Banning, *The Sacred Fire of Liberty*, 111–37.

40. See Madison, *Notes on Ancient and Modern Confederacies*, April–June 1786, in Founders Online; Madison, *Vices of the Political System*.

41. Madison to Jefferson, Oct. 24, 1787, in Founders Online; Broadwater, *Jefferson, Madison, and the Making of the Constitution*, 134–38; Jack N. Rakove, *The Beginnings of National Politics: An Interpretive History of the Continental Congress* (Baltimore: Johns Hopkins University Press, 1979), 392–93.

42. Madison, *Vices of the Political System*; Ketcham, *James Madison*, 186–88.

43. Federalist Papers, nos. 10, 51; Broadwater, *Jefferson, Madison, and the Making of the Constitution*, 136–38.

44. Rufus King to Elbridge Gerry, Feb. 10, 1787, in *Letters of the Delegates to Congress*, ed. Paul H. Smith (Washington, DC: Library of Congress, 1976–2000), 24:90–91.

45. James Madison, *Notes of Debates in the Federal Convention of 1787* (Athens: Ohio University Press, 1985), 30–33; Broadwater, *Jefferson, Madison, and the Making of the Constitution*, 139–40.

46. Robertson, *The Constitution and America's Destiny*, 96–98; Klarman, *The Framers' Coup*, 136–44; Madison to Jefferson, June 6, 1787, in Founders Online. Jefferson was miffed at the convention's secrecy, telling John Adams, "I am sorry they began their deliberations by so abominable

a precedent as that of tying up the tongues of their members. nothing can justify this example but the innocence of their intentions, & ignorance of the value of public discussions." Jefferson to Adams, Aug. 30, 1787, in Founders Online.

47. Madison, *Notes of Debates*, 209–11, 630; Klarman, *The Framers' Coup*, 548–49.

48. *The Records of the Federal Constitution of 1787*, ed. Max Farrand (New Haven, CT: Yale University Press, 1911), 3:599; Madison, *Notes of Debates*, 486, 561.

49. Luther Martin's Letter on the Federal Convention of 1787, in Elliot, *Debates in the Several State Conventions*, 1:385–86.

50. Burstein and Isenberg, *Madison and Jefferson*, 153–54. See Charles Pinckney to Madison, March 28, 1789; Madison to Edmund Pendleton, Oct. 28, 1787, in Founders Online.

51. Gerard V. Bradley, "The No Religious Test Clause and the Constitution of Religious Liberty: A Machine That Has Gone of Itself," *Case Western Reserve Law Review* 37 (1986): 674–747; Dreisbach, "The Constitution's Forgotten Religion Clause," 265–68; Pratt, *Religion, Politics and Diversity*, 93–97, 107–8; Curry, *First Freedoms*, 161–62.

52. Benjamin Franklin to Richard Price, Oct. 9, 1780; Benjamin Rush to Price, Oct. 15, 1785, April 22, 1786, in Founders' Constitution, vol. 4, docs. 5 and 8; Noah Webster, "On Test Laws, Oaths of Allegiance and Abjuration, and Partial Exclusions from Office" (March 1787), in Dreisbach and Hall, *Sacred Rights of Conscience*, 368–70.

53. See Jonas Phillips to President and Members of the Convention, Sept. 7, 1787, in Founders' Constitution, 4:11, and Morton Borden, *Jews, Turks, and Infidels* (Chapel Hill: University of North Carolina Press, 1984), 5, 10.

54. Bradley, "The No Religious Test Clause," 690, 693–94; Dreisbach, "The Constitution's Forgotten Religion Clause," 285–89.

55. Dreisbach, "The Constitution's Forgotten Religion Clause," 262–63; Wood, "'No Religious Test Shall Ever Be Required,'" 206; Isaac Kramnick and R. Laurence Moore, *The Godless Constitution: The Case against Religious Correctness* (New York: Norton, 1996), 26–45; Howard Gillman and Erwin Chemerinsky, *The Religion Clauses: The Case for Separating Church and State* (New York: Oxford University Press, 2020), 34 (through article 6, "the Constitution incorporated a separation of church and state").

56. *Freeman's Oracle*, Feb. 8, 1788, in Herbert J. Storing, *The Compete Anti-Federalist* (Chicago: University of Chicago Press, 1981), 4:242; McGarvie, *One Nation under Law*, 48–58.

57. "Essay by Samuel," *Virginia Independent Chronicle,* Oct. 31, 1787; Charles Turner, Convention Debates, Feb. 5, 1788, in Storing, *Compete Anti-Federalist,* 5:126, 4:221; Spencer W. McBride, *Pulpit Nation: Clergymen and the Politics of Revolutionary America* (Charlottesville: University of Virginia Press, 2016), 120–26.

58. Samuel Spencer, July 30, 1788, in Elliot, *Debates in the Several State Conventions,* 4:200. See also Oliver Wolcott (Connecticut), Jan. 9, 1788; Rev. Shute (Massachusetts), Jan. 30, 1788, in Elliot, *Debates in the Several State Conventions,* 2:202, 118.

59. "A Landholder," *Connecticut Courant,* Dec. 17, 1787, in *Debate on the Constitution,* ed. Bernard Bailyn (New York: Library of America, 1993), 1:521–25.

60. "Aristocrotis" (1788); "Elihu," Feb. 18, 1788, in Storing, *Compete Anti-Federalist,* 3:206–7, 4:248–49.

61. Zachariah Johnston, July 30, 1788; James Iredell, July 30, 1788, in Elliot, *Debates in the Several State Conventions,* 3:645–46, 4:192.

62. Madison to Jefferson, Oct. 24, 1787, in Founders Online. See also Madison to Edmund Pendleton, Oct. 28, 1787, and Madison to Edmund Randolph, April 10, 1788, in Founders Online.

63. Kramnick and Moore, *Godless Constitution,* 27–28; Stephen Botein, "Religious Dimensions of the Early American Republic," in *Beyond Confederation: Origins of the Constitution and American National Identity,* ed. Richard Beeman, Stephen Botein, and Edward C. Carter II (Chapel Hill: University of North Carolina Press, 1987), 317 (quotation). As Spencer McBride demonstrates, however, the putatively secular character of the new government did not stop Federalist clergy from claiming that the new Constitution was "agreeable to the will of Heaven." McBride, *Pulpit Nation,* 108–20.

7. THE SECOND COLLABORATION: THE BILL OF RIGHTS

1. McCollum v. Board of Education, at 213 (Frankfurter, J.); Sehat, *The Myth of American Religious Freedom,* 48–49.

2. "Address by Denatus," in Storing, *Complete Anti-Federalist,* 5:263.

3. "An Old Whig," in ibid., 3:36.

4. "Philadelphiensis," in ibid., 3:107.

5. "An Old Whig," in ibid., 3:37.

6. Federalist Papers, no. 84.

7. Thomas Tredwell, July 2, 1788; Henry Abbot, July 30, 1788, in Elliot, *Debates in the Several State Conventions,* 2:373; 4:191–92.

8. James Iredell, July 30, 1788, in ibid., 4:194.

9. "Essay by Deliberator," *Freeman's Journal,* Feb. 20, 1788, in Storing, *Complete Anti-Federalist,* 3:179.

10. James Madison, June 24, 1788, in Elliot, *Debates in the Several State Conventions,* 3:560.

11. Madison to Jefferson, Oct. 17, 1788, in Founders Online.

12. Ibid.; Federalist Papers, no. 51.

13. Jefferson to Madison, Dec. 20, 1787, in Founders Online.

14. Richard B. Morris, *The Forging of the Union, 1781–1789* (New York: Harper and Row, 1987), 300–305; Klarman, *The Framers' Coup,* 422–53.

15. Madison to Jefferson, Feb. 19, 1988; Jefferson to Edward Carrington, May 27. 1788; Jefferson to William Stephens Smith, Feb. 2, 1788, in Founders Online. See also Jefferson to Madison, Feb. 6, 1788, in Founders Online, expressing the same sentiment.

16. Klarman, *The Framers' Coup,* 453–59; Sehat, *The Myth of American Religious Freedom,* 42–43.

17. Edward Carrington to Jefferson, Oct. 23, 1787; Madison to Jefferson, Oct. 24, 1787; Madison to Jefferson, April 22, 1788; Dec. 9, 1787, in Founders Online; Klarman, *The Framers' Coup,* 455–56.

18. John Blair Smith to Madison, June 12, 1788, in Founders Online; Meyerson, *Endowed by Our Creator,* 158–60.

19. Patrick Henry, June 12, 1788, in Elliot, *Debates in the Several State Conventions,* 3:21–23, 55–56, 314–15, 317, 446–49, 460–62, 317; Kidd, *Patrick Henry,* 190–205.

20. James Madison, June 6, 1788; Edmund Randolph, June 10, 1788, in Elliot, *Debates in the Several State Conventions,* 3:93, 330, 469.

21. Elliot, *Debates in the Several State Conventions,* 3:654; Madison to Alexander Hamilton, July 20, 1788, in Founders Online; Klarman, *The Framers' Coup,* 479–80; Kidd, *Patrick Henry,* 206–7.

22. Klarman, *The Framers' Coup,* 469–81; Elliot, *Debates in the Several State Conventions,* 3:657–59. An accompanying resolution stated that "no right of [religious] denomination, can be cancelled, abridged, restrained, or modified by the Congress . . . and that among the other essential rights, the liberty of conscience and of the press cannot be cancelled, abridged, restrained or modified by any authority of the United States." Richard Labunski, *James Madison and the Struggle for the Bill of Rights* (New York: Oxford University Press, 2006), 113–14.

23. Madison to Alexander Hamilton, June 27, 1788, in Founders Online.

24. Madison to Jefferson, Aug. 10, 1788, in ibid. See also Madison to Jefferson, Sept. 21, Dec. 3, 1788, in ibid., expressing ongoing concern about the drive for a second constitutional convention.

25. Jefferson to Madison, July 31, 1788, in ibid.

26. Madison to Jefferson, Oct. 17, 1788, in ibid.; Paul Finkelman, "James Madison and the Bill of Rights: A Reluctant Paternity," *Supreme Court Review* (1990): 309–13.

27. Madison to Jefferson, Oct. 17, 1788, in Founders Online; Broadwater, *Jefferson, Madison, and the Making of the Constitution,* 182–83.

28. Madison to Jefferson, Oct. 17, 1788; Jefferson to Madison, March 15, 1789, in Founders Online; Finkelman, "James Madison and the Bill of Rights," 328–29; Burstein and Isenberg, *Madison and Jefferson,* 196. See Koch, *Jefferson and Madison,* 55, suggesting Madison changed his mind due to Jefferson.

29. See Jefferson to Madison, Dec. 20, 1787, Feb. 6, July 31, 1788; Jefferson to Joseph Priestley, June 19, 1802, in Founders Online. See also Jefferson to C. W. F. Dumas, Feb. 12, 1788; Jefferson to Edward Carrington, May 27, 1788; Jefferson to William Carmichael, June 3, Aug 12, 1788; and Jefferson to Thomas Lee Shippen, June 19, 1788, in Founders Online.

30. See George Lee Turberville to Madison, Nov. 10, 13, 1788, in ibid.; Kidd, *Patrick Henry,* 210–11; and Brant, *James Madison: Father of the Constitution,* 236–39.

31. George Lee Turberville to Madison, Oct. 27, 1788; Henry Lee to Madison, Nov. 19, 1788; Madison to Jefferson, Dec. 8, 1788; James Madison Sr. to Madison, Jan. 30, 1788; Madison to Washington, Jan. 14, 1789, in Founders Online; Brant, *James Madison: Father of the Constitution,* 240–42; Labunski, *James Madison and the Struggle for the Bill of Rights,* 158–61.

32. Madison to George Eve, Jan. 2, 1789, in Founders Online; Labunski, *James Madison and the Struggle for the Bill of Rights,* 162–67; Brant, *James Madison: Father of the Constitution,* 240–41.

33. Madison to George Eve, Jan. 2, 1789; Benjamin Johnson to Madison, Jan. 19, 1789, in Founders Online; Labunski, *James Madison and the Struggle for the Bill of Rights,* 165–67; Mark S. Scarberry, "John Leland and James Madison: Religious Influence on the Ratification of the Constitution and on the Proposal of the Bill of Rights," *Penn State Law Review* 113 (2009): 733–800.

34. John Leland to Madison, Feb. 15, 1789; Madison to George Eve, Jan. 2, 1789; Madison to Washington, Nov. 20, 1789, in Founders Online; Labunski, *James Madison and the Struggle for the Bill of Rights,* 170–77; Scarberry, "John Leland and James Madison," 737–39.

35. See George Washington, First Inaugural Address, April 30, 1789, in Founders Online; Burstein and Isenberg, *Madison and Jefferson,* 197.

36. Madison to Edmund Pendleton, April 8, 1789, in Founders Online; Labunski, *James Madison and the Struggle for the Bill of Rights,* 185–92.

37. *Daily Advertiser* (New York), June 9, 1789, 2, in *The Complete Bill of Rights: The Drafts, Debates, Sources, and Origins*, ed. Neil H. Cogan (New York: Oxford University Press, 1997), 57.

38. *The Annals of Congress: The Debates and Proceedings in the Congress of the United States* (Washington, DC: Gales and Seaton, 1834–56), 1:451. See also Amendments to the Constitution, June 8, 1789, in Founders Online.

39. *Annals of Congress*, 1:452.

40. Burstein and Isenberg, *Madison and Jefferson*, 197; Brant, *James Madison: Father of the Constitution*, 265; *Annals of Congress*, 1:784; Labunski, *James Madison and the Struggle for the Bill of Rights*, 202–3; Rakove, *The Beginnings of National Politics*, 152–54; Witte and Nichols, *Religion and the American Constitutional Experiment*, 68–69.

41. Amendments to the Constitution, June 8, 1789; Madison's Remarks, in Cogan, *The Complete Bill of Rights*, 53–57; Feldman, *Three Lives of James Madison*, 267–68.

42. Pierce Butler to James Iredell, Aug. 11, 1789; George Clymer to Richard Peters, June 8, 1789, in Cogan, *The Complete Bill of Rights*, 82, 80. See also James Sullivan to John Adams, July 2, 1789, in Founders Online: "I was myself, and still am, an advocate for amendments: but not for one half the *alterations* proposed by Mr. Madison."

43. Cogan, *The Complete Bill of Rights*, 57; Labunski, *James Madison and the Struggle for the Bill of Rights*, 194; Ketcham, *James Madison*, 289–92; Ragosta, *Religious Freedom*, 110–12; Banning, *Jefferson and Madison*, 16. See Madison to Richard Peters, Aug. 19, 1789, in Founders Online: "A constitutional provision in favor of essential rights is a thing not improper in itself and was always viewed in that light by myself. It may be less necessary in a republic, than a Monarchy, & in a federal Govt. than the former, but it is in some degree rational in every Govt., since in every Govt. power may oppress, and declarations on paper, tho' not an effectual restraint, are not without some influence."

44. Madison to Jefferson, June 30, 1789; Jefferson to Madison, Aug. 28, 1789, in Founders Online; Koch, *Jefferson and Madison*, 56.

45. *Annals of Congress*, 1:757–59, 1:796; Brant, *James Madison: Father of the Constitution*, 271; Meyerson, *Endowed by Our Creator*, 166–69. The House also approved Madison's proposal for what would become the Second Amendment, along with its exemption for people with religious scruples, but the exemption was removed by the Senate. Cogan, *The Complete Bill of Rights*, 169–77.

46. *Annals of Congress*, 1:755; Sehat, *The Myth of American Religious Freedom*, 46–47.

47. Madison to Edmund Randolph, Aug. 21, 1789, in Founders Online.

48. Senate Journal, 1:70, in Cogan, *The Complete Bill of Rights*, 3–6.

49. House Journal, 1:146; Senate Journal, 1:142, in Cogan, *The Complete Bill of Rights*, 6, 7–8; Brant, *James Madison: Father of the Constitution*, 271; Brant, "Madison: On the Separation of Church and State," 16; Labunski, *James Madison and the Struggle for the Bill of Rights*, 239–40.

50. Madison to Edmund Pendleton, Aug. 21, 1789, in Founders Online; Burstein and Isenberg, *Madison and Jefferson*, 195–96; Brant, *James Madison: Father of the Constitution*, 268–73; Feldman, *Three Lives of James Madison*, 276.

51. Madison to Edmund Pendleton, Sept. 14, 1789, in Founders Online; Sehat, *The Myth of American Religious Freedom*, 48–49.

52. Two scholarly works examining these arguments are Steven D. Smith, *Foreordained Failure: The Quest for a Constitutional Principle of Religious Freedom* (New York: Oxford University Press, 1995), and Donald L. Drakeman, *Church, State, and Original Intent* (New York: Cambridge University Press, 2010).

53. Hamburger, *Separation of Church and State*, 101–7, 144–80; Dreisbach, *Thomas Jefferson and the Wall of Separation;* Hall, "Madison's Memorial and Remonstrance"; Smith, *Foreordained Failure;* Drakeman, *Church, State, and Original Intent.*

54. Hall, "Madison's Memorial and Remonstrance," 42–48; Ragosta, *Religious Freedom*, 101, 114–16, 129.

55. Cord, *Separation of Church and State*, 7–8, 214; Drakeman, *Church, State, and Original Intent*, 262.

56. *Annals of Congress*, 1:758–59, 796.

57. Smith, *Foreordained Failure*, 12; Drakeman, *Church, State, and Original Intent*, 262.

58. Curry, *First Freedoms*, 217, 222.

59. Daniel O. Conkle, "Toward a General Theory of the Establishment Clause," *Northwestern University Law Review* 82 (1988): 1113, 1133–34; Smith, *Foreordained Failure*, 30; Elk Grove School District v. Newdow, 542 U.S. 1 (2004) (Thomas, J., concurring in the judgment).

60. See Steven K. Green, "Federalism and the Establishment Clause: A Reassessment," *Creighton Law Review* 38 (2005): 761–97; Drakeman, *Church, State, and Original Intent*, 229–49.

61. *Annals of Congress*, 1:757–59.

62. Ibid.

63. Drakeman, *Church, State, and Original Intent,* 229–49; Ragosta, *Religious Freedom,* 116–21.

64. Brant, "Madison: On the Separation of Church and State," 15–17.

8. THE WASHINGTON AND ADAMS PRESIDENCIES

1. Gordon S. Wood, *Empire of Liberty: A History of the Early Republic, 1789–1815* (New York: Oxford University Press, 2009), 1–4, 239–75.

2. Ibid., 576–619; Green, *Separating Church and State: A History,* 76–89.

3. Jefferson, *Autobiography,* 116; Burstein and Isenberg, *Madison and Jefferson,* 203.

4. Burstein and Isenberg, *Madison and Jefferson,* 126.

5. Jefferson to Peter Carr, Oct. 10, 1787; Marquis de Lafayette to Jefferson, Aug. 25, 1789, in Founders Online; Jefferson, *Autobiography,* 105, 113–14; Cunningham, *In Pursuit of Reason,* 123–28; Dumas Malone, *Jefferson and the Rights of Man* (Boston: Little, Brown, 1951), 223.

6. Hamilton to Edward Carrington, May 26, 1792, in Founders Online.

7. Jefferson to Madison, Oct. 28. 1785; Jefferson to Charles Bellini, Sept. 30, 1785; Jefferson to Madison, Dec. 16, 1786; Jefferson to George Wythe, Aug. 13, 1786, in ibid; John Ferling, *Adams vs. Jefferson: The Tumultuous Election of 1800* (New York: Oxford University Press, 2004), 33.

8. Andrew Shankman, *Original Intents: Hamilton, Jefferson, Madison, and the American Founding* (New York: Oxford University Press, 2018), 2–4 ("By 1793 Hamilton and Jefferson had concluded that they disagreed in every way about what sort of society the United States should be"); Koch, *Jefferson and Madison,* 98.

9. Washington, First Inaugural Address, April 30, 1789, in Founders Online (also containing the phrases "the propitious smiles of Heaven" and "the eternal rules of order and right, which Heaven itself has ordained").

10. Washington to Lafayette, Aug. 15, 1787, in ibid.; Paul Boller, *Washington and Religion* (Dallas, TX: Southern Methodist University Press, 1963), 118–28; James Thomas Flexner, *Washington: The Indispensable Man* (Boston: Little, Brown, 1974), 216.

11. Washington to George Mason, Oct. 3, 1785, in Founders Online; Boller, *Washington and Religion,* 118–19.

12. George Washington, "Undelivered First Inaugural Address: Fragments," April 1789, in Founders Online.

13. Boller, *Washington and Religion,* 123.

14. See appendix A, in ibid.; Washington to the Protestant Episcopal Church, Aug. 19, 1789; Washington to the Society of Quakers, Oct. 13, 1789; Washington to the United Baptists of Virginia, May 1789, in Founders Online; and Meyerson, *Endowed by Our Creator*, 187–94.

15. Washington to the Hebrew Congregation in Newport, Rhode Island, Aug. 18, 1790, in Founders Online.

16. Boller, *Washington and Religion*, 155–57.

17. The Presbytery of the Eastward to Washington, Oct. 28, 1789, in Founders Online.

18. Washington to the Presbyterian Ministers of Massachusetts and New Hampshire, Nov. 2, 1789, in ibid; Meyerson, *Endowed by Our Creator*, 193–94.

19. Boller, *Washington and Religion*, 162.

20. Washington to Madison, Sept. 8, 1789, in Founders Online; Meyerson, *Endowed by Our Creator*, 185–86.

21. George Washington, Thanksgiving Proclamation, Oct. 3, 1789, in Founders Online; Meyerson, *Endowed by Our Creator*, 186–87.

22. Lance Banning, *The Jeffersonian Persuasion: Evolution of a Party Ideology* (Ithaca, NY: Cornell University Press, 1978), 164–68.

23. "Property," *National Gazette*, March 27, 1792, in Founders Online; Ketcham, *James Madison*, 328–30; Burstein and Isenberg, *Madison and Jefferson*, 233–37.

24. See George Washington, "Draft of Proclamation and Proclamation," Jan. 1, 1795, in Founders Online, and Meyerson, *Endowed by Our Creator*, 196–97.

25. John Adams to Benjamin Rush, Sept. 4, 1812, in Founders Online.

26. William White, *A Sermon, on the Reciprocal Influence of Civil Policy and Religious Duty. Delivered in Christ Church, in the City of Philadelphia, on Thursday, the 19th of February, 1795, Being a Day of General Thanksgiving* (Philadelphia: Ormrod and Conrad, 1795), 3–7.

27. Meyerson, *Endowed by Our Creator*, 197. See also Tim LaHaye, *Faith of Our Founding Fathers* (Brentwood, TN: Wolgemuth and Hyatt, 1987), 106; Michael Novak and Jana Novak, *Washington's God: Religion, Liberty, and the Father of Our Country* (New York: Basic Books, 2006), 109–10; and American Legion v. American Humanist Association, 139 S.Ct. 2067, 2087 (2019).

28. George Washington, Farewell Address, Sept. 19, 1796, in Founders Online.

29. For background, see George S, Mott, "Formation of Washington's Farewell Address to the American People," *Pennsylvania Magazine of*

History and Biography 21 (1897): 392–408; Hamilton to Washington, July 30, 1796; Farewell Address, Sept. 19, 1796, in Founders Online; Boller, *Washington and Religion,* 46–49; Meyerson, *Endowed by Our Creator,* 198–99; and Richard Brookhiser, *Alexander Hamilton: American* (New York: Free Press, 1999), 127–28.

30. William White, "Address of the Philadelphia Clergy," March 3, 1797, in Founders Online.
31. Washington to William White, March 3, 1797; Jefferson, "Notes on a Conversation with Benjamin Rush," Feb. 1, 1800, in ibid.; Meyerson, *Endowed by Our Creator,* 195–96.
32. Boller, *Washington and Religion,* 64.
33. See generally Simon Schama, *Citizens: A Chronicle of the French Revolution* (New York: Knopf, 1989).
34. *Gazette of the United States,* July 29, Oct. 10, 1789, in *The Revolutionary Era Primary Documents on Events from 1776 to 1800,* ed. Carol Sue Humphrey (Westport, CT: Greenwood Press, 2003), 226, 224–25.
35. Enos Hitchcock, "An Oration" (1793), in Sandoz, *Political Sermons,* 1180; Jedidiah Morse, *The Present Situation of Other Nations of the World, Contrasted with our Own* (Boston: Samuel Hall, 1795), 11, 14; Gary B. Nash, "The American Clergy and the French Revolution," *William and Mary Quarterly,* 3rd series, 22 (1965): 392–422.
36. Nash, "The American Clergy and the French Revolution," 397–98; Noah Webster, *The Revolution in France* (New York: George Bunce, 1794), in Sandoz, *Political Sermons,* 1239, 1252–53.
37. James Turner, *Without God, Without Creed: The Origins of Unbelief in America* (Baltimore: Johns Hopkins University Press, 1985), 35–72; Christopher Grasso, *Skepticism and American Faith: From the Revolution to the Civil War* (New York: Oxford University Press, 2018), 25–26, 97–106; Kerry S. Walters, *Rational Infidels: The American Deists* (Durango, CO: Longwood Academic, 1992), 5–7; Eric R. Schlereth, *An Age of Infidels: The Politics of Religious Controversy in the Early United States* (Philadelphia: University of Pennsylvania Press, 2013), 44–76; Ethan Allen, *Reason the Only Oracle of Man* (Bennington, VT: Haswell and Russell, 1784).
38. Thomas Paine, *The Age of Reason* (1794), in Foner, *Life and Major Writings of Thomas Paine,* 498, 469, 477.
39. Nash, "The American Clergy and the French Revolution," 403; Lyman Beecher, *Autobiography of Lyman Beecher,* ed. Charles Beecher (New York: Harper, 1864), 1:43; Schlereth, *An Age of Infidels,* 49–55.
40. "Americus," *Porcupine's Gazette,* July 31, 1798, 2.

41. Timothy Dwight, *The Duty of Americans, at the Present Crisis,* in Sandoz, *Political Sermons,* 1374–75, 1380; Schlereth, *An Age of Infidels,* 130–37; Nash, "American Clergy and the French Revolution," 397–99.

42. John Smalley, "On the Evils of a Weak Government," in Sandoz, *Political Sermons,* 1438.

43. Banning, *The Jeffersonian Persuasion,* 208–45; Cunningham, *In Pursuit of Reason,* 200–205.

44. Burstein and Isenberg, *Madison and Jefferson,* 315–16; Smith, *Republic of Letters,* 940–41; Jefferson to Edward Rutledge, Dec. 27, 1796; Madison to James Monroe, Sept. 29, 1796, in Founders Online.

45. See Bernard A. Weisberger, *America Afire: Jefferson, Adams, and the Revolutionary Election of 1800* (New York: William Morrow, 2000), 160–69, and Ferling, *Adams vs. Jefferson,* 83–98.

46. *Gazette of the United States,* Oct. 29, 1792, 2; Robert M. S. McDonald, "Was There a Religious Revolution of 1800?" in *The Revolution of 1800: Democracy, Race, and the New Republic,* ed. James Horn, Jan Ellen Lewis, and Peter S. Onuf (Charlottesville: University of Virginia Press, 2002), 177–80; Kidd, *Thomas Jefferson,* 130–31.

47. *Aurora* (Philadelphia), Sept. 13, Oct. 29, 1796, in Humphrey, *Revolutionary Era Primary Documents,* 298–99; McDonald, "Was There a Religious Revolution of 1800?" 179; Cunningham, *In Pursuit of Reason,* 202–4; Jefferson to Edward Rutledge, Dec. 27, 1796; Madison to Jefferson, Jan. 8, 1797, in Founders Online.

48. Jefferson to Philip Mazzei, April 24, 1796, in Founders Online; Burstein and Isenberg, *Madison and Jefferson,* 323–25; Kidd, *Thomas Jefferson,* 132.

49. *Gazette of the United States,* May 4, 1797, 2.

50. Hamilton to James McHenry, January 27–February 11, 1798, in Founders Online; Charles Ellis Dickson, "Jeremiads in the New American Republic: The Case of National Fasts in the John Adams Administration," *New England Quarterly* 60 (June 1987): 187–207.

51. Hamilton to Theodore Sedgwick, March 1–15, 1798; Hamilton to Timothy Pickering, March 17, 1798, in Founders Online.

52. John Adams to the *Boston Patriot,* May 29, 1809, in ibid.

53. John Adams, Fast Day Proclamations, March 23, 1798; March 6, 1799; Madison to Jefferson, June 10, 1798, in ibid.; Dickson, "Jeremiads in the New American Republic," 193–95; Meyerson, *Endowed by Our Creator,* 199–201.

54. Nathanael Emmons, "A Discourse Delivered on the National Fast" (1799), in *American Political Writing during the Founding Era, 1760–1805,*

ed. Charles S. Hyneman and Donald S. Lutz (Indianapolis: Liberty Fund, 1983), 2:1030–32.

55. Jedidiah Morse, *A Sermon Delivered at the New North Church in Boston* (Boston: Samuel Hall, 1798), 23; Dickson, "Jeremiads in the New American Republic," 195–204.

56. *Aurora,* May 9, 1798, in *American Aurora: A Democratic-Republican Returns,* ed. Richard N. Rosenfeld (New York: St. Martin's Press, 1997), 113.

57. Morse, *A Sermon Delivered at the New North Church in Boston,* 12: Jedidiah Morse, *A Sermon Exhibiting the Present Dangers, and Consequent Duties of the Citizens of the United States of America* (Charlestown, MA: Charles Etheridge, 1799), 18.

58. Jefferson to James Lewis Jr., May 9, 1798; Jefferson to Madison, May 17, 1798; "A Friend to America and Truth," April 1798; "An Unfortunate Mislead Man, but a Real Friend to America," April 18, 1798, in Founders Online; Smith, *Republic of Letters,* 1005–6.

59. Jefferson to Madison, May 10, 1798, in Founders Online; *Aurora,* May 9, 1798, in Rosenfeld, *American Aurora,* 113–20; *Aurora,* May 10, 1798, in Rosenfeld, *American Aurora,* 118.

60. John Adams, "To the Inhabitants of the Town of Hartford, Connecticut," May 10, 1798; Adams to Jefferson, June 30, 1813; Madison to Jefferson, June 10, 1798, in Founders Online.

61. Wood, *Empire of Liberty,* 249–50; James Morton Smith, *Freedom's Fetters: The Alien and Sedition Laws and American Civil Liberties* (Ithaca, NY: Cornell University Press, 1956), 63–93.

62. *Philadelphia Gazette,* Jan. 2, 1795, in Founders Online; Ketcham, *James Madison,* 355.

63. Jefferson to Madison, May 31, 1798; Madison to Jefferson, May 20, 1798, in Founders Online; Wood, *Empire of Liberty,* 259–62.

64. Smith, *Freedom's Fetters,* 94–111, 435–42; Jefferson to Madison, June 7, 1798, in Founders Online.

65. Kentucky Resolution and Virginia Resolution; Jefferson to John Taylor, June 4, 1798, in Founders Online; Smith, *Republic of Letters,* 1066–73.

9. THE JEFFERSON AND MADISON PRESIDENCIES

1. See Ferling, *Adams vs. Jefferson,* 135–61; Weisberger, *America Afire,* 227–57; Banning, *The Jeffersonian Persuasion,* 273–88; and McBride, *Pulpit Nation,* 150–65.

2. *Aurora*, May 24, Jan. 1, March 29, 1800, in Rosenfeld, *American Aurora*, 799, 732, 765; *A Dialogue between a Federalist and a Republican* (Charleston, SC, Aug. 25, 1800), 23.

3. "A Layman," *The Claims of Thomas Jefferson to the Presidency* (Philadelphia: Asbury Dickins, 1800), 30–31; *Connecticut Courant*, Sept. 15, 1800, in Humphrey, *Revolutionary Era Primary Documents*, 339–40; Ferling, *Adams vs. Jefferson*, 146–53; Lerche, "Jefferson and the Election of 1800," 470–71, 477–79.

4. Alexander Hamilton to John Jay, May 1, 1800, in Founders Online.

5. Luebke, "Origins of Thomas Jefferson's Anti-Clericalism," 349; "A Layman," *The Claims of Thomas Jefferson to the Presidency*, 29–30.

6. John M. Mason, *The Voice of Warning to Christians on the Ensuing Election* (1800), in *The Complete Works of John M. Mason, D.D.*, ed. Ebenezer Mason (New York: Baker and Scribner, 1849), 551–53, 536–37.

7. Linn, *Serious Considerations on the Election of a President*, 4, 12, 21–28; Noah Webster, *A Rod for the Fool's Back* (Bennington, CT: William Stockwell, 1800), 10; Kidd, *Thomas Jefferson*, 142–45.

8. Randall, *Life of Thomas Jefferson*, 2:567; *Aurora*, Aug. 28, 1800, in Rosenfeld, *American Aurora*, 840–42; Luebke, "Origins of Thomas Jefferson's Anti-Clericalism," 349–50; McDonald, "Was There a Religious Revolution of 1800?" 173.

9. *Gazette of the United States*, Sept. 11, May 1, Oct. 9, 1800, in Rosenfeld, *American Aurora*, 782, 864.

10. *New-England Palladium*, Sept. 7, 1800, reprinted in Lerche, "Jefferson and the Election of 1800," 474n20.

11. "Clergy," *Gazette of the United States*, Oct. 7, 1800, n.p.

12. "Grotius," *Vindication of Thomas Jefferson against the Charges Contained in a Pamphlet Entitled, "Serious Considerations"* (New York: David Denniston, 1800), 6–7, 32; [John Beckley?], *Address to the People of the United States, with an Epitome and Vindication of the Public Life and Character of Thomas Jefferson* (Philadelphia: James Carney, 1800), 32.

13. "Marcus Brutus," *"Serious Facts Opposed to Serious Considerations"; or, The Voice of Warning to Religious Republicans* (N.p, October 1800), 12; Abraham Bishop, *An Oration on the Extent and Power of Political Delusion* (Philadelphia: Mathew Carey, 1800), 66–67.

14. "Marcus Brutus," *"Serious Facts,"* 11, 2.

15. *Gazette of the United States*, May 3, April 14, 1800, in Rosenfeld, *American Aurora*, 782, 770.

16. Mason, *Voice of Warning*, 570, 553; Linn, *Serious Considerations*, 18.

17. "Grotius," *Vindication of Thomas Jefferson*, 21–22; *A Test of the Religious Principles of Mr. Jefferson* (Easton, MD: Thomas Perrin Smith, 1800), preface.

18. *Aurora*, Aug. 1, 18, Sept. 9, 1800, in Rosenfeld, *American Aurora*, 829, 839, 846.

19. Tunis Wortman, "A Solemn Address to Christians and Patriots," in Sandoz, *Political Sermons*, 1488, 1482, 1489, 1494.

20. McDonald, "Was There a Religious Revolution of 1800?" 173–94; Kramnick and Moore, *Godless Constitution*, 88–101.

21. Jefferson to James Monroe, May 26. 1800; Jefferson to Moses Robinson, March 23, 1801, in Founders Online.

22. Jefferson to Joseph Priestley, March 21, 1801; Jefferson to Benjamin Rush, Sept. 23, 1800, in ibid.

23. John Adams to Benjamin Rush, June 12, 1812, in ibid.

24. Cunningham, *In Pursuit of Reason*, 234–37; Brookhiser, *Alexander Hamilton*, 151–53; Alexander Hamilton to James A. Bayard, Dec. 27, 1800, Jan. 16, 1801, in Founders Online.

25. Thomas Jefferson, First Inaugural Address, March 4, 1801, in Founders Online.

26. Ibid.; Meyerson, *Endowed by Our Creator*, 208.

27. Jefferson, First Inaugural Address, March 4, 1801; Thomas Jefferson, Second Inaugural Address, March 4, 1805, in Founders Online; Meyerson, *Endowed by Our Creator*, 208–9. Thomas S. Kidd overstates Jefferson's use of religious rhetoric in asserting that the address "envisioned an American civil religion based on enlightened Christian virtue and on God's providential guidance." Kidd, *Thomas Jefferson*, 151.

28. Jefferson to Joseph Priestley, March 21, 1801; Jefferson to Elbridge Gerry, March 29, 1801; Jefferson to Levi Lincoln, Aug. 26, 1801, in Founders Online.

29. Danbury Baptist Association to Jefferson, Oct. 1801, in ibid.; Kidd, *Thomas Jefferson*, 157–60.

30. Jefferson to Levi Lincoln, Jan. 1, 1802; Jefferson, "Draft Reply to the Danbury Baptist Association," Dec. [31?], 1801, in Founders Online.

31. McLoughlin, *New England Dissent*, 2:1004–17. Jefferson had earlier responded to a congratulatory letter from a group of Delaware Baptists where he had celebrated with them "the establishment here of liberty, equality of social rights, exclusion of unequal privileges civil & religious, & of the usurping domination of one sect over another." Jefferson to the Delaware Baptist Association, July 2, 1801, in Founders Online.

32. Levi Lincoln to Jefferson, Jan. 1, 1802; Gideon Granger to Jefferson, Dec. 31, 1801, in Founders Online. Jefferson's note to Granger does not exist, but language in Granger's reply suggests it was similar to the one to Lincoln.

33. Jefferson to Nehemiah Dodge, Ephraim Robbins, and Stephen S. Nelson, Jan. 1, 1802, in Founders Online.

34. James Burgh, *Crito, or Essays on Various Subjects* (London: J. Dodsley, 1767), 1:115–21, in Dreisbach and Hall, *Sacred Rights of Conscience,* 524–25; Green, *Separating Church and State,* 18–31.

35. Daniel L. Dreisbach, "'Sowing Useful Truths and Principles': The Danbury Baptists, Thomas Jefferson, and the 'Wall of Separation,'" *Journal of Church and State* 39 (1997): 491.

36. Jeremiah S. Black, "Religious Liberty: An Address to the Phrenakosmian Society of Pennsylvania College" (Sept. 17, 1856), in *Essays and Speeches of Jeremiah S. Black,* ed. Chauncy F. Black (New York: D. Appleton, 1883), 53; C. Peter Mcgrath, "Chief Justice Waite and the Twin Relic: Reynolds v. United States," *Vanderbilt Law Review* 18 (1965): 507–43; Reynolds v. United States, at 164.

37. Levy, *The Establishment Clause,* 182, 185. See also Gillman and Chemerinsky, *The Religion Clauses,* 62.

38. Cord, *Separation of Church and State,* 36–46; Dreisbach, "'Sowing Useful Truths and Principles,'" 455–501.

39. Cord, *Separation of Church and State,* 36–46; Dreisbach, "'Sowing Useful Truths and Principles,'" 473–74.

40. Robert M. O'Neil, "The 'Wall of Separation' and Thomas Jefferson's Views on Religious Liberty," *William and Mary Quarterly,* 3rd series, 56 (1999): 791–94. An additional critique asserts that by referring to the "legislature" of "the whole American people," Jefferson was making a statement about federalism and the limitations on the national government. Dreisbach, "'Sowing Useful Truths and Principles,'" 479–81. This critique is undermined by the extensive body of Jefferson's writings on church and state that contain no jurisdictional element.

41. James Hutson, "Thomas Jefferson's Letter to the Danbury Baptists: A Controversy Rejoined," *William and Mary Quarterly,* 3rd series, 56 (1999): 775–90, 776 (quotation); Edwin Corwin, "The Supreme Court as a National School Board," *Law and Contemporary Problems* 14 (1949): 14; Daniel L. Dreisbach, "Thomas Jefferson and the Danbury Baptists Revisited," *William and Mary Quarterly,* 3rd series, 56 (1999): 805–16.

42. Hutson, "Thomas Jefferson's Letter," 776; Meyerson, *Endowed by Our Creator,* 213.

43. Isaac Kramnick and R. Laurence Moore, "The Baptists, the Bureau, and the Case of the Missing Lines," *William and Mary Quarterly*, 3rd series, 56 (1999): 817–22; Edwin S. Gaustad, "Thomas Jefferson, Danbury Baptists, and 'Eternal Hostility,'" *William and Mary Quarterly*, 3rd series, 56 (1999): 801–4; Thomas E. Buckley, "Reflections on a Wall," *William and Mary Quarterly*, 3rd series, 56 (1999): 795–800; Johann N. Neem, "Beyond the Wall: Reinterpreting Jefferson's Danbury Address," *Journal of the Early Republic* 27 (2007): 139–54.

44. James Hutson, "A Wall of Separation," *Library of Congress Information Bulletin* 57, no. 6 (1998): 163. See also Hutson, "Thomas Jefferson's Letter," 785–87; James Hutson, "James H. Hutson Responds," *William and Mary Quarterly*, 3rd series, 56 (1999): 823–24; and Dreisbach, *Thomas Jefferson and the Wall of Separation*, 21–23.

45. Meyerson, *Endowed by Our Creator*, 218–19; Kramnick and Moore, "The Baptists, the Bureau, and the Case of the Missing Lines," 821–22.

46. Cord, *Separation of Church and State*, 38–39. The treaty is reprinted at 261–63.

47. Henry Warner Bowden, *American Indians and Christian Missions* (Chicago: University of Chicago Press, 1981); R. Pierce Beaver, *Church, State, and the American Indians* (St. Louis: Concordia, 1966); Gary B. Nash, *Red, White, and Black: The Peoples of Early America* (Englewood Cliffs, NJ: Prentice-Hall, 1974), 46–47.

48. Washington to the Moravian Society for Propagating the Gospel, Aug. 15, 1789, in Founders Online; Beaver, *Church, State, and the American Indian*, 63–65; Anson Phelps Stokes and Leo Pfeffer, *Church and State in the United States* (New York: Harper and Row, 1964), 185–86; Act of June 1, 1796, chap. 46, § 5, 1 Stat. 490, 491.

49. Jefferson to Marquis de Chastellux, June 7, 1785; Jefferson, Second Inaugural Address, March 4, 1805; Jefferson to James Pemberton, Nov. 16, 1807; Jefferson to James Jay, April 7, 1809, in Founders Online; Peter S. Onuf, "'We Shall All Be Americans': Jefferson and the Indians," *Indiana Magazine of History* 95 (June 1999): 103–41.

50. Meyerson, *Endowed by Our Creator*, 219–20; Cord, *Separation of Church and State*, 261–62.

51. Madison, Memorandum to Jefferson, Oct. 1, 1803, in Founders Online; Meyerson, *Endowed by Our Creator*, 220–21.

52. Jefferson, Second Inaugural Address, March 4, 1805.

53. Samuel Miller to Jefferson, Jan. 18, 1808, in ibid.

54. Jefferson to Samuel Miller, Jan. 23, 1808, in ibid.

55. Dreisbach, *Thomas Jefferson and the Wall of Separation*, 62–67; Dreisbach, "'Sowing Useful Truths and Principles,'" 476–81.

56. Jefferson to Samuel Miller, Jan. 23, 1808; Miller to Jefferson, Jan. 18, 1808, in Founders Online; Knoles, "The Religious Ideas of Thomas Jefferson," 187–88.

57. Jefferson to Peter Carr, Aug. 10, 1787, in Founders Online.

58. Jefferson to Richard Price, July 12, 1789; Price to Jefferson, Aug. 3, 1789, in ibid.; Conkin, "Religious Pilgrimage of Thomas Jefferson," 28–30.

59. Joseph Priestley, *An History of the Corruptions of Christianity* (Boston: William Spotswood, 1797); Conkin, "Religious Pilgrimage of Thomas Jefferson," 29–34; Gaustad, *Sworn on the Altar of God*, 112–13; Sheridan, *Jefferson and Religion*, 26–28; Eugene R. Sheridan, "Introduction," in Adams, *Jefferson's Extracts from the Gospels*, 14–16; Jefferson to Joseph Priestley, April 9, 1803, in Founders Online.

60. Jefferson to Mary Jefferson Eppes, April 25, 1803; Jefferson to John Adams, Aug. 22, 1813, in Founders Online.

61. Jefferson to Joseph Priestley, April 9, 1803; Jefferson to Edward Dowse, April 19, 1803, in ibid.

62. Benjamin Rush to Jefferson, Oct. 6, Aug. 22, 1800; Jefferson to Rush, Sept. 23, 1800, in ibid.; Stephen Fried, *Rush: Revolution, Madness, and the Visionary Doctor Who Became a Founding Father* (New York: Crown, 2018), 398–99.

63. Joseph Priestly, *Socrates and Jesus Compared* (Philadelphia: Shaw and Shoemaker, 1803); Jefferson to Joseph Priestley, April 9, 1803, in Founders Online; Sheridan, "Introduction," 19–21.

64. Jefferson to Benjamin Rush, April 21, 1803; Jefferson to Joseph Priestley, April 24, 1803, in Founders Online; Adams, *Jefferson's Extracts from the Gospels*, 331–38; Gaustad, *Sworn on the Altar of God*, 114–18.

65. Benjamin Rush to Jefferson, May 5, 1803; Joseph Priestley to Jefferson, May 7, 1803, in Founders Online.

66. Jefferson to Benjamin Rush, Sept. 23, 1800, in ibid.

67. Benjamin Rush to Jefferson, Aug. 22; Oct. 6, 1800, in ibid.

68. Jefferson to Moses Robinson, March 23, 1801, in ibid.; Sheridan, "Introduction," 16–19.

69. James Madison, First Inaugural Address, March 4, 1809; Madison, Second Inaugural Address, March 4, 1813, in Founders Online.

70. Benjamin Rush to John Adams, June 4, 1812, in ibid.

71. James Madison, Presidential Proclamations, July 9, 1812; July 23, 1813; Nov. 16, 1814; March 4, 1815, in ibid.; Sheldon, *Political Philosophy of James*

Madison, 104–6; Cord, *Separation of Church and State,* 31–36; Donald L. Drakeman, "Religion and the Republic: James Madison and the First Amendment," *Journal of Church and State* 25 (August 1983): 440–42.

72. Madison to Edward Livingston, July 10, 1822, in Founders Online.

73. Madison, Presidential Proclamation, July 23, 1813, in ibid.; Meyerson, *Endowed by Our Creator,* 223.

74. Madison, Detached Memoranda; "Madison's 'Detached Memoranda,'" ed. Elizabeth Fleet, *William and Mary Quarterly,* 3rd series, 3 (Oct. 1946): 534–68; Meyerson, *Endowed by Our Creator,* 222–23.

75. James Monroe to Madison, April 22, 1815; Madison to Monroe, April 24, 1815, in Founders Online.

76. Mordecai M. Noah to Madison, May 6, 1818; Madison to Noah, May 15, 1818, in ibid.; Jonathan D. Sarna, *Jacksonian Jew: The Two Worlds of Mordecai Noah* (New York: Holmes and Meir, 1981), 16–28.

77. Madison, Veto Messages, Feb. 21, 28, 1811, in Founders Online. Madison's second veto is consistent with Mark McGarvie's thesis that a leading separationist impulse involved the privatization of religious institutions and the removal of their traditional role of providing public services. McGarvie, *One Nation under Law,* 9, 48.

78. Madison, Detached Memoranda; Leo Pfeffer, "Madison's 'Detached Memoranda,'" in Peterson and Vaughan, *Virginia Statute for Religious Freedom,* 288–95.

79. Madison, Annual Message to Congress, Dec. 3, 1816, in Founders Online.

10. RETIREMENT

1. Wood, *Empire of Liberty,* 701; Henry Adams, *History of the United States during the Administration of Thomas Jefferson and James Madison* (New York: C. Scribner's Sons, 1889–91), 9:220–21.

2. Jefferson to John Adams, Jan. 21, 1812, in Founders Online; Wood, *Empire of Liberty,* 1–4, 701–2.

3. Jefferson to James Smith, Dec. 8, 1822, in Founders Online.

4. Wood, *Empire of Liberty,* 589; Foner, *Life and Major Writings of Thomas Paine,* xli–xliv; Eric Foner, *Tom Paine and Revolutionary America* (New York: Oxford University Press, 2005), 257–59; Grasso, *Skepticism, and American Faith,* 140.

5. Timothy Dwight, *Travels in New-England and New-York* (New Haven, CT: Timothy Dwight, 1822), 4:272–73; Lyman Beecher, "The Building of Waste Places" (1814); "Lectures on Political Atheism, and Kindred

Subjects," in *Beecher's Works*, ed. Lyman Beecher (Boston: John P. Jewett, 1852), 2:121–22; 1:56–58, 75–76; Grasso, *Skepticism, and American Faith*, 281–93; Green, *Separating Church and State*, 111–13.

6. Winthrop S. Hudson, *Religion in America*, 3rd ed. (1965; New York: Charles Scribner's Sons, 1981), 134–45; Nathan O. Hatch, *The Democratization of American Christianity* (New Haven, CT: Yale University Press, 1989), 67–101.

7. William G. McLoughlin, ed., *The American Evangelicals, 1800–1900* (Gloucester, MA: Peter Smith, 1976), 1–27; William G. McLoughlin, *Revivals, Awakenings, and Reform* (Chicago: University of Chicago Press, 1978), 98–140; Paul E. Johnson, *A Shopkeeper's Millennium* (New York: Hill and Wang, 1978); Robert Baird, *Religion in the United States of America* (Glasgow: Blackie and Son, 1844), 600–603, 606.

8. Lyman Beecher, "The Practicability of Suppressing Vice, by Means of Societies Instituted for That Purpose" (1804), in *Lyman Beecher and the Reform of Society* (New York: Arno Press, 1972), 16–20; Beecher, "A Reformation of Morals Practicable and Indispensable" (1812), in *Lyman Beecher and the Reform of Society*, 17–19.

9. Clifford S. Griffin, *Their Brothers' Keepers: Moral Stewardship in the United Sates, 1800–1865* (New Brunswick, NJ: Rutgers University Press, 1960), 47–49; Robert T. Handy, "The Protestant Quest for a Christian America, 1830–1930," *Church History* 22 (1953): 8–20; Mark A. Noll, *America's God: From Jonathan Edwards to Abraham Lincoln* (New York: Oxford University Press, 2002), 208.

10. See Green, *Inventing a Christian America*; Steven K. Green, *The Bible, the School, and the Constitution* (New York: Oxford University Press, 2012); and Sehat, *The Myth of American Religious Freedom*, 51–69.

11. Gaustad, *Sworn on the Altar of God*, 212; Jefferson to Jared Sparks, Nov. 4, 1820, in Founders Online.

12. Jefferson to Thomas Cooper, March 13, 1820, in Founders Online.

13. Jefferson to James Smith, Dec. 8, 1822; Jefferson to John Davis, Jan. 18, 1824, in ibid.; Gaustad, *Sworn on the Altar of God*, 213–14.

14. Jefferson to Miles King, Sept. 26, 1814, in Founders Online. See also Jefferson to Margaret Bayard Smith, Aug. 6, 1816, in Founders Online.

15. Goodwill/Anonymous/A Friend to the Christian Religion to Jefferson, June 20, 1809; April 28, 1811; April 13, June 1, August 24, 1812; between Dec. 19, 1818, and Jan. 7, 1819, in ibid.

16. Miles King to Jefferson, Aug. 20, 1814; Jefferson to King, Sept. 26, 1814, in ibid.

17. Jefferson to Charles Thomson, Jan. 9, 1816, in ibid.
18. Charles Thomson to Jefferson, May 16, 1816; Jan. 7, 1817, in ibid; McBride, *Pulpit Nation*, 165–67.
19. Joseph Delaplaine to Jefferson, Nov. 23, 1816, in Founders Online; Kidd, *Thomas Jefferson*, 206–8.
20. Margaret Bayard Smith to Jefferson, July 21, 1816; Jefferson to Smith, Aug. 6, 1816, in Founders Online.
21. Lester J. Cappon, introduction, in Cappon, *Adams-Jefferson Letters,* xlvii.
22. John Adams to Jefferson, Nov. 4, 1816; Jefferson to Adams, Nov. 25, 1816, in Founders Online.
23. Jefferson to John Adams, May 5, 1817; Adams to Jefferson, May 18, 1817, in ibid.
24. Jefferson to Charles Clay, Jan. 29, 1815; Jefferson to John Adams, Aug. 22, 1813; Jefferson to Francis Van der Kemp, July 30, 1816; Jefferson to Benjamin Waterhouse, June 26, 1822; Jefferson, "Essay on New England Religious Intolerance" (Draft), Jan. 10, 1816, in ibid.; Luebke, "Origins of Thomas Jefferson's Anti-Clericalism," 352–53.
25. Jefferson to Charles Clay, Jan. 29, 1815, in Founders Online.
26. Jefferson to Margaret Bayard Smith, Aug. 6, 1816, in ibid.
27. Jefferson to William Short, April 13, 1820, in ibid.; Burstein, *Democracy's Muse*, 162–64.
28. Samuel Greenhow to Jefferson, Nov. 11, 1813; Jefferson to Greenhow, Jan. 31, 1814, in Founders Online.
29. Jefferson, "Essay on New England Religious Intolerance" (as published), Jan. 27, 1816, in ibid. See Lyman Beecher, *On the Importance of Assisting Young Men of Piety and Talents in Obtaining an Education for the Gospel Ministry,* 1st ed. (New York: Dodge and Sayre, 1815); 2nd ed. (Andover, MA: Flagg and Gould, 1816).
30. Jefferson to Michael Megear, May 29, 1823, in Founders Online.
31. Dumas Malone, "The Correspondence of Thomas Jefferson and Thomas Cooper—A Previously Unpublished Manuscript," ed. Seymour S. Cohen, *Proceedings of the American Philosophical Society* 147 (2003): 39–64; Smith, *Freedom's Fetters*, 307–33.
32. Jefferson to Thomas Cooper, July 4, 1820; Cooper to Jefferson, July 12, 1820, in Founders Online.
33. Thomas Cooper to Jefferson, Oct. 18, 1822, in ibid.
34. Jefferson to Thomas Cooper, Nov. 2, 1822; Cooper to Jefferson, Nov. 22, 1822, in ibid.
35. Jefferson to Horatio G. Spafford, March 17, 1814, in ibid.

36. Jefferson to James Fishback, Sept. 1809; Jefferson to Thomas Cooper, March 13, 1820; Nov. 2, 1822; Jefferson to William Short, April 13, 1822, in ibid.
37. Baird, *Religion in the United States of America*, 240–41; Jefferson to Jared Sparks, Nov. 4, 1820, in Founders Online.
38. Madison to Robert Walsh Jr., March 2, 1819, in Founders Online.
39. Madison to Edward Everett, March 19, 1823; Madison to Charles Caldwell, Nov. 23, 1826, in ibid.; Pfeffer, "Madison's 'Detached Memoranda,'" 293.
40. Madison to Edward Everett, March 19, 1823, in Founders Online; "James Madison's Autobiography," 199.
41. Jedidiah Morse to John Adams, Thomas Jefferson, and James Madison, Feb. 16, 1822, in Founders Online; Annual Report of the American Society for Promoting the Civilization and General Improvement of the Indian Tribes, Feb. 6, 1824, in American Periodical Series II, https://www.proquest.com/americanperiodicals/advanced?accountid=15051.
42. Jefferson to Madison, Feb. 25, 1822; Madison to Jefferson, March 5, 1822, in Founders Online.
43. Madison to Jedidiah Morse, Feb. 26, 1822; Adams to Morse, March 2, 1822, in ibid.
44. Jefferson to Jedidiah Morse, March 6, 1822, in ibid.
45. Madison to Edward Livingston, July 10, 1822, in ibid.
46. Fleet, "Madison's 'Detached Memoranda,'" 534–68; Pfeffer, "Madison's 'Detached Memoranda,'" 283–312; Grunes, "James Madison and Religious Freedom," 115–21. Grunes calls the Detached Memoranda Madison's "most authoritative statement" of the relationship between church and state (115).
47. Fleet, "Madison's 'Detached Memoranda,'" 554–55; Grunes, "James Madison and Religious Freedom," 115–21.
48. Fleet, "Madison's 'Detached Memoranda,'" 555, 558–61.
49. Ibid., 554–56; Pfeffer, "Madison's 'Detached Memoranda,'" 283–312.
50. Jefferson to the Members of the Baltimore Baptist Association, Oct. 17, 1808, in Founders Online.
51. Jefferson to the Virginia Baptist Association of Chesterfield, Nov. 21, 1808, in ibid.
52. Thomas Jefferson, *The Jefferson Bible* (Washington, DC: Smithsonian Books, 2011); Adams, *Jefferson's Extracts from the Gospels*; Sheridan, "Introduction," 3–44; Gaustad, *Sworn on the Altar of God*, 123–31.
53. Jefferson to Joseph Priestley, April 9, 1803; Priestley to Jefferson, May 7, December 12, 1803; Jefferson to Priestley, Jan. 29, 1804, in Founders

Online; Sheridan, "Introduction," 26–27; Sheridan, *Jefferson and Religion,* 43–44.

54. Jefferson to Priestley, Jan. 29, 1804; Jefferson to Francis Van der Kemp, April 25, 1816; Jefferson to John Adams, Oct. 12, 1813, in Founders Online; Sheridan, *Jefferson and Religion,* 44–45; Sheridan, "Introduction," 27–28.

55. Jefferson to Benjamin Rush, Aug. 8, 1804; Rush to Jefferson, Aug. 29, 1804; May 5, 1803; Jefferson to Charles Thomson, Jan. 9, 1815, in Founders Online; Sheridan, *Jefferson and Religion,* 49–50; Sheridan, "Introduction," 29–30, 45; Gaustad, *Sworn on the Altar of God,* 118–20; Adams, *Jefferson's Extracts from the Gospels,* 45–122.

56. Jefferson to John Adams, Oct. 13, 1813; Jefferson to Charles Thomson, Jan. 9, 1815, in Founders Online. See also Jefferson to Charles Clay, Jan. 29, 1815; Jefferson to Francis Van der Kemp, April 25, 1816; Jefferson to William Short, Oct. 31, 1819, in Founders Online.

57. Francis Van der Kemp to Jefferson, March 24, April 26, June 4, July 14, Nov. 1, 1816; Jefferson to Van der Kemp, April, 25, July 30, Nov. 24, 1816; May 1, 1817, in Founders Online; Sheridan, "Introduction," 34–36.

58. Jefferson to William Short, Oct. 31, 1819; William Short to Jefferson, Dec. 1, 1819; May 2, 1820, in Founders Online.

59. Gaustad, *Sworn on the Altar of God,* 123–31.

60. See John Adams to Jefferson, July 18, Sept. 14. 1813; Jefferson to Adams, July 5, 1814; Adams to Jefferson, July 16, 1813, in Founders Online.

61. Jefferson to John Adams, Jan. 22, 1821; Adams to Jefferson, Jan. 23, 1825, in ibid.; Cappon, *Adams-Jefferson Letters,* xlvii, 343.

62. Jefferson to Adams, Aug. 22, Oct. 12, 28, 1813, in Founders Online; Cappon, *Adams-Jefferson Letters,* 344–45.

63. Adams to Jefferson, March 10, 1823; Jefferson to Adams, April 11, 1823, in Founders Online.

64. See Jefferson to Horatio G. Spafford, March 17, 1814; Jefferson to Timothy Pickering, Feb. 27, 1821; Jefferson to Benjamin Waterhouse, June 26, 1822, in ibid.

65. Jefferson to Charles Clay, Jan. 29, 1815; Jefferson to Francis Van der Kemp, July 30, 1816, in ibid.

66. Jefferson to Charles Clay, Jan. 29, 1815, in ibid.

67. Jefferson to James Smith, Dec. 8, 1822, in ibid.

68. Jefferson to George Logan, Nov. 12, 1816; Jefferson to William Canby, Sept. 18, 1813; Jefferson to Thomas Leiper, Jan. 21, 1809, in ibid.

11. THE FINAL COLLABORATION

1. Jefferson to George Wythe, Aug. 13, 1786; Jefferson to Pierre Samuel Du Pont de Nemours, April 24, 1816, in Founders Online.
2. Jefferson to Madison, Dec. 20, 1787; Jefferson to Joseph C. Cabell, Jan. 31, 1814; Jefferson to John Tyler, May 26, 1810, in ibid.; Mercer, "Thomas Jefferson," 19–25.
3. Jefferson to John Adams, Oct. 28, 1813, in Founders Online; Ramon Sanchez, "Thomas Jefferson: The Founder of the Ideology of Democratic Education," *Journal of Education* 155 (1973): 45–55.
4. "A Bill for the More General Diffusion of Knowledge"; Jefferson, *Autobiography*, 61; Gaustad, *Sworn on the Altar of God*, 148–52.
5. Jefferson, *Notes on the State of Virginia*, 146–49, 159; Green, *The Bible, the School, and the Constitution*, 13–16.
6. "A Bill for Amending the Constitution of the College of William and Mary."
7. Jefferson, *Autobiography*, 61; Madison to Jefferson, Feb. 15, 1787, in Founders Online; Gaustad, *Sworn on the Altar of God*, 152–56.
8. Jefferson to Joseph Priestley, Jan. 18, 27, 1800; Priestley to Jefferson, May 1, 1800, in Founders Online; Wenger, "Thomas Jefferson, the College of William and Mary, and the University of Virginia," 339–74.
9. See James Madison, Annual Message to Congress, Dec. 5, 1810; Madison, National University, Dec. 12 and 26, 1796, in Founders Online.
10. Jefferson to Hugh L. White et al., May 6, 1810, in ibid.
11. David P. Peeler, "Thomas Jefferson's Nursery of Republican Patriots: The University of Virginia," *Journal of Church and State* 28 (1986): 79–93; Smith, *Republic of Letters*, 1776–78; Gaustad, *Sworn on the Altar of God*, 171–72; Alan Pell Crawford, *Twilight at Monticello: The Final Years of Thomas Jefferson* (New York: Random House, 2008), 151–56; John Adams to Jefferson, May 26, 1817, in Founders Online.
12. Rockfish Gap Report of the University of Virginia Commissioners, Aug. 4, 1818, in Founders Online; Gaustad, *Sworn on the Altar of God*, 173.
13. Smith, *Republic of Letters*, 1794–96; Peeler, "Thomas Jefferson's Nursery of Republican Patriots," 87–88.
14. Jefferson to William Roscoe, Dec. 27, 1820, in Founders Online; Donald G. Tewksbury, *The Founding of American Colleges and Universities before the Civil War* (New York: Teachers College, 1932), 175–77, 180.
15. Madison to Samuel H. Smith, Nov. 4, 1826, in Founders Online; Peeler, "Thomas Jefferson's Nursery of Republican Patriots," 80, 83–84.

16. Principles of Government for the University of Virginia, Feb. 1825; Jefferson to Madison, Feb. 1, 1825; Jefferson to Joseph Cabell, Feb. 3, 1825; Madison to Jefferson, Feb. 8, 1825, in Founders Online.

17. Burstein and Isenberg, *Madison and Jefferson*, 585; Jefferson to Destutt de Tracy, Dec. 26, 1820; Madison to Jefferson, Feb. 8, 1825; Jefferson to John Adams, July 5, 1814, in Founders Online.

18. Ketcham, *James Madison*, 649; Smith, *Republic of Letters*, 1792; Jefferson to Albert Gallatin, Oct. 29, 1822; Jefferson to John Adams, Oct. 12, 1823; Jefferson to Evelyn Dennison, Nov. 9, 1825, in Founders Online.

19. Jefferson to Thomas Cooper, Sept. 1, 1817; Oct. 7, 1814; Thomas Cooper to Jefferson, Sept. 22, 1814; Jefferson to Joseph Cabell, March 1, 1819, in Founders Online; Crawford, *Twilight at Monticello*, 153–54; Malone, "The Correspondence of Thomas Jefferson and Thomas Cooper," 52–53.

20. David E. Swift, "Jefferson, John Holt Rice, and Education in Virginia, 1815–25," *Journal of Presbyterian History* 49 (1971): 32–58; Gaustad, *Sworn on the Altar of God*, 176–77.

21. *Virginia Evangelical and Literary Magazine* 3 (1820): 63–74; Thomas Cooper, *Memoirs of Dr. Joseph Priestley* (London: J. Johnson, 1806); Swift, "Jefferson, John Holt Rice, and Education in Virginia," 42–43; Thomas Cooper to Jefferson, March 1, 1820 (editors' note), in Founders Online.

22. Thomas Cooper to Jefferson, March 1, 1820; Jefferson to Cooper, March 13, 1820, in Founders Online.

23. Madison to Jefferson, March 6, 1819; Joseph C. Cabell to Jefferson, Feb. 22, 1819, in ibid.

24. Jefferson to Robert Taylor and Chapman Johnson, May 16, 1820; Jefferson to Thomas Cooper, April 8, 1820, in ibid.; Crawford, *Twilight at Monticello*, 190–91; Swift, "Jefferson, John Holt Rice, and Education in Virginia," 42–43; Malone, "The Correspondence of Thomas Jefferson and Thomas Cooper," 57–60.

25. Jefferson to Thomas Cooper, July 4, 1820; Jefferson to William Short, April 13, 1820; Cooper to Jefferson, Nov. 20, 1822; July 20, May 3, 1820, in Founders Online.

26. Cooper to Jefferson, Dec. 21, 1822; May 6, June 16, 1823, in ibid.

27. Jefferson to Madison, Jan. 7, 1824; Madison to Jefferson, Jan. 14, 1824, in ibid.

28. See the various letters of Joseph C. Cabell to Jefferson, Aug. 5, 1821; Jan. 7, 14, 1822, and Jefferson to Joseph C. Cabell, Jan. 28, 1823, in ibid.

29. Jefferson to Thomas Cooper, Nov. 2, 1822; Madison to Edward Everett, March 19, 1823, in ibid.; Gaustad, *Sworn on the Altar of God*, 178.

30. Jefferson to Madison, Aug. 8, 1824; Madison to Jefferson, Sept. 10, 1824, in Founders Online.

31. Jefferson to John Adams, Oct. 12, 1823, in ibid.

32. Jefferson to Madison, Feb. 17, 1826; Madison to Jefferson, Feb. 24, 1826; Madison to Samuel H. Smith, Nov. 4, 1826, in ibid.

33. Jefferson to Madison, Feb. 17, 1826, in ibid.

34. Madison to Jefferson, Feb. 24, 1826, in ibid.

35. Crawford, *Twilight at Monticello*, 241–46; Burstein and Isenberg, *Madison and Jefferson*, 599; George Tucker, *The Life of Thomas Jefferson, Third President of the United States* (Philadelphia: Carey, Lee and Blanchard, 1837), 2:496 (the simultaneous deaths "seemed to indicate the immediate agency of heaven"); Madison to Layfette, Nov. 1826, in Founders Online.

36. Jefferson to Madison, Feb. 17, 1826; Madison to William T. Barry, Aug. 4, 1822, in Founders Online; Ketcham, *James Madison*, 656–58.

37. Burstein and Isenberg, *Madison and Jefferson*, 600; Chapman Johnson to Madison, April 21, 1828, in Founders Online.

38. Madison to Chapman Johnson, May 1, 1828, in ibid.

39. Madison to Benjamin O. Peers, April 23, 1833, in ibid.

40. Burstein and Isenberg, *Madison and Jefferson*, 600; Madison to Edward Everett, March 19, 1823, in Founders Online.

41. Madison to Robert Walsh Jr., March 2, 1819, in Founders Online.

42. Madison to Frederick C. Schaeffer, Dec. 3, 1821, in ibid.

43. Madison to Edward Livingston, July 10, 1822, in ibid.

44. Madison to Edward Everett, March 19, 1823, in ibid.

45. Jasper Adams, *The Relation of Christianity to Civil Government in the United States* (Charleston: A. E. Miller, 1833), 6–7, 12–13, 15–16; Daniel L. Dreisbach, *Religion and Politics in the Early Republic* (Lexington: University Press of Kentucky, 1996), 11–12, 39–58.

46. Adams, *The Relation of Christianity to Civil Government*, 12–16, 21–22; Green, *Second Disestablishment*, 98–100.

47. Madison to Jasper Adams, Sept. 1833, in Founders Online.

48. Ibid.; Sidney E. Mead, "Neither Church nor State: Reflections on James Madison's Line of Separation," *Journal of Church and State* 10 (1968): 349–63; Dreisbach, *Religion and Politics in the Early Republic*, 157.

49. Ketcham, "Madison and Religion," 80–81; Burstein and Isenberg, *Madison and Jefferson*, 639; Madison to George Tucker, June 22, 1836, in Founders Online.

50. Photograph of Madison's tombstone, https://www.presidentsusa.net /madisongravesite.html; Ketcham, *James Madison*, 669–70.

12. THE LEGACY

1. Gaustad, *Sworn on the Altar of God,* 194–95.

2. See Steven K. Green, *The Third Disestablishment: Church, State, and American Culture, 1940–1975* (New York: Oxford University Press, 2019), 355–63, and Green, *Separating Church and State,* 97–105, 188.

3. David Reiss, "Jefferson and Madison as Icons in Judicial History: A Study of Religion Clause Jurisprudence," *Maryland Law Review* 61 (2002): 94–176, 95 (quotation).

4. Thomas Jefferson Randolph, *Memoirs, Correspondence, and Private Papers of Thomas Jefferson* (London: Colburn and Bentley, 1829), 4:460; Joseph Story to "Judge Fay," Feb. 15, 1830, in *Life and Letters of Joseph Story,* ed. William W. Story (Boston: Little and Brown, 1851), 2:33; Peterson, *Jefferson Image,* 29–33.

5. Tucker, *Life of Thomas Jefferson,* 1:97–102; Peterson, *Jefferson Image,* 122–26.

6. Peterson, *Jefferson Image,* 69–71; Jon Meacham, *American Lion: Andrew Jackson in the White House* (New York: Random House 2009), 87; Arthur M. Schlesinger Jr., *The Age of Jackson* (New York: Little, Brown, 1945), 350–60.

7. Richard R. John, "Taking Sabbatarianism Seriously: The Postal System, the Sabbath, and the Transformation of American Political Culture," *Journal of the Early Republic* 10 (Winter 1990): 517–67; James R. Rohrer, "Sunday Mails and the Church-State Theme in Jacksonian America," *Journal of the Early Republic* 7 (1987): 53–74; Wayne E. Fuller, *Morality and the Mail in Nineteenth-Century America* (Urbana: University of Illinois Press, 2003); Timothy Verhoeven, *Secularists, Religion and Government in Nineteenth-Century America* (Basingstoke, UK: Palgrave Macmillan, 2019), 33–62.

8. New Jersey Memorial, Jan. 8, 1830, in *American State Papers Bearing on Sunday Legislation,* ed. William Addison Blakely (Washington, DC: Religious Liberty Association, 1911), 277–78; Verhoeven, *Secularists, Religion and Government,* 45–48.

9. Senate Report on Sunday Mails, Committee on the Post Office and Post Roads, Jan. 19, 1829, 20th Cong., 2nd sess., and House Report on Sunday Mails, Committee on the Post Office and Post Roads, March 4 and 5, 1830, 21st Cong., 1st sess., in Blakely, *American State Papers,* 233–68; Verhoeven, *Secularists, Religion and Government,* 53–58; Green, *Second Disestablishment,* 110–18.

10. Grasso, *Skepticism and American Faith,* 281–93; Schlesinger, *The Age of Jackson,* 136–38; Bertram Wyatt-Brown, "Prelude to Abolitionism:

Sabbatarian Politics and the Rise of the Second Party System," *Journal of American History* 58 (1971): 316-41.

11. Meacham, *American Lion*, 206-7; Adam Jortner, "Cholera, Christ, and Jackson: The Epidemic of 1832 and the Origins of Christian Politics in Antebellum America," *Journal of the Early Republic* 27 (2007): 233-64; Peterson, *Jefferson Image*, 72-73; Schlesinger, *The Age of Jackson*, 353-54, 360.

12. Francis Lister Hawks, "The Life of Jefferson," *New York Review*, March 1837, 5; Peterson, *Jefferson Image*, 127-28.

13. Theodore Dwight, *The Character of Thomas Jefferson, as Exhibited in His Own Writings* (Boston: Weeks, Jordan, 1839), 344-64.

14. Schlesinger, *The Age of Jackson*, 351-52; Clifford S. Griffin, "Religious Benevolence as Social Control," *Mississippi Valley Historical Review* 44 (1957): 427-28; Richard J. Carwardine, *Evangelicals and Politics in Antebellum America* (New Haven, CT: Yale University Press, 1993), 76-77.

15. Theodore Frelinghuysen, *An Inquiry into the Moral and Religious Character of the American Government* (New York: Wiley and Putnam, 1838), 2-3, 14, 187, 198, 207.

16. Baird, *Religion in the United States of America*, 240-41, 258, 260-61.

17. Tayler Lewis, "Has the State a Religion?" *American Whig Review* 3 (1846): 273-89; Peterson, *Jefferson Image*, 87-89; Grasso, *Skepticism and American Faith*, 258-73.

18. See State v. Chandler, 2 Har. 553 (Del. 1838) (criticizing Jefferson while upholding a blasphemy statute); City Council of Charleston v. Benjamin, 2 Strobh. Law 508 (S.C. 1846) (criticizing Jefferson while upholding a Sunday law conviction).

19. Jefferson to Madison, Oct. 15, 1810 (calling Story a "tory"), in Founders Online; Green, *Second Disestablishment*, 193-96.

20. Jefferson to John Cartwright, June 5, 1824, in Founders Online; Green, *Second Disestablishment*, 193.

21. John Cartwright to Jefferson, July 28, 1824, in Founders Online; Joseph Story to Edward Everett, Sept. 15, 1824, in Story, *Life and Letters of Joseph Story*, 429-30.

22. Joseph Story, *Miscellaneous Writings* (Boston: James Munroe, 1835), 451.

23. Joseph Story, "Christianity a Part of the Common Law," *American Jurist* 9 (April 1833): 346-48; reprinted in Story, *Life and Letters of Joseph Story*, 431-33.

24. Joseph Story, *Commentaries on the Constitution of the United States* (Boston: Hilliard, Gray, 1833); R. Kent Newmeyer, *Supreme Court Joseph*

Story: Statesmen of the Old Republic (Chapel Hill: University of North Carolina Press, 1985), 182.

25. Story, *Commentaries on the Constitution*, 3:722–24.

26. Ibid., 3:724, 728, 726–27; Green, *Second Disestablishment*, 196–98.

27. Alexis de Tocqueville, *Democracy in America*, trans. Henry Reeve (New York: Adlard and Saunders, 1838), 308.

28. Louis Kossuth, *The Future of Nations, in What Consists Its Security: A Lecture Delivered in New York, June 21, 1852* (New York: Fowler and Wells, 1854), 32.

29. Adam G. De Gurowski, *America and Europe* (New York: D. Appleton, 1857), 323.

30. Randall, *Life of Thomas Jefferson;* Washington, *Writings of Thomas Jefferson.*

31. Randall, *Life of Thomas Jefferson,* 1:203, 219–23.

32. Ibid., 3:460–71, 553–61.

33. Peterson, *Jefferson Image*, 149–61. Andrew Burstein calls Randall's hagiographic portrayal of Jefferson's beliefs an "over the top defense." Burstein, *Democracy's Muse*, 164–67.

34. "To Messrs. Nehimiah Dodge, Ephraim Robbins, and Stephen S. Nelson, a Committee of the Danbury Baptist Association, in the State of Connecticut," Jan. 1, 1802, in Founders Online; Black, "Religious Liberty," 53; Mcgrath, "Chief Justice Waite and the Twin Relic," 525–28; Reynolds v. United States, at 164; George Bancroft, *History of the United States from the Discovery of the Continent to 1789* (New York: D. Appleton, 1883–85), 6:154–59.

35. *The Papers of James Madison*, ed. Henry D. Gilpin (New York: J. and H. G. Langley, 1841); *Letters and Other Writings of James Madison*, ed. Philip A. Fendall (Philadelphia: J. P. Lippincott, 1865), 1:108–69.

36. John Quincy Adams, *The Lives of James Madison and James Monroe, Fourth and Fifth Presidents of the United States* (Buffalo: Geo. H. Derby, 1850), 26–28.

37. Rives, *History of the Life and Times of James Madison,* 1:41–48, 33–36, 599–634.

38. Sydney Howard Gay, *James Madison* (Boston: Houghton, Mifflin, 1884), 11–17, 62–66, 139.

39. Gaillard Hunt, *The Life of James Madison* (New York: Doubleday, 1902), 10–12, 78–86, 177.

40. "Proclaims Jefferson Day," *New York Times*, April 7, 1943, 21; "Jefferson Ideals Lauded in Sermons," *New York Times*, April 11, 1943, 39;

"Birth of Jefferson to Be Marked Today," *New York Times,* April 13, 1943, 21; "Roosevelt, Hailing Jefferson, Looks to Gain in Liberty," *New York Times,* April 13, 1943, 1, 16; "Address by Roosevelt," *New York Times,* April 14, 1943, 16; Peterson, *Jefferson Image,* 377–79, 420–42.

41. West Virginia State Board of Education v. Barnette, 319 U.S. 624, 637, 640 (1943); 645–46 (Murphy, J., concurring); 653 (Frankfurter, J., dissenting).

42. Claude G. Bowers, *Jefferson and Hamilton: The Struggle for Democracy in America* (Boston: Houghton Mifflin, 1925); Claude G. Bowers, *Jefferson in Power: The Death Struggle of the Federalists* (Boston: Houghton Mifflin, 1936), 145; Peterson, *Jefferson Image,* 347–50.

43. Edward McNall Burns, *James Madison: Philosopher of the Constitution* (New Brunswick, NJ: Rutgers University Press, 1938).

44. Claude G. Bowers, *The Young Jefferson* (Boston: Houghton Mifflin, 1945); Koch, *The Philosophy of Thomas Jefferson.*

45. John M. Ferren, *Salt of the Earth, Conscience of the Court: The Story of Justice Wiley Rutledge* (Chapel Hill: University of North Carolina Press, 2004), 139–49.

46. Brant, *James Madison: The Virginia Revolutionist;* Brant, *James Madison: The Nationalist.*

47. Brant, *James Madison: The Nationalist,* 343–55. See also Brant, *James Madison: Father of the Constitution,* 265–71.

48. See Wiley Rutledge Papers, box 143, folders 8–12, Library of Congress, Washington, DC; Everson v. Board of Education, 330 U.S. 31–42 (Rutledge, J., dissenting).

49. See generally Green, *The Bible, the School, and the Constitution.*

50. Reynolds v. United States, at 145; Davis v. Beason, 133 U.S. 333 (1890).

51. Bradfield v. Roberts, 175 U.S. 291 (1899); Quick Bear v. Leupp, 210 U.S. 50 (1908); Cochran v. Louisiana State Board of Education, 281 U.S. 370 (1930).

52. Green, *The Third Disestablishment,* 101–28, 135–46.

53. Everson v. Board of Education, 44 A.2d 333 (N.J. 1945); Daryl R. Fair, "The Everson Case in the Context of New Jersey Politics," in *Everson Revisited: Religion, Education, and Law at the Crossroads,* ed. Jo Renee Formicola and Hubert Morken (Lantham, MD: Rowan and Littlefield, 1998), 1–21; Donald L. Drakeman, "*Everson v. Board of Education* and the Quest for the Historical Establishment Clause," *American Journal of Legal History* 49 (2007): 119–68; Sarah Barrington Gordon, *The Spirit of the Law* (Cambridge, MA: Belknap Press of Harvard University Press, 2010), 59–64.

54. Cochran v. Louisiana State Board of Education, at 374–75; Brief of Appellant in Everson v. Board of Education, at 5, 11, 15, 22.

55. Brief of the General Conference of Seventh-day Adventists et al., in Everson v. Board of Education, at 7, 18; Brief of ACLU in Everson v. Board of Education, at 8–14. ACLU's historical argument likely drew from the work of Vivian Thayer, who was a member of the ACLU board of directors. See V. T. Thayer, *Religion in Public Education* (New York: Viking Press, 1947).

56. Fair, "The *Everson* Case in the Context of New Jersey Politics," 9–10; Christine L. Compston, "The Serpentine Wall: Judicial Decision Making in Supreme Court Cases Involving Aid to Sectarian Schools" (Ph.D. diss., University of New Hampshire, 1986), 59–60; Brief of the National Council of Catholic Men and the National Council of Catholic Women in Everson v. Board of Education, at 25, 32–35.

57. Del Dickson, *The Supreme Court in Conference* (New York: Oxford University Press, 2001), 400–403.

58. Hugo Black Papers, box 285, folders 2–3, Library of Congress; Drakeman, "*Everson v. Board of Education*," 139–40; Compston, "The Serpentine Wall," 69–72.

59. Everson v. Board of Education, 330 U.S. 31–39 (Rutledge, J., dissenting).

60. Drakeman, "*Everson v. Board of Education*," 141, 149–58.

61. Everson v. Board of Education, 330 U.S. 11–14, 18.

62. McCollum v. Board of Education, at 212; 214, 216, 231 (Frankfurter, J.); 238–56 (Reed, J., dissenting).

63. See Daniel L. Dreisbach and Mark David Hall, *Faith and the Founders of the American Republic* (New York: Oxford University Press, 2014).

64. Thayer, *Religion in Public Education*; Milton R. Konvitz, "Separation of Church and State: The First Freedom," *Law and Contemporary Problems* 14 (1949): 44–60; R. Freeman Butts, *The American Tradition in Religion and Education* (Boston: Beacon Press, 1950); Frank Swancara, *The Separation of Religion and Government* (New York: Truth Seeker, 1950); Conrad Henry Moehlman, *The Wall of Separation between Church and State* (Boston: Beacon Press, 1951); V. T. Thayer, *The Attack upon the American Secular School* (Boston: Beacon Press, 1951).

65. Wilfrid Parsons, SJ, *The First Freedom: Considerations on Church and State in the United States* (New York: Declan X. McMullen, 1948); J. M. O'Neill, *Religion and Education under the Constitution* (New York: Harper and Brothers, 1949); Corwin, "The Supreme Court as a National

School Board," 3–22; Mark DeWolf Howe, *The Garden and the Wilderness* (Chicago: University of Chicago Press, 1965).

66. See generally Sehat, *The Myth of American Religious Freedom;* Gordon, *The Spirit of the Law;* and Wenger, *Religious Freedom.*

67. McGowen v. Maryland, at 420, 437, 443. The Supreme Court decided only one other establishment clause case in the interim, Zorach v. Clauson, 343 U.S. 306 (1952).

68. Engel v. Vitale, 370 U.S. 421 (1962); Abington School District v. Schempp, at 203; Flast v. Cohen, 392 U.S. 83, 103 (1968). Warren's statements led Justice John Marshall Harlan to remark that "to treat Madison's Remonstrance as authoritatively incorporated in the First Amendment is to take grotesque liberties with the simple legislative process, and even more with the complex and diffuse process of ratification of an Amendment by three-fourths of the states." Flast v. Cohen, at 126 (Harlan, J., dissenting).

69. Mark David Hall, "Jefferson Walls and Madisonian Lines: The Supreme Court's Use of History in Religion Clause Cases," *High Court Quarterly Review* 15 (2009): 103–47. See also David Sehat, *The Jefferson Rule: How the Founding Fathers Became Infallible and Our Politics Inflexible* (New York: Simon and Schuster, 2015), 1–2, and Reiss, "Jefferson and Madison as Icons in Judicial History."

70. Carson v. Makin, 142 S.Ct. 1987, 2005 (2022) (Breyer, J., dissenting). In 2019, Justice Ruth Bader Ginsburg referred to both the Danbury letter and the *Memorial and Remonstrance* in her dissenting opinion in American Legion v. American Humanist Association, at 2105.

71. Cord, *Separation of Church and State;* Hamburger, *Separation of Church and State;* Dreisbach, *Thomas Jefferson and the Wall of Separation;* Muñoz, *God and the Founders.* See also Bradley, *Church-State Relationships in America.*

72. Wallace v. Jaffree, at 38, 92, 106–7 (Rehnquist, J., dissenting).

73. Lee v. Weisman, 505 U.S. 577, 633–634 (1992) (Scalia, J., dissenting); Locke v. Davey, 540 U.S. 712, 727 (2004) (Scalia, J., dissenting); McCreary County v. ACLU, 545 U.S. 844, 895–96 (2005) (Scalia, J., dissenting); Hein v. Freedom from Religion Foundation, 551 U.S. 587, 634 (2007) (Scalia, J., concurring); Espinoza v. Montana Dept. of Revenue, 140 S.Ct. 2246, 2265–66 (Thomas, J., concurring).

74. Rosenberger v. University of Virginia, at 819; 863 (Souter, J., dissenting).

75. Ibid., 854–56 (Thomas, J., concurring); 868–72 (Souter, J., dissenting); Madison to Benjamin O. Peers, April 23, 1833, in Founders Online.

76. Town of Greece v. Galloway, 572 U.S. 565, 576 (2014); American Legion v. American Humanist Association, at 2087.
77. Van Orden v. Perry, 545 U.S. 677, 730 (2005) (Stevens, J., dissenting).
78. Mitchel v. Helms, 530 U.S. 793, 871 (2000) (Souter, J., dissenting); Zelman v. Simmons-Harris, 536 U.S. 639, 711–12 (2002) (Souter, J., dissenting); Van Orden v. Perry, at 724–25 (Stevens, J., dissenting); Van Orden v. Perry, at 737 (Souter, J., dissenting); Hein v. Freedom from Religion Foundation, at 638 (Souter, J., dissenting); Town of Greece v. Galloway, at 575–76 (Kagan, J., dissenting); Trinity Lutheran Church v. Comer, 582 U.S. 449, 482–83 (2017) (Sotomayor, J., dissenting); American Legion v. American Humanist Association, at 2105 (Ginsburg, J., dissenting); Espinoza v. Montana Dept. of Revenue, at 2284–87 (Breyer, J., dissenting); Carson v. Makin, at 2005 (Breyer, J., dissenting).

CONCLUSION

1. Jefferson, *Autobiography*, 20–21; Foote, *Religion of Thomas Jefferson*, 11–13; Peterson, *Thomas Jefferson*, 12, 14–15.
2. Ketcham, "Madison at Princeton," 40–45.
3. Miller, *First Liberty*, 61.
4. Jefferson, *Notes on the State of Virginia*, 160, 159; Jefferson, Danbury Letter, Jan. 1, 1802, in Founders Online.
5. "James Madison's Autobiography," 199; Madison, "Property," *National Gazette*, March 27, 1792, in Founders Online; Sehat, *The Myth of American Religious Freedom*, 48.
6. Jefferson to William Roscoe, Dec. 27, 1820, in Founders Online.
7. Rakove, *Beyond Belief, Beyond Conscience*, 67–68.
8. Madison, *Memorial and Remonstrance*, ¶ 12.
9. Statute for Establishing Religious Freedom, in Founders Online.
10. Madison to Jefferson, Oct. 15, 1788, in ibid.
11. Madison, Detached Memoranda.
12. Madison to Edward Livingston, July 10, 1822; Madison to Robert Walsh Jr., March 2, 1819, in Founders Online.
13. Rakove, *Beyond Belief, Beyond Conscience*, 99, 3.
14. McConnell, "The Origins and Historical Understanding," 1453 (arguing that Madison supported broad exemptions for religious practice).
15. Jefferson, Danbury Letter; Madison, *Memorial and Remonstrance*, ¶ 4.
16. Madison, *Memorial and Remonstrance*, ¶¶ 1, 8.
17. Rakove, *Beyond Belief, Beyond Conscience*, 178.

18. Ibid., 4; Feldman, *The Three Lives of James Madison,* 276.
19. Daniel L. Dreisbach, Mark David Hall, and Jeffry H. Morrison, eds., *The Forgotten Founders on Religion and Public Life* (Notre Dame, IN: University of Notre Dame Press, 2009).
20. Muñoz, *God and the Founders,* 207.
21. Hall, "Jeffersonian Walls and Madisonian Lines," 108; Rakove, *Beyond Belief, Beyond Conscience,* 96.
22. Muñoz, *God and the Founders,* 206.

⦿ INDEX ⦿

RELIGIOUS FREEDOM AND PUBLIC DIALOGUE

A Robert Nusbaum Center Series

Eric Michael Mazur and Kathleen M. Moore, Editors

Originally established in 1996 as the Center for the Study of Religious Freedom, the Robert Nusbaum Center at Virginia Wesleyan University encourages diversity, dialogue, and religious freedom and supports education and civil dialogue on issues related to race, religion, gender and gender identity, sexuality, and ethnicity. With its series Religious Freedom and Public Dialogue, the Nusbaum Center seeks to publish books that investigate historical and contemporary conceptualizations of religious freedom; books that interrogate the complex relationships between religion, race, and culture; and books that explore the impact that contested determinations of religious freedom have on public life.